International Advances in Adoption Research for Practice

International Advances in Adoption Research for Practice

Gretchen Miller Wrobel

and

Elsbeth Neil

⊛WILEY-BLACKWELL

A John Wiley & Sons, Ltd., Publication

This edition first published 2009
© 2009 John Wiley & Sons Ltd., except for chapter 7 (© 2007 Taylor & Francis Ltd)

Wiley-Blackwell is an imprint of John Wiley & Sons, formed by the merger of Wiley's global Scientific, Technical, and Medical business with Blackwell Publishing.

Registered Office
John Wiley & Sons Ltd, The Atrium, Southern Gate, Chichester, West Sussex, PO19 8SQ, UK

Editorial Offices
The Atrium, Southern Gate, Chichester, West Sussex, PO19 8SQ, UK
9600 Garsington Road, Oxford, OX4 2DQ, UK
350 Main Street, Malden, MA 02148-5020, USA

For details of our global editorial offices, for customer services, and for information about how to apply for permission to reuse the copyright material in this book please see our website at www.wiley.com/wiley-blackwell.

Library of Congress Cataloging-in-Publication Data has been applied for

A catalogue record for this book is available from the British Library.

ISBN 978-0-470-99817-5 (hbk) 978-0-470-99818-2 (pbk)

Set in 10/12.5 pt Sabon by SNP Best-set Typesetter Ltd., Hong Kong
Printed in Singapore by Markono Print Media Pte Ltd

1 2009

Contents

Contributors

Kay Asquith is a Course Tutor on the MSc in Psychoanalytic Developmental Psychology, Anna Freud Centre, London, UK.

Susan Ayers-Lopez is Senior Research Program Coordinator at The University of Texas at Austin, USA.

Celia Beckett is a research worker at the MRC Social, Genetic and Developmental Psychiatry Centre, Institute of Psychiatry, Kings College London, UK.

E. Wayne Carp holds the Benson Family Chair in History and is Professor of History at Pacific Lutheran University, Tacoma, Washington, USA.

Jenny Castle is a research worker at the MRC Social, Genetic and Developmental Psychiatry Centre, Institute of Psychiatry, Kings College London, UK.

Emma Colvert is a project coordinator at the MRC Social, Genetic and Developmental Psychiatry Centre, Institute of Psychiatry, Kings College London, UK.

Amy Chanmugam is a Graduate Research Assistant at the University of Texas at Austin, USA.

Kristin Dillon is a PhD student in the Department of Family Social Science, University of Minnesota, Minneapolis, USA.

Harold D. Grotevant holds the Rudd Family Foundation Chair in Psychology at the University of Massachusetts Amherst. He is also Professor Emeritus of Family Social Science at the University of Minnesota, Minneapolis, USA.

Saul Hillman is a Research Psychologist and Postgraduate Supervisor on the MSc in Psychoanalytic Developmental Psychology, Anna Freud Centre, London, UK.

Jill Hodges is Consultant Psychotherapist at the Brain and Behavioural Sciences Unit, Institute for Child Health, London; Anna Freud Centre, London; Department of Child and Adolescent Mental Health, Great Ormond Street Hospital, London, UK.

David Howe is Professor of Social Work at the University of East Anglia, Norwich, UK.

Femmie Juffer is Professor of Adoption Studies at the Centre for Child and Family Studies, Leiden University, the Netherlands.

Jeanne Kaniuk is head of the Adoption Service at Coram Family, an independent adoption agency based in London, UK.

Ruth Kelly is a Senior Social Work Practitioner, Health Service Executive, Wexford, Ireland.

Jana Kreppner is a lecturer in developmental psychology at the School of Psychology, University of Southampton, UK, and a visiting research fellow at the MRC Social, Genetic and Developmental Psychiatry Centre, Institute of Psychiatry, Kings College London, UK.

Leslie D. Leve is a Research Scientist at the Oregon Social Learning Center and a Senior Scientist at the Center for Research to Practice in Eugene, Oregon, USA.

Courtney J. Lynch is Assistant Professor at the University of North Carolina at Charlotte, USA.

Elissa Madden is a Graduate Research Assistant at The University of Texas at Austin, USA.

Ruth G. McRoy is Ruby Lee Piester Centennial Professor Emerita at The University of Texas at Austin, USA.

Mitul Mehta is a lecturer at the Centre for Neuroimaging Sciences, Department of Clinical Neuroscience, Institute of Psychiatry, Kings College London, UK.

Elsbeth Neil is a Senior Lecturer in Social Work at the University of East Anglia, Norwich, UK.

Adam Pertman is the Executive Director of the Evan B. Donaldson Adoption Institute, Associate Editor of *Adoption Quarterly* and author of *Adoption Nation: How the Adoption Revolution is Transforming America.*

Jesús Palacios is Professor of Developmental Psychology at the University of Seville, Spain.

David Reiss is Clinical Professor of Child Psychiatry at the Yale Child Study Centre, New Hallen, Connecticut, USA.

Michael Rutter is Professor of Developmental Psychopathology at the MRC Social, Genetic and Developmental Psychiatry Centre, Institute of Psychiatry, Kings College London, UK.

Peter Selman is Visiting Fellow in the School of Geography, Politics and Sociology at Newcastle University, UK.

Edmund Sonuga-Barke is Professor of Developmental Psychopathology at the MRC Social, Genetic and Developmental Psychiatry Centre, Institute of Psychiatry, Kings College London, UK; Director of the Developmental Brain-Behaviour Laboratory, School of Psychology, University of Southampton, UK; and Adjunct Professor at the Child Study Center, New York University, USA.

Howard Steele is Director of Graduate Studies and Associate Professor in the Department of Psychology, New School for Social Research, New York, USA.

Miriam Steele is Associate Professor and Assistant Director of Clinical Psychology, New School for Social Research, New York, USA.

Suzanne Stevens is a research worker at the MRC Social, Genetic and Developmental Psychiatry Centre, Institute of Psychiatry, Kings College London, UK, and a PhD student at the Developmental Brain-Behaviour Laboratory, School of Psychology, University of Southampton, UK.

Marinus H. van IJzendoorn is Professor in the Centre for Child and Family Studies, and Director of the Rommert Casimir Institute of Developmental Psychopathology, Leiden University, the Netherlands.

Amy Whitesel is a Senior Research Associate in the Department of Psychology at George Washington University, Washington, DC, USA.

Gretchen Miller Wrobel is Professor of Psychology, Bethel University, St. Paul, Minnesota, USA.

Foreword

As a former journalist, I'm always interested in my former colleagues' choice of 'experts' when they write stories relating to adoption. Typically, with all good intentions, they obtain their information and insights from people in three categories: the leaders of organizations with titles that project authority; practitioners in the field (usually attorneys or agency officials); and individuals whose knowledge derives primarily from personal experience (adopted people, birth parents and adoptive parents).

There's no problem, in principle, with seeking input from someone who has a specialized understanding about any subject, so it's perfectly reasonable that reporters would reach out to all the types of people I've just listed. In practice, however, there is indeed a problem. Owing largely to adoption's secretive history, journalists – like mental health professionals, medical personnel and many others who deal intimately with the issues and people in our not-so-little world – generally don't know as much about the subject as they do about many others. And so they too often fill in their blanks and, consequently, those of the consumers of their stories, without posing the kinds of critical questions they ask when deciding which 'experts' to use on other topics.

Do the people journalists select have personal biases, financial interests or ideological agendas, for example – factors that might not preclude conducting interviews with them or using their quotes, but may well alter the context in which their information is presented and understood? Or might they have limitations on their particular knowledge base – either because they're practitioners with a strong grasp of their own specific issues but perhaps not related ones, or because they have discrete experiences from which they should not be reasonably expected to extrapolate? To put it starkly, does a woman who has her child via Caesarian section then become an authority on Caesarian sections?

The most significant information in our own field often comes from women and men who are usually overlooked by journalists (and, in general, who get too little attention or credit for their achievements); they are the researchers who – to roughly follow the above analogy – are instrumental in creating the body of knowledge that allows us to determine which procedures work best for which patients. A large group of the most accomplished of these professionals convened in 2006 at the Second International Conference on Adoption Research, from which the contents of this insightful and useful book are derived.

None of this is intended as an attack on journalism, a profession of which I was proudly a part for 25 years, and one I continue to believe is vital to any free society. Rather, I am trying to provide perspective for reaching an obvious but critical conclusion – which I'll explain through this short joke:

> A mother took her son to his first American football game and, afterward, asked what he thought. "It was great," he replied. "I loved when they threw the ball, and ran around the field and jumped all over each other, but why all that fuss about 25 cents?" The mother, perplexed, asked her son what he was talking about. "You know," he said. "At the beginning, they threw a coin into the air, and the whole time after that, it was, "Get the quarter back, get the quarter back."

The point – and there is a point – is that if no one ever explains the rules of a game, who the players are (for anyone who needs to know, the quarterback is a key position on an American football team), what their motivations might be or what their actions mean, it can be difficult to understand what's happening in front of one's very eyes. That is precisely what happened with adoption. For generations, people discussed it only in guarded, hushed tones; single women were routinely instructed to pretend they never gave birth, while new parents were told not to disclose to their own children that they were adopted; and most laws, policies, practices and attitudes related to adoption were shaped, to put it charitably, more by good intentions than by good knowledge.

In a phrase, it's hard to learn much about secrets. So it's no wonder that most journalists – like most teachers, mental-health professionals, politicians and others who have a significant impact on the tens of millions of people for whom adoption is an everyday reality – don't yet know enough about this complex, fascinating, life-altering process. And they make mistakes as a result.

The very good news is that this reality is changing. To be sure, considerable progress still needs to be made, but greater honesty, transparency and pride are replacing the pretense, insularity and shame of the past; better

understanding of and respect for all the participants to adoption are suc-
ceeding the corrosive stereotypes and denigration that used to characterize
nearly all of us; and journalists – like teachers, mental-health professionals,
politicians, *et al.* – are doing a better and better job of reflecting, and
shaping, reality.

All of which, finally, brings me back to this insightful and important
book. The best policies, practices, laws and attitudes in any society are
informed by scrupulous research, broad experience and, as best as we
humans can achieve it, knowledge untainted by financial self-interest or
ideological bias. The authors whose writing you are about to read are
among the most talented, thoughtful and highly regarded scholars and
researchers in the field of adoption today. Their work is one of the primary
reasons why we have made so much progress over the past few decades,
and why I'm hopeful that we will continue on this positive path into the
future.

Anyone seeking important, reliable, research-based information – most
notably adoption, mental-health and medical professionals (oh, yes, and
journalists) – need look no further.

Adam Pertman

Adam Pertman is the Executive Director of the Evan B. Donaldson Adop-
tion Institute, Associate Editor of *Adoption Quarterly* and the author of
*Adoption Nation: How the Adoption Revolution is Transforming
America.*

Preface

Adoption is a global phenomenon that touches the lives of numerous families. Interest in the role of legal adoption as both a child welfare solution and as a means of alternative family formation for adults wanting to become parents has never been higher. Single persons and couples adopt children as infants and at older ages, domestically and internationally. There are few countries that are not involved in either intercountry adoption or domestic adoption, and the need for research to inform decisions about what is best for children is greater than ever.

Although adoption is a global phenomenon, it is not a uniform one. The cultural context is a huge determinant of the form that adoption takes. For example, in the United Kingdom adoption is currently primarily viewed as a means of providing new families for children in the public care system, and legal systems have evolved to allow for a child to be adopted without his or her birth parents' consent. In contrast most of the United Kingdom's European neighbours reject this use of adoption and have developed other means to secure permanence for children who cannot live with their birth parents. In some parts of the world, adoption is predominately about the receipt of children from other countries; in other places adoption is about the sending of children abroad. The relinquishment of babies by single mothers is very unusual in some countries (e.g. in Western Europe), infrequent but not rare in others (e.g. the United States) but is common in others (e.g. Korea). These examples about how adoption is used around the world also look different when viewed from a historical perspective, as adoption has changed and evolved to meet the needs of changing societies. For example, if we look back 40 years in the United Kingdom, we can see that adoption was primarily about the relinquishment of babies by single mothers and was not considered for children growing up in care.

The methodology used to study adoption reveals the phenomenon in different ways. For example, quantitative follow-up of intercountry adopted children can report on children's physical, behavioural and educational development but only qualitative research can reveal what it might feel like, for example, to be a Colombian child brought up by white Dutch parents in a small country town, and it is qualitative data that can reveal why and how various quantifiable effects occur. The 'outcomes' of adoption also differ if we ask the question 'outcomes for whom?' and it is important to consider how adoption affects not just children but also the adoptive and birth families and indeed the wider society.

Adoption researchers can be found in numerous different countries and different disciplines in the social sciences, arts and humanities, and psychological and behavioural sciences. Many adoption researchers are working in applied professional departments, such as child psychology or psychiatry, social work, education or the law. The opportunities for these different groups of people to come together and share their diverse perspectives are few and far between. Conferences specifically about adoption often focus on practice rather than research. Or they may have a focus on one aspect of adoption or one particular perspective – for example, post-adoption support services, child health outcomes, or new legislation about adoption. Of course adoption researchers often attend conferences within their own disciplines; for example, developmental psychologists may attend large international gatherings on child or adolescent development. The problem here is that other research on adoption is likely to form only a very small part of the programme, so again opportunities to interact with other people in the field are limited.

Because of this dispersal of adoption expertise across different countries, areas of interest, and disciplinary and methodological perspectives, opportunities for these various aspects of adoption to be put together as a whole are very limited. It was with the aim of addressing this issue that the Second International Conference on Adoption Research (ICAR2) was held in Norwich, England, in 2006. This conference built on the success of the First International Conference on Adoption Research, held at the University of Minnesota in 1999. The meeting was hosted by the University of East Anglia's Centre for Research on the Child and Family, one of the United Kingdom's leading research establishments in the field of child welfare and family placement. The Nuffield Foundation, London, generously agreed to sponsor the conference and additional resources followed from England's Department for Education and Skills, and the British Academy. The conference was organized and chaired by Elsbeth Neil. The 10 keynote speakers were invited with the aim of representing some of the different perspectives on adoption. The conference was aimed specifically at those actively involved in adoption research. The call for papers was distributed widely, and it was clear that the agenda for the meeting was wide open. All people hoping to attend were encouraged to submit an abstract to present their work in some form or another. Participation was limited to 150 people, to maximize interaction and retain focus.

The four-day conference took place in July 2006 in the middle of an unusual heat wave, the Wednesday of the meeting being the hottest July day ever recorded in England. The aim of attracting a diverse group of researchers was successfully met; the 150 delegates came from over 25 different countries with representatives from Europe, North and South America, South Africa, Asia and Australasia. Researchers working in a diversity of fields were represented and the spread of topics was wide. In addition to the 10 keynote papers, there were 12 paper symposia (43 papers), 8 poster symposia (48 posters) and 4 workshops (almost all of these are available on the conference web site: www.icar2.org.uk).

This book presents an edited collection of 13 papers (plus this introduction and a conclusion), 10 of which are by the conference keynote speakers and three by paper symposia presenters (3 papers). Each chapter is either the paper first presented at ICAR2, or an adaptation or evolution of this work. The goal of this conference was to bring together the worldwide, multidisciplinary community of distinguished and emerging adoption researchers, to enable sharing of research findings and to encourage interaction and debate about the future research agenda. The book shares many of the aims of this important international event with the additional goal of disseminating the messages from the presentations in a manner that is relevant and accessible to a wider audience, especially to practitioners working in adoption.

The first main section of the book brings together four papers that outline the importance of context in adoption. Chapter 1 is by David Howe, Professor of Social Work at the University of East Anglia, England. Howe's chapter explores adoption around the world and across the ages, outlining why it is a topic of fascination in both the sciences and the arts. The author of Chapter 2, E. Wayne Carp, is Professor of History at Pacific Lutheran University, Tacoma, USA. His contribution offers a careful analysis of the history of secrecy and openness in adoption records in England, the United States and New Zealand. This analysis reveals the extent to which attitudes towards openness in adoption in the Western world have fluctuated over the years in response to changes in broader attitudes about illegitimacy, infertility and the 'ideal' form of family. In Chapter 3, Peter Selman, visiting fellow at the University of Newcastle, England, presents an up-to-date analysis of the demography of intercountry adoption, focusing on sending countries and highlighting the dramatic rise of adoptions from China and the reasons behind this. Finally in this section, Jesús Palacios, Professor of Developmental Psychology at the University of Seville, Spain, utilizes Urie Bronfenbrenner's bio-ecological model of human development to shape an extensive review of what we know and what we still need to find out about adoption.

The second main section of the book consists of nine empirical papers, reporting the latest findings from key researchers. In Chapter 5, Ruth McRoy, Professor Emeritus at The University of Texas at Austin, USA, describes the early findings of her evaluation of the Collaboration to Adopt US Kids project. She reports on the barriers to adoption that can stand in the way of children in care finding a new family, and outlines the factors associated with successful special needs adoptions. In Chapter 6, David Reiss (Erik Erikson Scholar at the Austin Riggs Center, Stockbridge, Massachusetts, and Visiting Professor at Yale University, USA) focuses on how the adoptive rearing environment can moderate the risks of behaviour problems in children who may carry a genetic predisposition to such difficulties. Adoption has always been of interest as a means of studying the relative effects of nature and nurture, and the research discussed here offers a cutting-edge perspective on how genes and environment interact.

Michael Rutter, Professor of Developmental Psychopathology at the Institute of Psychiatry, Kings College, London, explores developmental outcomes for intercountry adoptees in Chapter 7. This chapter is based on his major study into the effect of early severe deprivation on Romanian children adopted into Britain, reporting on outcomes for the children at age 11. This research illuminates which children are most at risk of long-term problems, and discusses the implications for supporting children and their families. In Chapter 8, Femmie Juffer, Professor of Adoption, University of Leiden, the Netherlands, draws on both her own longitudinal follow-up of a group of intercountry adoptees in Holland, and the meta-analytical methods for which her department is renowned. Using this wealth of data she offers a comprehensive overview of what is known about the developmental outcomes for intercountry adoptees, arguing that there is empirical evidence to support the case for intercountry adoption as an intervention that generally promotes children's welfare.

Miriam Steele, Associate Professor at New School for Social Research, New York, USA, discusses her research (carried out with the Thomas Coram Institute in London, England) looking at the placement for adoption of older children who have experienced neglect and abuse (Chapter 9). Using attachment theory and methodologies, and following up both adoptive parents and children over time starting before the adoption placements began, she discusses how a secure state of mind in adoptive parents can help children with poor care experiences to change their own mental representations of attachment. Chapter 10 by Gretchen Miller Wrobel (Bethel University, St. Paul, Minnesota, USA) focuses on the subjective experience of the adopted persons themselves, providing a model for understanding adoption curiosity. Using data from the longitudinal Minnesota/Texas Adoption Research Project, she explores the expression of curiosity of adoptees in middle childhood and in adolescence.

Ruth Kelly, senior social work practitioner from Wexford, Ireland, contributes the important perspective of the birth family in adoption in Chapter 11. She summarizes her qualitative research with mothers who placed their children for adoption in Ireland. This chapter covers both the mothers' experiences of placing their babies for adoption, and the outcomes of reunions with the adopted adult many years later. Chapter 12 by Elsbeth Neil, Senior Lecturer in Social Work at the University of East Anglia, England, also includes the birth family perspective in adoption, in her analysis of how birth relatives' acceptance of the child's adoption relates to the openness of adoptive parents with whom they were having post-adoption contact. She reports on 30 'matched' cases where adoptive parents and birth relatives were both interviewed to explore some of the dynamics and transactions of post-adoption contact. Also drawing on research into openness in adoption in Chapter 13, Hal Grotevant who holds the Rudd Family Endowed Chair in Adoption at the University of Massachusetts – Amherst, uses his multi-perspective data from two waves of the Minnesota/Texas Adoption Research Project to explore how adoptive parents and birth parents manage distance and closeness in their relationships with each other. Finally, Chapter 14 by Gretchen Miller Wrobel and Elsbeth Neil summarizes some of the key messages for practice that are suggested by the previous contributions.

No one volume can cover every possible perspective on adoption and this collection is not exhaustive. Nevertheless this book does collect together the work of established and emerging adoption researchers from five different countries, giving an international perspective on the topic; research carried out into three key types of adoption are all covered (intercountry adoption, domestic special needs adoption, infant adoption); and a range of different theoretical and disciplinary perspectives are offered. Adoption is discussed from the point of view of the adoptive parents, the adopted person and the birth family. Furthermore, all contributions are written with the intention of making the latest research findings relevant and accessible to practitioners, as well as to identify implications for the future research agenda. It is our hope that the book will stimulate thinking both within and between the research and practice communities.

Acknowledgements

We would like to thank the Nuffield Foundation, London (and especially their deputy director Sharon Witherspoon) for their generous financial support, which made the Second International Conference on Adoption Research possible. Gratitude is also due to England's Department for Children, Schools and Families (formerly the Department for Education and Skills) who also helped fund the conference via their Adoption Research Initiative; and to the British Academy who sponsored two key international speakers in attending. Thank you to my colleagues at the University of East Anglia for all their help with hosting the adoption conference. Finally, thank you to my husband, Richard for your love and patience.

Elsbeth Neil

Thank you to my colleagues at Bethel University and the University of Minnesota who provided inspiration and support for this project. Most of all thank you to my family, John, Alex and Kathryn for your unending encouragement.

Gretchen Miller Wrobel
January 2008

Part 1

Adoption in Context

1

Nature, Nurture and Narratives

David Howe

I want to celebrate the part that adoption research and writing has played in our understanding of human experience and personal development. In the case of adoption at least, I want to show that Snow's (1956) two cultures of science and art have actually come together as men and women have pursued a shared fascination with adoption's ability to disturb the social and psychological landscape and in so doing, reveal the character of our human being. And as scientists and writers have developed their various researches and reflections, so adoption appears to have contributed much to our understanding of who we are, and what makes us who we are. I shall recognize four such contributions.

However, first I wish to begin with a little history.

It is a convention that most books on the adoption of children begin with its origins. These histories recognize that adoption, in some form or another, has occurred across time and place. And because adoption involves the care of children by parents and families other than those to whom infants were born, in Rowe's (1966) words, they are also stories of 'love and loss'. The three principal characters in these stories are the child, her genetic parents and her adoptive parents. It is the relationship between these three parties that has so intrigued artists and scientists alike.

Most accounts of adoption begin with the Biblical story of Moses. Soon after he was born, Moses was hidden by his birth mother to protect him from being killed. He was found in the bulrushes on the banks of the Nile and adopted by an Egyptian princess, a daughter of the Pharaoh. Forms of adoption are also recorded in ancient Greece and Rome.

In more recent times, the dislocation and break-up of extended families and old communities during the West's period of industrialization, coupled with disease, death and destitution, lead to increasing numbers of children born illegitimate or left orphaned and destined to become 'foundlings'. Many of these orphaned children were 'indentured' to families. There they would be fed and clothed and taught a skill or trade in return for helping out the family with its work or business. These arrangements represented a proto-form of adoption. Examples can be found in many countries including Scotland, the United States and England. Indeed, in some American states, many of these practices became regularized as legal adoptions as early as the middle of the nineteenth century. However, it was not until 1926 that England introduced its first adoption law, spurred on by the large number of orphaned and illegitimate children born during and after the First World War. There was a growing feeling that the quality of a child's parenting and upbringing could make as much difference to how he or she would turn out in life as family stock and heredity. To facilitate this belief in the importance of nurturing, and to protect the adoptive family from any potential interference from the biological family, adoptions became 'closed'. There could be no contact between the child's old and new families.

In their excellent book on adoption, Triseliotis, Shireman and Hundleby (1997) go on to recognize a third period of adoption philosophy and practice. This begins after the Second World War. The adoption of babies began to be seen as a solution to the problem of married couples' infertility. The so-called 'matching' of children to adoptive parents represented an attempt to ensure as much similarity as possible between the placed baby and her new family. But because in most Western countries the vast majority of childless, prospective adopters were white, then the matched child was a white, healthy, 'perfect' baby. The emphasis was on meeting the needs of infertile couples rather than those of the baby.

However, this period of adult-centred practices did not last long as adoption agencies began to shift towards more child-centred approaches, partly encouraged by the decreasing number of young babies available for adoption on the one hand, and the increasing number of couples wanting to adopt on the other. Other factors were also at play. Researchers recognized that many children were drifting, without thought or planning, in the public care system. If good quality family life was now recognized as fundamental to sound development, it seemed particularly important that these children, many of whom had suffered early adversity, should enjoy the benefits of permanent family care. So in the 1980s the mantra in the United States and United Kingdom became 'no child is unadoptable'. Older children, children with physical or learning difficulties, and non-white children were increasingly being placed for adoption with a variety of parents including those who might be infertile and childless, or might already have children, or be single, gay, separated, or divorced. Matters soon got complicated with ideological doubts about the correctness of white couples adopting black babies – a practice that became known as transracial adoption. In some countries, including Britain, this led to a drive to recruit more minority ethnic families as adopters, a policy and practice that has met with some success.

But as Triseliotis, Shireman and Hundleby (1997) observe, the latest phase in the history of adoption has witnessed a huge expansion of overseas adoptions with children from China, India, South America and many other countries being placed with predominantly Western families including adopters from America, the Netherlands, France and Italy. The rise of intercountry adoptions has revived many of the political issues that initially surrounded transracially placed children, with the old fault-lines of adult-centred versus child-centred adoptions being reopened.

Not surprisingly, these radical practices in which babies and young children born to one set of parents and raised by another, greatly fascinated philosophers and scientists. Adoption provided them with a 'natural experiment' to test whether nature or nurture, genes or environment determined children's development as they progressed from infancy to adulthood. And there was a further scientific bonus in the case of older-placed children, particularly those who had experienced deprivation and maltreatment in their first years of life – could the developmental harm suffered as a result of early adversity be overcome by later good-enough care? Is developmental recovery possible? The study of adopted children's development therefore became a major topic of enquiry for a whole variety of reasons.

Of course, there was also a straightforward child welfare policy question. Is adoption successful? How do adopted children compare developmentally with those who remain with families where the parenting is poor, or children who are reared in institutional care, or children who are looked after in foster care? The answer is generally that adopted children, particularly those placed as babies, do well (Howe, 1998). In most domains they compare favourably with normal populations of children matched socially and economically with those of their adoptive parents. In Brodzinsky's (2006) words, "the vast majority of adopted individuals are well within the normal range of adjustment." And although not quite so marked, many older-placed children, psychosocially speaking, also appear to fare comparatively well when adopted.

However, it was adoption's ability to throw light on questions of nature and nurture that captured the imagination of developmental scientists. Children raised by their genetic parents both inherit maternal and paternal genes *and* find themselves living in an environment created by those very same parents. In these situations it is difficult to disentangle the effect of biology and culture. But in the case of children adopted as young babies, genes and environment become separated. Thus, to the extent that adopted children resemble their biological parents and siblings, then genetic influences might be said to hold sway. And to the extent that children appear and behave similarly to their adoptive parents and non-related siblings, then the power of the environment might be seen to be at work. This field of study is known as behaviour genetics. Behaviour genetics is as much interested in nurture as it is in nature, environment as much as genes, and along with studies of identical twins, adoption has been a topic of key interest to the scientists in this field.

The adoption research carried out under the aegis of behaviour genetics has concentrated on four areas:

1. Intelligence, including education and occupational attainment
2. Temperament, personality and behaviour
3. Psychopathology and mental illness
4. Conduct disorders and criminal behaviour.

It is hard to do justice to the vast amount of research that has been generated by these scientists. Their research designs have grown in sophistication and their understanding of the relationship between genes and environment has become ever more subtle. Very broadly, these studies recognize the major part that genes play in our psychological, social and behavioural development. Across a wide range of abilities, attributes, characteristics and traits, adopted children's behaviour and development correlates with that of their genetic parents. But these correlations never reach levels commensurate with the child's degree of relatedness to their birth relative. This suggests that environment is also playing a part.

For example, several studies have shown that the cognitive abilities of adopted children correlate with those of their biological parents, but relatively these abilities are either raised or lowered depending on the social and economic circumstances of the adopters, that is, the quality of the environment (e.g. Capron and Duyme, 1989, 1996). Children born of lower IQ, educationally underachieved biological parents who are placed with educationally and economically advantaged adopters, have their expected IQ scores significantly raised compared with any brothers or sisters who might have remained in the biological family. Matched adopted children placed with adopters who have more modest educational and economic backgrounds do not show such pronounced gains. So although genes appear to underpin an individual's potential IQ score, environmental factors affect the extent to which that potential is achieved.

A similar story can be found in adoption studies of schizophrenia. In the general population, the risk of schizophrenia is about 1%. If your mother or father suffers the illness and you were brought up by them, the risk rises to somewhere between 6 and 13%. However, according to Lowing, Mirsky and Pereira (1983) and their work on the Danish Adoption Study, if you have a parent with schizophrenia but you are placed as a baby for adoption with non-schizophrenic adopters, this risk reduces to around 3% – still three times higher than normal but much lower than if you had lived with your schizophrenic parent. In this example, the birth family appears to pose both a genetic and an environmental risk, whereas the adoptive family offers some form of environmental protection against the onset of schizophrenia. Children born without the genetic risk would be unlikely to develop schizophrenia whatever the quality of the family environment.

The work of scientists such as Robert Plomin, Avshalom Caspi, Terrie Moffat, Michael Rutter, and David Reiss and his colleagues has explored gene–environment interaction, and how family relationships mediate or moderate the expression of genetic influences. This specific field of gene–environment interaction in which individuals appear to bring about their own environments is known as active or evocative gene–environment correlation. For example, Reiss et al's (2003) work has shown that heritable child characteristics influence parents' behaviour towards their child, and this applies equally well to adopters and the way they interact with their children. Paul (1998), writing a piece in *Psychology Today* based on a review of the work of Reiss and others, puts it almost poetically when she says that "as genes and environment interact in this way, they need to be in constant conversation, back and forth ... Even as genes are calling forth particular reactions, they're also reaching out for particular kinds of experience" (p. 2).

These studies, and many more like them, suggest that not only is the debate *not* one of nature *or* nurture, it is not even one of nature *and* nurture. Rather, we must look to the *interaction* of nature and nurture if we are fully to understand human development. Noble (2006), in his book *The Music of Life*, suggests that "genes are merely a data-base and cannot do anything without other systems interpreting them ... the environment affects the way genes work" (p. 5). This current way of thinking, partly based on the pioneering findings of so many adoption studies, offers a much more exciting, creative and insightful way of thinking about our psychological, indeed biological development. As Rutter (2006) has it in the title of one of his books, to understand the relationship between genes and behaviour, we need to look at the *interplay* between nature and nurture. Ridley (2003) titles his more populist book *Nature Via Nurture: Genes,*

Experience, & What Makes Us Human. He goes on to say "Genes are designed to take their cues from nature . . . nature is designed for nurture" (p. 4). Richardson (2000) sums up his position noting that "Precisely because humans (and other animals) are designed to be self-promoting, to continue to exist, they have evolved ways of incorporating information about the environment they encounter . . ." (p. 70).

> *So, adoption's first contribution to knowledge has been to play an integral part in helping us to understand how nature and nurture interact as children journey from infancy to adulthood.*

Most of the adoption gene–environment research has looked at children placed as babies. However, the number of very young babies now being adopted is relatively small, particularly in Britain. In the United Kingdom, older children with histories of abuse and neglect, rejection and trauma are much more typical of the kind of child being adopted. But there are also other adopted children whose pre-placement histories are equally unhappy. These children have experienced poor quality institutional care where many suffered severe neglect and global deprivation.

We know that children who remain with abusive and neglectful parents, and children who suffer institutional deprivation are at very high risk of seriously impaired psychosocial development. There is a high chance that they will develop a variety of psychopathologies and behaviour problems. In parenthesis, I do make a distinction between the developmental pathways followed by children who suffer abuse, neglect, rejection or trauma at the hands of their primary caregivers, and those children who have experienced extreme institutional neglect, typically failing to form a bond with a selective attachment figure.

The key research and policy question is to wonder at the fate of both groups of children when they are adopted. Having suffered major emotional setbacks and developmental impairment, can they achieve developmental recovery? When they experience good quality care, do they return to the normal pathways of psychosocial development, and in the case of severely neglected children, do they recover physically? In short, do they exhibit bio-behavioural catch-up?

The broad answer to these questions is yes, but there are qualifications. The general rule of thumb is that the earlier the age at which the child was first exposed to the maltreatment or deprivation, the more traumatic the experience, and the longer the child lived under those adverse conditions, the less complete is the level of psychosocial recovery and bio-behavioural catch-up (O'Connor *et al.*, 2000; Rutter, O'Connor and Beckett, 2000).

Even so, many severely neglected children show remarkable improvements, particularly in their physical and cognitive recovery, but also in many cases, in their emotional and behavioural progress, though here recovery is often less marked. The terrible pre-adoption experiences of these children speak of the power of hostile and helpless caregiving environments seriously to impair children's psychological development. They tell of the devastating consequences when children are starved of human relationships. But when adopted, these children also bear testimony to the healing power of warm, loving, attuned, empathic and sensitive caregiving, the kind of parenting provided by so many adoptive parents. Little wonder, then, so many researchers conclude that for these children adopters represent the most potent of therapeutic environments.

Our appreciation of the power of relationships to heal and the ability of children to bounce back when life does treat them kindly is therefore adoption's second major contribution to the sum of human understanding.

A rather different research tradition has formed around another of adoption's engrossing features – when you are not raised by your genetic parents, where do you feel you belong? Who are you? Who are your real parents? Issues of loss, identity, sense of self, and psychological connectedness are raised in stark relief when dealing with those who are adopted and those who adopt.

Aspects of this emerged in my own and Julia Feast's research when we studied adult adopted people who had decided to go on a journey and search for their birth parents (Howe and Feast, 2000). In many of these cases, the search led to direct face-to-face contact with a birth mother, sometimes a birth father, and often one or more birth siblings.

The two strongest themes in the search and reunion experience of adopted people were the wish to develop a more complete sense of self and identity, and the need to understand why one was placed for adoption. These two themes of 'roots' and 'reason' tap into (i) issues of self and the formation of identity; and (ii) feelings around loss, rejection and grief. Contact with a birth relative is for most people initially a means to an end. However, meeting someone who possesses so much information about you – in terms of what they know, how they look, how they behave, their personality – inevitably entails the development of some kind of relationship, one which may be charged with powerful feelings. But what we found in most cases was that the initial driving force behind the strong desire to search was curiosity, curiosity about who one might look like, behave like, move like. The emergence of a relationship with the birth relative, if one forms at all, is a secondary achievement. The relationship may or may not last once the primary goal of the search process has been reached.

So, not surprisingly, the most common reason given for conducting the search was 'to fill the gaps', 'to complete the jigsaw'. Adopted people who search are seeking to consolidate their identity by filling in a whole range of missing detail to do with looks, origins, accounts and explanations. Many of the dissonances experienced in adoption between nature and nurture, being born to one set of parents but chosen by another, the love of your adopters premised on a perceived rejection by your biological parents, and in the case of those placed transracially being black in a white family, belonging to your new family yet feeling somehow different – all of these splits can lead to a self which is experienced as divided, uncertain, incomplete, ambiguous, fluid, unanchored and shifting. "I feel like the whole of me is a dichotomy," said Sophie, an accomplished professional actor, "you know, there are many dichotomies and many dualities running through my life – I'm mixed race, I'm nearly ambidextrous, I am bisexual . . ." The search for self is part of the attempt to unite the fragmented pieces of experience, to ground what was previously drifting and loose.

When asked about being adopted, most respondents talked about their experiences in very positive terms, particularly those adopted as babies (Howe and Feast, 2000). The majority described their childhoods as happy. They said they felt loved. They felt they belonged in their families. However, about a half of all adopted people, including many of those who spoke positively, said that nevertheless they did feel slightly different – they were aware of physical and personality contrasts. This was not necessarily a negative observation, simply a statement of the way things were felt and perceived. We also found that women are twice as likely to search as men.

There was some evidence that those who were less positive about their adoption experience were slightly more likely to search, but this still left large numbers who had enjoyed very happy and successful adoptions also deciding to embark on the search and reunion journey, typically with the full support of their adoptive parents. In other words, because the majority of adopted people were content with their adoption experience, the majority of searchers were in fact positive about their adoptions, although of the minority who were less than happy, their decision to search was statistically marginally more likely.

Many searches lead to a reunion with the birth mother, and occasionally birth father. Eight years after their first reunion, about 50% of those who had met and established a relationship with their birth mother were still in some kind of contact (Howe and Feast, 2001). In some cases adoptive parents had also met the birth mother, and in one or two examples both sets of parents had become good friends and even gone on holiday together – without their child! But for most adopted people who had maintained some kind of relationship with their birth mother, the frequency and intensity of contact with their adoptive parents still remained much higher and greater. Only in a few cases, especially when the adoption experience had been described negatively, had relationships broken down with the adopters. In fact, there was some truth in the observation that adopted people who had the most secure childhoods seemed psychologically and emotionally sufficiently skilled to deal well with the challenges of the reunion experience, whatever its outcome.

Conversely, many of those who had suffered an unhappy adoption seemed less able to handle the emotional stresses of developing a relationship with their birth relatives. Although unhappy adoptions might spur the desire to establish an alternative relationship with the birth mother, the lack of emotional skill, ironically caused by the poor adoptive caregiving experience, meant that the individual was not well equipped to deal with the emotional and relationship needs, often experienced as very intense, generated by the reunion. In these cases, the relationship with the birth mother was at risk of breaking down, leaving the adopted person with no relationship with either mother (Howe and Feast, 2000, 2001).

Thus, the evidence of this study and others like it suggests that the social bonds of childhood tend to be much stronger than the ties of blood. Nurture is more potent than nature. The psychological self that developed in the care of the adopters, the family memories shared throughout childhood, the fabric of one's social identity, and the experience of being loved by parents over the early years appear to lay down deep and long lasting bonds between adopters and their children. This is not to say that adopted people don't have curiosity about and fascination with their genetic origins and their birth relatives – they do. Or that adopted people won't get on well with their birth mother – many will. But in terms of thinking about home and safety, love and understanding, comfort and familiarity, the social ties of early, sensitive caregiving, at least from the perspective of the adopted child, appear to outbid those of biology.

Thus, the insights generated into the nature of loss and identity, family and belonging, social bonds and genetic ties are adoption's third significant contribution to our understanding of the human experience.

The affiliative bond favouring stronger ties to the adoptive parents compared with the birth parents is often, but not always mirrored in literature.

There are many novels where the grown-up child does discover his or her birth parent but the first love is retained for the adopters to whom the child returns. This is the case in George Eliot's nineteenth century novel *Silas Marner*. Despite learning the identity of her true father, the son of a prosperous, land owning family, young Eppie chooses to live with the old man, the weaver Silas Marner, who raised her and came to love her as a daughter. Commenting on her novel, Eliot said that it was intended "to set in a strong light the remedial influences of pure, natural, human relations." Similar plot lines in which the social bonds of adoption win can be found in L.M. Montgomery's *Anne of Green Gables* and Charles Dickens' *Oliver Twist*. For example, Anne Shirley, an 11-year-old happy, cheerful and talkative orphan girl is adopted by 60-year-old Matthew and Marilla Cuthbert who live at Green Gables. Although they were expecting to adopt a boy to help Matthew run the farm, Anne's charms win them over and she brings them much happiness and devotion. Dickens, of course, uses adoption in a number of his novels as he examines the effects of poverty, the fate of orphans and foundlings, class and the family. *Bleak House* and *Great Expectations* as well as *Oliver Twist* all have adoption in some form or another cropping up in the plot.

Another adoption plot line involves a child who is abandoned because of maternal poverty, parental death or the stigma of illegitimacy and then raised by cruel, neglectful or exploitative carers. J.K. Rowlings's *Harry Potter* is but the latest in a long line of such characters. Harry's parents die while he is still a baby and he is brought up by his hostile and unloving aunt and uncle. In these stories nature generally triumphs over nurture. In spite of his aunt and uncle's attempts to suppress Harry's inherited tendency towards magic, nevertheless he is destined to become a wizard.

In other tales, the unhappily adopted child discovers his birth parents only for the reunion to lead to disastrous consequences. The classic example of adoption, identity and family is the story of *Oedipus*. Although there are several versions of the tale, traditionally Laius, King of the Thebes is warned by an oracle in the temple at Delphi that one day his son would slay him. When his wife, Iocaste gives birth to a boy, he takes the infant and leaves him exposed on a mountain with his feet bound together (hence the name Oedipus – swollen foot). A shepherd found the infant Oedipus – and incidentally, shepherds and similarly untainted, pastoral figures and artisans close to nature are frequently destined to become the adoptive parents of orphaned children – who was eventually adopted by King Polybus of Corinth and his wife. When Oedipus reached manhood, he too visited Delphi and upon learning that it was his destiny to kill his father and marry his mother, not knowing he was in fact adopted, he left Corinth. On his travels Oedipus met with Laius, they quarrelled and, as predicted by the Oracle, Oedipus killed his father. Later, as a reward for solving the riddle of the Sphinx, he received the throne of Thebes and the hand of the widowed queen, who unbeknown to Oedipus was his mother, Iocaste. They had four children and when his mother finally learned the truth, she committed suicide. Not a happy ending.

In her analysis of adoption in literature, Novy (2004), Professor of English Literature at the University of Pittsburgh and an adopted person herself, recognizes a third mythic adoption story in European and American culture, that of the adopted child who happily discovers her birth parents. Perdita in Shakespeare's *Winter's Tale* – whose name is derived from the Latin for 'lost' – is the example she cites to illustrate this myth.

The plot of a *Winter's Tale* is convoluted. Woven into the complex storyline is the jealousy of King Leontes. He believes that his wife, Hermione, has been having an affair with his boyhood friend, King Polixenes and that the daughter to whom she has just given birth is the love child of that adulterous relationship. However, no such affair has taken place and the baby is in fact King Leontes' own child. Not accepting Hermione's protestations of innocence, the baby is banished and is eventually adopted and raised by shepherds. The child is named Perdita – 'lost little girl'. After the passage of time and more twists and turns, the 16-year-old Perdita meets and falls in love with Florizel, the son of King Polixenes. Thinking Perdita to be the child of a lowly shepherd, Polixenes forbids the marriage of Florizel and Perdita. Yet more tortuous plot devices finally result in Perdita being recognized for who she truly is, the daughter of King Leontes and Queen Hermione. She is happily reunited with her royal birth parents, and of course fit to marry Florizel.

Novy (2004) believes these three basic types of adoption story – disastrous adoption followed by disastrous discovery, happy discovery in which the birth parent is the 'real and truly loving parent', and the happy adoption in which the adopters are confirmed as the 'real and truly loving' parents – these stories "act as paradigms . . . to shape feelings, thoughts, language, and even laws about adoption" (p. 1). Adoption plots in literature and in drama are explorations of nature and nurture, heredity and love, loss and identity, parenthood and childhood, culture and class. The tension that adoption sets up in the storyline allows a number of these basic human issues to be examined. Typically either the birth parents or adopters are good or bad. The adopted child moves between contrasting classes or cultures, between rich and poor, between one ethnic group or country and another. In Mike Leigh's film *Secrets and Lies*, after the death of her adoptive mother, the thirtyish something, black adopted middle-class child,

Hortense, an optometrist, meets her white working-class birth mother, a roadsweeper, and so the film bridges not only gaps of race but class too.

A more recent publishing trend has seen the appearance of autobiographies written by adopted people who have searched for, and in many cases had a reunion with their birth parent. For example, in the United Kingdom, several of these authors have been celebrities – Kate Adie (2003) the journalist, Nicky Campbell (2005) the TV presenter, Jeremy Harding (2007) author and journalist. Intriguingly, and perhaps tellingly, Harding calls his book *Mother Country* explaining that throughout his childhood, thinking about his two mothers was rather like straying into a tricky terrain. In a 2006 newspaper article, he says that "the contours of 'Mother Country' are sometimes daunting, and knowing where you are and who's out there can be hard, since to some extent, the child creates the mother in its mind, a charmed, unreliable place, where real people and events undergo strange transfigurations' (Harding, 2006).

Harding (2007) is by no means alone amongst adopted people who have become writers and actors in believing that the tendency to wonder and imagine, the feeling of being in between places and people, the sense of transience, the experience of seeing the world and one's place in it from different perspectives, is fertile ground for growing creative minds that are driven to reflect on uncertainty, identity, and the meaning of family and parenthood. The experience of the self as slightly dislocated, the sense of the self being both inside and outside of experience might provide the adopted individual with a peculiar sensitivity to many human situations. Edward Albee, the American playwright – the author of *Whose Afraid of Virginia Wolf?* – describes his adoption by a couple who managed vaudeville theatres, as difficult. "I never felt related to these people. I am a permanent transient . . . The only good thing about the adoption was that I was raised on live theatre . . . I was left pretty much to myself. I had a fairly active inner life" (Albee, 2005).

> *Adoption's fourth great contribution, therefore, has been to provide writers with the creative opportunity to explore many of life's fundamental questions – questions of who we are, of parenthood, of family, of belonging, of loss, of nature and nurture.*

These are the same questions posed by scientists but examined through the lens of the creative mind using one of humankind's most spell-binding techniques, that of story-telling.

Although this chapter has concentrated on the adopted child, similar avenues of thought, reflection and investigation could have been pursued with either the birth parent or adopter as the central character. They, of course, would have told rather different stories. But whether viewed by the scientist or the artist, we glimpse a little of the world's underlying character when things are out of place, not quite where they should be, not quite 'normal', in an unexpected alignment, fractured. Things being not how they should be, or how they were expected to be often drives scientific enquiry. Physicists note that distant starlight passing by the sun is bent by the gravitational warp exerted on space by the mass of the sun, thus confirming Einstein's 1915 prediction based on general relativity. Or, introduce a species from one continent into another and it plays havoc with the local ecology telling us much about the complex evolutionary balances found in nature. Or, create a plot-line where a stranger suddenly appears in the taken-for-granted world of a complacent community, or in which twins go their separate ways before they meet again as young adults, or when a child of noble birth is raised by shepherds in some pastoral idyll only to be reunited with the corrupt world of his birth – these narrative devices expose and throw into relief some of the more intriguing aspects of our deeper make-up.

Adoption, although born of loss, accident or tragedy, is also testimony to the resilience of the human spirit and the generosity of men and women towards one another.

References

Adie, K. (2003) *The Autobiography: The Kindness of Strangers*, Headline Books, London.

Albee, E. (2005) Interview, http://www.achievement.org/autodoc/page/alb1int-1 (accessed 22 August 2007).

Brodzinsky, D. (2006) Lecture, 20th Anniversary of the Post-Adoption Centre, London, May.

Campbell, N. (2005) *Blue-eyed Son: The Story of Adoption*, Pan Books, London.

Capron, C. and Duyme, M. (1989) Assessment of effects of socio-economic status on IQ in full cross-fostering study. *Nature*, 340, 552–3.

Capron, C. and Duyme, M. (1996) Effect of socio-economic status of biological and adoptive parents on WISC-R subtest scores of their French adopted children. *Intelligence*, 22 (3), 259–75.

Harding, J. (2006) Mother Country, *Observer*, 26 March 2006.

Harding, J. (2007) *The Mother Country*, Faber and Faber, London.

Howe, D. (1998) *Patterns of Adoption: Nature, Nurture and Psychosocial Development*, Blackwell Science, Oxford.

Howe, D. and Feast, J. (2000) *Adoption, Search and Reunion: The Long-term Experience of Adopted Adults*, BAAF, London.

Howe, D. and Feast, J. (2001) The long-term outcome of reunions between adult adopted people and their birth mothers. *British Journal of Social Work*, **31**, 351–68.

Lowing, P., Mirsky, A. and Pereira, R. (1983) The inheritance of schizophrenia disorder: A reanalysis of the Danish adoption study data. *American Journal of Psychiatry*, **1400**, 1167–71.

Noble, D. (2006) *The Music of Life: Biology Beyond the Genome*, Oxford University Press, Oxford.

Novy, M. (2004) *Imagining Adoption: Essays on Literature and Culture*, Michigan University Press, Michigan.

O'Connor, T.G., Rutter, M., Beckett, C. *et al.* (2000) The effects of global severe privation on cognitive competence: Extension and longitudinal follow-up. *Child Development*, **71**, 376–90.

Paul, A.M. (1998, Jan/Feb) The gene responsibility. *Psychology Today*, 1–5.

Reiss, D., Neiderhiser, J., Hetherington, E.M. and Plomin, R. (2003) *The Relationship Code: Deciphering Genetic and Social Influences on Adolescent Development*, Harvard University Press, Cambridge, MA.

Richardson, K. (2000) *Developmental Psychology: How Nature and Nurture Interact*, Macmillan, Houndmills.

Ridley, M. (2003) *Nature Via Nurture: Genes, Experience, & What Makes Us Human*, Fourth Estate, London.

Rowe, J. (1966) *Parents, Children and Adoption*, Routledge and Kegan Paul, London.

Rutter, M. (2006) *Genes and Behavior: Nature-Nurture Interplay Explained*, Blackwell, Oxford.

Rutter, M., O'Connor, T.G. and Beckett, C. (2000) Recovery and deficits following profound early deprivation, in *Intercountry Adoption: Developments Trends and Perspectives* (ed. P. Selman), BAAF, London, pp. 107–25.

Snow, C.P. (1956) The Two Cultures, *New Statesman*, 6 October.

Triseliotis, J., Shireman, J. and Hundleby, M. (1997) *Adoption: Theory, Policy and Practice*, Cassell, London.

2

How Tight Was the Seal? A Reappraisal of Adoption Records in the United States, England and New Zealand, 1851–1955

E. Wayne Carp

Introduction

The history of adoption has been one of the most neglected topics in the field of social history. There are several explanations for this lacuna. This is an intensely interdisciplinary subject, requiring scholars conversant in the law, social work, child and adult psychology, psychoanalysis, sociology, statistics, women's studies and anthropology.[1] In addition, the basic primary sources necessary for writing such a history – adoption case records – have been sealed by tradition and law. This has been an almost insurmountable barrier: no sources, no history. Finally, the relevant statutes, legislative debates, committee reports and departmental correspondence are often consigned to obscure archives. As a result, very little is known about the history of adoption records before the 1950s in the United States, England and New Zealand. In the past generation, however, scholars have become more interdisciplinary and have overcome the obstacle of inaccessible and difficult-to-access primary sources, producing a spate of new studies (Berebitsky, 2000; Carp, 1998; Carp and Leon-Guerrero, 2002; Cretney, 1998, 2003; Dalley, 1998; Griffith, 1997, 2005; Herman, 2002; Melosh, 2002; Nelson, 2003; Novy, 2001).

---

[1] It is, of course, possible to produce excellent work on the history of adoption within a single disciple. See for example, Grossberg (1985), Lowe (2000), Presser (1971-1972) and Zainaldin (1979).

This chapter will first demonstrate that in the United States, England and New Zealand, adoption records were open during the first half of the twentieth century or, if sealed, that a majority of adopted adults were able to access them fairly easily; and second, reveal when, why and how adoption records came to be sealed. In the United States, for example, the first adoption law, commonly known as the Massachusetts Children's Act enacted in 1851, was completely silent on the issue of secrecy and confidentiality and made no mention of adoption records. In fact, for the next century, the adoption records in the United States, with a few exceptions, were open to inspection by all members of the adoption triad (birth parents, adoptees and adoptive parents). Similarly, the history of English adoption and of adoption records reveals that before 1949, because of the way the law of informed consent was written, England practised a form of open adoption, where the birth mother and the adoptive parents knew each other's identities. And, in the era before the Second World War, although there were statutory prohibitions against triad members accessing their adoption records, informal pathways existed to allow birth mothers and adopted adults to discover information about their original families. Likewise, a large majority of New Zealand's adoption triad members were able to access their adoption agency records from the enactment of the Adoption of Children Act 1881 until the passage of the Adoption of Children Act 1955. From 1881 to 1955 the New Zealand court records and birth records were also open to all members of the adoption triad.

History of Adoption Records (United States)

There are three sources of family information about an adopted person: the records of the court that approved the final adoption; the case files of the adoption agency; and the repository for birth certificates (in the United States, usually the Bureau of Vital Statistics). What is perhaps the biggest surprise for anyone who studies this subject is that for a century after the enactment of the earliest adoption law in America, the Massachusetts Adoption Act of 1851, adoption records, with few exceptions, were open to inspection by members of the adoption triad. The story of how and when they were sealed is a complicated one. Adoption records were not all sealed at the same time because the 48 individual states, not the federal government, made that decision. Thus, in a few states, the court and adoption agency records might be sealed but the birth records open, while in another state all three categories of adoption records would most likely still be open. Because a strict chronological account would be confusing, the following account will proceed in a topical fashion, discussing adoption court records first, followed by adoption agency files, and ending with birth certificates.

In fact, adoption records have been sealed *twice* during the twentieth century. The first time, adoption triad members were *not* excluded from viewing their records. In 1917, lawmakers enacted the Minnesota Children's Code, which was the first law containing a clause making adoption court records confidential. The law was not intended to and did not prevent adopted adults from viewing their records. Rather, lawmakers stated explicitly that the goal of Minnesota's sealed adoption law was to keep the public from viewing the records. Because of the stigma of shame and scandal that surrounded adoption and illegitimacy during the first quarter of the twentieth century, they had in mind people like potential blackmailers who might threaten adoptive parents with telling the public about the child's adoption, or nosy neighbours who might discover the child's illegitimacy (Carp, 1998). Before the 1950s, half of the states had not even enacted confidentiality clauses into their adoption statutes. In 1942, for example, the founder of the Adoption Rights Movement, Jean Paton simply walked into the Probate Court in Detroit, looked up her adoption, and discovered her birth mother's full name. "There was no rigmarole then," Paton observed, "You were allowed to see your own paper in a kindly procedure" (Kittson, 1968, pp. 51–2).

Similarly, before the 1950s, adopted adults had little difficulty in accessing their files from adoption agencies. In general, state statutes remained silent on the regulation of adoption agency files, leaving it by default to the discretion of the agencies' executive directors and social workers. In the early twentieth century, social workers began keeping detailed files of adopted children for the sole purpose that they might return one day to the agency to recover their social history and make contact with their family of origin. For the next half-century, social workers cooperated with birth parents and adopted adults who returned to agencies requesting both non-identifying and identifying information. The Children's Home Society of Washington even conducted searches for adopted adults who were looking for original family members. Social workers routinely provided adoptive parents with information about their child (Carp, 1998).

Adopted adults could also access their original birth certificates, even after they had received an amended one. Good intentions led to amending and sealing the birth certificates of adopted children. Minnesota's 1917 Children's Code was also the first law in the United States to stipulate that when the court approved an adoption, the decree could reflect a change in the child's name, but birth certificates still carried the names of the adopted child's biological parents and were stamped with the word 'illegitimate' (Carp, 1998). How then could the public – in the guise of school officials and employers – be prevented from discovering the child's adoptive and illegitimate status? In 1930 two enterprising Illinois registrars of vital statistics put forth a concrete plan of issuing new birth certificates to adopted children with the names of the adopting parents, and proposed that the original certificate of birth be sealed with the decree of the court. However, they also suggested that the birth records were to be sealed from the prying eyes of the public, not from those directly involved in the adoption who were to be permitted to view them. The two registrars specifically recommended that the sealed records should be opened upon the demand of the child when he/she comes of age, or his or her birth or adopting parents, or by order of a court of record (Howard and Hemenway, 1931). By 1948, nearly every state in America had embraced the original recommendation of issuing a new birth certificate upon receiving a court-ordered decree of adoption (Carp, 1998; Huffman, 1949). Thus, during the first half of the twentieth century, adopted adults in the United States had no difficulty accessing their adoption court records, adoption agency records and birth certificates if they sought them (Carp, 1998; Samuels, 2001).

Secrecy Comes to Adoption Records (United States)

But this tradition of open records was slowly reversed during the 1950s as a movement to seal the records – this time *from* adoption triad members – gained momentum. Overall, war, demographic circumstances, changes in social work theory and practice, and the intellectual climate of opinion affected the adoption triad members' ability to access their adoption records. In addition to the continued large number of homes broken by death, divorce and desertion, there occurred a veritable demographic revolution in the number of children born out of wedlock. With social bonds loosened by World War II, illegitimacy rates, especially among non-whites, began to soar and continued their upward flight for the next 50 years. In 1938, 88 000 children were born out of wedlock; a decade later, 129 700; by 1958 the figure had climbed to 201 000, reaching 245 000 by 1962, a 306% increase in a quarter century. The largest increase in the number of out-of-wedlock births occurred among non-white mothers, climbing two and a half times, from 46 700 in 1938 to 130 900 in 1957 (Vincent, 1964).

But it was the baby boom, beginning in the mid-1940s and reaching its peak in the late 1950s, with its dramatic rise in marriages and births, which increased the demand for infants to adopt and resulted in adoption agencies being inundated with requests for children (Carp and Leon-Guerrero, 2002, pp. 198–9). The baby boom was both cause and effect of a profound change in the national culture that tied personal happiness to an ideology of domesticity and the nuclear family. Parenthood became a necessity. The media romanticized babies, glorified motherhood, and identified fatherhood with masculinity and good citizenship. The consequences of this celebratory pronatalism mood, as the historian May (1995) has written, "marginalized the childless in unprecedented ways." Uncomfortable at being childless and the subject of public opprobrium, many of these childless couples sought adoption in record numbers as one solution to their shame of infertility.

The crucial ingredient in the origins of the revolution in adoption practice was not the increase of 'supply' factors, though these were important, but on the 'demand' side, as childless couples besieged adoption agencies pleading for a baby to add to their household. Even before the war years, the nation found itself in an adoption boom. Startled Children's Bureau officials initially attributed the unexpected demand for adopted children to the low birth rate of the Depression years and subsequent wartime prosperity, as previously economically strapped couples found they could now afford to start adoptive families (MacKenzie, 1940). But with the baby boom and the new pronatalism culture, the number of applications to adopt a child soared. In 1937 child welfare officials used incomplete returns to estimate that there were between 16 000 or 17 000 adoptions annually; of which one-third to one-half were adoptions by relatives (Theis, 1937). By 1945 the Children's Bureau estimated that adoptions had increased threefold from 1937, to approximately 50 000 annually; a decade later the number of adoptions had nearly doubled again to 93 000 and by 1965 climbed to 142 000 (Reid, 1963). In less than 30 years, the number of adoptions had grown nearly ninefold.

In the decade after World War II, this new interest group – white, middle-class and childless couples – overwhelmed the understaffed and underfunded adoption agencies, which had failed to anticipate the increase in adoption applicants. The demand far exceeded the number of available children. By the mid-1950s one expert estimated that of the four and half million childless couples, fully one million were seeking the approximately 75 000 children available for adoption (Lake, 1954; Schapiro, 1956). By 1957, depending on what region of the nation a prospective adoptive couple inhabited, CWLA executive director Joseph P. Reid estimated that the odds were between 18 to 1 and 10 to 1 against receiving a child (Reid quoted in Barclay, 1957). Social workers accommodated adoptive parents' demand for infants by following the new advice of early placements advocated by the British psychiatrist John Bowlby (1951, pp. 15–51, 101–8; see also Bowlby, 1988, chapter 2). Citing a mass of clinical evidence, Bowlby demonstrated the adverse effect that 'maternal deprivation' – the lack of a mother's care – had on the development of infants' character and mental health. He recommended strongly that "the baby should be adopted as early in his life as possible" (p. 101), specifying that "the first two months should become the rule" (p. 103). By 1955 the Los Angeles County Bureau of Adoptions, one of the largest agencies in the country, reported its success of placing infants directly from the hospital (Lynch and Mertz, 1955).

With the tremendous increase in illegitimacy during World War II, coupled with the pronatalism and the baby boom of the post-war years, adoptions soared and so did the number of states passing laws sealing adoption court records.[2] By 1948 a majority of states had sealed their court records (Leavy, 1948). Why state legislators did so at this time is difficult to say because of a paucity of evidence. One legal historian Samuels (2001) has suggested that the sole reason lawmakers sealed adoption court records was to protect "adoptive parents and their adoptive children from being interfered with or harassed by birth parents" (p. 385).

Adoption agencies followed a similar path of preventing members of the adoption triangle from gaining access to the information in their adoption records, but the pattern of closure was more complex. Adoption agency records had never been completely open. That is because although there were no statutory prohibitions, executive directors of adoption agencies had discretion to withhold information from triad members. And, adoption agency officials viewed the relationship between birth mothers and adoptive parents with caution, favouring adoptive parents. They shared their fear, common in the early decades of the twentieth century that birth mothers would return to claim their children either out of love or money. Progressive Era social workers thus incorporated secrecy between birth and adoptive parents into the adoption agency case records they created. The Children's Home Society of Washington's relinquishment form dating from the 1910s, for example, contained a section prohibiting birth parents from searching for their children (Carp, 1998). In 1938 the Child Welfare League of America (CWLA), the leading private adoption organization in the nation, responding to complaints from unwed mothers and concerned about the loss of clients to commercial adoption agencies, issued Standards that recommended "adoption proceedings be completed without unnecessary publicity" (quoted in Carp, 1998, p. 27; see also p. 112). When adoption

---

[2]   By the mid-1930s, a few states such as New York (1935), Oregon (1939) and Maryland (1939) had already sealed their adoption court records (Leavy, 1948, p. 18).

agencies closed their records to unwed mothers in particular, these standards played an important role.

Two other factors were crucial to the decision by adoption agencies to close their records to birth mothers. One was the changing demographics of adoption agencies clientele: post-war unwed mothers were younger (a median age of 18 years instead of 22) as were their children (4 days old rather than 4 years). Secrecy was much easier to impose (Carp, 1998). The other factor was the uncritical acceptance by the social work profession of psychoanalytic theory, tenets of which by 1958 had been incorporated into the Child Welfare League of America's (1958) influential Standards for Adoption Service. It stated that unwed mothers "have serious personality disturbances [and] need help with their emotional problems" (p. 14). The solution to these 'problems' was to separate the unwed mother from her child, place the child for adoption, and make sure that if the mother ever returned to the agency for information, she be denied access (Carp, 1998). By the end of the 1950s, adoption agencies had shut birth mothers out from accessing information about the children they had relinquished.

Between the 1950s and the 1970s, adult adoptees also found access to their adoption agency records barred. The process was uneven; the reasons not always clear. And there were exceptions: Alabama did not seal its adoption records until 1991. Again, records were never totally accessible even to adopted adults. Social workers, acting in what they felt to be the best interests of the child, had always selectively withheld potentially damaging non-identifying facts about the child's background, such as racial (African American), birth (illegitimacy) or social (imprisonment of father) information. They believed such information to be 'useless' to the child. A sincere wish to spare the individual painful emotions or, as they saw it, from social stigma, motivated these omissions (Carp, 1998).

But beginning in the 1950s social workers began to refuse adult adoptees access to their records when they returned to the agency for identifying information based on a totally new argument: Freudian psychology. Adoption officials perceived adopted adults who sought such information as neurotic and pathological, and by extension their request as a sign of a failure of the adoptive process (Bernard, 1953; Clothier, 1939, 1943). In addition to psychoanalytic theory, adopted adults found that they had to overcome an increasing stress on social work professionalism, an unintended consequence of state lawmakers' desire to crack down on 'welfare cheats' by publishing the public assistance rolls. Social workers resisted these efforts by conservative legislatures to harass their clients, but in the process they often broadened the principle of confidentiality to include adopted adults as well as those on public assistance (Carp, 1998).

Birth records were eventually sealed, too. Responding to the pronatalism of the era, Children's Bureau officials began to justify keeping birth records secret by invoking the need to protect adoptive parents from possible interference by birth parents. They recommended that both sets of parents should remain unknown to each other. Such a concern reflected a long-standing fear by social workers. However, this was the first time that the Federal Children's Bureau or public health officials ever acted on this fear; the first time they had justified confidentiality for reasons other than the welfare of the adopted child (U.S. Department of Labor, 1949). State legislatures began following the Children's Bureau's advice. By 1960, in 29 states, adoptees could access their original birth certificates only by petitioning a court. But in 20 others, adopted adults were still free to inspect their records. In the 1960s, four more states closed their birth records; six more did so in the 1970s, and seven more after 1979. Only two states, Alaska and Kansas have never closed their birth records to adopted adults (Samuels, 2001).

Between the 1950s and 1980s, access to adoption court records was closed down first to birth mothers, then to adopted adults. Next came the denial of access to adoption agency records, followed at last by birth certificates. The seal was now tight.

History of Adoption Records (England and Wales)

Although adoption certainly existed as a social institution, in the sense of providing a home for a child who would be cared for as a member of the adopters' family, it was not until 1926 that England enacted the Adoption of Children Act 1926 (Cretney, 2003). Why did it take England until 1926 to provide for legal adoption? Scholars have advanced numerous reasons. First, opposition to adoption was deeply entrenched in England where property and inheritance rights were venerated. Second, adoption had to overcome the seemingly insurmountable obstacle of the common law, which held that parental rights and duties were inalienable (Lowe, 2000). But more importantly for understanding openness and secrecy in adoption, it is wise to concentrate on one long-range cause and one triggering event. The long-range cause was that for several generations before the Great War, there was a long-standing tradition of adoption being associated with the 'criminal treatment of illegitimate children', otherwise known as 'baby farming' (Behlmer, 2002). Newspaper exposés of unmarried mothers who wanted to rid themselves of their children repeatedly revealed that they paid foster parents or nurses to have them 'adopted'. These foster parents or nurses took the child in exchange for weekly payments or a lump sum at the time of transfer and then when payments stopped, they simply ended 'caring' for the child. The newspapers labelled the deaths of these children the 'slaughter of the innocents'. Between the 1860 and 1890, public health officials went underground and investigated these transactions. One official placed a single ad in a newspaper for an adoption of a child for five pounds and received 333 replies. Subsequent visits to the homes proved "beyond doubt" that many of these women "carried on the business [of adoption] with a deliberate knowledge that the children would die very quickly" (Behlmer, p. 83). The alarm over 'baby farming' lasted for more than a generation.

The triggering event that overcame England's officialdom's reluctance to grant *de facto* adoptions legal security was the Great War. Nearly three-quarters of a million soldiers died during World War I; another 150 000 more citizens, many of them young men, died during the influenza outbreak of 1918–1919. Thus, during that short, five-year period, a huge number of 'war orphans' lost at least one parent. Increasing their numbers were the 'war babies', the illegitimate children born of wartime liaisons, which reversed the long-time decline in illegitimacy rates (Behlmer, 2002). The result, as the historian, George Behlmer has written, was that "never in living memory had there been so many children who needed new homes or so many grieving parents ready to provide them" (p. 95).

The Tomlin Committee (1926)

Appointed in 1924, the Tomlin Committee eventually wrote the Draft Bill that became enacted as the Adoption of Children Act 1926. According to the Tomlin Report, the adoption societies believed that secrecy was essential to adoption. However, the Tomlin Committee was dead set against secrecy in adoption, noting disapprovingly that such a policy "deliberately [sought] to fix a gulf between the child's past and future" (quoted in Teague, 1989, p. 68). The Committee further observed, "we think that this system of secrecy would be wholly unnecessary and objectionable with a legalized system of adoption, and we should deprecate any attempt to introduce it" (quoted in Keating, 2001, p. 6).

The Tomlin Committee's lack of enthusiasm for adoption and secrecy was matched by a zealous concern for the rights of birth parents and their children. This manifested itself in ensuring that the birth parents' consent to the adoption was real and informed, which resulted in a policy tantamount to an open adoption that became embedded in the 1926 Adoption of Children Act. Acting on the association of adoption with surreptitious child placements and baby farming, the Committee assumed the High Court would want to see the birth parents and that the birth parents would want to know who was to adopt their child, what kind of people they were, and the condition of the home the child would be brought up in. Thus, the 1926 Adoption Act prescribed that the birth parents of the adopted child and the adoptive parents should physically be known to each other.

Moreover, Adoption Rules, drawn up for the county and local courts, required the mother to receive the address of the adoptive parents on the form used for the giving of parental consent (Cretney, 2003). As one senior civil servant wrote in January 1927:

> It is not intended that the name of the proposed adopter should be concealed from the natural parent. ... It is essential ... that before a legal adoption takes place, the natural parent should have sufficient knowledge with regard to the proposed adopter to give a real consent ... and it would not be possible for the Rules made under the Act to prescribe that the natural parent might purport to consent to the adoption without knowing who the proposed adopter is. (quoted in Keating, 2001, p. 7)

That these legislative conditions were put into practice is evident from the *Minute Book of the Bath Juvenile Court*, which reveals that between 1927 and 1933 there were occasional interim adoption orders made with conditions attached permitting birth parents to visit their children on an interim basis – in one case, a father was allowed to visit his daughter for two weeks every three months (Keating, 2001).

The Horsbrugh Report (1937)

The Government's suspicion of adoption societies' practices did not abate. If anything, it heightened: with the increase in adoptions – over 5000 a year by the mid-1930s – state scrutiny became intense. In 1935 the Home Office formed the Horsbrugh Committee, chaired by Florence Horsbrugh MP, to investigate the methods pursued by adoption societies and to recommend reforms to rectify what was believed to be "the evils associated with unlicensed, unregulated and unsupervised adoptions" (Teague, 1989, p. 70). In the course of its investigation, the Committee revisited the issue of consent orders and secrecy. Its Report noted that adoption societies' officials, pressing for secrecy in adoption, testified that many adopters displayed anxiety that their name and address were made known to birth parents. These witnesses claimed that adoptive parents feared that birth parents might disturb the child or engage in blackmail; some alleged that they knew of adoptive parents who had moved to a different part of the country to avoid being interfered with (Horsbrugh, 1937).

The needs of the birth parents weighed heavily with the Horsbrugh Committee members, also, but in a different way. In the Report, they countered the adoption societies' arguments for adoptive parents' need for secrecy by observing that they "had been told [that birth] parents are often very anxious to know where their children have been placed and to receive information as to their children" (Horsbrugh, 1937, p. 18).

The Report went on to rebuke the adoption societies, many of whom, in the interest of secrecy, had the consent form signed before the name and address of the adopters had been inserted or had the names of the adopters covered over (Horsbrugh, 1937; see also Cretney, 1998).[3] It reminded the societies that "no adoption order may be made under the Adoption of Children Act 1926 except with the consent of every person or body who is a parent or guardian of the infant" (Horsbrugh, 1937, p. 18). Committee members also accused adoption societies of desiring secrecy because they favoured adopters over birth parents. The Report chastised the societies for not being "sufficiently concerned to keep in touch with the mother once the child has been handed over to" the adoptive parents (Horsbrugh, 1937, p. 20). In some cases, the Report scolded, the societies were even known to have prevented a meeting between the mother and the adopters because the adopters expressed a wish to avoid the meeting or feared that the mother might regret the step she had taken and the adoption fail because of non-consent (Horsbrugh, 1937).

Condemning the societies' one-sided regard for adoptive parents, the Horsbrugh Report went on to justify the right of 'informed consent' for birth mothers. The practices of the adoption societies in regard to secrecy and consent, committee members noted,

> cannot be right, or after all it is the mother who supplies the child and the fact that her consent is required to the making of an order in favor of a particular person or persons implies that she should at least be placed in possession of information—certainly if she desires it—to enable her to decide whether to give or withhold her consent to the adoption of her child by these persons. (Horsbrugh, 1937, p. 21)

The Report recommended as a safeguard that upon first applying to an adoption society, birth parents should "fully understand the consequences of handing over a child for adoption and that they should be made aware

---

[3] The societies also feared that the possibility that the birth mother might disappear before the adoption could be arranged.

that they have both a duty and a right to attend court and by attending an opportunity to satisfy themselves personally as to the suitability of the prospective adopters and as to all other matters with which the court is concerned" (Horsbrugh, 1937, p. 22). To assure there is no misunderstanding, the Report further recommended that the societies provide birth parents with a printed form "explaining in simple language the effect of adoption and their rights and duties in connection with an application for an adoption order, and that the signature of the [birth] parent should be obtained to a prescribed form stating that she has read and understands the memorandum" (Horsbrugh, 1937, p. 22).

The resultant Adoption of Children (Regulation) Act 1939 preserved the notion that a mother could not reasonably consent to adoption unless she knew the identity of the adopter. Conversely, adopters were well aware of the identity of the birth parents. Thus, 'informed consent' led to a form of open adoption, which, as we shall see, became a vital source of information for adopted adults in search of their birth families.

History of Birth Records

If adoptions were not clothed in secrecy, what about adoption records? Let's look at birth records first. The Adopted Children Register was open to anyone who wished to examine it, but there existed an apparent insurmountable difficulty for adopted adults searching for his or her birth family: the adopted child would be referred to in the birth register by his or her biological family surname and in the Adopted Children Register by his or her adoptive family surname. To connect the two entries the Registrar General was required to maintain yet a third separate register, "to record and make traceable the connexion [*sic*] between any entry in the register of births which has been marked 'Adopted' pursuant to this Act and any corresponding entry in the Adopted Children Register" (Adoption of Children Act 1926). This separate file was sealed and no inspection was permitted without a court order (Ovsiowitz, 1986).

However, what many adoption researchers have failed to realize is that the Adoption of Children Act 1926 was contravened and an unknown number of adopted adults were able to discover the names of their birth parents. The reason for this is that the High Court frequently directed entries in the Adopted Child Register to be entered in the child's original surname. Apparently, the county courts were not consistent on the issue either, with some also contravening the letter of the law, much to the annoyance of the Registrar-General, Sir Claud Schuster, who believed that high matters of constitutional principle were at stake. Schuster failed to take any action, for fear the publicity would open more issues than he was willing to deal with (Cretney, 2003).

Informal Pathways to Birth and Family Information

Adopted adults were also capable of discovering the details of their birth families directly from their adoptive parents. This was possible because adoptive parents were usually aware of their child's original surname, because when they first filed the adoption application, the original birth certificate would have been lodged with it (Terry, 1979). Or their adoptive parents might have seen the document at one of the adoption societies. Discussing county welfare offices, Younghusband (1978) found that in the mid-1950s, confidentiality was not a high priority, "with the records kept on the counter at the reception desk with names and addresses clearly visible" (p. 23). In other cases, adopted adults might have stumbled upon the relevant documents after their adoptive parents had died. In addition, before World War II, third-party intermediaries, such as local doctors, nurses and birth parents arranged the majority of adoptions informally. These intermediaries sometimes gave the adoptive parents the birth details of the baby (Rushbrooke, 2001; Smith and Logan, 2004). Armed with this information about their birth families, adopted adults could simply apply directly to Somerset House for a copy of the original birth certificate.

Moreover, adoptees could sometimes receive facts about their birth if they made a claim directly to the adoption societies, which were woefully lacking in professional staff late into the 1950s (Rushbrooke, 2001). In one northern county borough in the mid-1950s, for example, of the 72 social workers employed, only five had had a professional training and 42 had no training of any kind; nor was training considered of much importance (Younghusband, 1978). In fact, not until the Children Act 1975 was the professionalization of the adoption process and the appointment of quali-fied children's officers in local authorities finally completed when that Act outlawed adoption by parents (except for relatives) and by third parties, such as a vicar or general practitioner (Ball, 2003). Moreover, as adoptions declined in the 1960s, many adoption societies closed up shop, and their records were transferred to the Local Authority, where birth information was given to adoptees who applied directly (Rushbrooke, 2001).

Quantifying these informal methods of how an adopted adult might have received information about one's family of origin before records were opened is difficult. However, a survey by Day (1980) of the first 500 coun-selling interviews at the General Register Office in London under Section 26 of the 1975 Children Act found that "in many instances, the applicant wanted to have official confirmation of details already in his possession" (p. 24). Similarly, a study conducted in 1983 by Haimes and Timms (1983), in which they interviewed 45 adoptees, revealed that 21 of these knew their original name and the name of their birth parents before they applied to the Register General for birth records under Section 26 of the 1975 Children Adoption Act. While not conclusive, these studies suggest that many adopted adults before the age of open records were in possession of identifying information about their family origin.

Secrecy Comes to England: The Adoption of Children Act 1949

The Children Act 1949 completely changed the law governing the requirement of parental consent to adoption and ushered in a regime of secrecy in adoption by effectively destroying the mother's right to know the identity of the adopters. Although the adoption societies naturally provided leadership in the campaign for secrecy, war and demographic circumstances again are crucial for understanding the genesis of the Adoption of Children Act 1949.

The Second World War placed an unprecedented strain on the family. As in the United States, illegitimacy soared, nearing an unprecedented 10% of all births in 1945 (9.3%); divorce petitions climbed from 5750 in 1937 to 48 501 in 1941, with adultery accounting for 71% of the divorces in 1947. Concomitant with the growing belief that marriage and family life was being seriously undermined by widespread promiscuity and marital infidelity, there was great concern about Britain's falling birth rate, which had been troubling policy makers since the 1930s. Consequently, according to Fink (2000) there was "a widespread belief that to ensure society's well-being in the postwar years, the family's moral, emotional, and material stability had to be restored" (p. 179). The well-being of children, including adopted children, became one of the government's highest priorities. Moreover, John Bowlby's work on maternal deprivation, which stressed the importance of the mother–child relationship, became enormously influential, especially for adoptions. Bowlby's work emphasized that children who could not be raised by their birth parents should be permanently placed with adoptive parents, if they were to form an attachment successfully (Welbourne, 2003).

As in World War I, there was a huge increase in the number of adoptions. In 1939, the courts granted 7926 adoption orders; after World War II, in 1946, the number more than tripled to 23 564, with the great majority of children being born out of wedlock. However, adoption societies arranged less than a quarter of the adoptions (Cretney, 1998, 2003).

Thus, the majority of adoptions in England were being made without state supervision or investigation, despite the recommendations of the Horsbrugh Report. According to Cretney (2003), as part of a massive reform that the Labor government instituted that placed adoption under state regulation, the Adoption of Children Act 1949 "completely rejected the notion, implicit in the 1926 Act, that a mother could not reasonably consent to adoption unless she knew the identity of the adopter" (p. 612). Instead the 1949 Adoption of Children Act permitted the adopters' identity to be concealed behind a serial number (Cretney, 2003). The increase in adoptions, the tilt towards adopters and their desire for secrecy heralds the true beginning of the 'fresh start' philosophy.

The secrecy in adoptions in England was matched by the growth in secrecy in adoption records, meaning birth certificates. This was because the vast majority of adoption orders were now being carried out not in the High Court but in county courts, where access to birth certificates could only be gained through a court order.

History of New Zealand Adoption

As in England and other countries, adoption had been in existence much earlier and had been taking place informally by Pākehā [Anglo/Europeans] foster parents who agreed to receive children as members of their families. Similar to England during the Victorian period, there was considerable opposition and suspicion of legal adoption in New Zealand, due to the evils of baby farming and the social stigma of illegitimacy. However, also like England, the perception of the growing need to give security to the adopted child and adopted parents eventually resulted in the early introduction of legal adoption, spurred on by the dynamic leadership of Prime Minister George Waterhouse. Thus, in 1881, New Zealand became the first country in the British Empire to legalize adoption with the passage of the Adoption of Children Act (Griffith, 2005).

History of Adoption Records (New Zealand)

From the Adoption of Children Act 1881 until 1915, anyone could obtain a copy of any adoptee's original birth entry – with birth names and birth parents' names. There were no restrictions on these adoption records (Griffith, 1997; Iwanek, 1987). With the passage of the Birth and Deaths Registration Amendment Act in 1915, New Zealand became the first country in the world to invent the amended birth certificate. The sole reason for this innovation was put forth during the House Debate by Mr E.P. Lee (from Oamaru, on the South Island of New Zealand), who first proposed that the adoptee's birth be reregistered in the adoptive parents' names and adoptees' new names. He stated (quoted in Griffith, 1997) "a certain amount of stigma exists in getting a certificate in another name than the legal one" (p. 348). There was no intent by the legislators to conceal the truth of the adoptees' origins, only to protect them from the stigma of illegitimacy (Griffith, 1997). Moreover, adopted persons were not restricted from inspecting or receiving their original birth certificates.

The amended birth certificate, however, might be seen as an impediment to access to adopted adults' birth certificate because, if while growing up, their parents never informed them of their adoption, it is conceivable that they would never know the truth of their origins. However, as in England before the Adoption of Children Act 1949, a number of factors ensured that a high percentage of adopted persons eventually found out that they were adopted and thus potentially had access to their birth records and identifying information. For example, before the passing of the Adoption Act 1955, which closed access to adoption records, consent to adoption could not take place unless the identity of the proposed adopters had been disclosed to the birth mother (Griffith, 1997). Also as in England, the forms that adopting parents signed included the child's birth surname and birth's mother's name and address. Because New Zealand's adoptive parents were often concerned about the genetic background of the birth parents and the child's background, these facts were important in calming fears and often remembered. Adoptions arranged by doctor, clergy, solicitor, friend, or even a response to a newspaper ad were far more common than adoption agency placements. These intermediaries knew the identity of the child and often passed it on to the adopting parents. A copy of the official adoption order, with the adoptee's full birth name, was issued to all adoptive parents, filed with family papers in most homes, and prone to adoptee discovery. There was also the gossip factor – if parents did not inform adoptees, someone would. An astounding one-half of adoptees were placed within the same district they were born in. As one adoption researcher (Griffith, 1997) has put it: "The age old 'Did you know' about illegitimate scandals was an efficient adoption information exchange" (p. 392). After analysing the statistics and thousands of pages of documents, the historian Sir Keith Griffith (1997) estimates that between 1881 and 1955, 60% of New Zealand's adopted adults "did or could know of their origins" (p. 393).

Secrecy Comes to New Zealand: Adoption Act 1955

After nearly 70 years of open records, New Zealand closed its adoption records with the passage of Section 23 of the 1955 Adoption Act. As in the

United States, important demographic changes in New Zealand's adoption population and social work theory and practice occurred that were responsible for the regime of secrecy and the restriction on adoptees' access to their records. Up until roughly 1940, Anglo/Europeans preferred to adopt young children, who were more 'useful' in the fields or around the home than babies who were viewed as 'uneconomic'. Only a third of the children adopted in New Zealand between 1920 and 1939 were under one year of age; a little over a third were between one and five years of age, and the rest were over five (Else, 1991). Thus, close to two-thirds of these children would retain memories of their birth parents and siblings, reinforcing statutes that gave triad members access to their records and making secrecy all but impossible. Up until the 1940s, the State did its best to keep unmarried women and illegitimate babies together as a fitting punishment for the mother's sin and as cost-cutting measure: institutional care was expensive. While even into the late 1940s, more mothers tried to keep their babies than placed them for adoption; most dependent children were placed in institutions. The babies placed for adoption were usually the result of a married woman's extramarital affair (Else, 1991; Goldson, 2003; New Zealand Law Commission, 2000).

By the early 1950s, an intellectual revolution had occurred in social work, fuelled by British developmental psychiatrist, John Bowlby's study *Maternal Care and Mental Health* (1951) on attachment theory. Bowlby recommended, "very early placing for adoption" to promote bonding with the new mother figure and to avoid the harmful effects of institutional care (Else, 1991). Bowlby's (1951) theory gave impetus to separating babies from their unwed mothers and placing them with childless couples. Adoption became the rage. As Lewis Anderson (quoted in New Zealand Law Commission, 2000), the Deputy Superintendent of the Department of Social Welfare stated in the 1950s:

> I am assuming that all who read this . . . think as I do that, in principle, adoptions are a good thing, and that I do not need to write about the emotional satisfaction for adoptive parents and child that can ensue from a good adoption. We will agree that adoptions should be encouraged rather than discouraged. (p. 16)

The press, such as *The Evening Post*, spread the pro-adoption message from the Child Welfare Department (quoted in Iwanek, 1987): "There is nothing to compare with successful adoption as a method of care for otherwise unwanted children. Nor is there anything to compare with it as a means of setting up happy family groups" (p. 11).

Consequently, many young pregnant mothers were smuggled into the city to live in a cheap or free private board or a Home and deliver their babies in secret, while prospective adoptive mothers were known to have faked their pregnancy with the help of an artfully positioned pillow months before the adoption (Else, 1991). In their own interests, it was believed, adoptees should be completely cut off from their own origins. Maternity institutions such as Bethany, Motherhood of Man, and Alexandra began to encourage single mothers to relinquish their babies and promote adoption. Child welfare services also began promoting adoptions. The culmination of these demographic trends, intellectual ideas, and social work theories and practice was the Adoption Act of 1955, which implemented the 'complete break' theory and imposed secrecy on adoption records denying adopted persons the right to inspect them (Goldson, 2003; Griffith, 1997). Section 23 of the Adoption Act stated that "Adoption records shall not be available for production or open to inspection except on order of the court" except for limited access to estate administrators and marriage celebrants (Griffith, 1997, p. 384).

Conclusion

Adopted adults in all three Anglophone countries were able to access their adoption records before the 1950s, but the reasons varied greatly. In the United States, a federal system of government traditionally left family matters to state governments and the private sphere. State legislators sealed adoption court proceedings from public scrutiny, followed the advice of public health officials and their allies in social work, and issued amended birth certificates to protect adopted persons from the stigma of illegitimacy. State laws, mostly silent on the issue of adoption records, left it to the discretion of adoption agencies, whose general policy was to dispense identifying information upon request. Thus, before the 1950s, most adopted adults and birth parents had little difficulty in accessing their records in the United States; only in a few states did laws prohibit triad members from accessing their court records.

In contrast, in both England and New Zealand, the parliamentary system of government provided a uniformity and purpose in adoption law that was often lacking in American administration. Although the system of government was different, the result was the same: many triad members were able to access their adoption records until the 1950s. In England, the Adoption of Children Act 1926 emphasized the birth mother's informed consent to the adoption, which led to a form of open adoption and knowledge of the identity of the birth parent, the result of the desire to prevent the long-standing practice of trafficking in children. Other informal pathways by which adopted persons became aware of information about their original families included the Adopted Child Register, birth and family information provided by adoptive parents and adoption agencies. Similarly, in New Zealand, the evils of baby farming led to the first law to make adoption legal, the Adoption of Children Act 1881, which permitted adopted adults the right to access their birth certificates. There were no restrictions on adoption agency or court records until 1955. Likewise, pathways such as local gossip and informal access to their adoptive parents' adoption orders provided a majority of New Zealand's adopted adults with information about their original families.

No one event led the curtain of secrecy to drop on adopted adults and birth parents, especially birth mothers, in these three countries. But there is no question that the 1950s represented a watershed era. In all three Anglophone countries, a huge increase in wartime illegitimacy, followed by the post-war baby boom, and its accompanying pronatalist ideology, resulted in a sharp rise in the demand for infant adoption. Similarly, in all three countries, social workers, influenced strongly by John Bowlby's theories on early infant placement and the dangers of 'maternal deprivation', advocated the sealing of birth, adoption agency and court records. In the United States, however, many states' birth records remained open until the 1960s and even 1980s.

"The past is a foreign country; they do things differently there," begins L.P. Hartley's novel *The Go-Between* (1953). Just as we travel to foreign countries to learn new things, we study history to introduce us to the values and perspectives of other times. The history of adoption records before the 1950s suggests that in countries where adoption records are still sealed, the practice of social work has lost something of value. In the early twentieth century, American social workers created adoption records on behalf of the adoption triad; later, the records became the tools for professionals' own training, treatment and publication, their origins forgotten in legal and bureaucratic restraints (Carp, 1998). In England before 1950, by contrast, adoption law was more humane, demanding informed consent from birth parents, thus assuring that they and the adoptive parents knew one another's identities. In the past, social workers assumed they would form a personal relationship with the members of the adoption triad, a relationship that would continue into adulthood. After the 1950s, with the popularity of psychoanalysis in America, social workers' benevolence changed to surveillance as they began to view adopted adults and birth mothers as neurotic patients rather than as clients. In England, the law made adoptive parents invisible behind serial numbers, thus depriving birth mothers of informed consent. Despite these swings in the pendulum, we should not romanticize the period before 1950. Without unemployment insurance or aid to dependent families in America or the social welfare state in England or New Zealand, family members all too often became separated from each other due to death, poverty or unemployment. Still, it is hoped that this essay will lead to a broader understanding of the little-researched history of adoption records before the 1950s in these three Anglophone countries, so that welfare workers, social workers and the international adoption community will have a useable past to which to travel.

References

Adoption of Children Act 1926, U.K. c 29, s 11.

Ball, C. (2003) The changed nature of adoption: A challenge for legislators, in *Frontiers of Family Law* (ed. G. Miller), Ashgate, London, pp. 6–22.

Barclay, D. (1957) Adoption Agencies: Pro and Con, *New York Times Magazine*, 17 February.

Behlmer, G.K. (2002) What's love got to do with it: "Adoption" in Victorian and Edwardian England, in *Adoption in America: Historical Perspectives* (ed. E.W. Carp), University of Michigan Press, Ann Arbor, pp. 82–100.

Berebitsky, J. (2000) *Like Our Very Own: Adoption and the Changing Culture of Motherhood, 1851–1950*, University Press of Kansas, Lawrence.

Bernard, V.W. (1953) The application of psychoanalysis to the adoption agency, in *Psychoanalysis and Social Work* (eds M. Heiman and M.R. Kaufman), International Universities Press, New York, pp. 160–209.

Bowlby, J. (1951) *Maternal Care and Mental Health*, World Health Organization, Geneva.

Bowlby, J. (1988) *A Secure Base: Parent Child Attachment and Healthy Human Development*, Basic Books, New York.

Carp, E.W. (1998) *Family Matters: Secrecy and Openness in the History of Adoption*, Harvard University Press, Cambridge, MA.

Carp, E.W. and Leon-Guerrero, A. (2002) When in doubt, count: World War II as a watershed in the history of adoption, in *Adoption in America: Historical Perspectives* (ed. E.W. Carp), University of Michigan Press, Ann Arbor, pp. 181–217.

Child Welfare League of America (1958) *Standards for Adoption Service*, Child Welfare League of America, New York.

Clothier, F. (1939) Some aspects of the problem of adoption. *American Journal of Orthopsychiatry*, **9**, 598–615.

Clothier, F. (1943) The psychology of the adopted child. *Mental Hygiene*, **27**, 222–30.

Cretney, S. (1998) *Law, Law Reform and the Family*, Clarendon Press, Oxford.

Cretney, S. (2003) *Family Law in the Twentieth Century: A History*, Oxford University Press, Oxford, England.

Day, C. (1980) General register office study, in *Access to Birth Records: The Impact of Section 26 of the Children Act 1975* (ed. T. Hall), Association of British Adoption and Fostering Agencies, London, pp. 21–33.

Dalley, B. (1998) *Family Matters. Child Welfare in Twentieth-Century New Zealand*, University of Auckland, Auckland.

Else, A. (1991) *A Question of Adoption: Closed Stranger Adoption in New Zealand, 1944–1974*, Bridget Williams Books, Wellington, New Zealand.

Fink, J. (2000) Natural mothers, putative fathers, and innocent children: The definition and regulation of parental relationships outside marriage, in England, 1945–1959. *Journal of Family History*, **25**, 178–95.

Goldson, J. (2003) Adoption in New Zealand: An international perspective, in *Adoption: Changing Families, Changing Times* (eds A. Douglas and T. Philpot), Routledge, London and New York, pp. 246–50.

Griffith, K.C. (1997) *New Zealand Adoption History and Practice, Social and Legal, 1840–1996*, K.C. Griffith, Wellington, New Zealand.

Griffith, K.C. (2005) *New Zealand Adoption History And Practice, Social And Legal, 1840–1996*, Rev. edn, vol. 2: history/rationale, CD-ROM in possession of the author.

Grossberg, M. (1985) *Governing the Hearth: Law and the Family in Nineteenth-Century America*, University of North Carolina, Chapel Hill, NC.

Haimes, E. and Timms, N. (1983) *Access to Birth Records and Counselling of Adopted Persons Under Section 26 of the Children Act, 1975*, University of Newcastle upon Tyne, Newcastle upon Tyne.

Hartley, L.P. (1953) *The Go-Between*, Hamish Hamilton, London.

Herman, E. (2002) The paradoxical rationalization of modern adoption. *Journal of Social History*, **36** (2), 339–85.

Horsbrugh, F. (1937) *Report of the Departmental Committee on Adoption Societies and Agencies*, Cmd 5499, HMSO, London.

Howard, S.L. and Hemenway, H.B. (1931) Birth records of illegitimates and of adopted children. *American Journal of Public Health*, **21**, 641–7.

Huffman, H.C. (1949) The Importance of Birth Records. *Proceedings of National Conference of Social Work*, pp. 351–60, Columbia University Press, New York.

Iwanek, M. (1987) *A Study of Open Adoption Placements*, Mary Iwanek, Petone, NZ.

Keating, J. (2001) Struggle for identity: Issues underlying the enactment of the 1926 adoption of children act. *University of Sussex Journal of Contemporary History*, **3**, 1–9.

Kittson, R.H. [Jean Paton] (1968) *Orphan Voyage*, Vantage Press, New York.

Lake, A. (1954) Babies for the Brave, *Saturday Evening Post*, 31 July 1954, pp. 25–7.

Leavy, M.L. (1948) *Law of Adoption Simplified*, Oceana, New York.

Lowe, N.V. (2000) English adoption law: Past, present, and future, in *Cross Currents: Family Law and Policy in the US and England* (eds S.N. Katz, J. Eekelaar and M. Maclean), Oxford University Press, New York, pp. 307–40.

Lynch, E.I. and Mertz, A.E. (1955) Adoptive placement of infants directly from the hospital. *Social Casework*, **36**, 450–7.

MacKenzie, C.A. (1940) Boom in Adoptions, *New York Times Magazine*, 6-7, 10 November 1940, p. 29.

May, E.T. (1995) *Barren in the Promised Land: Childless Americans and the Pursuit of Happiness*, Basic Books, New York.

Melosh, B. (2002) *Strangers and Kin: The American Way of Adoption*, Harvard University Press, Cambridge, MA.

Nelson, C. (2003) *Little Strangers: Portrayals of Adoption and Foster Care in America, 1850–1929*, University of Indiana, Bloomington.

New Zealand Law Commission (2000) *Adoption and Its Alternatives: A Different Approach and a New Framework*, New Zealand Law Commission, Wellington, New Zealand.

Novy, M. (ed.) (2001) *Imagining Adoption: Essays on Literature and Culture*, University of Michigan, Ann Arbor, MI.

Ovsiowitz, H.A. (1986) *The metamorphosis of adoption: A study of selected multidisciplinary approaches to the evolution of secrecy in the adoption process.* Queen's College, Faculty of Law, Unpublished LL.M. Thesis.

Presser, S.B. (1971–1972) The historical background of the American law of adoption. *Journal of Family Law*, **11**, 443–516.

Reid, J.H. (1963) Principles, values, and assumptions underlying adoption practice, in *Readings in Adoption* (ed. I.E. Smith), Philosophical Library, New York, pp. 26–37.

Rushbrooke, R. (2001) The proportion of adoptees who have received their birth records in England and Wales. *Population Trends*, **104**, 26–34.

Samuels, E.J. (2001) The idea of adoption: An inquiry into the history of adult adoptee access to birth records. *Rutgers Law Review*, **53**, 367–436.

Schapiro, M. (1956) *A Study of Adoption Practice*, vol. I, Child Welfare of America, New York.

Smith, C. and Logan, J. (2004) *After Adoption: Direct Contact and Relationships*, Routledge, London.

Teague, A. (1989) *Social Change, Social Work and the Adoption of Children*, Gower Hants, England.

Terry, J. (1979) *A Guide to the Children Act 1975*, 2nd edn, Sweet and Maxwell, London.

Theis, S.v.S. (1937) Adoption, in *Social Work Yearbook*, vol. 4, (ed. R.H. Kurtz) Russell Sage Foundation, New York.

U.S. Department of Labor, Children's Bureau (1949) *The confidential nature of birth records*, Pub. 332, Government Printing Office, Washington, DC.

Vincent, C. (1964) Illegitimacy in the next decade: Trends and implications. *Child Welfare*, **43**, 514–20.

Welbourne, P. (2003) Attachment theory and children's rights, in *Adoption: Changing Families, Changing Times* (eds A. Douglas and T. Philpot), Routledge, New York, pp. 60–9.

Younghusband, E. (1978) *Social Work in Britain: 1950–1975*, vol. 1, George Allen & Unwin, London.

Zainaldin, J.S. (1979) The emergence of a modern American family law: Child custody, adoption, and the courts. *Northwestern University School of Law*, 73, 1038–89.

3

From Bucharest to Beijing: Changes in Countries Sending Children for International Adoption 1990 to 2006

Peter Selman

Introduction

By the end of the 1980s the total number of intercountry adoptions seemed to be falling in many countries. In Sweden and the Netherlands a decline had been underway throughout the 1980s; in the United States numbers rose from 4868 in 1981 to 10 097 in 1987 (Altstein and Simon, 1991, pp. 15–16), but then fell to 7093 in 1990, following the sharp reduction in the number of children sent by South Korea in the aftermath of the Seoul Olympics. Only France and Italy showed a consistent upward movement throughout the decade. Then for two years, following the fall of dictator Ceausescu, Romania became the major source of children worldwide with an estimated 10 000 children sent for adoption between January 1990 and July 1991 (UNICEF, 1998).

However, to many this seemed likely to be a temporary interruption in a general decline and in 1991, Howard Altstein wrote that:

> As we enter the 1990s, a major question emerges: Are we witnessing the beginning of the end of wide-scale ICA *[Intercountry Adoption]*? Recent figures and statements from supplying countries seem to support the notion that ICA is waning. . . . Romanian orphans in 1990 are an example of a momentary addition to the world's pool of children available for adoption by foreigners. But as a long-term world-wide phenomenon whereby nonwhite children from poor nations are transferred to families in rich, white nations, ICA appears to be declining. (Altstein and Simon, 1991, p. 191)

For the United States at least this seemed to be the case. After a brief revival in 1991, when the annual total rose to 9050 – entirely due to adoptions from Romania, numbers fell to 6472 in 1992, the lowest figure for a decade. However, in 1992 two new countries – China and Russia – entered the United States top 10 sending countries and over the next 15 years became the major source of children to the United States and many other receiving countries. As a result, the annual number of children adopted internationally more than doubled between 1995 and 2004, although the last two years have seen a reversal of this decade of growth (see Table 3.1 below).

The aim of this chapter is to look in more detail at the changes in the source of children over the period 1990 to 2006, from the rise of intercountry adoption from Romania to the recent domination of China as the main

Table 3.1 Intercountry adoption to selected receiving countries from 1995 to 2006.

Country	1995	1999	2001	2003	2004	2006
United States	8987	16363	19237	21616	22884	20679
France	3034	3597	3094	3995	4079	3977
Italy	2161	2177	1797	2772	3402	3188
Canada	2045	2019	1874	2180	1955	1525
Spain	815	2006	3428	3951	5541	4472
Subtotal for five top states	17042	26162	29430	34514	37861	33841
Sweden	895	1019	1044	1046	1109	879
The Netherlands	661	993	1122	1154	1307	816
Germany	537	977	798	674	650	583
Norway	548	589	713	714	706	448
Denmark	488	697	631	523	528	450
Belgium	430	450	419	430	470	383
Australia	224	244	289	278	370	421
United Kingdom	154	312	326	301	334	364
Ireland	52	191	179	358	398	313
Total (number of countries)[a]	22161	32912	36376	41527	45287	39728
	(19)	(22)	(22)	(22)	(22)	(22)
% to top five	77	80	81	83	84	83
% to United States	41	49	53	52	51	52

[a]The other countries included in the overall totals are Finland, Iceland, Luxembourg, New Zealand and Switzerland – with the addition of Cyprus, Israel and Malta from 1999.

sending country. The chapter will also explore whether the recent downturn heralds the end to international adoption or a temporary retrenchment as was experienced in the late 1980s.

The Growth of Intercountry Adoption in the Twentieth Century

The Early History of Intercountry Adoption

Intercountry adoption is usually accepted as commencing as a global phenomenon in the years following the Second World War (Altstein and Simon, 1991), although the movement of children between countries has a much longer history – for example, the child migrants from the United Kingdom to Australia and Canada (Bean and Melville, 1989; Gill, 1997; Hubinette, 2006b; Parker, 2008). In the immediate aftermath of the war, international adoption was largely about movement of children from war-torn countries in Europe and Japan to the United States. The story of intercountry adoption as a large-scale phenomenon involving inter-racial placements is more commonly seen as commencing in the 1950s and in particular in the aftermath of the Korean War, which ended in July 1953. Between 1957 and 1969, "over twenty thousand children born outside the United States joined American families through adoption" (Ruggeiro, 2007a, p. 106), a third of these from South Korea.

European countries were also involved in intercountry adoption from an early stage, both as receiving countries and as sending countries. From the early 1960s children from Austria, Germany and Greece were adopted in the Netherlands (Hoksbergen, 1991). Norway, Sweden and the United Kingdom took children from Korea in the 1950s and by the early 1960s several other countries were taking significant numbers of children. Australia became involved in intercountry adoption in the 1970s, taking Korean children from 1969 (Hubinette, 2006a) and Vietnamese from the end of the Vietnam War in 1975 (Rosenwald, 2007).

By the 1970s intercountry adoption was well established in the United States and mainland Europe. Numbers were growing rapidly, fuelled by a demand for children from childless couples faced with a dwindling supply of infants available for domestic adoption (Hoksbergen, 2000). In the 1980s, Kane (1993, p. 234) was able to identify 21 countries "thought to receive more than 20 children per year through international adoption" and to obtain statistics from 14 of these. The statistics presented in this chapter

Table 3.2 Standardized rates of intercountry adoption between 1998 and 2004: increase in adoptions in 1998–2004.

Country	Number of adoptions 2004	Adoptions per 100 000 population 2004	Adoptions per 1000 live births 2004	Adoptions per 1000 live births 1998	% Increase in number of adoptions 1998–2004
Norway	706	15.4	12.8	11.2	+10
Spain	5541	13.0	12.4	4.2	+273
Sweden	1109	12.3	11.7	10.8	+20
Denmark	528	9.8	8.4	9.9	−15
Ireland	398	9.8	6.3	2.8	+171
The Netherlands	1307	8.1	6.9	4.6	+58
United States	22 884	7.8	5.5	4.2	+45
France	4079	6.8	5.5	5.3	+8
Australia	370	1.9	1.5	1.3	+51
United Kingdom	334	0.6	0.5	0.4	+29

Source: Selman (2006b).

are based on data from 22 countries identified as 'primarily receiving countries' (The Hague Conference on Private International Law, 2006) producing annual figures on the number of children received (see Table 3.1). Significant numbers of children are also known to be taken in Austria, Japan and the United Arab Emirates – and smaller numbers in Andorra, Greece, Singapore and Hong Kong.

Trends in Receiving Countries 1990–2006

Kane (1993) estimates a global movement of 170 000–180 000 children in the 1980s, based on her analysis of available data for 14 receiving countries with allowance for underestimates and missing countries. By the end of the decade annual numbers had risen to over 20 000 a year. Between 1995 and 2004 there was a marked increase in the global number of intercountry adoptions each year, doubling in number to an estimated *minimum* of 45 000 officially recorded annual adoptions by 2004 (Table 3.1). Between 1998 and 2004 numbers rose by 41% (Table 3.2) but figures for 2005 and 2006 suggest a clear reversal of this pattern, driven by major reductions in the number of children sent from Eastern European countries (Selman, 2007a) and new restrictions on adoptions in China (Bellock and Yardley, 2006; Hilborn, 2007b).

*Standardized Rates of Intercountry Adoption for
Receiving Countries*

Although the United States takes most children, other countries have a higher
level per 100 000 population or 1000 live births as shown in Table 3.2. In
1998 the highest level was found in the Nordic countries, but by 2004 Spain
had joined Norway and Sweden as one of the top three countries. The lowest
rates were found in Australia, Germany and the United Kingdom.

If we look further back, the highest rates historically were also found in
northern Europe where the number of adoptions peaked in the late 1970s.
In 1980 the number of adoptions per 100 000 population was 20.5 in
Sweden and more than two children adopted from abroad for every 100
children born in the country; in Denmark and the Netherlands the rate per
100 000 population was 15.0 and 11.0 respectively. In the same year the
adoption rate in the United States was 2.2 and in France 1.7.

*How Many Children Have Been Adopted Since the
Second World War?*

Between 1948 and 2006, over 400 000 children were sent for adoption to
the United States. In the same period over 160 000 children were sent
abroad for adoption by Korea alone. My estimate for 22 receiving countries
in the first seven years of the twenty-first century (2000–2006) is of a
minimum movement of 280 000 children. By 2010 the decade total is likely
to be over 400 000. If we add this to Kane's figure of 180 000 for 1980–
1989 and a probable total of at least 230 000 for the 1990s, the total for
the 31 years from 1980 to 2010 is about 850 000. Annual numbers were
less in the previous three decades – over 80 000 children went to the United
States between 1948 and 1979 (Altstein and Simon, 1991; Ruggeiro, 2007a)
and the number going to other countries will be at least 60 000, which
means that the global total for the period 1948–2010 is likely to be
approaching one million. It is the period 1990–2006 I wish to concentrate
on in the second part of this chapter looking in detail at the changes in
countries sending children for international adoption, with a briefer consideration of the patterns over the previous 40 years.

The Rise and Fall of Sending Countries

The longest sequences of reliable statistics on intercountry adoption for a
receiving country (1948 to date) are for the United States (Ruggeiro, 2007a).

Table 3.3 Countries sending most children for intercountry adoption in 1980–2006; listed in order of number of children sent.

1980–1989[a]	1995[b]	1998[c]	2003[d]	2006[d]
Korea	China	China	China	China
India	Korea	Russia	Russia	Russia
Colombia	Russia	Vietnam	Guatemala	Guatemala
Brazil	Vietnam	Korea	Korea	Ethiopia
Sri Lanka	Colombia	Colombia	Ukraine	Korea
Chile	India	India	Colombia	Colombia
Philippines	Brazil	Guatemala	India	Vietnam
Guatemala	Guatemala	Romania	Haiti	Haiti
Peru	Romania	Brazil	Bulgaria	Ukraine
El Salvador	Philippines	Ethiopia	Vietnam	India

[a]Kane (1993) – children sent to 14 countries.
[b]Selman (2002) – children sent to 10 countries.
[c]Selman (2006b) – children sent to 19 countries.
[d]Selman (2007d) – children sent to 22 countries.

These give us a quick snapshot of changes in sending countries over a period of nearly 60 years. Korea dominated until 1994, apart from a brief period when Romania reigned as the major source of children for the fiscal year 1991, but China and Russia have been on top since 1996. Table 3.3 shows the global pattern of international adoption by sending countries from the 1980s through to 2006, based on aggregation of data from receiving countries (Kane, 1993; Selman, 2002, 2006b, 2007d).

China is currently the major source of children worldwide; China and Russia together accounted for 51% of all adoptions to the 22 receiving countries in 2004. The last few years have seen a dramatic reduction in the number of children sent by Romania and Bulgaria as they sought entry into the European Union and there have been declines in other Eastern European States such as Belarus and the Ukraine. There are marked differences between major receiving countries in the countries of origin of the children sent (Selman, 2006b, 2007d). Guatemala continues to be a major source for the United States despite many concerns over child trafficking (Smolin, 2005b), which have led most other receiving countries to suspend adoptions from that country. South Korea is a major source only in North America. Italy receives children mainly from Eastern Europe and South America and none from China. Seventy percent of children sent to Spain in 2004 were from China. France takes larger numbers from Francophone countries such

Table 3.4 Standardized adoption ratios (per 1000 live births) in selected sending countries in 2003 and 2005; listed in order of ratio in 2005.

Country	Number of adoptions[b] 2005	Number of births[c] (1000s)	Adoption ratio[d] 2005	Adoption ratio[d] 2003
Guatemala	3857	437	8.8	6.4
Latvia	114	21	5.4	3.6
Russia	7471	1540	4.9	6.3
South Korea[a]	2115	457	4.6	4.7[a]
Ukraine	1705	392	4.4	5.0
Haiti	913	255	3.6	4.2
Kazakhstan	823	237	3.5	3.4
Bulgaria	115	67	1.7	15.5
Colombia	1434	968	1.5	1.8
Poland	397	365	1.1	0.95
China	14493	17310	0.84	0.6
Vietnam	1190	1648	0.72	0.57
Ethiopia	1713	3104	0.55	0.29
Belarus	23	91	0.25	7.2
Romania	15	211	0.07	2.0
India	857	25926	0.03	0.05

[a]Figures from the Korean Ministry of Health & Welfare show that the adoption ratio in Korea fell from 13.3 in 1985 to 3.0 in 1995 but subsequently increased by 50% as adoptions levelled out and births fell sharply (Selman, 2007d, p. 59).
[b]Adoptions to 22 receiving countries in 2005 (see Table 3.1).
[c]Data from UNICEF *State of the World's Children 2007*.
[d]Adoptions per 1000 live births.

as Haiti, Vietnam and Madagascar. Ethiopia emerges as a major source of children for all countries from 2004 onwards.

Standardized Rates of Intercountry Adoption for Sending Countries

Standardization shows that, although China sends the most children worldwide, the level of adoptions per 1000 live births is low. The highest ratios in 2005 were found in Guatemala, Korea and Eastern Europe (see Table 3.4).

In 1986 when Korean adoptions were at their highest, the adoption ratio was 13.3, similar to Bulgaria in 2003 but lower than Romania in 1991 when the ratio is over 25, if we use the UNICEF estimated total of 7000 worldwide (UNICEF, 1998). An analysis of Korean adoptions standardized against the changing number of live births (Selman, 2007d) shows that, although the annual number of adoptions remained static at about 2000 per annum from 1995 to 2005, the ratio rose from 3.0 to 4.7, as the total fertility rate fell to an all time low of 1.08, prompting the government to call for a reduction in overseas adoption.

Age and Gender in International Adoption

Many receiving countries do not routinely record the age and gender of children sent for adoption, but we have such data for the US and the EurAdopt agencies (mainly in the Netherlands and the Nordic countries) and for countries such as France, which responded to the Hague Special Commission questionnaire in 2005 (Selman, 2006b, pp. 196–7).

The Age of Children at Placement

There are major differences in the age at which children are adopted. Korea now sends almost entirely children under one year of age, while Brazil has now ended infant adoption to other countries and a majority of children sent are over age 5, with the younger children usually having special needs or being part of a sibling group. Ruggeiro (2007a) provides detailed tables of changes between 1990 and 2003 in the age and sex of children sent to the United States from a range of countries. The most striking change is in adoptions from Romania, which largely involved young babies in the peak year of 1991 but subsequently involved much older children. In contrast, adoptions from Korea have increasingly involved very young children under the age of 1 (94% in 2003 compared with only 71% in 1986, when over 6000 visas were granted).

Gender in International Adoption

That China sends mainly girls for intercountry adoption is widely known, but it is less recognized that Korea now sends mainly boys, whereas in the past the majority of children sent were girls (Ruggeiro, 2007a). The current pattern may reflect the preference for girls by in-country adopters in Korea, concerned with issues of lineage and inheritance. Other countries sending a preponderance of females include India and Vietnam (Selman, 2006b).

Sending Countries 1948 to 1989

Adoption from European Countries

From 1948 to 1970, European countries featured regularly in the top five countries sending children to the United States each year. Between 1948 and 1962 Greece accounted for 16% of children adopted from abroad and as late as 1967, Germany, Italy and England together accounted for over 40% (Altstein and Simon, 1991, p. 14). Adoption from West Germany continued longest with 6578 children going to the United States between 1963 and 1987. The experience of one child 'rescued' from a German orphanage is vividly portrayed by Peter Dodds (1997). It is often forgotten that many Finnish children moved to other Scandinavian countries during the Second World War, 70 000 to Sweden alone (Serenius, 1995). Many of these former 'war children' remained silent and then in their forties and fifties began to feel the need to give voice to their experiences and meet others who could understand what they had been through. Their experience mirrored the gradual emergence of the voice of the British child migrants and foreshadowed the Korean adoptee gatherings of today.

Adoption from Korea

The history of adoption from Korea has been well documented (Bergquist *et al.*, 2007; Hubinette, 2006a; Sarri, Baik and Bombyk, 2002). Beginning in the mid-1950s in the aftermath of the Korean War, when it largely involved mixed-race children, by the mid 1960s Korean adoptions were accounting for a third of all adoptions to the United States and from 1972 to 1987 for over half (Altstein and Simon, 1991). Total numbers peaked in 1985 when 8837 children were sent to other countries (5694 to the United States) and by then very few were mixed race. Adverse publicity in the years leading up to the 1988 Seoul Olympics led the Korean government to limit the numbers sent and to set a target for ending international adoption by the end of the century. By 1991 the total number sent had fallen to just over 2000 and remained at this level for the next 14 years – falling below 2000 only in 2006 (Selman, 2007d).

With the exception of 1991, when Romania sent the most children worldwide, Korea remained the major source of children in the United States until 1995 when China and Russia began to dominate. Even today it is the fourth largest supplier of 'orphans' to the United States, despite being one of the strongest economies and having one of the lowest birth rates in the world. The United Nations Committee on the Rights of the

Child has raised concerns about the level of intercountry adoption in Korea (Selman, 2007c) and there was much criticism from the local press and academics (Lae, 2007) during the 2007 Adoptee Gathering in Seoul, when adopted Koreans from several countries joined Korean birth mothers in calling for an end to international adoption (Trenka, 2007b).

New Sources of Children from 1970

Although Korea remained the most important source of children to the United States – and a major source for many other countries – until the late 1980s, the demand for children was growing and new sources of children emerged in Asia and South America in the 1970s and 1980s. Kane (1993) reports that the number of countries identified as sending children rose from 22 in 1980 to 68 in 1989.

The Philippines   The Philippines – a country with a long tradition of links to and dependence on the United States – began to send children to the United States in the late 1960s and featured in the top six sending countries through to 1992 and in the top 12 for the next 14 years. In the 1980s over 500 children a year were sent to the 14 countries in Kane's study and as late as 2005 the Philippines sent 480 children (0.24 per 1000 live births) to 13 different countries worldwide.

Vietnam   The adoption of Vietnamese 'orphans' began during the Vietnam War (1959–1975) and accelerated with the fall of Saigon on 30 April 1975, in the months leading up to which over 2000 infants and children were airlifted from Vietnam and adopted by families around the world in the notorious 'Operation Babylift' (Hubinette, 2006b; Martin, 2000; Willing, 2006). In the 1990s there was a sharp rise in the number of children sent, especially to France (from 65 in 1991 to 1393 in 1996) and the United States (from 110 in 1993 to 766 in 2002). In recent years adoption from Vietnam has been surrounded by controversy and accusations of corruption. France suspended adoptions in 1999 (Selman, 2000, p. 258) and the number received fell to only 3 in 2000, but by 2005 Vietnam had once more become the main source of children in France. Vietnam halted adoptions to many countries from 2003 to 2004 while it reviewed its policies and implemented bilateral agreements. In the United States the number of visas issued for Vietnam fell to 21 in 2004 and 7 in 2005; but rose again to 163 in 2006 after such an agreement was signed. By 2006 the global total had risen to over 1300, still well below the total of 2500 sent in 1998.

India   Intercountry adoption from India started in the mid 1970s. India was in the top five countries sending children to the United States from 1978 to 1995 and in the top 10 through to 2006. The adoption ratio in India is even lower than in the Philippines – 0.03 per 1000 in 2005 (see Table 3.4). However, there are many stories of corruption in some states in India and suggestions that the actual number of children sent may be higher (Smolin, 2005a). Adoption from India is explored in greater detail in Apparao (1997) and Bhargava (2005).

Other Asian Countries Sending Children in the 1970s and 1980s   In Kane's (1993) study Sri Lanka was the fifth most important source of children in the 1980s, sending a total of 6815 for international adoption, but numbers fell rapidly from the late 1980s. Three hundred children were sent to France alone in 1986 but from 1996 annual totals were below 10. Total numbers sent worldwide in 2005 and 2006 remain low, despite many pressures to restart after the tsunami in December 2004 (McGinnis, 2005). In 1980 Indonesia was the main source of children for the Netherlands, with a total of 669 children, but no adoptions were recorded after 1985 and, like Sri Lanka, Indonesia took steps to prevent any revival of international adoption in the aftermath of the tsunami (Hariyadi, 2005). In contrast Thailand sent under a thousand children in the 1980s, but over a hundred children a year to EurAdopt agencies between 1993 and 2006 and 50 or more a year to the United States over the same period. More than 500 children (0.5 per 1000 births) were sent to 22 receiving countries in 2004.

Countries of Latin America   In Kane's (1993) study of intercountry adoption in the 1980s, six of the top 10 sending countries were in Latin America (Table 3.3). By 2006 only two of these – Guatemala and Colombia – remained in the top 10. In the United States, 13 of the top 20 sending countries were in Latin America in 1990; by 2006 only five of these – Guatemala, Colombia, Haiti, Mexico and Brazil – remained in the top 20 and five (Chile, Costa Rica, Cuba, Honduras and Paraguay) sent few or no children. Many of the countries that have reduced the number of children sent for intercountry adoption have done so because they felt it inappropriate as they became richer and often from a deep sense of shame or because of a series of scandals.

Colombia was the first South American country to send significant numbers of children to the United States, featuring in the top five from 1974 to 1984. In the 1980s it sent nearly 15 000 children to Kane's 14 receiving countries and between 1979 and 2006 sent over 6000 children to France alone. Brazil continues to send children to the United States, but over 80%

now go to Europe, mainly to Italy and France. Total numbers fell from 1655 in 1993 (Fonseca, 2002) to under 400 in 2002, but have subsequently risen again to over 500 in 2006 (Selman, 2006a, 2006b). Infant adoption is now largely in-country but older and special needs children, including sibling groups, are sent for intercountry adoption.

From the mid-1990s the number of children sent for international adoption from Guatemala began to rise sharply reaching more than 4200 worldwide in 2006. Ninety-six percent of these children went to the United States (Selman, 2007a). Most European countries will not adopt children from Guatemala because of the known corruption in the system (Smolin, 2005b). The number sent to the United States has risen steadily from 257 in 1990 to 4135 in 2006, despite the State Department noting that its adoption procedures do not meet the standards of the Hague Convention (Guatemala's accession to the Convention has been challenged by five contracting states) and cautioning US citizens against adopting from Guatemala. It is expected that numbers may fall dramatically following the United States' ratification of the Hague Convention in December 2007 (Clemetson, 2007).

Intercountry Adoption Since 1990

By the end of the 1980s there was a growing belief that intercountry adoption had peaked. In Sweden and the Netherlands a decline had been underway throughout the 1980s and annual totals had been falling in the United States since 1987. There had been major reductions in the number of children sent by Korea and that country had set a target of ending international adoption by 2005 (Sarri, Baik and Bombyk, 2002). Then in 1990 a new source of children emerged with the fall of the Romanian dictator Ceausescu (DCI and ISS, 1991).

Romania

The impact of Romania on the world of international adoption has been well documented and frequently discussed from the onset in 1990 following the fall of Ceausescu in December 1989 (DCI and ISS, 1991; Kligman, 1992; Pullar, 1991; Reich, 1990). There had been adoption from Romania in the 1980s – as many as 792 in Kane's study, mostly going to France – but authorization had to come from the President himself (Dickens, 2002).

For nearly two years after the dictator's fall, Romania became the main focus for international adoption. UNICEF (1998) has estimated that more than 10 000 children were taken from the country between January 1990 and July 1991. In these two years Romania accounted for about a third of all international adoptions. The United States was the main recipient, but *Defence for Children International* suggests that, during the five months from August 1990 to February 1991, 500 or more children went to France, Germany and Italy and at least 200 to Canada, Greece, Switzerland and the United Kingdom (DCI and ISS, 1991).

The impetus for this massive movement of children was the media publicity around the conditions in Romanian 'orphanages', where many thousands of children were housed because of widespread abandonment during the dictator's pronatalist regime when abortion was made illegal (Kligman, 1992). But there were other factors at work, not least the falling numbers of children available from traditional sources such as Korea, Sri Lanka and many countries of South America. Although many couples travelled to Romania in response to images of older children in institutions, it soon became apparent that many of these were either not available for adoption or had "such severe mental or physical disabilities that all but the most committed adopters were deterred from taking them" (Dickens, 2002, p. 77). Instead, many who travelled turned to maternity hospitals where new mothers were subjected to pressures to relinquish their babies. As a result a majority of children adopted in the United States in 1990 and 1991 were under the age of 1 year (Ruggeiro, 2007b). In April 1991 a report from *Defence for Children International* and *International Social Service* said that intercountry adoption was "now seen as a national tragedy in Romania" (DCI and ISS, 1991, p. 9) and in July 1991 a nine-month moratorium was imposed.

In 1992 the moratorium was lifted and children were once again able to be adopted but the numbers were much lower – 700 to the United States in the next four years, compared with 2553 in 1991 – and only 10% under age 1 (Ruggeiro, 2007b). A similar story is found in France – 1000 children adopted in 1990–1991 but less than 300 between 1992 and 1995. Greene *et al.* (2007) report that between 1980 and August 2005 over 800 children were adopted from Romania by Irish parents, about a third of those adopted internationally in that period. In the United Kingdom the Home Office identified 324 Romanian children adopted by families living in England between February 1990 and September 1992 (Beckett *et al.*, 1998). These were to be the sample used in the longitudinal study of 165 Romanian adoptees by Michael Rutter and his team at the Institute of Psychiatry (see Chapter 7). In the following eight years there were only 113 approved applications for Romanian children in the whole of the United Kingdom.

Table 3.5 Adoption from Romania to 22 receiving states from 1999 to 2005; ranked by number sent in 2001.

Country	1999	2000	2001	2002	2004	2005
United States	895	1119	782	168	57	2
Spain	280	583	373	38	48	3
France	302	370	223	42	16	n/a
Italy	243	23	173	40	119	0
Ireland	n/a	69	48	12	2	0
Switzerland	31	38	43	45	22	n/a
Germany	64	56	33	22	10	6
Total	2065	2452	1809	413	287	15

The number of children leaving Romania to some countries began to rise again from 1996, with 1103 going to the United States and 370 to France in the year 2000. Official Romanian figures show a rise from 1315 children sent in 1996 to 2290 by 1998. Renewed attempts to control what was clearly becoming a flourishing market in children (Post, 2007) were made in 2002, as a result of which the number entering the United States fell sharply from 782 in 2001 to 57 in 2004. In France only 45 children were taken between 2002 and 2005. Official data from the Romanian government record a total of 10 936 international adoptions between 1997 and 2004 (Chou, Browne and Kircaldy, 2007). Table 3.5 shows the rapid decline in global numbers from 2000 to 2005.

In 2005 the Romanian government finally announced that intercountry adoptions were to end: only biological grandparents living in another country will be able to adopt Romanian orphans, and then only if no other relative or Romanian family will adopt the child (Dickens, 2006; Family Helper, 2006). Many argue that the effect of intercountry adoption in Romania has been negative, delaying the reform of institutional care and the development of in-country adoption (Dickens, 2002). Social workers preferred to work in international adoption and orphanages could make financial gains. This charge was repeated in a recent book by Roeli Post (2007) who kept a diary on her work for the European Commission helping Romania reform its child protection system. Post argues that intercountry adoption in Romania had become a market in children, riddled by corruption. But in America angry voices were raised about the EU's lack of consideration for the "many thousands still housed in appalling conditions" (Wolfe-Murray, 2006) and as early as 2001, a Korean reporter on the

Table 3.6 International adoptions from selected Eastern Europe countries to 22 receiving states in 2003–2006; ranked by number sent in 2003.

	2003	2004	2005	2006
Russia	7746	**9425**	7471	6752
Ukraine	**2052**	2021	1705	1031
Bulgaria	**962**	368	115	96
Belarus	**636**	627	23	34
Romania	**465**	287	15	0
Poland	345	**408**	397	375
Lithuania	85	**103**	78	91
Hungary	69	68	24	**90**
Latvia	65	124	114	**140**

International Herald Tribune condemned the Romanian authorities citing South Korea's wisdom in not banning adoption by foreigners (Che, 2001). Meanwhile, in 2006 there were more than 1100 'pending' cases, which had still not been finalized (Family Helper, 2006).

Other Countries of Eastern Europe

Russia became one of the top 20 countries sending children to the United States in 1992, when 324 orphan visas were granted. From 1993 to 1996 it was the second largest supplier of children, and from 1997 to 1999 it sent more children than did any other country. From 2000 Russia was second to China until 2006, when both China and Guatemala sent more. The largest number sent to the United States in a single year was 5865 in 2004, which also marked the point when adoptions from Russia worldwide peaked at 9425 (see Table 3.6). Since then numbers have fallen as there have been growing concerns in the media over the fate of children sent for adoption, following reports of the murder of Russian children by their adoptive parents in the United States (Khabibullina, 2006) and the case of the five-year-old girl adopted by a paedophile for purposes of sexual exploitation (Smolin, 2007, pp. 20–31). In 2006 Russia announced that it intended to re-accredit all foreign agencies involved in the placement of children and by 2007 there were rumours of a complete end as in Romania.

Before the collapse of Communism, adoption from Eastern and Central European countries had been rare, with the exception of Poland, which sent 1480 children in the 1980s to Kane's 14 receiving countries. But from 1992 several other countries began to send children to Western Europe or Northern America, gradually replacing Romania as the main source of children from Europe after Russia. Bulgaria was in the top 20 sending countries for the United States from 1992 to 2003 (Ruggeiro, 2007b). In 2003 Bulgaria was the ninth most important source of children worldwide and recorded the highest adoption ratio of all sending countries with 15 adoptions per 1000 live births (see Table 3.4), but thereafter numbers fell as Bulgaria, like Romania, was subject to pressures from the EU in the build-up to their membership in 2007.

Table 3.6 shows a similar reduction in the number of children sent from Belarus; little change in Russia and the Ukraine; and growth in Poland, Latvia and Lithuania, all longer standing members of EU. In these countries intercountry adoption is now focused on older and special needs children. Although Russia and the Ukraine continue to feature in the top 10 countries sending children, some have speculated that the second wave of 'European' adoptions initiated from Romania and Russia, and spreading throughout Eastern Europe in the 1990s, may now be coming to an end.

Cambodia

Adoptions from Cambodia began in the early 1990s, more than 10 years after the end of the Pol Pot regime in 1979. The first children went to France and the United States in 1991, and from 1997 to 2002 Cambodia was in the top 20 countries sending children to the latter country. But by the end of the 1990s concerns were growing about corruption in dealings with the country (Selman, 2006a), and many countries had refused to become involved. From 1998 to 2002 a large majority of the children sent went to two countries – the United States and France (Selman, 2007d, p. 65). Evidence of corruption was growing and in the aftermath of the exposure and prosecution of Lauren Gallindo for visa fraud (ABC News, 2004; Smolin, 2007), the United States State Department announced a suspension of adoptions from 2002, and from 2004 to 2006 only seven visas were granted (U.S. Department of State, 2007). Cambodia acceded to the Hague Convention in April 2007 and there is speculation that it may once again become a significant source of children for receiving countries, but Germany, the Netherlands and the United Kingdom have objected to the accession.

The Rise of Intercountry Adoption from China

In the period 1980–1989, Kane (1993) reported less than 100 children sent abroad from mainland China, although three times that figure were sent

Table 3.7 Adoptions from China to 22 receiving states, 1998–2006; ranked by number sent in 2006.

Country[a]	1998	2002	2003	2004	2005	2006[a]
United States	4206	5053	6859	7044	7906	6493
Spain	196	1427	1043	2389	2753	1759
Canada	901	771	1108	1001	973	606
The Netherlands	210	510	567	800	666	362
Sweden	123	316	373	497	462	314
France	23	210	360	491	458	314
United Kingdom	123	111	108	165	188	187
Total	6115	9135	11230	13408	14493	10743

[a] In 2006 the China Centre for Adoption Affairs reported links with 16 countries – in addition to those shown in the table above, children have been sent to Australia, Belgium, Denmark, Finland, Iceland, Ireland, New Zealand, Norway and Switzerland.

from the island of Hong Kong to a range of countries including the United Kingdom (Bagley, 1993). The People's Republic of China began to allow foreigners to adopt orphaned children on *ad hoc* basis in the late 1980s (Tessler, Gamache and Liu, 1999), but formal approval did not come until 1992, when China passed a law "officially granting foreigners the right to adopt and setting up protocols for doing so" (Evans, 2000, p. 17). From that year the number of children going to the United States began to rise sharply and by 1995 China had become the main sender of children, replacing Korea. By 2003 over 6000 children a year were arriving with a peak of 7906 in 2005.

By 1998 China had become the main source of children for adoption in Canada, Denmark, the Netherlands and the United Kingdom, while in Spain numbers rose from 196 in 1998 to 2753 by 2005 (see Table 3.7). Of the major receiving countries only Italy receives no children from China. Although there has been some reduction in the number of children sent in 2006, it seems likely that China will continue to dominate international adoption throughout the first decade of the twenty-first century, and by 2010 the total number of Chinese adoptees worldwide could exceed the 160 000 sent by Korea over a much longer period of time. However, China is a huge country and the adoption ratio remains relatively low (Table 3.4). China ratified the Hague Convention in 2005.

The remarkable rise seems to be associated with the opening up of China to the West and growing revelations about the huge number of abandoned children resulting from the One-Child Policy, which had been enacted a decade earlier in 1979 (Johansson and Nygren, 1991). This had resulted in large numbers of babies being abandoned in public places (Johnson, Bangham and Liyao, 1998), as there was no legal avenue by which birth parents could place their children for adoption. The modification of the policy to "one son/two child" (Rojewski and Rojewski, 2001, p. 5) did little to reduce the rate of child abandonment, but ensured that those abandoned were girls, predominantly second daughters (Johnson, 2004). It is of course this pattern that has made China unique in sending such a huge preponderance of girls for adoption.

Why Is Adoption from China So Popular?

The arrival of China as a source of children for adoption coincided with the end to the huge influx of Romanian children described above. It met, therefore, a growing demand for children stimulated by that Romanian influx of children. Just as the interest in Romania was stimulated by media coverage of the country's orphanages, so too China was to come to the attention of Western film-makers in the notorious 'Dying Rooms' shown on British television in 1996. Prospective adopters around the world saw international adoption as a way of helping such children and also "enriching the multicultural landscape of the receiving countries" (Luo and Bergquist, 2004, p. 25).

But in the early years China had a particular appeal for many Westerners because of its unique perception of appropriate adopters. In contrast to most other sending countries there was a preference for older parents and an acceptance of single women as suitable to adopt. Furthermore, most available children were babies and in relatively good health. The fact of 'abandonment' was cited as a positive by some US agencies as it seemed to make it unlikely that birth parents could ever intrude on the adopted family – at a time when domestic adoption in the United States was increasingly stressing open adoption, and search and reunion was a major feature of the lives of older adoptees.

The Single Mother and China

Although there are no definitive statistics, it has been estimated that as many as a third of all 'Chinese' adoptions in the United States in the 1990s were by single women. Thus a new source of 'demand' was developing that was a key factor in the growing popularity of international adoption in many countries. The Chinese authorities had always made it clear that adoption by gay and lesbian couples was not acceptable, but it became clear that at least some single applicants were in a same-sex relationship. In 2001 the Chinese Centre for Adoption Affairs (CCAA), which was established in 1996 to take charge of foreign adoptions, announced a restriction of the number of single applicants – to a maximum of 5%. Then in 2006 CCAA announced new guidelines intended to recruit adoptive families with qualities that Chinese believed would provide the greatest chance that children will be raised by healthy, economically stable parents (Bellock and Yardley, 2006). The new guidelines state that prospective adopters must be a couple of one male and one female who have been married for at least two years and have had no more than two divorces between them. If either spouse was previously divorced, the couple cannot apply until they have been married for at least five years. Priority is to be given to applicants aged 30–45. The guidelines include a requirement that one applicant must be in stable employment with an income of $10 000 for each family member and neither must have a criminal record. Other requirements include a body mass index of less than 40, a high school diploma and to be free of certain health problems like AIDS, cancer and mental disorders (Hilborn, 2007b). The new rules, which came into effect on 1 May 2007, will make it impossible for single women to apply for a child and will also make it difficult for many married couples to adopt a second child.

What Is the Future for Adoption from China?

The last two years have seen a fall in the number of children sent from China to most countries, but it remains unclear whether this is a retrenchment or whether it heralds the beginning of a steady reduction and early ending to adoption from China, and what this would mean for the overall incidence of intercountry adoption. China has concrete benefits from a continuation of adoption in the short term, as a solution to the continuing abandonment of girls and through savings on the cost of institutional care and the substantial amount of revenue adoption brings in – $3000 per child. It also seems that Chinese attitudes towards intercountry adoption remain positive. Luo and Berquist (2004, pp. 21–2) found that government and welfare institution personnel viewed it as "an appropriate response to an overburdened system".

How Are Internationally Adopted Children Faring?

There is an increasing number of studies of the outcome of international adoptions and to date, large-scale surveys show that such children do as well as children in general or same race adoptions (Haugaard, Wojslawowicz and Palmer, 2000a, 2000b; Simon and Altstein, 2000; van IJzendoorn and Juffer, 2006), but that there are problems associated with late placement from an institution. In Chapter 8 Juffer and van IJzendoorn report on a longitudinal study of children from Colombia, Sri Lanka and South Korea, and a meta-analysis of 270 empirical studies on adjustment, noting the "massive catch-up and gains in all developmental domains" and concluding that "adoption – as an alternative for institutional care – is a very successful intervention in children's lives".

The adoption of children from Romania has attracted particular attention, not least because it was seen as offering a 'natural experiment' in the possibility of recovery from extreme institutional deprivation (Haugaard and Hazan, 2003). In Chapter 7 Rutter and his colleagues examine findings from the longitudinal study of 165 children adopted in the United Kingdom, reporting on their progress at age 11. The study shows a remarkable 'catch-up' following placement in a family, but continuing problems in a minority and especially those adopted at an older age. Misca (2006) has argued, however, that all the Romanian studies are flawed because they do not look at the development of children who remained in institutions and that many of the problems of the children pre-dated admission to an orphanage.

International adoption from China has already generated more publications, especially in the United States (Dorow, 2006; Johnson, 2004; Tessler, Gamache and Liu, 1999; Volkman, 2005) than any other sending country, including Korea. Much of the writing has come from adoptive parents (Buchanan, 2005; Evans, 2000; Klatzkin, 1999) or focused on adoptive parents' experiences (Rojewski and Rojewski, 2001; Tessler, Gamache and Liu, 1999). Most of the children are still quite young so that there are no longitudinal studies that have followed them into their older years, although empirical research on younger children is emerging.

Tan (2004) compared 126 single mother adoptive families with 415 dual-parent adoptive families, using the *Child Behaviour Checklist* (CBCL) and found no evidence that single parenting was a risk factor for Chinese adoptees' adjustment. Pre-school girls scored significantly lower than the US norms on the internalizing and externalizing problem scale as did school-age girls on the externalizing scale. In Norway a study by Dalen and Ryvgold (2006) found no difference in educational achievement between adopted children from China and a matched sample of Norwegian-born children. As most of the Chinese children have been adopted at younger ages, it may be that the problems noted in other studies will be less evident. Although interest in adoption from China was influenced by images of poor institutional care, there is little evidence that children were coming from the situations of extreme deprivation faced by institutionalized Romanian children (Dalen and Ryvgold, 2006). However a study by Tan (2006) found that a history of neglect in infancy was associated with lower 'social competence' for a minority of Chinese girls adopted in the United States.

Some argue that problems of identity will be less for the new generation of Chinese adoptees as compared with the children adopted from Korea in the 1970s and 1980s. They are being brought up in a much more open atmosphere where parents pay more attention to such issues by encouraging their children to learn about their culture and often taking them back to their country of origin. But evidence from the personal stories of adult Korean adoptees (Trenka, 2003; Trenka, Oparah and Shin, 2006) and the findings from Sweden on the problems of adopted people in early adulthood (Hjern *et al.*, 2002; Lindblad, Hjern and Vinnerljung, 2003) should remind us that a true picture of the 'success' of Chinese adoptions will only emerge in the future. What will this large cohort of adoptees feel when they reach adulthood? How will these young women feel about their early history of 'abandonment' because of their gender? Will those adopted by single women have a different experience from those adopted into more conventional two-parent families? Even if the objective outcomes are good, there may be anger about the process of intercountry adoption, just as today adult Koreans are returning to their country and calling for an end to international adoption (Trenka, 2007a).

Africa – A New Untapped Source with Huge Capacity?

This chapter is concerned with the rise and fall of sending countries. At a time when adoption from Latin America and Eastern Europe seems unlikely to increase and the messages from Asia remain mixed, the one clear growth area is Africa where the potential numbers seem large. To date this is most evident in Ethiopia where numbers have been rising rapidly in recent years. Adoptions from Ethiopia trebled between 2001 and 2006, when the annual total was over 2100 (Selman, 2006b, 2007d). Ethiopia is now in the top 10 sources of children for all the major receiving countries, and in 2005 and 2006 was second only to China in the numbers sent to the EurAdopt agencies. In the United States the number of adoptions from Ethiopia doubled between 2004 and 2006, fuelled, some would say, by publicity surrounding the adoption of an Ethiopian child by actress Angelina Jolie, but also reflecting the end of adoption from Romania and the restrictions on Chinese adoptions which have affected single applicants especially.

Ethiopia is not a typical African country and had a history of adoption for many years before this recent rise, as had Madagascar where intercountry adoptions to France reached 259 in the late 1980s and currently account for 3% of all French intercountry adoptions. More significant is the fact that Mali, which has recently acceded to the Hague Convention, is now the tenth largest supplier of children to France; that Liberia and Nigeria are amongst the top 20 sending countries for the United States; and that South Africa has been the fifth most important source for EurAdopt agencies in 2005 and 2006. However, most African countries send few or no children, including Malawi, which came to the front of attention following the 'adoption' of a young boy by pop star Madonna. Muslim countries seem unlikely to send significant numbers as the Koran is usually interpreted as forbidding adoption. But the impact of HIV/AIDS on Africa has been immense. Most of the AIDS 'orphans' are cared for by their wider family, but it is easy to see that international adoption could become an attractive option for poor countries struggling to provide for those children who cannot be supported by family or community care. However, many receiving countries will not approve the adoption of a child who is HIV positive and most prospective adoptive parents are still seeking healthy infants (Selman, 2007b).

The Future of Intercountry Adoption

The sharp fall in the number of adoptions in 2006 has led to much speculation about the future of international adoption (Hilborn, 2007a). Adoptions from Romania have ended and in 2006 China sent 4000 fewer children worldwide than in 2005 (Table 3.7). Reports from adoption agencies in North America suggest that Korea is now releasing fewer children for international adoption and that adoptions from Belarus and the Ukraine will remain closed in 2007 (Hilborn, 2006). Furthermore, the international community is now united in seeking to ensure that war and natural disaster are no longer a trigger for new waves of international adoption, as was seen in the reaction to the 'rescue' of children from Darfur by the French agency, Zoe's Ark (Chrisafis, 2007; Crumley, 2007; Duval Smith and Rolley, 2007). However, in the United States, in 2006, the number of visas issued for 'orphans' from Ethiopia and Liberia rose by 75 and 93%, respectively, and for the EurAdopt agencies Ethiopia was the second most important sending country in 2005 and 2006, suggesting that Africa may now be becoming the new source for a market facing supply problems when demand is as high as ever.

In the Netherlands Ina Hut, head of the Dutch Agency Wereldkinderen (World Children), has asked "is the end of adoption near?" (Hut, 2007) noting the growing waiting lists for intercountry adoption and the rising 'price' of children. Meanwhile criticism of the whole process of international adoption has increased in recent years both from adult adoptees (Dodds, 1998a, 1998b; Hubinette, 2005; Trenka, 2007a; Westra, 2007) and also from adoptive parents who have found corruption in the placement of their own children (Smolin, 2004, 2005b, 2007).

In 1991 Rene Hoksbergen expressed the hope that

> ... culture and economic circumstances in all Third-World countries change to the extent that it will be the exception when a child's only chance for a satisfactory upbringing exists with a family thousands of miles from its birthplace. (Hoksbergen, 1991, p. 156)

Writing 13 years later, by which time the number of international adoptions had more than doubled, David Smolin, adoptive father of two Indian girls whom he later discovered had not been freely given up by their mother, has written

> ... the recurrent cycle of scandal, excuse, and ineffective "reform" will probably continue until intercountry adoption is finally abolished, with history labelling the entire enterprise as a neo-colonialist mistake. It does not have to be this way, but it will take more than legal fictions and illusory restrictions on child trafficking to prevent the ultimate demise of the intercountry adoption system. (Smolin, 2004, p. 325)

Many sending countries have ended the practice, some with major regrets over their reliance on it for so many years. What this chapter has sought to show is that in recent years, this has usually been followed by other countries becoming a source for children in what has come to be an international market (Kapstein, 2003; Masson, 2001; Saclier, 2000; Triseliotis, 2000).

This trend is most evident in the United States and much depends on how far the ratification in December 2007 of the 1993 Hague Convention will lead to tighter controls on adoption agencies and individuals involved in overseas adoption (Hansen and Pollack, 2006; Hollinger, 2004). However, as Greene *et al.* (2007, p. 3) have noted, "If those arranging the adoption are running a business, the birth parents are in dire financial circumstances and the prospective adopters are desperate for a child, it is ... difficult to see who is putting the child's needs first." If sub-Saharan Africa is to replace China and Russia as the main source of children for this market, there must be even greater vigilance to ensure the best interests of the child, as any payments offered will have even more impact than on countries such as Romania.

References

ABC News (2004) *Adoption Scammer Gets 18 Months in Jail: Seattle Woman Took Babies from Poor Cambodians, Told Americans They Were Orphans.* ABC World News 19 November 2004, http://abcnews.go.com/WNT/ (accessed 18 January 2008).

Altstein, H. and Simon R. (1991) *Intercountry Adoption: A Multinational Perspective*, Praeger, New York.

Apparao, H. (1997) International adoption of children: The Indian scene. *International Journal of Behavioural Development*, **20** (1), 3–16.

Bagley, C. (1993) Chinese adoptees in Britain: A twenty-year follow-up of adjustment and social identity. *International Social Work*, **36**, 143–57.

Bean, P. and Melville, J. (1989) *Lost Children of the Empire*, Unwin Hyman, London.

Beckett, C., Groothues, C., O'Connor, T.G. and the English and Romanian Adoptees Study Team (1998) Adopting from Romania: The role of siblings in adjustment. *Adoption and Fostering*, **22** (1), 25–34.

Bellock, P. and Yardley, J. (2006) China Tightens Adoption Rules for Foreigners, *New York Times*, 20 December 2006.

Bergquist, K., Vonk, M., Kim, D. and Feit, M. (eds) (2007) *International Korean Adoption: A Fifty-Year History of Policy and Practice*, Haworth Press, New York.

Bhargava, V. (2005) *Adoption in India: Policies and Experiences*, Sage, London.

Buchanan, E. (2005) *From China with Love: A Long Road to Motherhood*, John Wiley & Sons, Ltd, Chichester.

Che, E. (2001) Adoptions by Foreigners Can Be Fine, *International Herald Tribune*, Thursday 23 August.

Chou, S., Browne, K. and Kircaldy, M. (2007) Intercountry adoption and the internet. *Adoption & Fostering*, **31** (2), 22–31.

Chrisafis, A. (2007) Eight Years' Hard Labour for Charity Group in Bogus Orphans Scam, *Guardian Unlimited*, 27 December 2007, http://www.guardian.co.uk (accessed 18 January 2008).

Clemetson, L. (2007) Adoptions from Guatemala Face an Uncertain Future, *New York Times*, 16 May 2007.

Crumley, B. (2007) Charges Made in Darfur 'Adoptions', *TIME Magazine*, 29 October 2007, http://www.time.com/time/world/article/0,8599,1677231,00.html (accessed 18 January 2008).

Dalen, M. and Ryvgold, A. (2006) Educational achievement in adopted children from China. *Adoption Quarterly*, **9** (4), 45–58.

DCI and ISS [Defence for Children International and International Social Services] (1991) *Romania: The Adoption of Romanian Children by Foreigners*, DCI and ISS, Geneva.

Dickens, J. (2002) The paradox of inter-country adoption: analysing Romania's experience as a sending country. *International Journal of Social Welfare*, **11**, 76–83.

Dickens, J. (2006) *The social policy context of inter-country adoption*. Paper presented at the Second International Conference on Adoption Research, University of East Anglia, Norwich, 17–21 July.

Dodds, P. (1997) *Outer Search/Inner Journey; An Orphan and Adoptee's Quest*, Aphrodite Publishing Company, Washington, DC.

Dodds, P. (1998a) The case against international adoption, keynote speech, *National Adoption Conference of New Zealand*, Christchurch, http://peterfdodds.com/keynote.htm (accessed 18 January 2008).

Dodds, P. (1998b) International adoption: Opening Pandora's Box, *Bastard Quarterly*, Spring-Summer 1998, http://www.bastards.org/bq/dodds1.htm (accessed 18 January 2008).

Dorow, S.K. (2006) *Transnational Adoption: A Cultural Economy of Race, Gender, and Kinship*, New York University Press, New York.

Duval Smith, A. and Rolley, S. (2007) Did they plot to steal Africa's orphans of war? *The Observer*, 4 November 2007, pp. 28–29.

Evans, K. (2000) *The Lost Daughters of China: Abandoned Girls; Their Journey to America and the Search for a Missing Past*, Tarcher/Putnam, New York.

Family Helper (2006) Country News; Romania, http://www.familyhelper.net/news/romania.html (accessed 18 January 2008).

Fonseca, C. (2002) An unexpected reversal: Charting the course of international adoption in Brazil. *Adoption & Fostering*, **26** (3), 28–39.

Gill, A. (1997) *Orphans of the Empire: The Shocking Story of Child Migration to Australia*, Millennium, Alexandria, New South Wales.

Greene, S., Kelly, R., Nixon E. *et al.* (2007) *A Study of Intercountry Adoption Outcomes in Ireland*, Children's Research Centre, Trinity College, Dublin.

Hansen, M. and Pollack, D. (2006) The regulation of intercountry adoption. *bepress Legal Series*, Working Paper 1385 (20 May 2006), http://law.bepress.com/expresso/eps/1385 (accessed 15 January 2008).

Hariyadi, M. (2005) Jakarta Blocks Tsunami Orphan Adoptions. *AsiaNews.it*, http://www.asianews.it/index.php?art=2246&1=en (accessed 18 January 2005).

Haugaard, J. and Hazan C. (2003) Adoption as a natural experiment. *Development and Psychopathology*, **15**, 909–26.

Haugaard, J., Wojslawowicz, J. and Palmer, M. (2000a) International adoption: Children predominantly from Asia and South America. *Adoption Quarterly*, **3** (2), 83–93.

Haugaard, J., Wojslawowicz, J. and Palmer, M. (2000b) International adoption: Children from Romania. *Adoption Quarterly*, **3** (3), 73–84.

Hilborn, R. (2006) International adoption: Beware slow processes and closed countries. *Family Helper*, 20 September 2006, http://www.familyhelper.net/news/summary.html (accessed 18 January 2008).

Hilborn, R. (2007a) Adoption slowdown in China starts the great decline of 2006. *Family Helper*, 5 August 2007, http://www.familyhelper.net/news/070825stat.html (accessed 18 January 2008).

Hilborn, R. (2007b) May 1: Nine New Adoption Rules Start in China. *Family Helper*, 1 May 2007, http://www.familyhelper.net/news/070501chinarules.html (accessed 18 January 2008).

Hjern, A., Lindblad, F. and Vinnerljung, B. (2002) Suicide, psychiatric illness and social maladjustment in intercountry adoptees in Sweden: A cohort study. *The Lancet*, 360, 443–8.

Hoksbergen, R. (1991) Intercountry adoption coming of age in the Netherlands: Basic issues, trends and developments, in *Intercountry Adoption; a Multinational Perspective* (eds H. Altstein and R. Simon), Praeger, New York.

Hoksbergen, R. (2000) Changes in attitudes in three generations of adoptive parents, in *Intercountry Adoption; Development, Trends and Perspectives* (ed. P. Selman), BAAF, London, pp. 295–314.

Hollinger, J.F. (2004) Intercountry adoption: Forecasts and forebodings. *Adoption Quarterly*, 8 (1), 41–60.

Hubinette, T. (2005) Korea Must Stop Overseas Adoption, *Korea Herald*, 3 March 2005, http://www.tobiashubinette.se/adoptionstop.pdf (accessed 18 January 2008).

Hubinette, T. (2006a) *Comforting An Orphaned Nation: Representations of International Adoption and Adopted Koreans in Korean Popular Culture*, Jimoondang Publishers, Seoul.

Hubinette, T. (2006b) From orphan trains to babylifts: Colonial trafficking, empire building and social engineering, in *Outsiders Within: Writing on Transracial Adoption* (eds J. Trenka, J. Oparah and Sun Yung Shin), South End Press, Cambridge, MA, pp. 139–49.

Hut, I. (2007) Interview on Radio Netherlands Worldwide, 8 July 2007, romania-forexportonly.blogspot.com (accessed 23 November 2007).

Johansson, S. and Nygren, O. (1991) The missing girls of China: A new demographic account. *Population and Development Review*, 17 (1), 35–51.

Johnson, K.A. (2004) *Wanting A Daughter, Needing A Son: Abandonment, Adoption, and Orphanage Care in China*, Yeong & Yeong Book Co., St. Paul, Minnesota.

Johnson, K., Banghan, K. and Liyao, W. (1998) Infant abandonment and adoption in China. *Population and Development Review*, 24 (3), 469–510.

Kane, S. (1993) The movement of children for international adoption: An epidemiological perspective. *The Social Science Journal*, 30 (4), 323–39.

Kapstein, E.B. (2003) The Baby Trade, *Foreign Affairs*, November/December.

Khabibullina, L. (2006) *Circulation of Russian children in Europe (case study of transnational adoption of children from Russia to Catalonia)*. Paper presented at the Second International Conference on Adoption Research, University of East Anglia, Norwich, 17–21 July.

Klatzkin, A. (ed.) (1999) *A Passage to the Hear: Writings from Families with Children from China*, Yeong & Yeong Book Co., St. Paul, Minnesota.

Kligman, G. (1992) Abortion and international adoption in post-Ceausescu Romania. *Feminist Studies*, **18** (2), 405–19.

Lae, C.J. (2007) The Shame of Korea's Orphan Exportation, *The Hankyoreh*, 18 September 2007, http://english.hani.co.kr/arti/english_edition/e_opinion/237090.html (accessed 18 January 2008).

Lindblad, F., Hjern, A. and Vinnerljung, B. (2003) Intercountry adopted children as young adults – A Swedish cohort study. *American Journal of Orthopsychiatry*, **73** (2), 190–202.

Luo, N. and Bergquist, K. (2004) Born in China: Birth country perspectives on international adoption. *Adoption Quarterly*, **8** (1), 21–39.

Martin, A. (2000) The Legacy of Operation Babylift, *Adoption Today*, **2** (4), http://www.adoptvietnam.org/adoption/babylift.htm (accessed 18 January 2008).

Masson, J. (2001) Intercountry adoption: A global solution or a global problem. *Journal of International Affairs*, **55** (1), 141–68.

McGinnis, H. (2005) *Intercountry Adoption in Emergencies: The Tsunami Orphans*, The Evan B. Donaldson Adoption Institute, New York, http://www.adoptioninstitute.org/publications/ (accessed 12 November 2007).

Misca, G. (2006) *The "Romanian orphans" adopted internationally – Reflections on research studies over the past decade*. Paper presented at the Second International Conference on Adoption Research, University of East Anglia, Norwich, 17–21 July.

Parker, R. (2008) *Uprooted: The Shipment of Poor Children to Canada, 1867–1917*, Policy Press, Bristol.

Post, R. (2007) *Romania – For Export Only: The Untold Story of the Romanian 'Orphans'*, EuroComment Diffusion, the Netherlands.

Pullar, V. (1991) *Romanian Babies: Robbery or Rescue*, Daphne Brasell Press, New Zealand.

Reich, D. (1990) Children of the nightmare. *Adoption & Fostering*, **14** (3), 9–14.

Rojewski, J. and Rojewski J. (2001) *Intercountry Adoption from China: Examining Cultural Heritage and Other Post Adoption Issues*, Bergin & Garvey, Westport, CT.

Rosenwald, T. (2007) The Devil is in the Detail: Adoption Statistics as a Post Adoption Service in Australia, *Adoption Australia*, Spring 2007, pp. 18–22.

Ruggeiro, J.A. (2007a) Adoptions in and to the United States, in *Adoption: Global Perspectives and Ethical Issues* (ed. J. Pati), Concept Publishing Company, New Delhi, pp. 102–36.

Ruggeiro, J.A. (2007b) *Eastern European Adoption: Policies, Practice and Strategies for Change*, Transaction Publishers, New Brunswick.

Saclier, C. (2000) In the best interests of the child? in *Intercountry Adoption: Development, Trends and Perspectives* (ed. P. Selman), BAAF, London, pp. 53–65.

Sarri, R., Baik, Y. and Bombyk, M. (2002) Goal displacement and dependency in South Korean-United States intercountry adoption. *Children and Youth Services Review*, 20, 87–114.

Selman, P. (ed.) (2000) *Intercountry Adoption: Development, Trends and Perspectives*, BAAF, London.

Selman, P. (2002) Intercountry adoption in the new millennium: The 'quiet migration' revisited. *Population Research and Policy Review*, 21, 205–25.

Selman, P. (2006a) *The movement of children for international adoption: Developments and trends in receiving states and states of origin 1998–2004*. Paper presented at the First International Forum on Childhood and Families, "On philias and phobias", Barcelona, 29 September–3 October 2006.

Selman, P. (2006b) Trends in intercountry adoption 1998–2004: Analysis of data from 20 receiving countries. *Journal of Population Research*, 23 (2), 183–204.

Selman, P. (2007a) *The impact of intercountry adoption on the well-being of children in Europe*. Paper presented at the final conference of the WELLCHI network, Barcelona, 8–10 February 2007.

Selman, P. (2007b) *The growth of intercountry adoption in the 21st century*. Paper presented at 3rd International ACTION Conference on Post Adoption Services, Cambridge, MA, 19–21 February.

Selman, P. (2007c) Chapter 4: The UK's experience and status on the rights of children, in *Adoption: Global Perspectives and Ethical Issues* (ed. J. Pati), Concept Publishing Company, New Delhi, pp. 57–81.

Selman, P. (2007d) Intercountry adoption in the twenty-first century: An examination of the rise and fall of countries of origin, in *Proceedings of the First International Korean Adoption Studies Research Symposium* (eds K. Nelson, E. Kim and M. Petersen), International Korean Adoptee Associations, Seoul, pp. 55–75.

Serenius, M. (1995) The silent cry: A Finnish child during World War II and 50 years later. *International Forum of Psychoanalysis*, 4, 35–47.

Simon, R.J. and Altstein, H. (2000) *Adoption Across Borders*, Rowman & Littlefield.

Smolin, D. (2004) Intercountry adoption as child trafficking. *Valparaiso Law Review*, 39 (2), 281–325, http://works.bepress.com/david_smolin/3 (accessed 22 November 2007).

Smolin, D. (2005a) The two faces of intercountry adoption: The significance of the Indian adoption scandals? *Seton Hall Law Review*, 35, 403–93, http://works.bepress.com/david_smolin/2 (accessed 22 November 2007).

Smolin, D. (2005b) How the intercountry adoption system legitimizes and incentivizes: The practices of buying, trafficking, kidnapping, and Children. *ExpressO Preprint Series*, no. 749, http://law.bepress.com/expresso/eps/749/ (accessed 22 November 2007).

Smolin, D. (2007) Child laundering as exploitation: Applying anti-trafficking norms to intercountry adoption under the coming Hague regime. *ExpressO*, http://works.bepress.com/david_smolin/4 (accessed 22 November 2007).

Tan, X.T. (2004) Child adjustment of single-parent adoption from China: A comparative study. *Adoption Quarterly*, **8** (1), 1–20.

Tan, X.T. (2006) History of early neglect and middle childhood social competence: An adoption study. *Adoption Quarterly*, **9** (4), 59–72.

Tessler, R., Gamache, G. and Liu, L. (1999) *West Meets East: Americans Adopt Chinese Children*, Bergin & Garvey, Westport, CT.

The Hague Conference On Private International Law (2006) *Report of the Special Commission to review the practical operation of the 1993 Hague Convention*, HCCH, The Hague, http://www.hcch.net/upload/wop/adop2005_rpt-e.pdf (accessed 18 January 2008).

Trenka, J. (2003) *The Language of Blood: A Memoir*, Minnesota Historical Society Press, Minneapolis.

Trenka, J. (2007a) Fool's gold: International adoption from South Korea, http://jjtrenka.wordpress.com/2007/07/10 (accessed 22 November 2007).

Trenka, J. (2007b) Korean Adoptees from Abroad and Birth Mothers Protest Overseas Adoption, *The Hankyoreh*, 5 August 2007, http://jjtrenka.wordpress.com/category/resistance/ (accessed 22 November 2007).

Trenka, J., Oparah, J. and Shin S.Y. (2006) *Outsiders Within; Writing on Transracial Adoption*, South End Press, Cambridge, MA.

Triseliotis, J. (2000) Intercountry adoption: Global trade or global gift? *Adoption & Fostering*, **24** (2), 45–54.

UNICEF (1998) Intercountry Adoption. *Innocenti Digest*, no. 4, Florence: UNICEF International Child Development Centre, http://www.unicef-icdc.urg/publications/index.htm (accessed 18 January 2008).

U.S. Department of State (2007) *Immigrant Visas issued to Orphans coming to the United States*, http://travel.state.gov/family/adoption/stats/stats_451.html (accessed 22 November 2007).

van IJzendoorn, M. and Juffer, F. (2006) Adoption as intervention: Meta-analytic evidence for massive catch-up and plasticity in physical, socio-emotional, and cognitive development. *Journal of Child Psychology and Psychiatry*, **47** (12), 1228–45.

Volkman, T. (2005) *Cultures of Transnational Adoption*, Duke University Press, London.

Westra, H. (2007) The market of adoption. Radio Netherlands 21 and 23 October 2007, http://romania-forexportonly.blogspot.com (accessed 23 November 2008).

Willing, I. (2006) Beyond the Vietnam War adoptions, in *Outsiders Within* (eds J. Trenka *et al.*), South End Press, Cambridge, MA, pp. 259–66.

Wolfe-Murray, R. (2006). International adoptions: An update. 3 December 2006, *VIVID – Romania Through International Eyes*, http://www.vivid.ro/index.php (accessed 18 January 2008).

4

The Ecology of Adoption*

Jesús Palacios

Urie Bronfenbrenner was a well-known and highly reputed scholar in the field of developmental psychology. His work has greatly shaped this field of research. As Bronfenbrenner's own historical analysis puts it, developmental psychology during the first decades of the twentieth century was basically descriptive, mainly analysing babies, children and adolescents' developmental milestones. The theoretical analysis models prevailing during those years were quite elementary and were described by Bronfenbrenner as the 'social address model' (differences in development explained by social class, ethnic origin or any other label that serves to compare a group with another one) and the 'personal attributes model' (the comparing element here is more individual than social: age, gender, premature birth, etc.). The main drawback of these models is that "personal characteristics present early in life will have the same consequences for later development irrespective of the environment in which such later development takes place" (Bronfenbrenner, 2005, p. 71).

The model proposed by Bronfenbrenner is noticeably more complex. There are three main interrelated contributions in his legacy: the Process-Person-Context-Time (PPCT) model, his proposal of a perspective named 'ecology of human development', and the necessity of connecting research and social policy. This connection will be addressed later in this chapter. Now, as a way of introduction, the components of the PPCT model and the ecological perspective of human development will be briefly analysed.

Developmental research always has the developing *person* as its main subject. Each individual has his or her own personal characteristics (biology, biography, behavioural style) playing a significant role in the shape and content of his or her own psychological development. When researchers, Bronfenbrenner among them, wanted to explain individual differences, they

---

* To the memory of Urie Bronfenbrenner (1917–2005), mentor, colleague and friend.

became increasingly immersed in the analysis of *processes* and dynamic interactions between individuals and their context. These processes are posited as the primary mechanisms producing human development.

As far as the analysis of *context* is concerned, one of the most lucid contributions made by Bronfenbrenner was revealing the intertwined system of contexts in which human development takes place. We owe him the idea of the ecology of human development, with a distinction between microsystem (contexts in which the child spends significant time and has significant relationships), mesosystem (analysis of the relationships and overlaps between the different microsystems in which the child participates), exosystem (contexts in which it is not the child who participates directly, but it is rather the people caring for him/her who participate) and macrosystem (the larger cultural context, law, rules, habits, prevailing beliefs, etc.). Lastly, the model proposed by Bronfenbrenner includes the *time* factor (chronosystem) as another essential ingredient with effects on the individual under development (childhood, adolescence, adulthood . . .) as well as on each of the context systems mentioned before (e.g. changes in the family system, in law or social habits).

The ecological systems model proposed by Bronfenbrenner is therefore a complex, multi-levelled model emphasizing the individual, interactions, contexts and time. It is a model in contrast with the 'social address models' and 'personal attributes models' mentioned before. The 'ecological systems approach' – as it is called – has been a very useful tool in the understanding of human development. The goal of this chapter is checking adoption research against the template of the ecological systems approach, in an effort to assess the scope and limits of our knowledge on adopted people, and on the processes taking place in the complex reality of adoption. Schweiger and O'Brien (2005) have also applied the ecological systems approach to the analysis of research on special needs adoption.

It is not the goal of this chapter to make an exhaustive account of adoption research. On the contrary, specific research contributions will be purposely selected which are relevant to illustrate the ideas that will be presented. A good part of the chapter will refer not to available research, but to areas in which research-based information is scarce or missing.

The Adopted Person

At the very core of the ecological systems model we find the person (in our case, the adopted person) under development. On his first descriptions of the ecological systems model, Bronfenbrenner had thoroughly criticized that type of research on development that did not pay attention to context. However as the ecological systems model gained popularity, so much interest was taken in developmental contexts that Bronfenbrenner pointed out that it was not a question of replacing developmental models with no contexts with context models with no development. He then began talking of the 'bioecological' model as a way of emphasizing the personal characteristics of the developing person. Among these we can find antecedents such as biological traits (e.g. genetic characteristics), personal biography, individual style and behavioural expressions.

Research on adoption has been, and still continues to be, dominated by research on adoption outcomes. In all likelihood, the issue most researched on has been the presence of behavioural problems in adopted children. As shown by Palacios and Sánchez-Sandoval (2005), the research paradigm most frequently used has been comparing adopted and non-adopted subjects (a good example of the 'social address model' described by Bronfenbrenner), with the well-known conclusion that most adoptees seem to function well within normal ranges, even if several research studies have found a greater incidence of behavioural problems (especially, attention and hyperactivity problems) among adopted children when compared with their non-adopted age mates (see the meta-analysis by van IJzendoorn and Juffer, 2005b). The 'personal attributes model' has also been used quite extensively, usually focusing on aspects such as early versus late adoption and short versus long exposure to institutional life.

Fortunately, adoption research focusing on outcomes has become more interesting in recent years, for at least three reasons:

- Firstly, besides that of behavioural problems, other outcome areas have been added to adoption research. Some of these areas are physical development and health, cognitive and academic abilities. Attachment-related issues are also gaining significance in adoption research, as shown in Chapter 9.
- Secondly, another important novelty is that in recent years there have been several longitudinal research projects offering data on the changes taking place over time in groups of adoptees, adding a chronosystem perspective on individual development (see Chapters 7 and 8).
- Thirdly, research on outcomes is becoming more theoretically informed, as can be seen in studies inspired in the resilience paradigm.

Studies on adoption outcomes are of great interest even if they evidence that adoption research is still in a phase that is mostly descriptive, attempting to document facts and connect them with specific antecedents. One of our problems is that research on adoption outcomes has children's experiences prior to adoption as one of its black holes. Data on children's genetic background, history of abuse, specific features of their institutional experiences and of their individual vulnerability are usually missing or are very limited. This is especially true in the case of international adoptions. It is frequently the case that the main sources of information are adoptive parents who, in turn, were given very little information when adopting their children. And then researchers find themselves trapped in a very limited perspective, with little or no information on processes and taking for granted that all children adopted from Romanian orphanages were exposed to the same conditions of institutionalization, and that all Chinese adoptees shared similar circumstances before their adoption. Research on adoption outcomes will greatly improve when we are able to add more detailed information on the characteristics of the adopted person before joining the adoptive family.

Unfortunately, things do not change much when it comes to what happens once the child has been adopted. The emphasis on processes is again quite limited as it is shown by the fact that time spent with the adoptive family (not the type of experiences lived during that time) is sometimes used as an index with which to analyse changes over time. Research relating to processes is then more the exception than the rule. The ecological systems model gives us the opportunity of improving this analysis by distinguishing between processes in different context systems: microsystem, mesosystem, exosystem and macrosystem.

In summary, most research focusing on adopted persons' development is centred on outcomes and is descriptive in nature. For many years, behavioural problems were the target of comparisons between adopted and nonadopted persons. Recently, other outcome topics have become part of the researchers' interest, longitudinal projects are being carried out and more theoretically informed research programmes have emerged. Data on children's background are very scarce and emphasis on processes is lacking.

Microsystem

Microsystem refers to "the immediate setting containing the person" (Bronfenbrenner, 1977, p. 515). In the case of Western children and adolescents, family, peers and school are the fundamental microsystems all children participate in.

According to Bronfenbrenner, human development takes place through processes of progressively more complex reciprocal interactions between an active, evolving psychosocial human organism and the persons, objects, and symbols in its immediate external environment. For the family microsystem, for instance, the ecological system analysis encompasses taking into account simultaneously children's individual characteristics, interaction processes with parents and siblings, consideration of the specifics of the family style (home environment, rearing practices . . .) and the changes over time in all these components.

Very few research projects on adoption can be identified as following the requirements of a model that simultaneously takes into consideration processes, personal characteristics, contexts and time. Of the very few research projects that fulfil these requirements, two will be now summarized.

Rushton (Quinton *et al.*, 1998; Rushton and Dance, 2006; Rushton *et al.*, 2003) is the principal investigator of a prospective adoption study examining the development of 61 children who joined permanent unrelated families during middle childhood (between 5 and 11 years). From an outcomes perspective, the main findings after one year after placement were:

- 72% of placements were working out well and appeared stable, 23% were not going well and 5% disrupted in the course of the first year (outcome analysis).
- The proportion of children exhibiting problem behaviour was much higher than in the general population, both a month after placement and a year later ('social address model' type of analysis).

But the authors went beyond this type of analysis. First, they managed to explore *individual characteristics* of the children involved. Some had been the object of a particular type of emotional abuse consisting of selective rejection by biological parents, and they had been adopted alone while their siblings remained in the biological family. Although 72% of the placements were working well one year after adoption for the whole sample, 60% of the preferentially rejected children were classified as progressing unsatisfactorily. This nicely illustrates how the more we know about the personal circumstances and the individual profile of the children, the better is our understanding of their progress and difficulties.

The analysis of the microsystem also requires taking into consideration *interaction processes*. According to the adopters' reports, 73% of children had formed an attached relationship with the parents by the end of their first year in placement. The remaining 27% had failed to develop an attached relationship with either parent after a year of placement or the relationship was described as superficial. In most cases, non-attached relationships were mutual. From antecedents, only a history of active rejection by birth parents was associated with this outcome. But history before adoption was not all. Two process-related aspects of child behaviour towards adoptive parents were predictive of attachment problems: difficulties in the expression of interpersonal emotions (such as care, trust, affection . . .) and the expression of 'false affection' (children's expression of affect felt by parents as unconvincing, unnatural and forced). These difficulties were hardly present in the group that formed attachments while they were over-represented in the non-attached group.

Children's *context* also matters and parents, parental feelings and behaviour count. The key factor on the parents' side was in processes and interactions: adoptive parents of the non-attached children showed more difficulties in responding to them in a warm and sensitive manner as early as one month into placement, and the situation had worsened by the end of the year. The *time* dimension is also important in other regards: after a year post-placement, the non-attached group of children showed an increase in the number of conduct difficulties, whereas the attached group did not change significantly in this aspect.

Rushton *et al.*'s (2003) study has been summarized in some detail because it is a nice illustration of an approach that goes beyond description of outcomes depending on some 'social address' or 'personal attributes' variables. It shows the viability and the interest of the process-person-context-time perspective required in the ecological systems model. It also shows that this type of approach takes us much further than the outcomes oriented research.

I will refer more briefly to another illustration of these principles: our study of disruptions of internationally adopted children in Spain between 1997 and 2000 (Palacios, Sánchez-Sandoval and León, 2005b). Either in the child or in the parents, there was no single factor that was predictive of the final negative outcome of adoption disruption. But when certain children's characteristics (age at adoption, behavioural difficulties . . .) were associated with certain parents' characteristics (inadequate motivation, poor preparation, rigid and inflexible rearing styles) and when there were initial relationship problems (coldness, distance . . .), then the situation deteriorated over time and the outcome of disruption was much more likely to occur. Also, it is interesting that in many cases of disruption there were instances of professional malpractice (in home assessment, matching, follow-up and post-adoption support). I shall return to issues of professional intervention when discussing exosystem matters.

Some studies have also illustrated the interest of adding time as a relevant factor in the analysis of the adoptive family microsystem. Seen from a chronosystem perspective, the adoptive family microsystem has undergone important changes in the last years. When we first studied adoption in Spain, most adoptions were infant domestic adoptions. One of our findings about 10 years ago was that by age 6 about 50% of adopted children had not been told about their adoption (Palacios, Sánchez-Sandoval and Sánchez, 1996). We have studied this same matter in a more recent research (Palacios, Sánchez-Sandoval and León, 2005a) and the picture is quite different: 95% of adopted children aged 6 have been told about their adoption. This does not imply that communication about adoption is now an easy and well-resolved problem for all adoptive families, as 30% of the parents report having talked about adoption with their child only once, and when children are interviewed they depict their parents as being less communicative about adoption than parents' self-reports suggest. But there is no doubt that families are now more open about adoption with their adopted children, a change that is related to some macrosystem issues to be discussed later on.

Let me now turn to what we ignore about adoption in the microsystem. From sibling relationships to communication about adoption, for instance, different adoption-related issues could be chosen to illustrate how much we still need to learn about the adoptive family microsystem. Given its normative character in adoptive families, communication about adoption can be taken as a case in point. The complexities of adoption communication are nicely illustrated in Wrobel *et al.*'s (2003) Family Adoption Communication model. Being a key aspect in their life, information about adoption becomes a major component of adopted children's and adolescents' emotions and identity. What a child is told about his or her adoption and the emotional climate of the communication about adoption (Brodzinsky, 2005) can be postulated to have an impact on the adopted person's feelings about himself or herself, about their birth- and their adoptive parents. Given the centrality for the adopted person of the 'adoption story' and of parent–child communication about adoption circumstances, it is amazing how little we know from research about the impact on the adopted person of the different ways to handle the sharing or withholding of information. Actually, most of what we know comes from clinical or case-based evidence, but we have almost no empirical knowledge about the impact of circumstances such as too little versus too much telling (Kaye, 1990), early versus late telling, or emotionally open versus emotionally closed information sharing. Do these circumstances affect the adopted child's well-being, adaptation, behavioural problems, search for information and contact, family relationships, and another developmental and relational aspects? We largely ignore it.

Similar comments seem appropriate regarding attachment processes. Adopted children join their new families with internal working models of attachment that reflect the difficulties derived from past experiences. Hodges *et al.* (2005) and Steele (Chapter 9) have shown that new relational experiences with adoptive parents are not going to simply erase the sequelae of previous emotional adversity. In fact security and insecurity (about self, others, or relationships) will coexist in these children's internal working models. There is interesting clinical literature in this area and we also have some outcome information, but much less is known from the perspective of the transactional model of parent–child interactions proposed by Howe and Fearnley (2003) for the analysis of attachment processes. How do children's initial internal working models interact with their adoptive parents' attachment strategies and internal working models? How do bonding processes change over time once a new 'emotional literacy' and new transactions in the family environment take place? Research evidence on these important matters remains very limited.

There is a notable dearth of information on how adopted children fare in the other microsystem where they spend a good part of their life, namely the school. The little we know about adopted children in schools is clearly outcome oriented, showing a better school performance in adopted children compared with their siblings and peers left behind, but a higher incidence of school difficulties in adopted children compared with their non-adopted classmates (see meta-analysis by van IJzendoorn and Juffer, 2005a). Research on adopted children in the school microsystem seems not to have gone much further than this type of descriptive research on academic performance. A study by Juffer and her Leiden research group (Juffer, Stams and van IJzendoorn, 2004; Stams *et al.*, 2000) has extended this type of analysis to issues of social integration, showing that, among the adoptees, the percentage of popular children was higher (and the proportion of rejected children was lower) than among their non-adopted classmates. These differences were mainly due to the high proportion of adopted girls who were rated by their peers as popular and the low proportion of them in the rejected group. This social address type of knowledge is what we have about adopted children at school, and it shows how much we still need to learn.

In summary, very few research projects on adoption can be identified as simultaneously taking into consideration person-process-context-time in the analysis of the adoptive family microsystem. The few existing studies show the viability and the interest of this approach. Critical areas have not been empirically explored from this perspective. And we know even less about what happens to the adopted child in the school microsystem. Research in the microsystem calls for a consideration of processes, as most of what we know about the adopted persons' microsystems is still outcome oriented.

Mesosystem

The mesosystem comprises "the relations among two or more settings in which the developing person becomes an active participant" (Bronfenbrenner, 2005, p. 80). Two aspects are relevant in the analysis of this contextual level: the transitions from one setting to another (called ecological transition) and the connections between the settings.

As far as the ecological transition is concerned, it is quite astonishing to realize how little we know from research. Adopted children are undertaking a major transition which in the case of intercountry adoptions implies that they travel from one country to another, from one culture to another, from one language to another, from an institution to a family . . . and we simply take for granted that they adapt very quickly. Although many adoptive children were in institutions before being adopted, others were with substitute families. Are there differences between them in the process of adaptation depending on the nature of their placement prior to adoption? How do children really adapt? Are there aspects in which the process is more difficult for them? How do children's and parents' personal characteristics interact in the first weeks of life together? Some work has been done on the transition to adoptive parenthood, but it is not easy to identify any empirical study on the transition to adoptive filiation, although insights in Rosnati's (2005) work in Italy are valuable.

Concerning another relevant aspect in the transition to being adopted, I am not aware of any empirical evidence regarding the preparation of children for adoption. And, once the child is in his or her new home, we have only very little empirical evidence on the process of mutual adaptation. Pinderhughes (1996) developed a model of family readjustment following older child adoptions, with adjustments and readjustments being described as part of the process. This model was illustrated with a case study, but I believe that we have no empirical evidence on how the transition process actually goes. There is talk of a 'honeymoon period' right after the child's arrival to the new home, for instance, but this has not been empirically documented. There is some evidence that in cases of adoption failure there was a lack of attachment and of violated expectations in the early days of the new relationship, but, once again, the evidence tends to be more clinical than research grounded.

With regard to the connections between the different settings in which the adopted child takes part, there is very limited evidence on the family–school overlap and interactions, which is not surprising given the little knowledge we have on adopted children at school, as mentioned before.

Two studies have shown the connection between experiences at home and social competence (Grotevant *et al.*, 2001; Stams, Juffer and van IJzendoorn, 2002). A third study, more in keeping with the mesosystem type of analysis, including a chronosystem dimension, can be mentioned. It is the longitudinal analysis of school achievement and adult qualifications in an investigation comparing a large sample of adoptees with two contrast groups: those born in very similar circumstances and who remained with their biological mothers, and those from the general population of children in the same cohort (Maughan, Collishaw and Pickles, 1998). Adopted children performed at school at levels that compared with the general population of children and got significantly better scores than those of similar children who remained with their mothers. The mesosystem component in the study lays in the confirmation that the strongest predictors of attainment on all measures of achievement were teachers' ratings of parental interest in education, on the one hand, and the child's emotional and behavioural problems on the other. Here we see personal characteristics (behavioural problems) and contextual factors (parents' interest in education) in one microsystem (family) having an impact over time on children achievement in another microsystem (school).

To illustrate the areas of ignorance in adoption research in the mesosystem, social competence issues can be mentioned. From developmental literature we know that child–parent attachment has a significant impact on children's peer relations (Schneider, Atkinson and Tardif, 2001). How does this work in the case of adopted children, whose attachment development has been more complex in many cases? As with many other questions at the mesosystem level of analysis, this issue has not been explored.

Seen from another angle, adopted children look different from many of their peers (physical traits) or are known to be different (because they are known to be adopted). What is the impact of this perception of differences by peers? Are adopted children treated differently by their peers? Is there any experience of rejection? These questions are by no means trivial and we simply seem not to have clear answers from research.

If we know little on the connections between the family and the school microsystems, there is another mesosystem where the research information available is considerably richer. It is the case of research on open adoption, in which connections between biological and adoptive families are analysed and taken into consideration. In most cases, the adopted child is not an active participant in the birth family microsystem, at least physically. However, even if to a diverse degree, adopted children are 'psychologically present' for birth mothers (Fravel, McRoy and Grotevant, 2000) and connect the biological and the adoptive microsystems, giving rise to the idea of the 'adoptive kinship network' or the 'adoption triangle' to which I will refer to later on.

Given the expectation of negative consequences of open adoption, it is not surprising that part of the interest of open adoption researchers has been oriented to document its outcomes (see, for instance, Grotevant, Perry and McRoy, 2005). But in keeping with the requirements of the ecological systems model, researchers have also paid attention to issues related to processes, persons, context and time. According to Siegel (1993), the four basic dimensions in open arrangements are type, frequency, timing and participants. Changes in contact arrangements over time are a fifth dimension to be added, as contact arrangements are an evolving reality. All these five dimensions have been analysed thoroughly, as can be seen in Chapters 12 and 13. One conclusion that derives from the research on open adoption is that a 'one size fits all' type of approach is not adequate in a matter in which the flexibility to accommodate over time the personal needs, attitudes and skills of all parties involved is essential.

In summary, the mesosystem or connections between the different microsystems in which the adopted child participates remain largely unexplored. The very important ecological transition from the previous context to the adoptive family should allow for fascinating explorations of the adaptation process. The same is true for the connections between family and school. In contrast, the connections between birth and adoptive family have been studied in detail by open adoption researchers, showing the relevance and the viability of empirical explorations of the adoption mesosystems.

Exosystem

According to Bronfenbrenner's definition, the exosystem is "a setting that does not ordinarily contain the developing person, but in which events occur that influence processes within the immediate setting that does contain that person" (1989, p. 238). If we imagine an adoptive family with regular contact with grandparents who are used as a source of support and advice, that would be a good example of an exosystem for such a family. In fact research has shown that parents who adopt children with special needs report finding the highest level of supportive contact in their informal network, including their own parents, other extended family members, best friends ... (Kramer and Houston, 1998; Rosenthal, Groze and Morgan, 1996). If this network is so important for adoptive parents, it is interesting to note that no research has been devoted to the 'adopting' grandparents, their attitudes, their role and influence.

Out of all exosystem contexts that could be thought of as being relevant for the adopted person and the adoptive family, I would like to concentrate now on one of special importance: adoption professionals. I use this label to refer to an unorganized army of professionals working at any stage of the adoption process, from preparation to placement to post-adoption services. These professionals perform such critical tasks as decision making about type of placement, home study, preparation of children and parents, matching, follow-up during the pre-adoption period, post-adoption support, children and family therapy when needed . . . Just as an illustration, research on adoption disruptions has shown that professional intervention (be it by virtue of action or of omission) very often plays a role when adoptions go wrong (Palacios, Sánchez-Sandoval and León, 2005b).

Traditionally, adoption matters were considered to refer to the 'adoption dyad', encompassing the adopted child and the adoptive parents. In part influenced by research on open adoption, we have become used to thinking of the adoption kinship network, which is an adoption triangle including the adoption dyad plus the biological family. I would like to propose here an 'adoption quadrangle' to include adoption professionals and their interventions. In what follows I would like to see what adoption research has to say to professionals to assist them in performing their multiple and very complex tasks. Later on I will consider whether adoption researchers should be regarded as part of this unorganized army of adoption professionals or not.

The analysis could start with a general statement valid for most of the contents to be covered: there is very little research-based evidence to be used by adoption professionals when working at any stage of the adoption process. Standard research strategies in the assessment of interventions, such as trial designs comparing the efficacy of different approaches, are exceptional rather than usual. Although not true for all professional activities around adoption, there is a good amount of practice literature, but much less assessment of efficacy, long-term impact, cost . . . Many critical decisions seem to be based more on professional consensus, personal or cultural biases and preferences, than on sound research data.

This is the case, for instance, with adopters' preparation. Packages with training materials for prospective adopters are available, but there is no research to show what works best. Is group training more effective than activities tailored individually? Is there any critical duration of training for it to be effective? Are approaches oriented to learning behavioural management more advisable than approaches oriented towards understanding children's behaviour? A research project now going on (Rushton *et al.*, 2006) should cast light on some of these issues, but so far, there is no research-based evidence to answer the questions.

The shortcomings of our knowledge about the home study can be illustrated with a very simple matter: age of prospective adopters or, as it is more often put in adoption practice, age difference between adopters and adoptees. In Holland, professionals work under the assumption of an age difference of 40 years between adopters and adoptee, as the oldest you can be to adopt is 46 and the oldest the child can be to be adopted is 6. In Spain, depending on the region, age difference is 40, 42 or 45. But in the United Kingdom age is not defined in terms of a specific figure, but as "the health and vigour to meet the many and varied demands of children in their growing years and be there for them into adulthood" (Adoption Act, 1976, sections 14 and 15). What is the research evidence supporting age restrictions in Holland or in Spain as opposed to the more open approach in the United Kingdom? None, I believe. If we had sound research evidence on this, we would not expect to find these differences in policies and regulations between European countries or between different regions within the same country.

Let us now turn to matching issues. It has been written that "too often the (matching) process may appear to be a gamble, with successful outcome due to chance rather than good planning in matching child and family" (Ward, 1997, p. 257). In her analysis of 80 special needs adoptions, McRoy (1999) found that "rationale for placement in the (analyzed) cases tended to be based more on finding a family willing to try the placement than a comprehensive assessment of the fit or match between the specific child and family" (p. 133). Some authors have proposed that matching decisions should be made on the grounds of psychological testing of children and families. Valdez and McNamara (1994), for instance, believe that matching should be made on the grounds of a 'goodness-of-fit' kind of approach and they are in favour of using a temperament test with both prospective adopters and children to establish successful matching. Others (The Hadley Centre for Adoption and Foster Care Studies, 2002) prefer 'compatibility' (between child's needs and family strengths) rather than matching. Clear-cut criteria as to how to establish this compatibility are not available except in the form of general principles.

The concept of 'stretching' is linked to matching. Stretching of adoptive parents' preferences occurs when prospective adopters are offered the adoption of a child whose characteristics do not match their original preferences: the child is older or more difficult or comes with a sibling, and so on. As McRoy (1999) has put it, "rushed placements, encouraging 'stretching' by adoptive parents, allowing adoptive parents to take on much more than they can obviously handle, and minimizing behaviors of a child may serve to facilitate movement of children from foster care to adoption, but set the stage for disruption or dissolution of the adoption" (p. 137). Had we more research on all these issues, we would be better able to assist professionals in their difficult decisions.

Finally, on adoption support. There has been some research on adopters' need, use and helpfulness of services (e.g. Brooks, Allen and Barth, 2002; Sturgess and Selwyn, 2007) but most of what we know on adoption support is related to post-adoption services (percentages of adoptive parents who have used different services, the types of services missed, the level of satisfaction with the services and so on). In their assessment of our knowledge on such services, Barth and Miller (2000) and Rushton and Dance (2002) have concluded that available research on post-adoption services is largely descriptive and based on few projects. According to Rushton (2003), further evaluative studies are urgently needed to test the value of those interventions that look promising and are theoretically sound. Such studies should meet criteria that are now basically missing in research on adoption support: use of random allocation methods, interventions tailored for adoptive families with clearly defined targets and established measures, interventions that are replicable and with sufficient sample size, and adequate follow-up length to test for long-term benefits.

We also lack analysis of adoption professional practices over time. The chronosystem approach could be very informative here as it could cast light on the dynamic connections between research, professional practice and changes in the macrosystem to be analysed later on. I still remember seeing, some 20 or 25 years ago, in a Spanish orphanage now dismantled, the label 'Non adoptable' on some children's files. These were special needs children, and the label was probably written by the professional in charge. Also, even more recently, I remember times when adoption professionals decided not to share with the adoptive parents part of a child's background information, considering this was a way of protecting the child from being stigmatized, or of preventing the parents from being frightened. These practices have now disappeared from professional practice, and it would be of great interest to document the process of change and the factors influencing it.

Once the research evidence on the matters that affect the daily activities of adoption professionals has been reviewed, one may wonder whether adoption researchers are part of the exosystem including adoption professionals. From what has been shown in this section, it is my impression that, more than an integral part of this body, adoption researchers are a distant exosystem of the adoption professionals' exosystem. There would be much to gain out of a closer cooperation and a partnership between research and professional intervention, since, as Bronfenbrenner (1974) wrote, social policy needs science, and science needs social policy, as well, in order to provide researchers with two essential elements for any scientific endeavour: vitality and validity.

In summary, as part of the adoptive family microsystem, professional interventions on adoption have been used to analyse research exploring the exosystem level. Adoption professionals perform a number of critical activities, but their practices seem more guided by peer consensus, or by personal or cultural biases, than by sound research evidence. Standard research strategies, such as designs comparing the efficacy of different intervention approaches, have not been used to study professional interventions on adoption, and very basic questions remain empirically unexplored. More than an integral part of professional activities around adoption, adoption research can be considered to be a distant exosystem of the adoption professionals' exosystem.

Macrosystem

The macrosystem was defined by Bronfenbrenner as "the overarching pattern of micro-, meso- and exosystem characteristic of a given culture (. . .), with particular reference to the developmentally instigative belief systems, resources, hazards, lifestyles, opportunity structures, life course options, and patterns of social interchange that are embedded in such overarching systems" (1989, p. 242). If we add the chronosystem perspective, we then have history as well as part of the picture. In what follows there is an analysis of what adoption research tells us about the anthropology, the history and the sociology of adoption. And I would like to add some comments on adoption researchers and adoption research as active contributors to shape the macrosystem, with which I will close the circle of my analysis.

Starting with the anthropology of adoption, as shown in the volume edited by Bowie (2004b), the practice of circulating children to be raised by non-biogenetic parents is present in different parts of the world. There are societies in which the exchange of children from fertile to infertile women is seen as a way of bringing order out of chaos by rectifying the mistake of infertility made by nature (Talle, 2004). Societies are described in which social parenthood (i.e. adoption) is seen as more desirable than biological parenthood (Alber, 2004), or in which adoption of a child from another family is a way to gain rights over the land (Treide, 2004). In other words, contrary to our Western current mentality, the interests of children or the desires of adoptive parents are not the main or the only reasons for circulating people (not only children) between families and social groups: inheritance, performance of religious duties, rights in land, absorption of someone into a particular group, formation of strategic alliances or the politics of marriage (Bowie, 2004a) are motives behind adoption and foster-age in some contemporary cultures. In some of these cultures, the majority of families are involved in the adoption of a child, in others half the popula-tion is adopted, still in others most children have spent at least part of their childhood in one or more different homes.

In reality, we don't need to travel far to find these contrasts with our current adoption practices. It is enough to travel backwards. Although still to be written in a more systematic form, the history of adoption has many illustrations of ways of thinking about adoption, which contrast with our current beliefs and practices (see Burguière *et al.*, 1996). In ancient Meso-potamia, for instance, it was possible to adopt a son or a daughter, a daughter-in-law, a brother or a sister, even a father; adoption could take a variety of forms with different functions: emancipation of a slave, choosing a wife for a son, concluding a sale, legitimating children or creating descen-dants in the event of a line dying out (Glassner, 1996). The Hammurabi Code (around 1700 BC), the first set of laws in history, included regulation on adoption procedures; adoption was practised in the best interest of adults who were childless or whose children had grown up and married away, a child or young person being then adopted to care for the parents in their old age. In ancient Athens, most adoptions involved relatives and adoption was only justified as the consequence of a lack of heirs (Sissa, 1996). In classical Rome, adoption was a way to ensure an heir, to reinforce inter-family ties or to promote alliances; a common practice in upper classes, adoption was not secretive or considered shameful, nor was the adopted boy expected to cut ties with his original family. The adopted child was often in a privileged situation, enjoying both original and adoptive family connections. Several Roman emperors were adopted by acting emperors as their successors and adoption was the most common way of gaining access to the throne without use of force; actually, Marcus Aurelius' succession by his natural son is considered to be the beginning of the Roman Empire decline (Thomas, 1996). Among the Celts of Britain and England, adoption was a common institution used to foster political links between wealthy families (Patterson, 1994).

In fact, we do not need to travel so far in time to see adoption from a historical perspective. In Chapter 2, Carp illustrates this point for the history of open adoption. The recent history of transracial adoption could also be taken as a case in point. In the United States, at the beginning of the 1970s there was a strong position against transracial adoption (basically, against black children being adopted by white families), whereas in our days ethnicity cannot automatically be considered the primary factor when making placement decisions, although this by no means implies that it should not be part of the decision making. Outside the United States, there are some countries where basically only transracial adoptions exist (e.g. Holland or the Scandinavian countries) to the point that if transracial adoptions were banned, there would be no adoptions. The transracial adoption debate is of interest because what is implied is far more than psychological matters, sociological and political arguments being also involved. It is also of interest because adoption research has made a significant contribution to changes in the way transracial adoption is perceived and practised, a point to which I shall return to later on.

After anthropology and history, the sociology of adoption can now be considered. Sociological analysis of adoption has in attitudes towards adoption one of its central interests. A good example of this approach could be a national adoption attitudes survey carried out in the United States in 2002 (Dave Thomas Foundation for Adoption, 2002). Attitudes towards adoption seem to be quite positive:

- 80% of US adults think the country should be doing or encouraging adoption.
- 75% believe adoptive parents are very likely to love their adoptive children as much as children born to them.
- 80% think that parents get as much or more satisfaction from raising adoptive children as from raising biological children.
- 94% perceive adoptive parents as lucky.

According to the survey, 40% of US adults have considered adopting a child at one time in their lives. But if only 0.2% of these adults actually pursued and completed the adoption process all 135 000 children in foster care would be adopted. In other words, there seems to be an important discrepancy between favourable attitudes and actual behaviour. Another illustration of this same fact can be found in a study of adolescent perceptions of adoption (Daly, 1994). When asked if they would select adoption if they or their partner became pregnant, 6% of the students said they definitely would; when asked what advice they would give to a friend with an unwanted pregnancy, 43% considered adoption to be the best solution. In other words, adoption seems to be a good idea ... for someone else to do.

How can this discrepancy be explained? Part of the explanation may be in the social construction of kinship and adoption (Miall, 1996). Traditionally, kinship has been defined on the basis of blood continuity, with blood relationships then being at the core of parent–child connections. In case of infertility, adoption was considered to be 'second best'. More recently, as Lebner (2000) has pointed out, genes have also entered the symbolic picture of kinship definitions as part of what Wegar (2000) calls "western fascination with genes and genetic explanations" (p. 363). According to Lebner's (2000) analysis, despite more diversity in family forms, "the preference for genetic connectedness is currently and continually being fed by the medicalization and geneticization of our society" (p. 374). The first alternatives to infertility are then medical treatments, adoption becomes 'third best' and adoption is still perceived by many as "not quite as good as having your own" (Fisher, 2003b). Adoption would carry with it a certain level of social stigmatization as part of the biologically related definitions of parenthood. According to Leon (2002), the way adoption is lived and felt by many of those touched by it (biological parents, adoptive parents, adopted persons) is highly dependent on these socially constructed notions of kinship and parenthood.

Perhaps as a reaction to the old stigma against adoption, the former secrecy about adoption is being substituted by a certain pride in being an adoptive parent (a kind of 'outing' to some extent similar to what has happened in the case of gay and lesbian people). Part of it may have to do with the increase in intercountry adoption and the visibility that adoption has gained in some societies that formerly used only or mainly domestic infant adoptions. Online adoption-related shops sell T-shirts for adults with the logo 'Expecting from China', for instance; there are others for children: 'Just arrived from Russia', 'Just arrived from Guatemala', and so on.

The changing attitudes of adoptive parents towards adoption have been analysed by Hoksbergen and ter Laak (2005) in their proposition of four generations of adoptive parents in recent times: the 'traditional-closed generation' before 1970, the 'open and idealistic generation' between 1971 and 1981, the 'materialistic-realistic' generation between 1982 and 1992, and the 'optimistic-demanding' generation since 1993. According to this analysis, the change in attitudes from one generation to another was in part fuelled by research findings. Thus, for instance, the idealistic approach of the second generation was difficult to sustain once research results during the 1980s and early 1990s were describing adopted children as having serious problems in different areas. I will use this connection between adoption research and public attitudes about adoption to bring my analysis to an end.

The attitude survey reported before showed that one of the main concerns to adopt a child out of foster care is the mental health of the child.

Interestingly enough, Fisher's (2003a) analysis of how adoption is portrayed in college textbooks and readers on families has revealed two major facts. One, that adoption has a very poor coverage in these books (in average, 1 out of every 200 pages is devoted to adoption). Second, that adoption is more frequently described negatively as it is more frequently associated with problems and difficulties than with positive outcomes. Probably, part of the reason why adoption is depicted this way has to do with the tone and content of a good amount of adoption research.

As Palacios and Brodzinsky (2005) have pointed out, for many years, adoption research focused on the increased risk of adopted children for psychological, social and academic problems; the pathologization of adoption ultimately culminated in the now repudiated concept of the 'adopted child syndrome'. These negative views about adoption find easily their way to the news, books and magazines, which are the main source of information about adoption for 45% of the population, according to the research survey (Dave Thomas Foundation for Adoption, 2002). Adoption research has also told many positive things about adoption, about the benefits and the gains of adoption for both children and parents, but this research is less known and perhaps less attractive to be reported in news and magazines. In any case, I agree with Miall (1996) in her appreciation that "there is a pressing need for researchers to theoretically normalize the examination of developmental issues within the adoptive family" (p. 316). What has happened with open adoption is a good example, as the way open adoption is now perceived and practised is highly dependent on the way its functioning and its outcomes have been described by researchers, in sheer contrast with the very negative prospects and fears of previous attitudes.

Through its impact on professionals who then influence adoptive parents and adopted children; through its influence on legal and policy issues; through its translation in the news and the media, adoption research contributes to shaping our macrosystem in adoption and family-related matters. If we now take a chronosystem perspective, adoption research seems to be changing and the 'normality' and resilience perspectives are also finding its place in adoption research. Of course, it is not the task of adoption researchers to hide problems and difficulties, but to place them in the context of the otherwise many positive assets of adoption. That could be part of the research agenda awaiting us and delineated in this chapter.

In summary, the adoption macrosystem has been recently illuminated by a number of studies exploring the anthropology, the history and the sociology of adoption. This knowledge is very helpful, as the way adoption is lived by those touched by it is highly dependent on this macrosystem dimension. Through its focus and findings, adoption research is an active macrosystem shaper, and this calls for our responsibility and our efforts to more fully understand the very complex ecology of adoption.

References

Alber, E. (2004) 'The real parents are the foster parents': Social parenthood among the Baatombu in Northern Benin, in *Cross-Cultural Approaches to Adoption* (ed. F. Bowie), Routledge, London, pp. 33–47.

Barth, R.P. and Miller, J.M. (2000) Building effective post-adoption services: What is the empirical foundation? *Family Relations*, **49**, 447–55.

Bowie, F. (2004a) Adoption and the circulation of children: A comparative perspective, in *Cross-Cultural Approaches to Adoption* (ed. F. Bowie), Routledge, London, pp. 3–20.

Bowie, F. (ed.) (2004b) *Cross-Cultural Approaches to Adoption*, Routledge, London.

Brodzinsky, D.M. (2005) Reconceptualizing openness in adoption: Implications for theory, research, and practice, in *Psychological Issues in Adoption: Research and Practice* (eds D.M. Brodzinsky and J. Palacios), Praeger, Westport, CT, pp. 145–66.

Bronfenbrenner, U. (1974) *Is Early Intervention Effective? A Report on Longitudinal Evaluations of Preschool Programs*, vol. **2**, Department of Health, Education and Welfare, Office Child Development, Washington, DC.

Bronfenbrenner, U. (1977) Toward an experimental ecology of human development. *American Psychologist*, **32**, 513–30.

Bronfenbrenner, U. (1989) Ecological systems theory. *Annals of Child Development*, **6**, 187–249.

Bronfenbrenner, U. (2005) *Making Human Beings Human: Bioecological Perspectives on Human Development*, Sage, Thousand Oaks, CA.

Brooks, D., Allen, J. and Barth, R. (2002) Adoption services use, helpfulness, and need: A comparison of public and private agency and independent adoptive families. *Children and Youth Services Review*, **24**, 213–8.

Burguière, A., Klapisch-Zuber, C., Segalen, M. and Zonabend, F. (eds) (1996) *A History of the Family. Vol. 1: Distant Worlds, Ancient Worlds*, The Belknap Press of Harvard University Press, Cambridge, MA.

Daly, K.J. (1994) Adolescent perception of adoption. Implications for resolving an unplanned pregnancy. *Youth and Society*, **25**, 330–50.

Dave Thomas Foundation for Adoption (2002) *2002 National Survey*, The Evan B. Donaldson Adoption Institute, New York.

Fisher, A.P. (2003a) A critique of the portrayal of adoption in college textbooks and readers on families, 1998–2001. *Family Relations*, **52**, 154–60.

Fisher, A.P. (2003b) Still "Not quite as good as having your own"? Toward a sociology of adoption. *Annual Review of Sociology*, **29**, 335–61.

Fravel, D.L., McRoy, R.G. and Grotevant, H.D. (2000) Birthmother perceptions of the psychologically present adopted child: Adoption openness and boundary ambiguity. *Family Relations*, 49, 425–33.

Glassner, J.J. (1996) *From Sumer to Babylon: Families as landowners and families as rulers*, in *A History of the Family. Vol. 1: Distant Worlds, Ancient Worlds* (eds A. Burguière, C. Klapisch-Zuber, M. Segalen and F. Zonabend), The Belknap Press of Harvard University Press, Cambridge, MA, pp. 92–127.

Grotevant, H.D., Perry, Y. and McRoy, R.G. (2005) Openness in adoption: Outcomes for adolescents within their adoptive kinship networks, in *Psychological Issues in Adoption: Research and Practice* (eds D. Brodzinsky and J. Palacios), Praeger, Westport, CT, pp. 167–86.

Grotevant, H.D., Wrobel, G.M., van Dulmen, M.H. and McRoy, R.G. (2001) The emergence of psychosocial engagement in adopted adolescents: The family as context over time. *Journal of Adolescent Research*, 16, 469–90.

Hodges, J., Steele, M., Hillman, S. *et al.* (2005) Change and continuity in mental representations of attachment after adoption, in *Psychological Issues in Adoption: Research and Practice* (eds D. Brodzinsky and J. Palacios), Praeger, Westport, CT, pp. 93–116.

Hoksbergen, R. and ter Laak, J. (2005) Changing attitudes of adoptive parents in Northern European countries, in *Psychological Issues in Adoption: Research and Practice* (eds D. Brodzinsky and J. Palacios), Praeger, Westport, CT, pp. 27–46.

Howe, D. and Fearnley, Sh. (2003) Disorders of attachment in adopted and fostered children: Recognition and treatment. *Clinical Child Psychology and Psychiatry*, 8, 369–87.

Juffer, F., Stams, G.J.J.M. and van IJzendoorn, M.H. (2004) Adopted children's problem behavior is significantly related to their ego resiliency, ego control, and sociometric status. *Journal of Child Psychology and Psychiatry*, 45, 697–706.

Kaye, K. (1990) Acknowledgment or rejection of differences? in *The Psychology of Adoption* (eds D.M. Brodzinsky and M.D. Schechter), Oxford University Press, New York, pp. 121–43.

Kramer, L. and Houston, D. (1998) Supporting families as they adopt children with special needs. *Family Relations*, 47, 423–32.

Lebner, A. (2000) Genetic "mysteries" and international adoption: The cultural impact of biomedical technologies on the adoptive family experience. *Family Relations*, 49, 371–7.

Leon, I.G. (2002) Adoption losses: Naturally occurring or socially constructed? *Child Development*, 73, 652–63.

Maughan, B., Collishaw, S. and Pickles, A. (1998) School achievements and adult qualifications among adoptees: A longitudinal study. *Journal of Child Psychology and Psychiatry*, 39, 669–85.

McRoy, R.G. (1999) *Special Needs Adoption: Practice Issues*, Garland, New York.

Miall, C.E. (1996) The social construction of adoption: Clinical and community perspectives. *Family Relations*, **45**, 309–17.

Palacios, J. and Brodzinsky, D.M. (2005) Recent changes and future directions for adoption research, in *Psychological Issues in Adoption: Research and Practice* (eds D. Brodzinsky and J. Palacios), Praeger, Westport, CT, pp. 93–116.

Palacios, J. and Sánchez-Sandoval, Y. (2005) Beyond adopted/nonadopted comparisons, in *Psychological Issues in Adoption: Research and Practice* (eds D. Brodzinsky and J. Palacios), Praeger, Westport, CT, pp. 257–68.

Palacios, J., Sánchez-Sandoval, Y. and León, E. (2005a) *Adopción Internacional en España: Un Nuevo País, Una Nueva Vida (Intercountry Adoption in Spain: A New Country, A New Life)*, Ministerio de Trabajo y Asuntos Socialesm, Madrid.

Palacios, J., Sánchez-Sandoval, Y. and León, E. (2005b) Intercountry adoption disruptions in Spain. *Adoption Quarterly*, **9**, 35–55.

Palacios, J., Sánchez-Sandoval, Y. and Sánchez, E. (1996) *La Adopción en Andalucía (Adoption in Andalusia)*, Consejería de Asuntos Sociales, Sevilla.

Patterson, N.T. (1994) *Cattle Lords and Clansmen: The Social Structure of Early Ireland*, University of Notre Dame Press, Notre Dame.

Pinderhughes, E.E. (1996) Toward understanding family readjustment following older child adoptions: The interplay between theory generation and empirical research. *Children and Youth Services Review*, **18**, 115–38.

Quinton, D., Rushton, A., Dance, C. and Mayes, D. (1998) *Joining New Families: A Study of Adoption and Fostering in Middle Childhood*, John Wiley & Sons, Ltd, Chichester.

Rosenthal, J.A., Groze, V. and Morgan, J. (1996) Services for families adopting children via public child welfare agencies: Use, helpfulness, and need. *Children and Youth Services Review*, **18**, 163–82.

Rosnati, R. (2005) The construction of adoptive parenthood and filiation in Italian families with adolescents: A family perspective, in *Psychological Issues in Adoption: Research and Practice* (eds D. Brodzinsky and J. Palacios), Praeger, Westport, CT, pp. 187–210.

Rushton, A. (2003) Support for adoptive families: A review of current evidence on problems, needs and effectiveness. *Adoption & Fostering*, **27**, 41–50.

Rushton, A. and Dance, C. (2002) *Adoption Support Services for Families in Difficulty: A Literature Review and Survey of UK Practice*, BAAF, London.

Rushton, A. and Dance, C. (2006) The adoption of children from public care: A prospective study of outcome in adolescence. *Journal of the American Academy of Child and Adolescent Psychiatry*, **45**, 877–83.

Rushton, A., Mayes, D., Dance, C. and Quinton, D. (2003) Parenting late placed children: The development of new relationships and the challenge of behavioural problems. *Clinical Child Psychology and Psychiatry*, **8**, 389–400.

Rushton, A., Monck, E., Upright, H. and Davidson, M. (2006) Enhancing adoptive parenting: Devising promising interventions. *Child and Adolescent Mental Health*, **11**, 25–31.

Schneider, B.H., Atkinson, L. and Tardif, C. (2001) Child-parent attachment and children's relations. *Developmental Psychology*, 37, 86–100.

Schweiger, W.K. and O'Brien, M. (2005) Special needs adoption: An ecological systems approach. *Family Relations*, 54, 512–22.

Siegel, D.H. (1993) Open adoption of infants: Adoptive parents' perceptions of advantages and disadvantages. *Social Work*, 38, 15–23.

Sissa, G. (1996) The family in ancient Athens (fifth-fourth century BC), in *A History of the Family. Vol. 1: Distant Worlds, Ancient Worlds* (eds A. Burguière, C. Klapisch-Zuber, M. Segalen and F. Zonabend), The Belknap Press of Harvard University Press, Cambridge, MA, pp. 194–227.

Stams, G.J.J.M., Juffer, F., Rispens, J. and Hoksbergen, R.A.C. (2000) The development and adjustment of 7-year-old children adopted in infancy. *Journal of Child Psychology and Psychiatry*, 41, 1025–37.

Stams, G.J.J.M., Juffer, F. and van IJzendoorn, M.H. (2002) Maternal sensitivity, infant attachment, and temperament predict adjustment in middle childhood: The case of adopted children and their biologically unrelated parents. *Developmental Psychology*, 38, 806–21.

Sturgess, W. and Selwyn, J. (2007) Supporting the placements of children adopted out of care. *Clinical Child Psychology and Psychiatry*, 12, 13–28.

Talle, A. (2004) Adoption practices among the pastoral Maasai of East Africa: Enacting fertility, in *Cross-Cultural Approaches to Adoption* (ed. F. Bowie), Routledge, London, pp. 64–78.

The Hadley Centre for Adoption and Foster Care Studies (2002) *Matching Children and Families in Permanent Family Placement. Research Summary*, School for Policy Studies, University of Bristol.

Thomas, Y. (1996) Fathers as citizens of Rome, Rome as a city of fathers (second century BC-second century AD), in *A History of the Family. Vol. 1: Distant Worlds, Ancient Worlds* (eds A. Burguière, C. Klapisch-Zuber, M. Segalen and F. Zonabend), The Belknap Press of Harvard University Press, Cambridge, MA, pp. 228–69.

Treide, D. (2004) Adoptions in Micronesia: Past and present, in *Cross-Cultural Approaches to Adoption* (ed. F. Bowie), Routledge, London, pp. 127–42.

Valdez, G.M. and McNamara, J.R. (1994) Matching to prevent adoption disruption. *Child and Adolescent Social Work Journal*, 11, 391–403.

van IJzendoorn, M. and Juffer, F. (2005a) Adoption is a successful natural intervention enhancing adopted children's IQ and school performance. *Current Directions in Psychological Science*, 14, 326–30.

van IJzendoorn, M. and Juffer, F. (2005b) The Emanuel Miller Memorial Lecture 2006: Adoption as intervention. Meta-analytic evidence for massive catch-up and plasticity in physical, socio-emotional, and cognitive development. *Journal of Child Psychology and Psychiatry*, 47, 1228–45.

Ward, M. (1997) Family paradigms and older-children adoption: A proposal for matching parents' strengths to children's needs. *Family Relations*, 46, 257–62.

Wegar, K. (2000) Adoption, family ideology, and social stigma: Bias in community attitudes, adoption research, and practice. *Family Relations*, **49**, 363–70.

Wrobel, G.M., Kohler, J.K., Grotevant, H.D. and McRoy, R.G. (2003) The Family Adoption Communication Model (FAC): Identifying pathways of adoption-related communication. *Adoption Quarterly*, **7**, 53–84.

Part 2
Research Perspectives

5

Children from Care CAN Be Adopted

Ruth G. McRoy, Courtney J. Lynch, Amy Chanmugam,
Elissa Madden and Susan Ayers-Lopez

Introduction

In the past decade, extensive efforts have been made by federal and state officials in the United States to increase the overall number of adoptions from the public child welfare system, particularly among older children and youth. In response to recent public awareness campaigns and various legislative initiatives, the number of adoptions has steadily increased since the mid-1990s. Between 1995 and 2005, the annual number of adoptions from the public child welfare system doubled, rising from approximately 25 700 to over 51 000 (U.S. Department of Health and Human Services, 2005a, 2008). Federal officials estimate that approximately 85% of all adoptions from the U.S. public child welfare system meet the criteria for 'special needs adoptions' (U.S. Government Accounting Office, 2002). That is, the child has at least one special need or characteristic that might impede or delay placement with an adoptive family (U.S. Government Accounting Office, 2002). While the definition varies slightly from state to state, the term 'special needs adoptions' generally refers to adoption of children who have physical, mental or emotional problems, as well as children who are from minority ethnic groups, are older or who belong to a sibling group (McRoy, 1999; Reilly and Platz, 2003; Ryan and Nalavany, 2003).

Despite the dramatic increase in the number of children adopted from care in the last decade, thousands of U.S. children still await adoption. According to the most recent statistics available, adoption is the permanency goal for an estimated 129 000 of the 510 000 children in the U.S. foster care system (U.S. Department of Health and Human Services, 2008). Of the 129 000 children awaiting adoption in 2006, approximately 50 000 of these children have been in continuous foster care for three years or more. Nineteen percent of waiting children have been in the public child welfare system for over five years. Currently, older children comprise the largest percentage of children in the public child welfare system waiting for adoption. In 2006, approximately 43 394 (33%) of children in the United States awaiting adoption were 11 years of age or older (U.S. Department of Health and Human Services, 2008). At that time, the majority of waiting children were living in a foster family (54%), with a relative (21%), or in a group home or institution (10%). Only 13% of children waiting in 2006 were living in a pre-adoptive home.

Caucasian children comprised 38% of children awaiting adoption and disproportionately high numbers of the children awaiting adoption in 2006 were children of colour. According to the 2000 Census, African American children represented less than 15% of the total U.S. child population (U.S. Census Bureau, 2004); yet they represented almost one-third (32%) of all children awaiting adoption from the U.S. public child welfare system (U.S. Department of Health and Human Services, 2008). Hispanic children represented 20% of children awaiting adoption in 2006 (U.S. Department of Health and Human Services, 2008).

This chapter will briefly review the literature on adoptions from foster care with particular emphasis on older child adoptions in the United States, the United Kingdom and Canada. Key research findings from a recent study of U.S. families who adopted older children from the foster care system will be discussed, and implications for practice and research will be provided.

Overview of Older Child Adoptions

Foster Care Adoptions in the United States

In 2006, approximately 51 000 children were adopted from the U.S. public child welfare system. These children were an average of 6.6 years old at the time of adoption. 57% percent of all adoptions from the public child welfare system in 2006 were consummated within a year of the child becoming legally free for adoption. Most children were adopted by their foster parents (59%) or by a relative (26%). Although efforts have been made in recent years to increase the number of 'general adoptions'[1] from the child welfare system, data from the last decade indicate that the proportion of

---

[1] The term 'general adoption' refers to adoptions of children by individuals with whom the child did not have a prior relationship.

children adopted by non-relatives, has steadily declined from 21% in 1998 to 15% in 2006. The ethnic breakdown of children adopted in the United States in 2006 was as follows: 45% were Caucasian, 27% were African American, 19% were Hispanic, 5% were of two or more ethnicities, 2% were of 'unknown' ethnicity, 1% were Native American and 1% were Asian American (U.S. Department of Health and Human Services, 2008).

Foster Care Adoptions in Canada and the United Kingdom

Because adoption record keeping remains at the provincial level and with the ministries responsible for facilitating adoptions, it is difficult to get a clear overall picture of adoption in Canada. However, it is estimated that thousands of children are waiting to be adopted in Canada. In 2005, the Adoption Council of Canada (ACC) estimated that 22 000 children in foster care were eligible for adoption. Of these, approximately 1700 are adopted in a given year (Department for Children, Schools and Families, 2007).

Similar to the disproportionately high representation of African American children in the foster care system in the United States, there is a disproportionately high number of Aboriginal children in Canada and the number continues to rise. Of the approximately 76 000 children residing in out-of-home care, 30 to 40% are estimated to be Aboriginal (Manning and Zandstra, 2003), although Aboriginal children only make up an estimated 5% of the Canadian child population (Scarth, 2004).

The United States has a much higher proportion of children in foster care than the United Kingdom, with 74 children per 10 000 in care in the United States, and 47 children per 10 000 in care in the United Kingdom (Sargent, 2003). While there was an increase in the number of children entering care in the United States in the 1990s, the number of children entering care in England during that same time did not increase dramatically. What did increase since the mid-1990s in England however, was that children were more likely to come into care because of child protection concerns and remain in care for longer periods of time (Selwyn and Sturgess, 2002).

In the year ending in March 2007, there were 60 000 children who were 'looked after' in England, compared with 60 300 in 2006. Of the 60 000 child placements, 71% were foster care placements. In this same year (2007), 3300 children were adopted, which represented an 11% decrease from the previous year's figure of 3700. Of those adopted, 64% were between 1 and 4 years of age, 27% were between 5 and 9 years of age, 5%

were between 10 and 15 years of age, and a mere 10 youths were age 16 and over (Department of Children, Schools, and Families, 2007).

Older Child Adoptions in the United Kingdom

Adoption Policy in the United Kingdom   In the 1970s, as the 'permanency movement' emerged and grew in the United States, ideas about permanency also garnered increased attention and emphasis in the United Kingdom. Research that demonstrated the success of older child adoptions, the identification of the foster care drift phenomenon, and the Houghton Committee's review of adoption all culminated in the passage of two key pieces of adoption legislation: The Children Act of 1975 and The Adoption Act of 1976. A key feature of this legislation was the introduction of 'Freeing Orders', which made it easier to terminate birth parent consent and easier for foster parents to adopt (Performance and Innovation Unit, 2000).

By the late 1980s, there was growing disillusionment with the 'investigate, rescue, remove' approach that developed and predominated in the 1970s and early to mid-1980s. In 1989, the Children Act of 1989 was passed. Although the Act was intended to create simultaneous emphasis on partnership of parents and family as well as on child protection, the Act was ultimately seen as de-emphasizing permanence and adoption. In the 1990s, there was a reduction in the number of adoptions of 'looked after' children, and although a Bill was proposed to make the child's best interest a central consideration in the adoption decision, the Bill was never introduced into Parliament (Performance and Innovation Unit, 2000).

The Adoption and Children Act of 2002 represented the most significant overhaul of UK adoption law in 26 years (Department of Education and Skills, 2003), in part because it aligned adoption law with the Children Act of 1989 to make the child's welfare and needs the paramount consideration in the adoption process. Furthermore, the Act ensured the needed support for people who were considering adoption, it allowed for unmarried couples to adopt jointly, and it established independent review in the assessment of prospective adoptive parents. The Act also strengthened the entitlement of the child, adoptive parents and birth parents to post-adoption support services. It also allowed for the arrangement of child advocacy services and increased supervision of the local authority's review of child cases (Department of Education and Skills, 2003).

Adoption Outcomes in the United Kingdom   In a review of adoption outcome literature, Triseliotis (2002) found that far more adolescents were likely to be placed in long-term foster care than in adoption. Although exact figures related to this finding were not available, only 179 (or 6.6%) of the 2700 children who left care through adoption in 1999 through 2000 were age 10 and older (Department of Health, 2001). In addition, breakdown rates in adoption and foster care were found to be very high, with one-third to more than one-half of placements disrupting within a three- to five-year period (e.g., fostering studies: Berridge & Cleaver, 1987; Parker, 1966; Rowe, Hundleby & Garnett, 1989; Thoburn, 1991; adoption studies: summary of U.S. studies; Borland, O'Hara & Triseliotis, 1991; Lowe *et al.*, 1999; Strathclyde Regional Council, 1991). In the Prime Minister's Review of Adoption (2000), the adoption disruption rate was roughly cited as 20%, with age at placement crucially impacting the chances of disruption (Fratter, Rowe, Sapsford & Thoburn, 1991). Several studies summarized in the Prime Minister's Review found disruption rates for children placed for adoption at age 7 or 8 at 20%. For children who were placed at age 11 or 12, disruption rates were as high as 40 to 50%, and for children who were placed for adoption in their 'late teens', disruption rates were slightly lower at 30 to 40% (Sellick & Thoburn, 1996). Additional risk factors identified by Fratter *et al.* (1991) include that the child is institutionalized (36%), the child has a history of behavioural/emotional difficulties (30%), has a history of abuse/neglect (25%) and is placed away from his/her siblings (29%). Physical and learning disabilities were not found to make a significant difference in the chance of disruptions (Fratter *et al.*, 1991).

Older Child Adoptions in the United States

Adoption Policy in the United States   A number of federal legislative initiatives have been enacted in the last three decades in order to promote permanency for children in the U.S. public child welfare system. In response to growing public concern regarding the number of children in care, Congress passed The Adoption Assistance and Child Welfare Act of 1980 (AACWA), also known as 'The Family Reunification' Act. As a condition of receiving federal matching funds, AACWA stipulated that states must make 'reasonable efforts' to prevent the removal of children and to reunify children removed from their homes with their birth families in a timely manner. In addition, AACWA required states to establish permanency plans for all children placed in out-of-home care and to place children in the most 'least restrictive' setting appropriate to meet their needs. While the primary goal of AACWA was to preserve and support families, AACWA also promoted adoption as a permanency option for children unable to return to their birth families. AACWA addressed financial barriers to the adoption of children with special needs through the provision of adoption subsidy payments and ongoing Medicaid coverage for children with special needs, as well as children who were eligible to receive welfare assistance through Aid to Families with Dependent Children (AFDC) or Supplemental Security Income (SSI) at the time they were removed from their birth family (Avery & Mont, 1997).

Although the implementation of AACWA was initially deemed a success, by the mid-1980s progress in reducing the number of children in the U.S. public child welfare system slowed (Barbell & Wright, 1999). Uncertainty by states of what constituted 'reasonable efforts' led to prolonged stays in care for many children as states exhausted all avenues to reunify children with their families. Hoping to facilitate quicker placement of children into permanent homes and reduce the growing number of children in the public child welfare system, Congress enacted the Adoption and Safe Families Act (ASFA), Public Law 105-89 in 1997. As with previous legislation, states were required to make reasonable efforts to reunify children with their birth families. However, under the new legislation, states were now encouraged to concurrently plan for adoption while working towards the goal of family reunification so that permanency might be established more quickly should it be determined that the child could not safely return to the parent's care. Concurrent planning typically includes early, individualized family assessment, with special focus on the issues leading to foster care placement, and development of a reunification prognosis. Families assessed as having a poor prognosis for reunification are given a concurrent plan (D'Andrade, Frame & Berrick, 2006; Katz, 1999; Schene, 2001). Also associated with the practice of concurrent planning is the early placement with a 'resource family' (or fost-adopt parents, foster/adoptive parents) who are asked to be prepared to provide a permanent home for a child, and at the same time to actively support the birth parents and sincerely work towards reunification (Katz, 1999; Schene, 2001).

Also, as required by ASFA, Congress instituted stringent timelines for state agencies working with birth parents who had children in care. Under the new legislation, states were required to pursue termination of parental rights for children in care for 15 out of the most recent 22 months. In addition, Congress authorized exceptions to the reasonable efforts clause in order to allow states to expedite termination of rights in extreme circumstances where the child's safety and well-being would likely be in jeopardy.

Additional programmes have also been instituted to enhance adoptions of children in care. Initially authorized as part of the Adoption and Safe Families Act of 1997, the Adoption Incentive Program was established to provide states with a financial incentive to increase the number of adoptions above established baselines (U.S. Department of Health and Human Services, 2006a). Also, in 2002, another federal initiative, the Collaboration to AdoptUsKids was funded by the U.S. Children's Bureau to (i) recruit adoptive families for waiting children, (ii) provide training and technical assistance to states and tribes to develop comprehensive recruitment plans and support for adoptive families, (iii) conduct research on barriers and factors associated with successful adoptions from care, and (iv) administer a national photolisting web site, AdoptUsKids.

The following year, in 2003, Congress passed the Adoption Promotion Act (P.L. 108-145) to increase the number of adoptive placements for older youth in care. This legislation re-authorized the Adoption Incentive Program and included additional provisions that would allow states the opportunity to receive additional incentive funds for increasing the number of children age 9 and older adopted from the public child welfare system. With the legislative focus on increasing the likelihood of children being adopted from care, it is also important to assess the outcomes of these adoptions. The following section presents a brief review of the recent U.S. research.

Adoption Outcomes in the United States   The number of adoption disruptions (breakdowns before finalization) and dissolutions (breakdowns after finalization) that occur each year in the United States is difficult to accurately quantify, as states are not required to report either the number of disruptions or the number of dissolutions that occur each year (Child Welfare Information Gateway, 2004). Thus, most states cannot provide accurate estimates of the number of children who re-enter the foster care system, as in most cases the child's last name has changed and the case is assigned a different identification number (Evan B. Donaldson Adoption Institute, 2004). According to a survey of 15 states, four states were able to provide data on the number of disruptions that occurred during the year and only five states could provide data on the number of dissolutions that occurred. Only two states, Oklahoma and Rhode Island, were able to provide annual data for both the number of adoption disruptions and dissolutions (Evan B. Donaldson Adoption Institute, 2004).

Although estimates of adoption disruptions vary across studies, the estimated rate of disruption for children generally falls between 9 and 15% (Festinger, 2005). However, there is evidence that disruption rates may increase with the child's age. Barth and Miller (2000) report the older a child is at the time of adoption, the higher the risk for disruption. In a study examining outcomes of adoption of children with special needs, Rosenthal (1993) reported disruption rates among children adopted at older ages to be between 10 and 15%. Yet, some research suggests that disruption rates for older children may be significantly higher (Ryan and Nalavany, 2003).

Much of the available research on adoption disruption and dissolution has focused on the identification of child and family factors associated with adoption instability and disruption (Freundlich and Wright, 2003; McRoy, 1999). Findings of studies evaluating contributing factors to adoption disruption and dissolution often vary and can appear somewhat contradictory, depending on the population studied and the number of years post-placement at the time of the study (Rosenthal, Schmidt and Conner, 1988; Smith *et al.*, 2006). However, Freundlich and Wright (2003) identified three of the more commonly cited characteristics reported in studies on adoption disruption (e.g. Barth and Berry, 1988; Festinger, 2002; McDonald *et al.*, 1991), including the child's age at the time the adoptive placement is made; the number of placements the child experienced prior to the adoption; and the presence of severe and persistent emotional/behavioural problems, such as attachment difficulties, sexually acting out and aggressive behaviour.

Several family characteristics predictive of disruption have been identified for adoptive families. One of the more concerning characteristics relates to the educational level of the adoptive parents; the adoptive mother in particular. Mothers with more education (college degree or higher) were found to be more likely to experience adoption instability or disruption than mothers with less education (Barth and Miller, 2000). This is thought to be a product of increased and subsequently unfulfilled parental expectations of the child's abilities (Partridge, Hornby and McDonald, 1986). In a survey of 249 adoptive families in Nevada examining characteristics and challenges of families who adopt children with special needs, Reilly and Platz (2003) concluded that realistic parental expectations of the child had the strongest influence on parental satisfaction with parenting and the overall quality of the parent–child relationship of the family-related factors examined. Other family factors leading to disruptions that have been identified include the absence of a prior relationship to the child as well as inadequate social support from relatives (McRoy, 1999).

Challenges to Achieving Permanency for Older Youth in the United States

In 2006, youth age 11 and older accounted for 35% of all children in care with a permanency goal of adoption; yet, they accounted for only 19% of all children adopted from the US public child welfare system (U.S. Department of Health and Human Services, 2008). According to the U.S.

Children's Bureau, on average, older youth in care typically remain in the child welfare system three times longer than children who exit care to join permanent families (U.S. Department of Health and Human Services, 2006b). Although federal and state officials have placed increased emphasis on promoting permanency for older youth in care, it is clear that much work remains.

A 2005 report to Congress (U.S. Department of Health and Human Services 2005b) identified six challenges to achieving permanency for older youth in the public child welfare system: (i) shortage of adoptive families, (ii) lack of supportive services for children and prospective adoptive families, (iii) inadequate permanency planning for youth in care, (iv) youth resistance to adoption, (v) child welfare staffing issues such as staff turnover and unmanageable workloads, and (vi) court-related barriers.

Strategies to Address Barriers to the Adoption of Older Youth

A number of strategies have been identified in the literature to promote the adoption of older youth. For example, Flynn, Welch and Paget (2004) conducted a study to determine youth, family and systemic factors associated with successful adoptions of older youth from the child welfare system. Despite encountering many obstacles throughout the adoption process, most families indicated satisfaction with their decision to adopt an older youth from the child welfare system. Researchers identified four 'keys to success' including (i) commitment – families reported the need for the parents and the adopted youth to commit to make the adoption work no matter what difficulties arise; (ii) personality – adopted youths and parents noted the importance of having a positive attitude and willingness to be flexible; (iii) support – the support of friends, family and professionals for parents, as well as the adopted youths, was also reported to be another important component of a successful adoption; and (iv) assistance when needed – parents insisted that when problems do arise, families must be willing to seek help and agencies must respond to the family's needs with appropriate, supportive services and in a timely manner. Adopted youths indicated that finding a compatible match is extremely important, as the adoption is more likely to go smoothly when parents and youth share common interests.

In order to improve adoption practice and outcomes for children and families, in 2002, the U.S. Children's Bureau funded a study to examine the experiences of families who had adopted children from the child welfare system. This nationwide study was conducted by our research team at the Center for Social Work Research at the University of Texas at Austin, as part of the Collaboration to AdoptUsKids.[2]

Overview and Methodology

A four-year prospective study of a nationwide sample of 161 adoptive families from 34 states and the District of Columbia who had adopted children with special needs, was conducted in order to identify factors associated with their successful outcomes. This research project is generally referred to as the 'Success Factors Study'. Special attention was placed on families who had adopted older children (particularly between the ages of 12 and 16 years), sibling groups, and children who had been in the foster care system for several years, in order to glean information on how these families and children were adjusting and what factors contributed to positive outcomes.

Adoptive parents were interviewed by phone by research staff and answered two annual follow-up surveys after the interview, including the Parenting Stress Inventory (Abidin, 1995) and a marital satisfaction scale adapted from the ENRICH Marital Satisfaction Scale (Fowers and Olson, 1993). Also, permission was obtained from Reilly and Platz (2003) who had conducted a similar study of successful special needs adoptions to adapt, for the purposes of this study, selected questions on the adoptive parents' knowledge of the child's background and history as well as the child's medical, physical and behavioural challenges.

Sample Description

Family Demographics There were 161 families and a total of 270 individual adoptive parents who participated in the study. Public agencies facilitated the adoptions for 58% of the families, and private agencies facilitated placements for 42% of the families. The majority of the families (n = 104, 65%) were married couples. There were also two (1%) unmarried same-sex couples and three (2%) unmarried opposite-sex couples. Forty-seven single female adopters composed 29% of the sample, and single males represented 3% (n = 5) of all adoptive parents.

[2] The Collaboration to AdoptUsKids, whose mission is to recruit and connect foster and adoptive families with waiting children, consists of six partners – The Adoption Exchange Association, The Child Welfare League of America, The Northwest Adoption Exchange, The Adoption Exchange Education Center, Holt International Children's Services, and the Center for Social Work Research at The University of Texas at Austin.

At the time of data collection, the average age of the adoptive mothers was 45 years and of adoptive fathers was 46 years. The adoptive families had an average income of $61 991. More than half of the sample of adoptive parents had completed either a bachelor's or graduate degree.

The majority, 80%, of families identified their ethnic background as Caucasian (n = 128). Eleven percent (n = 18) were African American and 3% (n = 5) were Hispanic and 4% (n = 10) were interracial couples. Overall, the majority (n = 105, 65%) of families adopted children of the same ethnic background as one parent (n = 8) or both parents: (n = 97; 78 Caucasian (non-Hispanic); 14 African American; 5 Hispanic). However, 56 (35%) families transracially adopted. Of the transracial adopters the majority were Caucasian families, who had adopted 50 minority children.

Of the 161 families, 106 (66%) had adopted more than one child. Forty-four percent (n = 47) of the multiple adopters had adopted two children (including the child who was the focus of the study), and 39% (n = 42) had adopted between three and five children in total. However, 17 (17%) families had adopted between 6 and 10 children. Fifty-three percent of families had adopted at least one sibling group.

Almost half (48%) of the focus children were placed with at least one biological sibling (n = 78). Of the 78 placed with siblings, 60 (77%) were placed at the same time as their siblings and 18 (23%) were placed at different times than their siblings. Thirty-four percent (n = 55) of the focus children were single child adoptions.

Almost all of the families in this study (97%) were parenting children who were school age or older. Only 2% were parenting only children less than 5 years of age. Two-thirds (67%) of the sample were parenting at least one teenager at the time of the study.

Of the 161 families who participated in the Success Factors Study, 58% (n = 94) of these families were general adopters (not adopting a specific child they were fostering, were related to, or knew before placement). Of the remaining families, 41 (25%) had adopted a child they had fostered, 6 (4%) adopted a relative, and 20 (12%) adopted a specific child but one who had not been in their home for foster care. In this latter group, families had initially come into contact with these children due to the parents' roles as therapist, teacher, residential treatment worker, or through family friends who were fostering the children. After meeting and interacting with the children, the families decided they wanted to adopt them.

Of the 161 families, 32 (20%) adoptive families were also fostering children in their home. Most had one or two foster children living in the home in addition to their adopted child(ren).

Motivation for Adopting   Parents in the study provided a number of different reasons for adopting from the foster care system including a recognition of the large number of U.S. children needing families (37%), financial reasons (37%); didn't want a baby (27%); wanted an older child (14%), wanted to adopt a forever child (17%) or wanted to help a disadvantaged child (22%).

Adopted Children's Demographics   One adopted child from each participating family was selected as the 'focus child' for the family. Criteria used to determine the focus child included the age of the child at placement, the quality and severity of the child's special needs, the highest level of challenge the child presented to the parents, and the length of time the child had been in the adoptive home. The purpose was to select a child to 'focus' on who presented the greatest challenges to the family.

Of the 161 focus children, 55% (n = 89) were male and 45% (n = 72) were female. They were an average of 6.5 years of age at time of placement (range = 0 to 17 years) in the adoptive home and had typically been in the home an average of 6 years at the time of the interview (range = 1 to 14 years).

The majority, 74% of focus children in the study were between 5 and 17 at placement. Of this number, six (4%) were between 13 and 17 when placed, 39 (24%) were between 9 and 12 at placement, and 74 (46%) were between 5 and 8 at placement. The average length of time between the time of finalization of the adoption and the time of the interview was 3.5 years.

Fifty percent of the focus children were Caucasian (non-Hispanic) (n = 80) and half were minority. Nineteen percent of the focus children were African American (n = 31), 12% were Hispanic (n = 20), 2% were Native American (n = 3) and 17% were of mixed race (n = 27).

Reasons for Removal and Experiences in Care   According to the parents, the children came into the foster care system for a number of reasons including neglect (63%), parental substance abuse (11%), emotional abuse (37%), physical abuse (39%), sexual abuse (29%), medical neglect (25%), prenatal exposure to drugs or alcohol (28%) and parental incarceration (20%).

Parents indicated that the time in foster care for the children ranged between 0 and 13 years with a mean of 3.7 years. Nine percent were placed at less than 1 year, 17% were placed between 1 and 4 years, 62% were placed between 5 and 10 years, and 12% were placed between 11 and 17 years. The number of placements in foster care ranged from 0 to 32. Nineteen percent of the sample had had at least one adoption disruption/

dissolution before being placed in their current home. One child experienced four prior disruptions.

Findings

Parental Challenges   The adoptive parents in the study indicated they were parenting a total of 437 children with 726 special needs. They indicated that 49 of their children had no special needs, while 348 children had at least one special need. For the children who were the focus of the study (n = 161), parents indicated that only 10 children had no special needs, while 104 had multiple special needs, and 42 had one special need.

Parents were asked to report on what types of attributes the focus children exhibited and behaviours the children engaged in that made the children difficult to parent. The most common child attributes parents addressed were anger (64%), defiance (60%), impulsiveness (60%) and manipulation (46%). The most common types of behaviours were violating rules of conduct (49%), lying (49%), arguing with peers (45%) and tantrums (45%).

Children in the study exhibited an average of 10 difficult behaviours. In fact, only 32 parents (20%) described the focus child as easy or very easy to parent. Thirty-six (22%) described the child as somewhat easy. However, over half, 93 parents (58%) described their child as difficult or very difficult to parent.

Children described as difficult to parent displayed behaviour challenges including violating rules of conduct (70%), verbal (55%) and physical (48%) aggression, stealing (48%), and vandalism (31%). This group was also more likely to be defiant, manipulative and/or depressed. Children in this category also were reported to have an average of five disabilities/challenges, with the majority having some type of attention deficit diagnosis.

The two most commonly mentioned child challenges were behavioural problems and emotional problems. Over three-quarters of the children were characterized by the adoptive parents as having behavioural problems, while 68% of the children were characterized as having emotional problems. Half of the sample of adopted children had learning disabilities (50%).

The level of difficulty that parents had in parenting the focus child was measured in several different ways. In the interview, parents were asked to rate how difficult the focus child had been to parent. Parents rated difficulty on a 1 to 5 scale, with 1 being very easy and 5 being very difficult. In the survey, parents were asked to identify the number of difficult behaviours and attributes the child exhibits out of a list of 35 behaviours, and parents were asked to complete four Parenting Stress Index (PSI) sub-scales – child reinforcement, adaptability, demandingness and acceptance.[3]

On each of the four PSI subscales, more than half of the parents' PSI scores fell into the high stress range. The highest percentage of parents, 69%, fell into the high stress range in the child demandingness subscale as compared with 15% in the general public (Abidin, 1995).

Pearson correlations were used to measure the association between the parents' assessment of how difficult the focus child was to parent and the more objective measure, 'Total Number of Behavior Problems', and with the four normed PSI measures. All of the measures were significantly associated with the parent's assessment at $p < 0.01$. The PSI scores 'Child is Demanding' and the 'Total Number of Behavior Problems' had the highest correlations at $r = 0.67$ and $r = 0.68$, respectively.

Parental Satisfaction   Despite the challenges of these adoptions, almost all of the 161 families viewed these adoptions as being successful. In fact, 71% indicated that they were very satisfied with the adoption, 22% were satis-fied, 6% were moderately satisfied, only 2% were dissatisfied and none were very dissatisfied with the adoption.

Post-Adoption Services for Children and Parents   Given the challenges these families were experiencing, we asked what post-adoption services they were receiving. The most commonly reported post-adoption services identi-fied by families in this study were financial supports, including adoption subsidies (89%), and help with routine medical (79%) and dental (77%) care. Seventy-seven percent also reported receiving financial supports other than a subsidy, such as health insurance, medical subsidies and social secu-rity benefits. The next most common set of services families used addressed the child's psychological and educational needs. Seventy-one percent of families reported using individual child therapy post-adoption, 60% had educational assessments completed and 59% of the children had psycho-logical evaluations.

In addition to utilizing post-adoption services for their children, many families also identified supports for themselves. For example, 56% of families reported spending time with other adoptive parents as a support

[3] Abidin (1995, p. 5) has normed the PSI subscales and identified cut-off points for each scale. The lower cut-off is at the 15th percentile or below. The higher cut-off is at the 85th percentile or above. He describes families whose scores are higher than the cut-off point as manifesting high levels of stress on that scale. He suggests that the families who fall below may be under-reporting their levels of stress due to social desirability pressures.

Table 5.1 Reasons for adopting an older child (n = 19).

	n	%
Child is a member of a sibling group	4	21
Wanted this particular child after becoming acquainted	3	16
Inability to have biological children	3	16
Wanted a child/more children regardless of gender	2	11
Wanted to give a child they knew a home	2	11
Matched with child by adoption agency	1	5
Saw child on waiting child programme	1	5
Knew the biological parents of child	1	5
Wanted to help a child who needed a home	1	5
Missing information	1	5
Total	19	100

mechanism, and 47% reported using family therapy. Only 3% of the families indicated they did not use any post-adoption services. Findings from this research suggested that families also had a number of unmet needs, particularly around respite care, and support groups for adopted children and for themselves.

Characteristics of Families Who Adopted Older Children

To gain further knowledge of success factors, we took a closer look specifically at the families who adopted children older than 11 who had the greatest challenges. Children age 11 or older at adoptive placement had a median of 7.3 prior placements, and spent an average of 4.9 years in foster care before placement in an adoptive home, with a range of 1 to 13 years. Twenty-six percent had at least one prior adoptive home disruption/dissolution.

The majority of the 19 families who adopted children age 11 and older in the sample were married couples, had a family member with a college degree, and an average income of $82 333 for couples and $31 477 for singles. Fifty-three percent had no other biological children in the home, 63% were general adopters, 5.2% were foster adopters, 26.3% were child-specific adopters and 5.2% were relative/kin adopters.

The 19 families who adopted an older child were asked what was the most important reason they decided to adopt. Their primary reasons are provided in Table 5.1. Six of the families had a prior connection with the child. In addition, four others adopted an older child because he or she was a member of a sibling group whom they wanted to adopt. Of those who had no prior connection to a sibling or child, they chose to adopt because either they were unable to have biological children (3), wanted another child (2), were matched with the child by an adoption agency (1) or saw the child on a waiting child programme (1).

Family Perspectives

Seven families were chosen randomly from our sample to illustrate the needs and services received by families adopting older, higher-needs children. The focus children in these families were older than 11 years old and exhibited multiple behavioural, medical and physical challenges. Among this small group of families who adopted older children, four parents felt very attached or attached and three felt somewhat attached to their children. Three parents felt the child was very attached or attached to them, two felt the child was attached, but somewhat guarded, one described the child as somewhat attached and one family acknowledged that the child was not attached. These seven families described the process of attachment as involving the following: being there for the child, building a relationship, adoptive parent's commitment and persistence, providing for the child's needs, and family activities. Several of the families in this group noted that attachment just happens naturally, and it happens when the child wants to be there.

When these families were asked about some of the most satisfying times they experienced when the child was first placed in their home, they mentioned the following:

> We told them if they ever needed a hug to just ask, and they both come for hugs every night.

> We remember when she would let her guard down and really talk to us and let us know who she was; Watching her play with other kids and being able to be a kid; Hearing "I love you Mom."

> I remember the little things, like the letters he wrote me for Mother's Day.

In order to learn from the experiences of these successful families, we inquired in what ways the family had contributed to the success of the adoption. Among the many ideas mentioned were the following: commitment to child and/or the adoption process; parent persistence in working with systems (i.e. child welfare, school, legal, health); adoptive parent advocates for child outside the family (i.e. school); being open to parenting a child with special needs; meeting the needs of the child; fully integrating the child into the family; having realistic expectations of the child's strengths and weaknesses; enjoyment of parenting and/or children; having unconditional love and acceptance of the child; a willingness or openness to resources (being willing to learn/ask for help); and having open and honest communication with the child about his or her thoughts/feelings in general.

Families, when asked what advice they would give when considering adoption of a child from the foster care system, suggested the following:

- Don't give up on the child.
- Hold the agency accountable (for services, background information, etc.).
- Be prepared to advocate for the child.
- Just do it, I recommend adopting.
- Have patience.
- Listen to the worker/counsellor when they tell you what to expect and be prepared to be committed.
- Not all kids in foster care are problems.
- Don't let the agency bully you – wait for the child you want.
- Don't wait for them to call you, be proactive about getting a child.
- Know this is a permanent decision.
- Be willing to learn about what the kids have gone through.
- Getting to know the child before bringing him/her into your home.
- Have realistic expectations of the child's strengths and weaknesses.

Finally, in reflecting on their parenting experiences, three families noted:

> Well, I just want to tell them that they have no idea what wonderful kids are out there. And sometimes you have to pick them up and brush them off and work with them, and oh, is it ever worth it! When you save their lives, they turn right around and save yours.

> He does give back. And he has grown into being a more complete person. So I think it's that reward of seeing that things have changed and there has been growth. And this sounds a little global, but if someone doesn't reach these kids, these are the kids that do damage in the world later. So I felt that he was one of those kids that needed real intervention in his life.

> She has her moments when she'll say, 'my life was so messed up before, this should have happened sooner, I'm having such a great life now'. You know deep down in her heart she really appreciates it.

Families also emphasized the positive impact adoption has had on them as parents. For example, two families noted:

> He's fulfilled my need to be a mom.

> She's definitely made us stronger, as people and as a family.

Implications for Practice and Research

Despite the long held belief of many that families want to adopt young children and that older children are 'hard to place', recent policy changes in the United States, the United Kingdom and Canada are leading to increases in older child adoptions from care. Many of these children are older, are members of sibling groups, are children of colour, have experienced multiple moves in care and have a myriad of behavioural challenges. However, the research suggests that most adoptions remain intact and families view their adoptions as successful.

The findings from the Success Factors Study described in this chapter, are very similar to those of Flynn, Welch and Paget (2004) who noted that a successful adoption involves commitment by parents and the youth, flexibility, a positive attitude and a sense of humour. Clearly, support from friends and professionals and the availability of post-adoption services are central. It is important for agencies to be available to provide support to families as they often are dealing with challenges for which they may not be prepared.

As Atkinson and Gonet (2007) note, "families have to 'learn the ropes'." They have to learn to "navigate the bureaucracies of school systems, departments of social services and juvenile justice and mental health systems" (p. 100). Adoption is a lifelong commitment and families must have access to funded services to maintain these placements. Just as federal funding to facilitate recruitment of families, adequate funding is also needed to provide for post-adoption services so families can receive ongoing support for the adoptions.

It is critical for the child welfare system to try to reduce the number of moves and disruptions children often experience in care as well as link these youth, while in care, to appropriate mental health service providers to address these issues prior to and after the adoption. Mental health practitioners need to become 'adoption competent' to increase the likelihood that they have the training needed to address the multiple challenges with which adoptive families may need help.

Some agencies, as part of their provision of post-adoption services, have begun to offer weekend marriage retreats and support networks to give adoptive families an opportunity to focus not only on adoption issues but to strengthen their marriages, communication and problem-solving skills. These retreats often provide respite for the children and time for parents to get away as well as get support from other adoptive families and clinically trained experts on marriage as well as adoption.

Moreover, based upon the research data on the types of families who adopt children from care, we must design effective recruitment campaigns to target this population and encourage more families to adopt. Successful adopters are among the best recruiters so agencies must find innovative ways to involve adoptive families as recruiters and as mentors for prospective and new adoptive families to prepare them for adoption. Through the Collaboration to AdoptUsKids national advertising campaign, television and radio advertisements are being used to enhance recruitment of potential families. The advertisements with themes like, 'You don't have to be perfect, to adopt' have attracted many potential adopters. Other advertisements feature teenagers to demonstrate that 'teens are adoptable too'. Through the advertisements, individuals and families who might have never previously thought about adopting or who have no idea about the need for adoptive families for older children, learn about the children needing permanence. In some states, 'Heart Galleries' consisting of enlarged professional photos of children needing placement are displayed in locations that attract large audiences, such as theatres. Also, through the Collaboration, Recruitment Response Teams (RRT's) consisting of adoption professionals as well as adoptive parents, have been established to respond to phone inquiries from families who have seen the advertisements or photos and are seeking more information about adoption. All of these strategies have proven to be very successful in promoting the adoption of older children in foster care.

More research is needed on families adopting children from care, which includes the voices of children and birth families as well as adoptive families. Much can be learned from interviews with children about what a 'forever family' means to them. As many of these older child placements involve ongoing relationships with previous caregivers, research that includes the birth parent as well as foster parent perspectives and experiences with adoption is needed. Research findings on the effectiveness of various approaches to child preparation and family preparation for adoption would also offer more evidence-based strategies for facilitating the transition process from foster care to adoption.

Thousands of children are waiting to be adopted in the United States, in the United Kingdom and in Canada. We must continue to overcome barriers to placements, facilitate these adoptions, and provide needed services and support to those who choose to adopt.

References

Abidin, R.R. (1995) *Parenting Stress Index*, 3rd edn, Psychological Assessment Resources, Odessa, FL.

Atkinson, A. and Gonet, P. (2007) Strengthening adoption practice, listening to adoptive families. *Child Welfare*, **86** (2), 87–104.

Avery, R.J. and Mont, D.M. (1997) Federal financial support of special needs adoption, in *Adoption Policy and Special Needs Children* (ed. R.J. Avery), Auburn House, Westport, CT, pp. 153–70.

Barbell, K. and Wright, L. (1999) Family foster care in the next century. *Child Welfare*, **78** (1), 3–14.

Barth, R.P. and Berry, M. (1988) *Adoption and Disruption: Rates, Risks, and Responses*, Aldine de Gruyter, Hawthorne, NY.

Barth, R.P. and Miller, J.M. (2000) Building effective post-adoption services: What is the empirical foundation? *Family Relations*, **49** (4), 447–55.

Berridge, D. and Cleaver, H. (1987) *Foster Home Breakdown*, Basil Blackwell, Oxford.

Borland, M., O'Hara, G. and Triseliotis, J. (1991) Placement outcomes for children with special needs. *Adoption & Fostering*, **15** (2), 18–28.

Child Welfare Information Gateway (2004) *Adoption Disruption and Dissolution: Numbers and Trends*, http://www.childwelfare.gov/pubs/s_disrup.cfm (accessed 30 November 2007).

D'Andrade, A., Frame, L. and Berrick, J.D. (2006) Concurrent planning in public child welfare agencies: Oxymoron or work in progress? *Children and Youth Services Review*, **28**, 78–95.

Department of Children, Schools, and Families (2007) *National Statistics: First Release*, http://www.dfes.gov.uk/rsgateway/DB/SFR/s000741/index.shtml (accessed 18 December 2007).

Department of Education and Skills (2003) The Children Act 2002.

Department of Health (2001) *Annual Statistics of Looked After Children*, Department of Health, London.

Evan B. Donaldson Adoption Institute (2004) *What's Working for Children: A Policy Study of Adoption Stability and Termination*, Evan B. Donaldson Adoption Institute, New York.

Festinger, T. (2002) After adoption: Dissolution or permanence? *Child Welfare*, **81** (3), 515–33.

Festinger, T. (2005) Adoption disruption: Rates, correlates and service needs, in *Child Welfare for the 21st Century: A Handbook of Children, Youth, and Family Services—Practices, Policies, and Programs* (Eds. G.P. Mallon and P. Hess), Columbia University Press, New York.

Flynn, C., Welch, W. and Paget, K. (2004) *Field-initiated Research on Successful Adolescent Adoptions: Final Report 2004*, http://www.sc.edu/ccfs/research/fullfinalreport.pdf (accessed 14 February 2005).

Fowers, B.J. and Olson, D.H. (1993) ENRICH Marital Satisfaction Scale. *Journal of Family Psychology*, **7** (2), 176–85.

Fratter, J., Rowe, J., Sapsford, D. and Thoburn, J. (1991) *Permanent Family Placement: A Decade of Experience*, British Association for Adoption and Fostering, London.

Freundlich, M. and Wright, L. (2003) *Post Permanency Services*, Casey Family Programs, Washington, D.C.

Katz, L. (1999) Concurrent planning: Benefits and pitfalls. *Child Welfare*, 78 (1), 71–87.

Lowe, N., Murch, M., Borkowski, M. *et al.* (1999) *Supporting Adoption: Reframing the Approach*, British Agencies for Adoption and Fostering, London.

Manning, C.F. and Zandstra, M. (2003) *Children in Care in Canada*. Child Welfare League of Canada, http://www.nationalchildrensalliance.com/nca/pubs/2003/Children_in_Care_March_2003.pdf (accessed 6 December 2007)

McDonald, T.P., Lieberman, A.A., Partridge, S. and Hornby, H. (1991) Assessing the role of agency services in reducing adoption disruptions. *Children and Youth Services Review*, 13 (5-6), 425–38.

McRoy, R.G. (1999) *Special Needs Adoptions*, Garland Publishing, Inc., New York.

Parker, R. (1966) *Decision in Foster Care*, Allen & Unwin, London.

Partridge, S., Hornby, H. and McDonald, T. (1986) *Learning from Adoption Disruption: Insights for Practice*, University of Southern Maine, Portland, ME.

Performance and Innovation Unit (PIU) (2000) *Prime Minister's Review of Adoption*, Cabinet Office, London.

Reilly, T. and Platz, L. (2003) Characteristics and challenges of families who adopt children with special needs: An empirical study. *Children and Youth Services Review*, 25 (10), 781–803.

Rosenthal, J.A. (1993) Outcomes of adoption of children with special needs. *The Future of Children*, 3 (1), 77–88.

Rosenthal, J.A., Schmidt, D. and Conner, J. (1988) Predictors of special needs adoption disruption: An exploratory study. *Children and Youth Services Review*, 10 (2), 101–17.

Rowe, J., Hundleby, M. and Garnett, L. (1989) *Child Care Now*, Batsford/British Agencies for Adoption and Fostering, London (BAAF), London.

Ryan, S.D. and Nalavany, B. (2003) Adopted children: Who do they turn to for help and why? *Adoption Quarterly*, 7 (2), 29–52.

Sargent, S. (2003) Adoption and looked after children. A comparison of legal initiatives in the UK and the USA. *Adoption & Fostering*, 21 (2), 44–52.

Scarth, S. (2004) *Adoption Canada Newsletter: Straight Talk about Aboriginal Children and Adoption*, http://www.adoption.ca/news/050101edab0411.htm (accessed 18 December 2007).

Schene, P. (2001) *Implementing Concurrent Planning: A Handbook for Child Welfare Administrators*, National Resource Center for Organizational Improvement, Maine.

Sellick, C. and Thoburn, J. (1996) *What Works in Family Placement?* Barnardos, Ilford.

Selwyn, J. and Sturgess, W. (2002) Achieving permanency through adoption. Following in US footsteps? *Adoption & Fostering*, 26 (3), 40–9.

Smith, S.L., Howard, J.A., Garnier, P.C. and Ryan, S.D. (2006) Where are we now? A post-ASFA examination of adoption disruption. *Adoption Quarterly*, 9 (4), 19–44.

Strathclyde Regional Council (1991) Fostering and adoption disruption. *Adoption and Fostering*, 45–123.

Thoburn, J. (1991) Family placement, in *Family Placement* (Ed. J. Fratter), British Agencies for Adoption and Fostering, London, pp. 19–57.

Triseliotis, J. (2002) Long-term foster care or adoption? The evidence examined. *Child and Family Social Work*, 7, 22–33.

U.S. Census Bureau (2004) *Characteristics of Children Under 18 Years by Age, Race, and Hispanic or Latino Origin, for the United States: 2000*, http://www. census.gov/population/cen2000/phc-t30/tab01.pdf (accessed 1 December 2006).

U.S. Department of Health and Human Services (2005a) *Adoptions of Children with Public Child Welfare Agency Involvement by State: FY 1995–FY 2003*, U.S. Department of Health and Human Services, Washington, D.C.

U.S. Department of Health and Human Services (2005b) *A report to Congress on adoption and other permanency out comes for children in foster care: Focus on older children*. U.S. Department of Health and Human Services, Washington D.C.

U.S. Department of Health and Human Services (2006a) *Adoption Incentives and AFCARS Penalties; Adoption Promotion Act of 2003 (Public Law 108-145): Information Memorandum*, http://www.acf.hhs.gov/programs/cb/laws_policies/policy/im/2004/im0404.htm (accessed 18 December 2007).

U.S. Department of Health and Human Services (2006b) *Enhancing Permanency for Older Youth in Out-of-Home Care*, http://www.childwelfare.gov/pubs/focus/enhancing/enhancing.pdf (accessed 18 December 2007).

U.S. Department of Health and Human Services (2008) AFCARS Report – Preliminary FY 2006 estimates as of January 2008 (14), http://www.acf.hhs.gov/programs/cb/stats_research/afcars/tar/report14.htm.

U.S. Government Accounting Office (2002) *Foster Care: Recent Legislation Helps States Focus on Finding Permanent Homes for Children, but Long-Standing Barriers Remain (GAO-02-585)*, U.S. Government Accounting Office, Washington, D.C.

6

Understanding Links Between Birth Parents and the Child They Have Placed for Adoption: Clues for Assisting Adopting Families and for Reducing Genetic Risk?*

David Reiss, Leslie D. Leve and Amy L. Whitesel

Researchers in the field of adoption research have designed studies to understand more fully the grief and recovery in parents who place their children and the intertwined processes of parenting and child development in adopting families. Rarely are these two domains linked in a single study. However, as studies are now showing (Dunbar *et al.*, 2006) the birth parents and adopting parents are often linked to each other through actual social contact in open adoptions and, even in more closed adoptions, they may be emotionally linked as each set of parents might think about the other over the course of time. Thus, one may consider the birth parents, the placed child, and the adoptive parents as a single social unit in the same sense that step parents, children and divorced birth parents can also be regarded as a single social unit, even if there is little or no face-to-face contact among some members of this unit. Indeed, social units of this kind may be thought of as yoked together by circumstances. In the case of the adoption 'yoke', ongoing social ties between birth and adoptive parents may vary from pure fantasy to frequent contact but the genetic relationship between birth parents and the adopted child is invariant across time. Grotevant has provided an elegant synthesis of research in this domain (Grotevant, 2006).

* Some sections of this chapter first appeared in the following article, and have been reproduced with the permission of the publishers, Cambridge University Press: Reiss, D. and Leve, L. (2007) Genetic expression outside the skin: Clues to the mechanisms of genotype X environment interaction. *Development and Psychopathology*, **19** (4), 1005–27.

Thus, studies of the 'adoption yoke' can provide us with very important information on central psychobiological process in child development, including the effects of prenatal exposure to drugs and toxins and genetic influences acting directly on the adopted child, as well as indirectly through the child's behaviour on his or her adoptive parents. Of particular importance, the study of adoption yokes allows us to distinguish between genetic and social influences on child development and to study their interplay across development. These potentials in the study of adoption yokes are already being pursued by several investigative groups (Deater-Deckard and Plomin, 1999; Petrill *et al.*, 2004; Plomin *et al.*, 1998; Wadsworth *et al.*, 2002). However, one potential in this promising line of investigation has been overlooked. The study of yoked adoption units provides one of the most powerful methods available for developing and planning interventions, designed to reduce genetic risk in child development and the secondary effects of genetically influenced developmental psychopathology on the adopting parents and other children in the adoptive family. We focus here on investigations of how naturally occurring variation in the adoptive rearing environment may moderate the expression of genetic influence in the child, and discuss planned intervention work with adoptive families that might attenuate genetic risk. We consider how the yoked adoptive family system may serve as a model for the interplay of genetic and social processes in child development, in families where biological parents rear their own children.

To serve these ends we are in the midst of conducting the Early Growth and Development Study (EGDS), which thus far has enrolled 359 yoked adoption units for extended study over the first seven years of the adopted child's development. All these units contain the adopting parents, the adopted child and the birth mother; about one-third (114) also contain the birth father, and we have collected extensive information about birth fathers who did not participate. The details of our study have been reported elsewhere (Leve *et al.*, 2007). In this chapter we will summarize the thinking that led to this study with a special emphasis on the role of genetic influences in shaping relationships within the family.

Genetic Questions for the Early Growth and Development Study

For at least two decades, mounting evidence has suggested that the social environment can moderate the expression of genetic influences on adaptive and pathological human behaviour. This broad set of phenomena is known as genotype × environment interaction. The evidence is drawn from two sources. First, the moderating effect of the social environment has been inferred from quantitative analyses of data from genetically informed studies, particularly twin and adoption studies. For example, an important set of adoption studies has shown that psychopathology in birth parents predicts psychopathology in their adopted offspring only when the adoptive rearing environment is adverse (Cadoret and Cain, 1981a, 1981b; Cadoret, Cain and Crowe, 1983; Cadoret *et al.*, 1990, 1995, 1996; Cloninger, Bohman and Sigvardsson, 1981; Sigvardsson, Bohman and Cloninger, 1996; Tienari *et al.*, 2004). Although this literature has been a part of recent research in genetics, it is not as widely appreciated among adoption professionals and birth and adoptive parents. However, the implications are important: even in the face of considerable genetic risk in their children, adoptive parents provide a milieu that offsets these risks. It is the burden of current research to understand how this happens.

Twin studies provided corroborating data. In many instances, they have suggested that individuals with a genetic liability are more likely to develop disorders when subjected to stress (Kendler *et al.*, 1995; Silberg *et al.*, 2001). These studies neither reveal whether one or more genes are involved nor do they identify the specific polymorphisms involved; rather, they focus on the phenotypic expression of the individual's genotype.

In the last five years an impressive range of studies has identified specific genes involved in interactions of this type (e.g. Caspi *et al.*, 2002; Gillespie *et al.*, 2005; Kendler *et al.*, 2005; Kim-Cohen *et al.*, 2006). Some of these studies have been followed up by sophisticated brain imaging studies to identify genetic influences on brain systems that are sensitive to and vulnerable to stressful life circumstances across a broad span of the life course. This work has been reviewed elsewhere (Caspi and Moffitt, 2006) and is clarifying the mechanisms whereby less efficient forms of particular genes may render individuals more vulnerable to their social environment. Its relevance for studies we describe here is currently being examined; however, in this chapter, we will not review it further.

Quantitative genetic studies, using twin and adoption designs, promise to open up a second line of inquiry on mechanisms of gene–environment interaction, and (as is shown below) pave the way for the development of specified preventive interventions that can help buffer against genetic risk and enhance genetically influenced resilience. They offer the promise of documenting how some adoptive families may be offsetting or reducing the genetic risk the child brings to the family. These studies derive their power from their capacity to estimate the impact of the individual's entire genotype rather than the smaller effects of single, measured genes. Research examining genotype × environment mechanisms across the last two decades in a broad range of domains has highlighted several major findings: genetically influenced characteristics of children and adults reliably evoke specific responses from parents and broader social environments; genetically influenced characteristics favour the selection of children and adolescents into peer groups (Iervolino *et al.*, 2002; Manke *et al.*, 1995); and genetically influenced characteristics influence marital adversity (Spotts *et al.*, 2004), the exposure to stressful life events and securing social support (Kessler *et al.*, 1992, 1994; Plomin *et al.*, 1990; Saudino *et al.*, 1997), and the selection of individuals into occupational or educational strata (Lichtenstein and Pedersen, 1997; Lichtenstein, Pedersen and McClearn, 1992). Thus, measures of parenting, sibling and peer relationships, marital quality and social class – formally believed to assess qualities of the social environment – are now understood to partially reflect genetic influences.

These data have led to a fundamental question: if genetic factors influence the social environment and these same factors also influence individual adjustment, might the association between the social environment and individual adjustment be attributable, in part, to genetic mechanisms rather than purely environmental mechanisms? The startling finding, in a broad range of studies, is that genetic factors account, in part, for a notable portion of covariance between 'environmental' measures and adjustment. For example, in one large study, the association between carefully measured negative relationships between mothers and antisocial behaviour in their adolescent children was observed to be 0.59 (Reiss *et al.*, 2000), a finding that, by itself, simply replicates many previous studies linking family processes to conduct problems in children and adolescents (Dishion, Patterson and Kavanagh, 1992; Forgatch, Patterson and Ray, 1996; Larzelere and Patterson, 1990; Patterson, 1982; Stoolmiller, Patterson and Snyder, 1997). However, genetic factors accounted not only for most of the variance in mother–child negativity and antisocial behaviour but also for 69% *of the covariance* between the two (Reiss *et al.*, 2000). Such findings suggest that genetic factors play an entirely unanticipated role in observed links between measures of the social environment and adolescent adjustment. In some cases, genetic factors might be a primary influence on measures of individual adjustment, such as antisocial behaviour; family difficulties might then serve both as a *consequence* and as a *cause* of children's adjustment problems. In other cases, genetic factors might evoke or select salient characteristics of the social environment prior to the advent of psychopathology. The adverse social environment might then amplify the adverse heritable trait, a process that, over time, might lead to pathological development. The sequence from genes to pathological behaviour to difficulties in the social environment can be considered to be a *reactive pathway*. This pathway suggests that disruptions in the social environment are secondary epiphenomena arising through genetic influences on socially disruptive behaviour of individuals. The sequence from genes to social environment to adjustment can be considered a *social mediation pathway*. In this case, disruptions in the social environment may precede and *mediate* the expression of genetic influence on disruptive behaviour.

Mediating effects of the social environment can occur in at least three ways. First, heritable characteristics of children (and adults) can evoke adverse or favourable responses from the social environment. For example, heritable fussiness in a child can evoke irritability from a caretaker. Second, heritable characteristics may favour an individual's choice of and engagement in social settings, such as schools and after-school activities, with consequent success and advancement to higher education and better employment. Third, heritable characteristics not only may influence people's choice of a particular social group, but also may be appealing to the group and influence the group's choice of them; the heritable feature influences the responses of the social group rather than just the active strivings of the children under study. Social mediation occurs if the response of the social environment to the heritable characteristics then plays an important role in the evolution of the problem or adaptive behaviour. For example, if irritable parenting – originally evoked by children's characteristics – amplifies impulsivity in children that is not yet at the problem level, then it becomes integrated or recruited into the mechanisms of expression of genetic influence on children's subsequent problem behaviour.

Evidence supporting the social mediation pathway elevates the role of the social environment. This evidence would suggest that, in many pathways of social and cognitive development, the social environment has an importance beyond its main effects on adjustment, independent of genotype. Indeed, genetically informed studies, in many cases, have supported these main effects although their magnitude is sometimes less than previously supposed. Evidence supporting the social mediation pathway suggests that the social environment, in addition to its main effects, is a crucial final pathway in mechanisms by which genetic influence is expressed in normal and pathological development. The implications of this possibility suggest that planned interventions to alter the response of the social environment to heritable characteristics of children and adults might improve individual adjustment by *blunting a critical mechanism of genetic expression*. There is now accumulating evidence supporting the idea of social mediation.

For example, at least seven studies have suggested that the social mediation pathway might account for the important role of genetic factors in the covariance between family structure or parent–child conflict on the one hand and antisocial behaviour on the other (Burt *et al.*, 2003, 2005; Cleveland *et al.*, 2000; Ge *et al.*, 1996; Narusyte *et al.*, 2007; O'Connor *et al.*, 1998; Reiss *et al.*, 2000). The pathway starts with heritable patterns of behaviour in the child that have not reached levels of clinical significance. Data suggest that genetically influenced aggressive temperament or patterns in children, below clinical thresholds, may evoke harsh parental responses (Ge *et al.*, 1996; Narusyte *et al.*, 2007).

The second step is that the evoked parental negativity intensifies the aggressive trait. Thus, over time the reciprocal influence of heritable aggressiveness in the child and harsh parental response will lead to conduct problems well above clinical thresholds. As we review below, several factors are known to intensify adverse parental responses to difficult children. These include economic adversity, marital conflict and parental psychopathology. The latter two are known, from adoption studies, to interact with genetic factors in the aetiology of conduct problems, severe aggression, and antisocial behaviour in adolescents and adults (Cadoret, Cain, and Crowe, 1983; Cadoret *et al.*, 1995). If economic distress, marital conflict and parental psychopathology are severe, we might expect the social mediation of genetic expression to be enhanced. Social mediation may diminish or vanish in the context of no economic distress, high marital satisfaction with little conflict, and no parental psychopathology.

Evidence for the social mediation pathway constitutes the spine for investigations of mechanisms of genotype × environment interaction. The implication of this work is that preventive interventions will be successful if they *decrease the sensitivity of the environment to genetically influenced characteristics in children*. With respect to adoptive families, this research will point more specifically to the specific and heritable patterns of behaviours that adopted infants and toddlers exhibit that may provoke their parents. Moreover it promises to provide data on the impact of equally well-studied reactions of the parents on subsequent behaviour of their children. In the next section, we describe how research to date has made substantive progress in the search for mechanisms of genotype × environment interaction, with an eye towards the development of preventive interventions to improve outcomes for individuals exposed to adverse environments and/or who are at genetic risk for problems. These steps bring us closer to being able to identify for adopting families what they can observe both in their children and in themselves that might amplify or reduce the risk that adverse heritable patterns in their infants and toddlers become problems of clinical concern.

Steps in the Search for Mechanisms of Gene × Environment Interaction

Genetically Influenced Characteristics of the Individuals Impact Their Social Environment

Genetic influences of individuals on their social environments have been observed across the lifespan. At age 5 months, there is a notable influence of an infant's genotype on hostile parenting behaviour, an effect that appears to be mediated by genetic influences on child's temperament, particularly irritable, unsoothability (Boivin *et al.*, 2005). Substantial effects have also been observed in the toddler period on measures of cognitive stimulation from the HOME measure (Braungart, Fulker and Plomin, 1992), for video coded affection and control at age 3 (Dunn and Plomin, 1986), and for maternal control and for competitive and positive sibling behaviour from ages 4 to 7 (Rende *et al.*, 1992). Similar genetically influenced evocative processes have been observed in the transition to adolescence (Deater-Deckard, Fulker and Plomin, 1999; O'Connor *et al.*, 1998). For adolescents, genetically influenced evocative effects have been reported using adoption (Ge *et al.*, 1996) and twin and sibling designs (Reiss *et al.*, 2000). Substantial influences have been reported for hostile and negative parenting, as well as for parental warmth and control on positive and negative responses to the target adolescent. These evoked parental responses seem to reflect both generalized dispositions of the adolescent for aggressive behaviour (Ge *et al.*, 1996) and specific interactive behaviours directed at a particular parent (O'Connor *et al.*, 1995). The genetic influences on how older adolescents and adults actively shape their own environments have also indicated substantial heritable influences on the quality of peer groups that adolescents select or heritable qualities lead them to be selected by peers (Iervolino *et al.*, 2002; Manke *et al.*, 1995). Further, women across a broad range of ages from early to later adulthood show substantial genetic influence on their active engagement in social groups, their perceived support from friends and relatives (Kessler *et al.*, 1992), and their involvement with satisfying marriages as measured from the women's and their spouses' perspectives and from the probability of divorce (D'Onofrio *et al.*, 2005; McGue and Lykken, 1992; Spotts *et al.*, 2004). Together, this large body of research provides strong evidence that genetically influenced characteristics of the individual impact the social environment, a key clue in guiding the search for mechanisms of genotype × environment interaction.

From the perspective of adoptive parents, these data suggest that they have many opportunities to observe the evolution of genetically influenced social behaviour in their growing child; not only do these unfold in the child relationships with them but in their interaction with siblings, teachers, friends and peers. Correspondingly there may be many opportunities across the span of childhood for interventions by parents or by informed practitioners to help amplify favourable inherited patterns of behaviour or reduce the risks that these behaviours become clinical problems.

Genetic Influences on the Environment May Mediate the Influences of Genes on Adjustment

The next body of research guiding the search for genotype × environment mechanisms has shown that, in many instances, there is substantial overlap in the genetic factors that influence the social environment and those that influence child, adolescent, and adult adjustment. The most thorough analyses are from the Nonshared Environment in Adolescent Development (NEAD) study, a comprehensive, longitudinal, genetically informed study that has measured a broad range of relationships (parent–child, sibling, marital and peer) using self-reports, informant reports, and observational measures across a broad range of adjustment (depression, antisocial behaviour, social responsibility, sociability, cognitive competence, and engagement and autonomy; Reiss *et al.*, 2000). Across numerous behavioural constructs, data from NEAD indicate a central role of genetic factors in accounting for the sizable association between measures of the social environment and of adjustment. Genetic factors played a major role in the association between maternal and paternal negativity, maternal and paternal positivity, and maternal and paternal strategies for controlling their adolescents on the one hand, and negative and the positive adolescent adjustment on the other. The major results of the NEAD study have been reported in Reiss *et al.* (2000).

Although no study has been designed to replicate the NEAD study, there have been many reports on the role of genetic factors in accounting for a substantial component of the covariation between the social environment and child, adolescent, and adult adjustment. For example, genetic factors account for the covariance of family structure (two-parent versus mother only) or family closeness and adolescent problem behaviour (Cleveland *et al.*, 2000; Jacobson and Rowe, 1999). A substantial role for genetic factors in the covariation between harsh parenting and externalizing in 11-year-olds has also been confirmed (Burt *et al.*, 2003). Studies of adults have shown similar results (Kendler, 2001; Lichtenstein *et al.*, 1993; Lichtenstein and Pedersen, 1995).

These mediation findings pose several questions about the nature of genotype × environment mechanisms. First, does this evidence support the proposed social mediation pathway from genotype to heritable trait to evoked social response to psychopathology? Or, might the pathway lead from genotype to psychopathology to evoked family response, as suggested by the reactive pathway? Neiderhiser *et al.* (1999) reported the first evidence to support the former pathway, a finding that was replicated many times for other variables in the NEAD study (Reiss *et al.*, 2000). By adolescence, there is evidence for reciprocal relationships among heritable trait, family response and emerging psychopathology, a finding replicated by Burt *et al.* (2005).

A second question posed by these mediation findings is whether the effects of heritable traits on relationships are specific or non-specific. For example, in the non-specific case, genetically influenced irritability in children might elicit high parental negativity, low parental warmth and reduced parental monitoring. In contrast, specific effects might make it more likely that social systems can mediate genetically specific effects on major indices of adjustment. For example, we know that social support, physical health and substance abuse are each influenced by distinct genetic factors (Kendler, Myers and Neale, 2000), with little overlap of genetic influences. Likewise, genetic factors that are common to major depression and anxiety disorders are distinct from those that influence situation phobias and animal phobias (Kendler *et al.*, 2003). Similarly, in adolescence, the genetic influences on antisocial behaviour are distinct from the genetic influences on self-worth. Genetic influences on sociability are distinct from those on social responsibility and from those on antisocial behaviour (Reiss *et al.*, 2000). This distinctiveness of genetic influences on different lines of development suggests an important requirement for any theory of social mediation. Specifically, if family relationships and other specifiable components of the social environment play a mediating role in the expression of these distinctive genetic influences, then evocative effects of the genotype must be distinct rather than general.

These data are of special relevance to adoptive parents. They emphasize that both genetically influenced risks and genetically influenced strengths are distinctive and varied. Moreover, children are likely to inherit a range of these.

The NEAD study is the sole source of data on this point, as no other longitudinal, genetically informed study to date has measured such a wide range of social relationships and dimensions of adjustment. Results suggest a high degree of genetic specificity for heritable evocative effects in adolescence. For example, heritable characteristics of adolescents that evoke warmth from mothers are almost completely uncorrelated with those that evoke warmth from fathers. Indeed, of 78 such comparisons, 72 showed more genetic specificity than genetic overlap (Reiss *et al.*, 2000).

In a re-analysis of NEAD data, Loehlin, Neiderhiser and Reiss (2005) conducted a factor analysis of the correlations among the latent genetic influences on three measures of parenting (parental negativity, positivity and control) and five dimensions of adolescent adjustment (antisocial behaviour, autonomy, depressive symptoms, cognitive competence, sociability and social responsibility). This revealed underlying associations between specific evocative effects and specific dimensions of adolescent adjustment. For example, the latent genetic influences on parental negativity loaded on a factor that had loadings only from antisocial behaviour and depressive symptoms and not from other measures of parenting or adjustment. A similarly specific pattern of loadings (both positive) was found for parental monitoring and adolescent sociability. The latent genetic influences on adolescent autonomy were the only ones to load on a factor defined primarily by parental positivity.

These findings delineate at least three sets of genetic factors that may initiate three different developmental pathways. Each may be a single polymorphism, as yet undiscovered, or a set of polymorphisms. This approach centres on the discovery of *evocative phenotypes*: distinctive features of children that evoke strong responses from others and that are genetically influenced and genetically distinct.

A third major question stemming from these mediation studies is whether social mediation is restricted to particular periods in development. This is crucial for planning preventive interventions and has practical implications for adoptive parents. During what periods in their child's development are new genetic influences playing a role in their child's relationships? These may be periods when their interventions, or those of mental health professionals, are most effective.

As is reviewed above, social mediation processes appear to occur across the lifespan starting in early childhood. However, as development unfolds, many of these mediational pathways reflect the cumulative effects of genetically influenced differences in personality features. For example, genetic influences on the traits of neuroticism, extraversion and openness account for all of the genetic influences of stressful life events of older adults (Saudino *et al.*, 1997), and genetic influences on cognitive abilities account for a notable portion of genetic influences on education and occupational status (Lichtenstein and Pedersen, 1997).

Indeed there are now many published studies on the balance between the expressions of new genetic influences versus stable genetic influences on a range of psychological factors across the lifespan. These studies can estimate, using twin designs and latent variable analyses, whether genetic or environmental factors contribute to change or to stability in a trait across time. For example, suppose a trait is highly heritable at two time periods, is moderately stable across time, but shows no correlation between its genetic factors at times 1 and 2. We can conclude that the genetic factors influencing the trait at time 1 'turn off' and that the genetic factors influential at time 2 'turn on' in the interval between times 1 and 2. This might occur at the molecular level or might reflect alterations in the social system in response to heritable traits (or both). Two studies (Plomin *et al.*, 1993; Reiss *et al.*, 2000) have suggested substantial changes in genetic expression during toddlerhood and adolescence, respectively. A third study found smaller but notable changes in genetic expression for personality in adolescence (Gillespie *et al.*, 2004). One study (Rietveld *et al.*, 2004) suggested modest change in genetic expression during the school age years, but another suggested very little change (van den Oord and Rowe, 1997). Six studies of long periods of adult life (Johnson, McGue and Krueger, 2005; Kendler *et al.*, 1993; McGue and Christensen, 2003; Pedersen and Reynolds, 1998; Plomin *et al.*, 1994; Viken *et al.*, 1994) have suggested little or no change in genetic expression during this period. In terms of new genetic influences, toddlerhood and adolescence are periods of substantial genetic innovation, whereas broad spans of adult are more likely to be quiescent.

Taken together, this body of work suggests that new genetic influences appear early in development, particularly toddlerhood, but that, by adulthood, genetic influences on many traits are typically the same as those expressed earlier in development. These data support the hypothesis that adverse social responses to heritable traits across broad spans of adult development are *responding to stable genetic influences that exert unchanging influences across broad spans of time* and possibly across widely different cultural contexts (Furukawa and Shibayama, 1997). However, in earlier development, the intimate social environment (i.e. parents, siblings and the parents' marriage) is *responding to fresh or novel genetic influences and/or may be eliciting new genetic influences to be expressed in the young child*; changes in heritable behavioural traits may be the socially relevant signals that herald these new genetic influences. Data from the NEAD study suggest that these heritable signals might be quite *specific for specific relationships at specific points in development*. Thus, social mediation of genetic influence across broad spans of adult development may show the 'social scars' of the hardening and stabilization of adverse genetic influences on cognition and personality that spoil broad areas of academic, economic and social achievement with serious consequences for psychopathology. Earlier in development, social mediation may be more fluid, reciprocal and specific. Changes in adverse heritable traits may 'recruit' specific qualities in specific family relationships. Family members may enlist in a third process by responding to these heritable traits with adverse responses or may disengage from the adverse behaviour of the child. Such parent–child interactions resulting from genotype × environment processes have clear implications for the design of preventive interventions; by specifying such sequences, genotype × environment interaction work can help to identify parent–child interactions at specified points in development that may be most malleable.

The Early Growth and Development Study: Focusing on the Mechanisms of Genetic Expression

The research we have just reviewed leads to three closely linked hypotheses. First, in several areas of child development genetic influences first emerge as temperamental features of children that have an impact on their caregivers. These features may be fully apparent to adoptive parents. Indeed, data suggest that parents more accurately perceive the temperaments of other children but put a very positive gloss on the temperaments of their own children (Seifer *et al.*, 2004). Thus, the help of other parents or professionals may be useful in this phase.

Second, the response of caregivers to this impact may amplify genetic influences. When the child's trait has the potential to lead to adverse outcomes, the parental reaction may amplify this risk. When the child's trait may lead to positive outcomes, such as a tendency to smile and laugh, parental reactions can enhance the prospect of a genetically influenced positive outcome.

Third, while most parents respond to this evocative behaviour in their children in more or less the same way, there are some parents who are unusually reactive ('over-reactors') and some parents who react little, if at all ('under-reactors'). This natural variation in parental reaction to genetically influenced behaviour in the child may substantially moderate the likelihood that genetic influence is expressed in patterns of child adjustment. This is one of several explanations for genotype × environment interaction. Thus, at this stage of research, we seek to learn directly from adoptive parents who 'over-react' to positive social behaviours in the sense they are effectively encourage them; we also seek to learn from parents who 'under-react' to adverse behaviours. That is, parents who do not respond to adverse behaviours of their children with non-productive negative behaviours of their own. As implied above, parents may not be able to report fully their own behaviour so our direct observation of their interaction with their children will help elucidate their successes and problems.

Fourth, if our first three hypotheses are correct then a door is open to a fourth hypothesis: if we can help parents respond differently to adverse, evocative behaviour from their children we may accomplish two ends: improve the quality of parent–child relationships and moderate the probability that adverse genetic influences are expressed fully, if at all, in the patterns of the child's adjustment.

Research on the adoption family unit – both birth parents, the child who is placed and the adopting parents – is best suited to examine the first three hypotheses. If these three are confirmed then the adoption design is a singular vehicle for testing the fourth hypothesis.

Hypothesis 1: heritable characteristics of the child evoke responses from caretakers. As outlined above, most of what we know about this phenomenon comes from twin studies. These have not only documented significant influence of heritable child characteristics on response of caretakers but have begun to identify what characteristics of children may evoke those responses. However, in twin studies parents and children share individual difference genes: each parent shares exactly 50% of these genes with each child. Thus, for example, the covariation of aggressive behaviour in the child with negative parental style may reflect a set of genes common to both. In the parent, these genes influence their irritability and negativity in social behaviour including their parenting styles. In the child, these same genes influence patterns of aggressive behaviour. By definition, children adopted by parents who are not related to them share no individual difference genes with their parents beyond similarities by chance alone. Links between heritable characteristics of children and parental responses are easier to interpret. In fact, the fundamental statistic is the correlation between a heritable characteristic of a *birth parent* and the parenting behaviour of the *adoptive parent*.

Hypothesis 2: amplification of heritable characteristics. The strength of the adoption design here follows from considerations above. We can follow the hypothesized reciprocal process longitudinally. Does the magnitude of parental response to child's heritable traits at time 1 predict the increase in intensity of that trait at time 2? Does the magnitude of the child's trait at time 2 predict the magnitude of parental response at time 3? Does the magnitude of this parental response at time 3 predict the magnitude of increase in the trait at time 4, and so on? Longitudinal studies have been carried out with twins and some of these have helped shape the hypothesis of amplification. However, as was the case for hypothesis 1, the use of the adoption design eliminates the possibility that genetic similarity between parents and children might be attributed to genes common to both.

Hypothesis 3: natural variation in response of parents to their children. As noted, we already know some of the broad classes of influence on parental response to children: economic stress, marital conflict and parental psychopathology are chief among them. In the context of an adoption study, we can focus on whether such factors alter response to heritable evocative behaviour in children. Might we see, for example, greater correlation between birth parent psychopathology and adoptive parent response when the adoptive parent is depressed than we might when the adopted parent is neither depressed nor has a history of depression? The adoption design deepens our understanding of the effect of the social context on parenting because it focuses on parent response to heritable behaviour in their children and allows us to study the consequence, for the children, of this response. Thus, the adoption design allows us to look for this sequence: (i) child exhibits evocative behaviour in direct proportion to birth parent's psychopathology, (ii) adoptive parents respond to this evocation especially if they are distressed and (iii) subsequent to this more intense reaction by a distressed parent, the child's evocative behaviour becomes more intense and provocative. Such reciprocal, amplifying patterns of child–parent behaviour have been theorized and tested in models developed with biological families, such as the Coercion Theory (Patterson, 1982; Patterson, Reid and Dishion, 1992; Reid, Patterson and Snyder, 2002).

Further work: interventions with adopting parents. Further along the road our knowledge of parental response to child evocation and its consequences will allow for a highly tailored intervention: helping the parent recognize the evocative adverse behaviour as well as evocative episodes of behaviour that are positive. We hope to aid parents in broadening their repertoire of responses to evocative behaviour through a combination of enhancing their skills as well their empathy for the child's experiences both before and after episodes of evocative behaviour. An intervention of this kind has a dual purpose: (i) to use current knowledge of behavioural genetics to focus on specific mechanisms highly relevant to development of children, and (ii) to test a theory of the social mechanisms by which genetic influences are fully expressed.

The major goal of our work is to lay the groundwork for this genetically informed intervention. The adoption design is central to this work: it allows us to know not only whether our intervention was successful but to learn whether or not it *attenuates the transmission of genetic risk from birth parents to children*. In order to conclude that an intervention had achieved this aim, we would need to obtain two findings. First, we would have to show not only that children in our intervention group developed more adaptive behaviour than those in the control condition, but that the differences in adaptation between those at genetic risk (risk is indexed by birth parent psychopathology) and those not at risk had been reduced or eliminated in the intervention condition but not in the control condition. Second, we would have to show that the reduction in this difference between those high and low in genetic risk (in the treated group) was proportional to the degree we were able to alter parental response to evocative behaviour of the child.

A Model for Understanding Complex Phenomena

In scientific investigations of complex phenomena it is often helpful to simplify the complexity by constructing a model that has most or all of the essential parts required for the investigation, but clears away some complexity that may obscure the key processes at work. Currently, we are familiar with mathematical and computer simulation models of complex phenomena ranging from weather patterns to predator–prey relationships. However, a more simple kind of model is worth considering and perhaps its best example is the tide predictor developed by Lord Kelvin in 1876. An avid sailor (and pre-eminent physical scientist) Kelvin recognized that predicting patterns of tidal changes in his favourite waterways required knowledge not only of the cycles of the moon and sun but of critical details of the shorelines. He tried to simplify the complex components of tidal variation into a small set of harmonic fluctuations and to represent these in a system of pulleys and dials ultimately attached to a pen and rotating drum. By turning a crank to activate this apparatus, the pen would draw the predictions of tidal flow for a given location for an entire year. The pulley system helped Kelvin both visualize and compute the interplay between astronomical events and earthly geography.

In this same sense, the adoption design is a way of visualizing and computing the complex relationships among genes, their timing of expression and the interplay of their influences with social processes in the family, while at the same time helping to pinpoint targets for intervention that may make a major difference in the lives of both children and parents. The fundamental simplification is focusing on parents and children who do not share any individual difference genes. This enables us to estimate the child's genetic risk using knowledge about birth parent characteristics. Even more uniquely, it enables us to identify behaviour in childhood that expresses genetic risk associated with adult psychopathology. For example, depression in childhood cannot be observed unambiguously until several years after birth. Moreover it may not be until mid-adolescence that genotypic variation among children manifests themselves in depressive symptoms (Silberg, Rutter and Eaves, 2001). How then is the genetic risk for depression in adulthood manifested in a 9-month-old? Associations between theory-derived characteristics of adult birth parents and their infants can help address this question. Third, we can estimate the impact of the genetic component of children's behaviour on their caretakers. A child may be irritable or inattentive for many reasons and these patterns can evoke parental responses. However, we are – for the purposes of this model – interested only in the genetic component of these complex behaviours. As noted earlier, in an adoption design the influence of this component can be estimated by a correlation of birth parent characteristics with adoptive parent reaction patterns.

However, in order to draw valid conclusions on these critical processes, certain features of the adoption model system are required. We list them here schematically:

1. Sample size. We must have a large sample of birth parents linked to their child they have placed for adoption and the child's adoptive parents in order to reliably estimate complex interactions.
2. Representativeness. The sample studied should be representative of a well-defined population of birth parent and adoptive family units.
3. Selective placement. The procedures of the adoption itself should not selectively place children in an adoptive home according to heritable characteristics of the birth parents.
4. Genetic effects and confounding. We must be able to distinguish the effects of genetic transmission of risk from parent to child from other mechanisms, principally prenatal exposure of the child to toxins, substance abuse and maternal anxiety; knowledge that the adoptive parents have about birth parents and their characteristics, and actual contact between birth parents and their child after placement.
5. Variation in genetic and environmental risk. There needs to be adequate variation in genetic risk among birth parents and this risk needs to be assessed as precisely as possible with in-person assessments of as many birth mothers and birth fathers as possible. There also needs to be adequate variation in the reactive patterns of adoptive parents in order to estimate the impact of this variation on the expression of genetic influence on the children's development.
6. Extended observation of birth parents and adoptive families. The study of birth parents needs to be longitudinal so that the emergence of

genetic risk, often delayed in the case of some psychiatric disorders, becomes apparent. The study of the adopting family also must have at least three waves in order to test fully the amplification pattern where child evocation is measured at time 1, parental response is measured at time 2, and the child's development, consequent to parental response can be observed at time 3. A robust study must measure putative heritable evocative patterns both by direct observation and by questions related to rearing patterns. It must do the same in its study of parental reaction patterns.

7. Developmental timing. Children must be studied during a time in development where there are known pathological behaviours that can be reliably measured, or alternatively, known, reliable, risk behaviours that lead to such pathological outcomes.

As in any model, there are caveats about generalizing: here it remains a critical question about how well findings can be applied to non-adoptive families who, in general, have children at younger ages, cover a broader spectrum of economic disadvantage and advantage, have not – for the most part – dealt with problems of infertility, who have not engaged in months and years of stressful and expensive efforts to have a child, and where some of the residual stigma surrounding adoption is not present. Moreover, it is unclear whether parents' responses to children might be different if they share genes with that child or they have clear knowledge that the child is their 'own' in a biological sense.

The Early Growth and Development Study: Is It a Valid Model?

At this early phase in our work we can only provide a preliminary report. We are constantly evaluating and testing the validity of the model as we analyse our data and report our first findings. We follow the same schema here as in the preceding section to evaluate our model. We have reported on some of these details elsewhere (Leve *et al.*, 2007):

1. Sample size. We drew our sample of 359 adoption family units from 33 adoption agencies in 10 states; these included public, private and religious agencies with varying policies on openness in adoption. After the adoptive placement, birth parents and adoptive parents settled in 43 states. We began our recruitment with 1796 eligible adoptive family triads, where the child had been placed at birth or within 90 days thereafter, but did not seek to recruit adoptive families until the agency received permission for us to contact them (18% declined), and until

we had recruited the matched birth mothers. The participating agencies located 737 of these birth mothers but 21% declined to be contacted by our project. Of the remaining 582 birth mothers, we could not locate 52, but of the remainder, 98% agreed to participate. From this set, we then attempted to recruit matched adoptive families. Of the 447 we could locate, 83% agreed to participate, giving us 359 matched birth mothers and adoptive families. Seeking birth fathers from this subset, we were unable to locate 235 of them. Of the 124 we could locate, 92% or 114 agreed to participate.

2. Representativeness. As noted, once we contacted birth and adoptive parents, our recruitment rate was very high (and our retention rates across three waves of data collection are equal or greater than these). However, we anticipated problems in locating our sample and thus all participating agencies were asked to provide us with basic demographic information on all eligible adoption units in order to ascertain possible biases in our sample. We compared recruited and non-recruited birth mothers, birth fathers, adoptive mothers and adoptive fathers on age, education and income. Of these comparisons there were only two significant but trivial differences for birth father age (non-participants 2 years older on average) and adoptive mother education (non-recruited adoptive mother has 0.5 years less education). Despite the large number of birth and adoptive families we could not contact, we conclude that our sample represents an agency facilitated, non-relative infant adoption in the United States.

    As is typically the case there is a striking difference in our sample between the socio-economic status and parental age of our sample of birth parents and adoptive parents. For example, our birth mothers have a mean age of 23.8 and birth father, 25.3. Of the birth mothers and birth fathers, respectively, 22 and 26% are non-white but only 9 and 10% of our adoptive mothers and fathers are. This means there a number of inter-racial adoptions in our sample. Finally, birth parents typically have a high school or trade school education whereas the typical adoptive parent has graduate college. Income differences reflect both differences in age and education with our young birth parents average less than $20 000 per year income and adoptive families over $100 000.

3. Selective placement. Some similarities between birth parents and adoptive parents could reflect the evocative processes that are the focus of our investigation. These could include affective states and even some psychiatric diagnoses. However, it is hard to imagine a child 'evoking' such factors as parental education (at the outset of the study),

income or age, which showed no evidence of selective placement in our study.

4. Unconfounded estimates of genetic influence. This is an aspect of our model that needs constant monitoring. We carefully measured fetal exposure to maternal use of toxins and substances of abuse, we estimated perinatal complications from maternal reports and systematic coding of medical records, and we also used maternal self-report and medical records to estimate psychiatric problems during pregnancy. However, the effects of these risk factors, which might explain some similarities between birth parents and the adopted child, can appear later in development. Thus, in each wave of assessment of child development these factors must be considered. Compounding the difficulty of these assessments is the fact that mothers may use drugs or have serious anxiety during pregnancy for genetic reasons. Thus, simple partialing of prenatal exposure will spuriously reduce estimates of genetic effects. We have developed more nuanced statistical models to separately estimate the effects of genetic from exposure effects.

    The same challenges face estimates of the effects of openness in the adoption process. We found remarkably unanimity among reporters – particularly birth mothers and both adoptive parents in their detailed reports of the level of openness of the adoption and we have continuously monitored variation in openness across our waves of assessment teasing apart effects, which so far have been trivial, on our estimates of the transmission of genetic risk.

5. Variation in genetic and adoptive family risk. It was no surprise to us that there is much psychological distress and a substantial prevalence of diagnosable psychiatric problems among the birth parents in our study. Many, but by no means all, are prompted to carry out an adoption plan by a myriad of social and psychological problems. However, variation in adoptive families was less assured. Almost all have adequate financial resources, although some are worried about them, and all were selected after some screening by adoption agencies. Nonetheless, in our initial assessments of psychiatric symptoms of birth parents using the Beck Anxiety and Depression Scales, we found that at least one adoptive parent was likely to have clinical levels of depression or anxiety in 24% of our adoptive families and by child age 18 months there was a divorce or a single parent in 9% of our adoptive families. The cumulative experience of psychiatric and marital problems among adoptive parents will certainly increase across time. This assures a wide range of factors that are likely to influence the reactivity of parents to evocative behaviour in their adopted children.

6. Extended observations. Our study planned two waves of data collection from birth parents and three waves of in-home assessments for adoptive families, as well as numerous follow-up phone interviews between and after the major waves of data collection. Moreover, our in-home assessments included extensive videotaping of child behavioural patterns and interaction patterns between the mother, father and child. We have been highly successful in retaining our sample. Recent estimates indicate retention rates up to 99% for our adoptive families, 92% for our birth mothers and 89% for our birth fathers, although these estimates are periodically revised as we lose some subjects and reclaim others (Leve *et al.*, 2007).

     We have already begun two new extensions of the study. The first is a lateral extension of the study to increase the sample size to 550 or more family units to more fully distinguish genetic and prenatal effects on early childhood development. The second is an extension in time to follow birth parents and adoptive families through the child's seventh year. This extension of the study gives new emphasis to cognitive and social skills relevant to successful school entry and explores the interplay of genetic factors and the Hypothalamic Pituitary Axis for a more complete understanding of the psychobiology of early childhood development. Encouraged by the current indicators of the validity of the adoption model, we are also planning our first intervention studies for which an entirely new sample will be required.

7. We have an ongoing process of testing and evaluating longitudinal developmental models with our infant and toddler data, as well as reviewing and examining the most recent findings in the published literature, to identify specific behaviours in early childhood that are predictive of psychopathology in later childhood and adolescence.

Implications for Adoptive Families and Professionals Who Work With Them

Our research is just beginning so its practical implications must wait until another day. However, the genetic research we have reviewed here is, for the most part, drawn from excellent studies and many of the results have been replicated. We draw three implications from this work.

First, the influences of a child's genotype may be first manifest in early childhood and be observed in the child's initial patterns of interaction with his or her parents. For any given child there is no way to know whether such patterns are heritable or not. Our study, with its detailed examination of these behaviours, may provide some clues but still there will be no way to know for certain, based on our data, how large a role genes play for any specific child. Based on studies of parents' observations of their own children, some of a child's negative or troubling patterns may slip beneath the radar of parents who understandably want to see their child in a positive light. Our study may help provide more specific clues and perhaps some aids to parents for early detection of these patterns. It must be emphasized that many of these patterns will be ones that favour a child's successful adjustment and parents will need to savour these and be as vigilant for their occurrence.

Second, already-published data convey two important messages to adoptive families. First, in the United States, adoptive families can often provide a child with material resources and financial and intellectual resources that would not have been provided had these children remained with their birth parents. In our experience, birth parents are often aware of this and seek adoptive parents; here they have a choice, which will provide these benefits for the children they are placing. Beyond that, published studies suggest that many adoptive families provide rearing environments that reduce and offset the risk of adverse genetic influences. In particular, current evidence suggests that the economic and educational resources of rearing families contribute substantially to the intellectual development of their adopted children, independent of their genotype (Capron and Duyme, 1989, 1991, 1996; Duyme and Capron, 1992). A very close inspection of some published data on behavioural self-regulation, for example that of Cadoret already cited, suggests that in a few instances rearing families may encourage the development of genetically at-risk children so that their achievements exceed those of children who are at little risk for behavioural problems.

Third, we are still in the dark as to exactly how these successes are achieved. We are hopeful that our research will clarify two major points. What is that adoptive parents do when they, in effect, override the effects of adverse genetic influences? Second, at what ages do these parenting patterns and strategies seem to have the greatest yield?

Summary

Recent genetic research is setting aside long-standing concepts of genetic influence. Data suggest that we should no longer limit our thinking to genes as influencing child vulnerability to adverse circumstances although this is certainly the case for some genetic effects. Moreover, genetic influences are not manifested only in the earliest stages of child development. Rather, genetic influences are persistent across the life course and during early childhood, and adolescence genes that have not been previously expressed manifest across a wide range of behaviours. Further, research suggests we can add a social dimension to our understanding of genetic influences. In many instances, genes influence how children enter, act, probe and influence their immediate social world. These new concepts of genetic influence on development paint a more hopeful picture than traditional findings. They suggest genetic factors not only make us more sensitive to social adversity and hence more vulnerable, but they also suggest some environments are more sensitive to genetic influences on patterns of social initiative in children, and this sensitivity perpetuates or amplifies the role of genes in child development. It may be that the sensitivity of the environment will be the first targets of preventive intervention.

If this picture is true, then studies focusing on the links between birth parents and adoptive families provide a unique model for examining variation in genetically influenced child initiation and parental response as a major arena for the interplay of genes and environment in shaping child development and parenting. Adoption samples of this kind are very expensive and difficult to recruit. However, attention to the validity of this unique model may yield a rich harvest of information of great value to adoptive families, as well as all families earnestly attempting to do the best for their children.

References

Boivin, M., Perusse, D., Dionne, G. *et al.* (2005) The genetic-environmental etiology of parents' perceptions and self-assessed behaviours toward their 5-month-old infants in a large twin and singleton sample. *Journal of Child Psychology and Psychiatry*, **46** (6), 612–30.

Braungart, J.M., Fulker, D.W. and Plomin, R. (1992) Genetic mediation of the home environment during infancy: A sibling adoption study of the HOME. *Developmental Psychology*, **28** (6), 1048–55.

Burt, S., Krueger, R.F., McGue, M. and Iacono, W. (2003) Parent-child conflict and the comorbidity among childhood externalizing disorders. *Archives of General Psychiatry*, **60** (5), 505–13.

Burt, S., McGue, M., Krueger, R.F. and Iacono, W.G. (2005) How are parent-child conflict and childhood externalizing symptoms related over time? Results from a genetically informative cross-lagged study. *Development and Psychopathology*, **17** (1), 145–65.

Cadoret, R.J. and Cain, C.A. (1981a) Environmental and genetic factors in predicting adolescent antisocial behavior in adoptees. *Psychiatric Journal of the University of Ottawa*, **6** (4), 220–5.

Cadoret, R.J. and Cain, C.A. (1981b) Genotype-environmental interaction in anti-social behavior. *Psychological Medicine*, **12**, 235–9.

Cadoret, R.J., Cain, C.A. and Crowe, R.R. (1983) Evidence for gene-environment interaction in the development of adolescent antisocial behavior. *Behavior Genetics*, **13** (3), 301–10.

Cadoret, R.J., Troughton, E., Bagford, J. and Woodworth, G. (1990) Genetic and environmental factors in adoptee antisocial personality. *European Archives of Psychiatry & Neurological Sciences*, **239** (4), 231–40.

Cadoret, R.J., Winokur, G., Langbehn, D. and Troughton, E. (1996) Depression spectrum disease, I: The role of gene-environment interaction. *American Journal of Psychiatry*, **153** (7), 892–9.

Cadoret, R.J., Yates, W.R., Troughton, E. *et al.* (1995) Genetic-environmental interaction in the genesis of aggressivity and conduct disorders. *Archives of General Psychiatry*, **52** (11), 916–24.

Capron, C. and Duyme, M. (1989) Assessment of effects of socio-economic status on IQ in a full cross-fostering study. *Nature*, **340**, 552–4.

Capron, C. and Duyme, M. (1991) Children's IQs and SES of biological and adop-tive parents in a balanced cross-fostering study. *Cahiers de Psychologie Cognitive/Current Psychology of Cognition*, **11** (3), 323–48.

Capron, C. and Duyme, M. (1996) Effect of socioeconomic status of biological and adoptive parents on WISC-R subtest scores of their French adopted children. *Intelligence*, **22** (3), 259–76.

Caspi, A., McClay, J., Moffitt, T. *et al.* (2002) Role of genotype in the cycle of violence in maltreated children. *Science*, **297** (5582), 851–4.

Caspi, A. and Moffitt, T.E. (2006) Gene-environment interactions in psychiatry: Joining forces with neuroscience. *Nature Reviews Neuroscience*, **7** (7), 583–90.

Cleveland, H.H., Wiebe, R.P., van den Oord, E.J.C.G. and Rowe, D.C. (2000) Behavior problems among children from different family structures: The influ-ence of genetic self-selection. *Child Development*, **71** (3), 733–51.

Cloninger, C.R., Bohman, M. and Sigvardsson, S. (1981) Inheritance of alcohol abuse: Cross-fostering analysis of adopted men. *Archives of General Psychia-try*, **38** (8), 861–8.

D'Onofrio, B.M., Turkheimer, E., Emery, R.E. *et al.* (2005) A genetically informed study of marital instability and its association with offspring psychopathology. *Journal of Abnormal Psychology*, **114** (4), 570–86.

Deater-Deckard, K., Fulker, D.W. and Plomin, R. (1999) A genetic study of the family environment in the transition to early adolescence. *Journal of Child Psychology and Psychiatry and Allied Disciplines*, **40** (5), 769–75.

Deater-Deckard, K. and Plomin, R. (1999) An adoption study of etiology of teacher and parent reports of externalizing behavior problems in middle childhood. *Child Development*, **70** (1), 144–54.

Dishion, T.J., Patterson, G.R. and Kavanagh, K.A. (1992) An experimental test of the coercion model: Linking theory, measurement, and intervention, in *Preventing Antisocial Behavior. Interventions from Birth through Adolescence* (eds J. McCord and R. Tremblay), Guilford, New York, pp. 253–82.

Dunbar, N., van Dulmen, M.H., Ayers-Lopez, S. *et al.* (2006) Processes linked to contact changes in adoptive kinship networks. *Family Process*, **45** (4), 449–64.

Dunn, J. and Plomin, R. (1986) Determinants of maternal behaviour towards 3-year-old siblings. *British Journal of Developmental Psychology*, **4** (2), 127–37.

Duyme, M. and Capron, C. (1992) Socioeconomic status and IQ: What is the meaning of the French adoption studies? *Cahiers de Psychologie Cognitive/ Current Psychology of Cognition*, **12** (5-6), 585–604.

Forgatch, M., Patterson, G.R. and Ray, J.A. (1996) Divorce and boys adjustment problems: two paths with a single model, in Stress, Coping and Resiliency in *Children and the Family* (ed. E.M. Hetherington), Lawrence Erlbaum Associates, Hillsdale, NJ.

Furukawa, T. and Shibayama, T. (1997) Intra-individual versus extra-individual components of social support. *Psychological Medicine*, **27** (5), 1183–91.

Ge, X., Conger, R.D., Cadoret, R.J. *et al.* (1996) The developmental interface between nature and nurture: A mutual influence model of child antisocial behavior and parent behaviors. *Developmental Psychology*, **32** (4), 574–89.

Gillespie, N.A., Evans, D.E., Wright, M.M. and Martin, N.G. (2004) Genetic simplex modeling of Eysenck's dimensions of personality in a sample of young Australian twins. *Twin Research*, **7** (6), 637–48.

Gillespie, N.A., Whitfield, J.B., Williams, B. *et al.* (2005) The relationship between stressful life events, the serotonin transporter (5-HTTLPR) genotype and major depression. *Psychological Medicine*, **35** (1), 101–11.

Grotevant, H.D. (2006) *Emotional distance regulation over the life course in adoptive kinship network*. Paper presented at the International Conference on Adoption Research-2.

Iervolino, A.C., Pike, A., Manke, B. *et al.* (2002) Genetic and environmental influences in adolescent peer socialization: Evidence from two genetically sensitive designs. *Child Development*, **73** (1), 162–74.

Jacobson, K.C. and Rowe, D.C. (1999) Genetic and environmental influences on the relationships between family connectedness, school connectedness, and adolescent depressed mood: Sex differences. *Developmental Psychology*, **35** (4), 926–39.

Johnson, W., McGue, M. and Krueger, R.F. (2005) Personality stability in late adulthood: A behavioral genetic analysis. *Journal of Personality*, **73** (2), 523–51.

Kendler, K.S. (2001) Twin studies of psychiatric illness: An update. *Archives of General Psychiatry*, **58** (11), 1005–14.

Kendler, K.S., Kessler, R.C., Walters, E.E. *et al.* (1995) Stressful life events, genetic liability, and onset of an episode of major depression in women. *American Journal of Psychiatry*, **152** (6), 833–42.

Kendler, K.S., Kuhn, J.W., Vittum, J. *et al.* (2005) The interaction of stressful life events and a serotonin transporter polymorphism in the prediction of episodes of major depression. *Archives of General Psychiatry*, **62** (5), 529–35.

Kendler, K.S., Myers, J.M. and Neale, M.C. (2000) A multidimensional twin study of mental health in women. *American Journal of Psychiatry*, **157** (4), 506–13.

Kendler, K.S., Neale, M.C., Kessler, R.C. *et al.* (1993) A longitudinal twin study of 1-year prevalence of major depression in women. *Archives of General Psychiatry*, **50** (11), 843–52.

Kendler, K.S., Prescott, C.A., Myers, J. and Neale, M.C. (2003) The structure of genetic and environmental risk factors for common psychiatric and substance use disorders in men and women. *Archives of General Psychiatry*, **60** (9), 929–37.

Kessler, R.C., Kendler, K.S., Heath, A. *et al.* (1992) Social support, depressed mood, and adjustment to stress: A genetic epidemiologic investigation. *Journal of Personality & Social Psychology*, **62** (2), 257–72.

Kessler, R.C., Kendler, K., Heath, A. *et al.* (1994) Perceived support and adjustment to stress in a general population sample of female twins. *Psychological Medicine*, **24** (2), 317–34.

Kim-Cohen, J., Caspi, A., Taylor, A. *et al.* (2006) MAOA, maltreatment, and gene-environment interaction predicting children's mental health: New evidence and a meta-analysis. *Molecular Psychiatry*, **11** (10), 903–13.

Larzelere, R.E. and Patterson, G.R. (1990) Parental management: Mediator of the effect of socioeconomic status on early delinquency. *Criminology*, **28**, 301–24.

Leve, L.D., Neiderhiser, J.M., Ge, X. *et al.* (2007) The early growth and development study: A prospective adoption design. *Twin Research and Human Genetics*, **10** (1), 84–95.

Lichtenstein, P., Harris, J.R., Pedersen, N.L. and McClearn, G.E. (1993) Socioeconomic status and physical health, how are they related? An empirical study based on twins reared apart and twins reared together. *Social Science & Medicine*, **36** (4), 441–50.

Lichtenstein, P. and Pedersen, N.L. (1995) Social relationships, stressful life events, and self-reported physical health: Genetic and environmental influences. *Psychology & Health*, **10** (4), 295–319.

Lichtenstein, P. and Pedersen, N.L. (1997) Does genetic variance for cognitive abilities account for genetic variance in educational achievement and occupational status? A study of twins reared apart and twins reared together. *Social Biology*, **44** (1-2), 77–90.

Lichtenstein, P.L., Pedersen, N.L. and McClearn, G.E. (1992) The origins of individual differences in occupational status and educational level: A study of twins reared apart and together. *Acta Sociologica*, **35**, 13–31.

Loehlin, J.C., Neiderhiser, J.M. and Reiss, D. (2005) Genetic and environmental components of adolescent adjustment and parental behavior: A multivariate analysis. *Child Development,* **76** (5), 1104–15.

Manke, B., McGuire, S., Reiss, D. *et al.* (1995) Genetic contributions to adolescents' extrafamilial social interactions: Teachers, best friends, and peers. *Social Development,* **4** (3), 238–56.

McGue, M. and Christensen, K. (2003) The heritability of depression symptoms in elderly Danish twins: Occasion-specific versus general effects. *Behavior Genetics,* **33** (2), 83–93.

McGue, M. and Lykken, D.T. (1992) Genetic influence on risk of divorce. *Psychological Science,* **3** (6), 368–73.

Narusyte, J., Andershed, A.-K., Neiderhiser, J.M. and Lichtenstein, P. (2007) Aggression as a mediator of genetic contributions to the association between negative parent-child relationships and adolescent antisocial behavior. *European Child & Adolescent Psychiatry,* **16** (2), 128–37.

Neiderhiser, J.M., Reiss, D., Hetherington, E.M. and Plomin, R. (1999) Relationships between parenting and adolescent adjustment over time: Genetic and environmental contributions. *Developmental Psychology,* **35** (3), 680–92.

O'Connor, T.G., Deater-Deckard, K., Fulker, D. *et al.* (1998) Genotype-environment correlations in late childhood and early adolescence: Antisocial behavioral problems and coercive parenting. *Developmental Psychology,* **34** (5), 970–81.

O'Connor, T.G., Hetherington, E.M., Reiss, D. and Plomin, R. (1995) A twin-sibling study of observed parent-adolescent interactions. *Child Development,* **66** (3), 812–29.

Patterson, G. (1982) *Coercive Family Process: A Social Learning Approach,* Castalia, Eugene, OR.

Patterson, G.R., Reid, J.B. and Dishion, T.J. (1992) *A Social Learning Approach. IV. Antisocial Boys,* Castalia, Eugene, OR.

Pedersen, N.L. and Reynolds, C.A. (1998) Stability and change in adult personality: Genetic and environmental components. *European Journal of Personality,* **12** (5), 365–86.

Petrill, S.A., Lipton, P.A., Hewitt, J.K. *et al.* (2004) Genetic and environmental contributions to general cognitive ability through the first 16 years of life. *Developmental Psychology,* **40** (5), 805–12.

Plomin, R., Corley, R., Caspi, A. *et al.* (1998) Adoption results for self-reported personality: Evidence for nonadditive genetic effects? *Journal of Personality and Social Psychology,* **75** (1), 211–8.

Plomin, R., Emde, R.N., Braungart, J.M. *et al.* (1993) Genetic change and continuity from fourteen to twenty months: The MacArthur Longitudinal Twin Study. *Child Development,* **64**, 1354–76.

Plomin, R., Pedersen, N.L., Lichtenstein, P. and McClearn, G.E. (1994) Variability and stability in cognitive abilities are largely genetic later in life. *Behavior Genetics,* **24** (3), 207–15.

Plomin, R., Pedersen, N.L., Lichtenstein, P. *et al.* (1990) Genetic influences on life events during the last half of the life span. *Psychology and Aging*, 5 (1), 25–30.

Reid, J.B., Patterson, G.R. and Snyder, J. (2002) *Antisocial Behavior in Children and Adolescents: A Developmental Analysis and Model for Intervention*, American Psychological Association, Washington, DC.

Reiss, D., Neiderhiser, J., Hetherington, E.M. and Plomin, R. (2000) *The Relationship Code: Deciphering Genetic and Social Patterns in Adolescent Development*, Harvard University Press, Cambridge, MA.

Rende, R.D., Slomkowski, C.L., Stocker, C. *et al.* (1992) Genetic and environmental influences on maternal and sibling interaction in middle childhood: A sibling adoption study. *Developmental Psychology*, 28 (3), 484–90.

Rietveld, M., Hudziak, J., Bartels, M. *et al.* (2004) Heritability of attention problems in children: Longitudinal results from a study of twins, age 3 to 12. *Journal of Child Psychology and Psychiatry*, 45 (3), 577–88.

Saudino, K.J., Pedersen, N.L., Lichtenstein, P. *et al.* (1997) Can personality explain genetic influences on life events? *Journal of Personality and Social Psychology*, 72 (1), 196–206.

Seifer, R., Sameroff, A., Dickstein, S. *et al.* (2004) Your own children are special: Clues to the sources of reporting bias in temperament assessments. *Infant Behavior and Development*, 27 (3), 323–41.

Sigvardsson, S., Bohman, M. and Cloninger, C. (1996) Replication of the Stockholm Adoption Study of alcoholism: Confirmatory cross-fostering analysis. *Archives of General Psychiatry*, 53 (8), 681–7.

Silberg, J., Rutter, M. and Eaves, L. (2001) Genetic and environmental influences on the temporal association between earlier anxiety and later depression in girls. *Biological Psychiatry*, 49 (12), 1040–9.

Silberg, J., Rutter, M., Neale, M. and Eaves, L. (2001) Genetic moderation of environmental risk for depression and anxiety in adolescent girls. *British Journal of Psychiatry*, 179, 116–21.

Spotts, E.L., Neiderhiser, J.M., Towers, H. *et al.* (2004) Genetic and environmental influences on marital relationships. *Journal of Family Psychology*, 18 (1), 107–19.

Stoolmiller, M., Patterson, G.R. and Snyder, J. (1997) Parental discipline and child antisocial behavior: A contingency-based theory and some methodological refinements. *Psychological Inquiry*, 8 (3), 223–9.

Tienari, P., Wynne, L.C., Sorri, A. *et al.* (2004) Genotype-environment interaction in schizophrenia spectrum disorder. *British Journal of Psychiatry*, 184, 216–22.

van den Oord, E.J.C.G. and Rowe, D.C. (1997) Continuity and change in children's social maladjustment: A developmental behavior genetic study. *Developmental Psychology*, 33 (2), 319–32.

Viken, R.J., Rose, R.J., Kaprio, J. and Koskenvuo, M. (1994) A developmental genetic analysis of adult personality: Extraversion and neuroticism from 18 to 59 years of age. *Journal of Personality and Social Psychology*, **66** (4), 722–30.

Wadsworth, S., Corley, R., Hewitt, J. *et al.* (2002) Parent-offspring resemblance for reading performance at 7, 12 and 16 years of age in the Colorado Adoption Project. *Journal of Child Psychology and Psychiatry*, **43** (6), 769–74.

7

Effects of Profound Early Institutional Deprivation: An Overview of Findings from a UK Longitudinal Study of Romanian Adoptees*

Michael Rutter, Celia Beckett, Jenny Castle, Emma Colvert, Jana Kreppner, Mitul Mehta, Suzanne Stevens and Edmund Sonuga-Barke

When the Ceauceşcu regime in Romania fell in 1989, there was widespread media coverage of the plight of children being reared in profoundly depriving institutions. The concern aroused over their suffering led to a humanitarian response that involved a substantial number of children being adopted. The situation was highly unusual in several respects. First, although some of the adopting parents adopted in response to their own infertility, a substantial proportion already had biological families of their own and adopted for altruistic reasons. Second, the degree and pervasiveness of the institutional deprivation was unusually severe by any standards (Castle *et al.*, 1999; Children's Health Care Collaborative Study Group, 1992; Reich, 1990). Third, unlike the usual situation in institutions, almost all the children had been placed there in early infancy (and hence were unlikely to have been admitted because of their own handicaps). Fourth, prior to 1989, so far as is known, there had been no adoptions from institutions in

* This chapter is an adapted version of 'Effects of profound early institutional deprivation: An overview of findings from a UK longitudinal study of Romanian adoptees' by Rutter *et al.* (2007). First published in the *European Journal of Development Psychology*, **4** (3), 332–50. The material has been reproduced with permission of the publishers, Taylor & Francis Ltd, http://www.informaworld.com.

Romania and probably almost no return of children to their biological families. Accordingly, there was not the usual problem of selectivity in the children remaining in the institutions.

The situation posed both policy issues and theoretical challenges. With respect to policy and practice, there was very little knowledge on what might be expected. Would the children make a developmental recovery if they were adopted into well-functioning families? How long would the recovery process take? What would be the challenges for the children and for their adoptive families? What would be the service implications in the short term and in the long term? Would particular kinds of remedial interventions be needed and, if they were needed, what form would they take? What implications, if any, would there be for the procedures that should be followed in the case of intercountry, as distinct from domestic, adoptions?

From the scientific, or theoretical, perspective, it was appreciated from the outset that the circumstances constituted an extremely valuable 'natural experiment' (see Haugaard and Hazan, 2003; Rutter, in press ; Rutter, Pickles, Murray and Eaves, 2001). To what extent would recovery be possible when extremely depriving conditions in early life were followed by generally good conditions in middle childhood? Insofar as there were enduring adverse consequences, would they be largely a function of pre-adoption deprivation or variations in the post-adoption rearing environment? What mechanisms might be involved in any enduring deficits that occurred? Would such deficits or impairments be of a kind ordinarily associated with stress or adversities or would there be specificities associated with the fact that institutional deprivation was involved?

The UK study was established to tackle both these policy and scientific questions. For both purposes, it was essential to have a representative sample of the legal adoptions from Romania, and this was obtained using Department of Health and Home Office records (see Rutter and the English and Romanian Adoptees Study Team, 1998). In order to examine possible institutional effects, it was decided to focus on variations in duration of institutional care and, hence, an age-stratified random sampling design was employed within the range of 0 to 42 months of age for UK entry. Because we wished to focus on the possible effects of institutional deprivation, whilst controlling for the possible effects of adoption, we chose to use a comparison group of domestic adoptions of children who had *not* experienced a depriving institutional rearing, and were less than 6 months of age at the time of adoption. This group was of interest in its own right in terms of representing one of the last cohorts of children adopted before open adoption became the norm. The choice of this sample meant that, by deliberate design, we were in a strong position to examine the effects of institutional deprivation. Equally, however, because we did not have a general population comparison group, we could not examine the effects of adoption as such; the rationale was that this had been well dealt with in numerous previous studies. Similarly, we could not examine the effects of variations in the age of adoption for children who had not experienced institutional deprivation. Many children adopted from abroad are physically distinctive because of their ethnicity. This was not the case with our sample. We found that raters of videotapes were unable to make an accurate judgement on which group the child came from. There were only a very few Roma children who were more distinctive.

In our published papers, we have considered the extent to which our findings agree with those produced by other research groups studying somewhat comparable samples (e.g. Ames, 1997; Gunnar, van Dulmen and The International Adoption Project Team, 2007; MacLean, 2003; Marcovitch *et al.*, 1995), but here we focus on bringing together our own findings up to the age of 11 years. In brief, however, it is clear that there is generally good agreement across studies. We should add that, this paper does not cover children's responses to being adopted. That is the most important issue that we are addressing in our research but the findings are reported elsewhere (Hawkins *et al.*, 2007).

The overall sample of Romanian adoptees numbered 165, of whom 144 were reared in institutions. We had a very high participation rate (circa 90%) of those eligible for selection among the Romanian adoptees. Because of the confidentiality of adoption records, we were unable to obtain information on the families of domestic adoptees who chose not to participate, but findings indicated that the participation rate was probably above 50%. There were 52 within-UK adoptees. Because participation was decided before outcomes could be known, it is unlikely that there was an important selection bias, but inevitably there were uncertainties on this, in a fashion that did not apply to those adopting from Romania.

As with almost all studies of adoptees, the adopting families were both socially and educationally advantaged as compared with the general population (Ivaldi, 2000), but the two groups did not differ in those respects. The only differences were those expectable on the basis of altruistic inter-country adoptions; thus, the parents adopting from Romania were slightly older and were much more likely to have biological children of their own. Those primarily adopting for altruistic reasons also tended to adopt slightly older children. Analyses were undertaken to determine if any of these differences were associated with variations in outcome and it was found that they were not (Beckett *et al.*, 2006; Kreppner *et al.*, 2007).

Conditions in the Institutions in Romania

Romanian records did not allow any satisfactory ratings of the quality of different institutions and, hence, we had to rely on reports from parents (all of whom had visited the institutions, sometimes making video recordings of conditions), together with reports from non-governmental organizations (NGOs) operating in Romania at the time (Children's Health Care Collaborative Study Group, 1992). It was clear that, although there were variations among institutions, the variation was from poor to abysmal, with none providing good conditions. Staffing levels were very low (about 1 staff per 30 children), there were virtually no toys or educational activities, staff–child interaction and communication was minimal, feeding was mainly by means of propped-up bottles with large teats, and washing involved being hosed down with cold water. Some of the children had lived in more than one institution and, for practical reasons, ratings were possible only for the institutions from which the children were drawn at the time of selection for adoption, and no systematic data were available on the institutions caring for the children when younger. It was known that the mortality rate in some of the institutions was substantial but quantitative data were not available. On the basis of all available information, ratings were made for the qualities of different aspects of institutional care (Castle *et al.*, 1999).

Conditions of the Children at the Time of UK Entry

Assessments at the time of UK entry indicated that the majority of the children were severely subnourished as indicated by a weight below the third percentile of UK norms. Height and head circumference were similarly grossly impaired. There was no systematic contemporaneous developmental assessment at the time of UK entry but retrospective reports (for which there was good evidence of validity) indicated that the majority of children were functioning in the intellectually impaired range (Rutter and the English and Romanian Adoptees Study Team, 1998). Both skin lesions and intestinal infections were common (Beckett *et al.*, 2003) and many of the children showed stereotypies and other behaviours typical of children in institutions (Beckett *et al.*, 2002).

Physical and Developmental Catch-up

Both groups of children were first assessed at 4 years of age using a combination of parental reports, direct observations and psychometric assessments. The only exception was that this was not possible for those entering the United Kingdom after the age of 2 years because they were already past the age of 4 at the first wave of data collection. Comparable data were collected for them at the second wave at 6 years, which involved all children in both groups. A further third wave assessment was undertaken at 11 years of age and this paper primarily focuses on findings at this age, in conjunction with changes between 6 and 11. At the time of writing, a fourth wave of data collection, at age 15, has just been completed.

The developmental catch-up of the children from Romania following UK entry was spectacular. For example, the mean Denver developmental quotient at entry to the United Kingdom was about 50, whereas the mean WISC IQ at age 11 was over 90. We could not chart the course and pace of the cognitive gains in detail (because we had measures only at 4, 6 and 11 years) but it was clear that they continued over periods of up to two years or so. In the group as a whole, there was no appreciable further cognitive catch-up between 6 and 11 years but there were significant, albeit slight, further gains for those with the lowest scores at age 6 (Beckett *et al.*, 2006). The marked improvement in functioning following entry to the UK adoptive families provided good evidence that the initial deficits were due to some aspect of the institutional deprivation that they had experienced.

In order to understand better the meaning of this catch-up, we need to turn to the indices of physical growth. By 6 years of age there had been virtually complete catch-up in the children's weight and height as judged by UK population norms. By contrast, however, although there had been similar major catch-up in head circumference (a reasonable index of brain size – Wickett, Vernon and Lee, 2000), it was much less complete at 6 years of age. In addition, whereas there was no further catch-up in weight and height between 6 and 11 (because catch-up was already almost complete by age 6), there *was* further catch-up in head circumference, albeit remaining below the normal range (Sonuga-Barke *et al.*, submitted). At 11, head circumference was still a standard deviation or so below population means but the recovery process had continued between 6 and 11. It may be concluded, first, that both brain size and IQ (see below) were more susceptible than height and weight to persisting deficits following profound institutional deprivation, and second, that the recovery process (although maximal in the first year or so) continued to some extent even some half a dozen years after leaving the institution.

Cognitive Deficits and Other Sequelae

Despite the major catch-up in psychological functioning in the first few years after the radical move from a profoundly depriving institution to a generally well-functioning adoptive family, cognitive deficits and other sequelae were evident in some children at ages 4, 6 and 11. Strikingly, the sequelae applied to four rather unusual patterns (quasi-autism, disinhibited attachment, inattention/overactivity and cognitive impairment), and not to the three more common patterns (emotional disturbance, conduct problems and peer relationship difficulties) seen in non-institutionalized groups (Rutter, Kreppner, O'Connor and the ERA Study Team, 2001). We approached this issue in several different ways. The first basic question was whether these persisting problems were a consequence of the early deprivation, of adversities in the adoptive family environment, or of periods of maladjustment that might be found in any group of young people as they grew up. The last point could be checked by means of comparison with the non-institutionalized early-adopted domestic adoptees. The findings were clear-cut in showing large between-group differences on a range of different domains of functioning at age 6 (Rutter, Kreppner, *et al.*, 2001) and again at 11 (Kreppner *et al.*, 2007). Moreover, there was substantial continuity in which children exhibited impairment at each age. For none of the adverse consequences was there any association between their presence and any variations in the measured qualities of the adoptive homes. Of course, the huge catch-up must have been attributable in part to the positive experiences provided by the adoptive families. On the other hand, as is typical of most groups of adoptive families, they had been selected to be relatively free of major environmental risks, they were socially and educationally advantaged compared with the general population, and the range of variation among the families was fairly small. We should not conclude, therefore, that the particular family qualities do not matter but rather that within the relatively narrow range in this sample, the variations (insofar as we were able to measure them) did not account for the persisting sequelae in the Romanian adoptees.

By contrast, the institutional deprivation was an important predictor of these unusual outcomes. Six findings were critical. First, the adverse outcomes were much less marked (and less specific) in the children adopted from Romania who had not experienced institutional care, although they had been deprived in other ways. In short, the main deficits were a function of *institutional* deprivation. Second, across all seven domains of functioning mentioned above, there was *no* measurable increase in the rate of deficits in children who were aged 6 months or less at the time of entering their adoptive family (although there were occasional deficits in individual children). Third, at age 6 years, for four out of the seven domains of functioning there was a dose–response relationship between the duration of institutional deprivation and the negative outcomes. That is, the longer the duration, the greater the probability of that outcome. These four domains were quasi-autism, disinhibited attachment, inattention/overactivity and cognitive impairment – all of which were quite uncommon in the group of domestic adoptees. In other words, the fourth feature was that institutional deprivation was not a risk factor for all types of psychopathology, but only for just a few that were infrequent in the general population. These four findings all point strongly to a causal effect (see Rutter, 2007, for a discussion of proceeding from a correlational observation to a causal inference). Fifth, despite the long passage of time, the effects of institutional deprivation were just about as marked at age 11 as they had been previously at 4 and 6. This applied to impairment generally (Kreppner *et al.*, 2007), but also it applied to individual features such as cognition (Beckett *et al.*, 2006), disinhibited attachment (Rutter *et al.*, 2007a) and inattention/overactivity (Stevens *et al.*, 2008). The sixth feature was the most surprising; although there had been a dose–response relationship with duration of deprivation at ages 4 and 6, this was no longer apparent at age 11. Rather, around about an age of placement of 6 to 12 months, there was a marked jump up to a level of some 40 or 50% of the children showing impairment (Kreppner *et al.*, 2007). The implications of this finding for mediating mechanisms (meaning those that are responsible for the effect) are considered further below.

Validating the Assessment of Impairment

Before considering the meaning of the variations in functioning at age 11, we need to ask whether the assessment of normality, on the one hand, and multiple areas of impairment, on the other, were truly valid. We approached this in three different ways. First, we checked by means of validation across informants and across measures. Thus, for example, standardized diagnostic interview and observation measures for autism (the Autism Diagnostic Interview-Revised – ADI-R and the Autism Diagnostic Observation Schedule – ADOS) were used to evaluate the quasi-autistic patterns (Rutter *et al.*, 2007b). Somewhat similarly, investigator observation ratings and blindly scored videos of interactions were used to validate disinhibited attachment (Rutter *et al.*, 2007). Second, we examined continuities in time – finding that, of the children without impairment at age 6, over two-thirds were similarly without impairment at 11 (Kreppner *et al.*, 2007). The proportions showing stability for multiple impairment were similar. Third, we examined patterns of service usage (Castle *et al.*, 2006). Of the children with multiple domains of impairment at 11, nearly 90% had used professional educational or psychological/psychiatric services compared with only about 1 in 10 of those showing apparently normal functioning. It may be concluded that the individual variations in outcome were truly valid. The half of the group of Romanian children who had experienced at least 6 months of institutional deprivation, who showed multiple domains of impairment, were truly malfunctioning to a degree that had led to service usage. Conversely, it was also the case that a substantial minority of the children suffering profound institutional deprivation seemed to be functioning normally in all respects at age 11 in spite of their seriously adverse early experiences.

Mechanisms Responsible for Individual Variations in Outcome

As noted, heterogeneity of outcome (meaning marked individual variations) was a pervasive element of all psychological features that we examined. This was not just evident at the extremes; rather it applied throughout the range. Thus, across the total range of duration of institutional deprivation, there was a wide spread of IQ scores (Beckett *et al.*, 2006) and of inattention/overactivity scores (Stevens *et al.*, 2008). Moreover, the degree of spread was as great for very prolonged deprivation (at least up to the age of 42 months, the oldest age for leaving the institutions in our sample) as it was for very short deprivational experiences. The challenge was to identify the mechanisms that accounted for the heterogeneity.

The first possibility was that the answer might lie in some aspect of the institutional experience. Accordingly, we sought to determine whether subnutrition was a key feature, given the seriousness of the subnutrition experienced by so many of the children. The findings showed that it was not (Kreppner *et al.*, 2007; Sonuga-Barke *et al.*, in press). Within the group who were aged at least 6 months when they left the institution, there was no significant effect of subnutrition on the proportion with multiple impairments. With respect to individual psychological features, there were none for which subnutrition had a major effect; in some there was no significant effect and for two (cognition and inattention/overactivity) there was a minor, just significant effect. The bottom line, however, was that subnutrition (perhaps surprisingly) played, at most, a minor role in the overall heterogeneity of outcome. There was some tendency for the cognitive deficits to be marginally greater in the presence of severe subnutrition, but the main predictor was whether institutional deprivation had extended beyond the age of 6 months.

Another possibility was that the variations in outcome were a function of the severity of the children's impairment at the time of entering their adoptive family in the United Kingdom. We examined this possibility in terms of the children's developmental quotient and their head circumference, and neither had a significant effect on psychological outcome. The one exception was the presence of minimal language (Croft *et al.*, 2006). Almost all of the children were entirely without language, in keeping with their overall severe developmental impairment, but of those aged at least 18 months a minority were able to imitate speech – an indication that perhaps they were nearly at the point when spoken language might be about to be evident. These children had a significantly higher mean IQ (both verbal and non-verbal) at 11. The query was what this might mean. The association was not just an index, or measure, of duration or quality of institutional care because it held even when these were taken into account. Conversely, there was no effect of duration/quality of institutional care (however measured) once minimal language had been taken into account. Moreover, the minimal language could not be considered just an index or reflection of the severity of deprivation because it did not predict non-cognitive/language outcomes. Thus there was no association, for example, with disinhibited attachment, despite the fact that this was particularly strongly associated with institutional deprivation. On the other hand, minimal language was significantly associated with our ratings of the quality of the institutional environment. What this means is that it was likely that in some way the variations in language were a consequence of some aspect of the institutional experience rather than some independent influence (such as the ordinary effects of genetic influences on variations in IQ). The specificity of effects to cognitive outcomes suggests that the minimal language constituted some kind of cognitive reserve made possible as a result of limitations in some aspect of the deprivation.

A further possibility was that the heterogeneity reflected the effect of specifically *institutional* deprivation. The consistent finding that the outcome of the Romanian adoptees who had not experienced institutional care, although less good than the domestic adoptive comparison group, was better than the group of institutional adoptees indicates that this was the case.

Yet another possibility was that the heterogeneity in outcome might be a consequence of variations in the quality of the adoptive family rearing environment. We found no evidence that this was the case – either in terms of the adoptive parents' IQ or educational background or in terms of psychological features. The implication is that for children as deprived as these children had been, the major variations in outcome were not likely to be due to the minor variations in the qualities of the adoptive families. Of course, that does not mean that the adoptive home qualities were without effect. The massive improvement in psychological functioning post-adoption provides a powerful testimony to their importance; also the family qualities may well have made an important difference to details of the children's psychological functioning. It is just that it did not account for the presence or absence of major deficits or impairments.

The final possibility is that variations in outcome reflected genetically influenced differences in susceptibility to environmental deprivation (Stevens *et al.*, 2006). The results of gene–environment interactions have been well demonstrated (Rutter, 2006; Rutter, Moffitt and Caspi, 2006) and it may be expected that, although genetic main effects are not likely, differences in genetic susceptibility could play a role in outcome differences. We have collected DNA on the sample to test this possibility.

The Role of Brain Growth

As already noted, head circumference lagged behind weight and height in recovery following removal from the institutional environment and placement in an adoptive family. We need, therefore, to consider what that might mean. One possibility was that it might reflect no more than a consequence of a general impairment in overall body growth as a result of subnutrition. The evidence suggested that this did constitute part of the story. In the sample as a whole, the children who experienced less than 6 months' institutional deprivation showed a much reduced height, weight and head circumference compared with other children, even though there were no measurable long-term effects on cognitive functioning (Sonuga-Barke *et al.*, in press). Within the subnourished group with an age of entry under 6 months, head circumference was far below normal. This seemed to be part of an overall effect of subnutrition on body size. By contrast, there was no impairment in head growth for those children experiencing less than 6 months' institutional care whose weight was within the normal range. There was, on the other hand, a major effect on head growth if the institutional deprivation lasted longer than 6 months.

In short, it seemed that it took some months for psychological deprivation to affect head size but it had a major effect if the deprivation persisted. Nevertheless, despite strong effects of institutional deprivation and subnutrition on head growth, within both the subnourished and relatively normally nourished groups, low head circumference had a negligible mediating effect on the long-term psychological impairments – that is, the degree to which the head was unusually small did not account for adverse psychological outcomes. What was, perhaps, unexpected was that the improvements in head growth extended over so many years. The mechanisms involved remain obscure and both our sample size and the extent of the variations in head growth recovery prevented us from examining possible biological mediating mechanisms. A surprise, however, is that, although head size was associated with several of the psychological outcomes, the psychological deficits and recovery were not explicable on the basis of head size. We should note, however, that it is certainly possible that there were brain changes that mediated (i.e. accounted for) the psychological deficit, but which were not reflected in overall head circumference.

Up to this point, we have treated head size as an indirect measure of brain size. However, we undertook a small pilot magnetic resonance imaging (MRI) study that provided a more direct test (Mehta *et al.*, submitted). The findings were clear-cut in showing a substantial positive correlation between head circumference and whole brain volume with respect to both grey and white matter – that is, the two main types of brain substance. The findings with respect to mediators of outcome were more complex. When the findings were corrected for total white matter volume, a significant finding was that the Romanian adoptees *without* deprivation-specific problems had a *larger* corpus callosum than both the controls and the Romanian children with deprivation-specific problems (Mehta, personal communication). The implication would seem to be that this increase in size represented a successful compensatory response to deprivation. Despite the statistical significance of the findings, there must be considerable caution in inferring mechanisms (because of the sample size) but the results do highlight the importance of considering possible compensatory mechanisms as well as damaging effects.

Cognitive/Language Impairment

Over the years, there has been speculation over whether different forms of deprivation might have differential effects on different aspects of cognitive development. A meta-analysis of cross-sectional findings on cognitive outcome suggested that the recovery of scholastic attainment might tend to lag behind recovery of IQ (van Ijzendoorn and Juffer, 2006). Our findings, by contrast, showed that the impairment of IQ and of scholastic attainment at 11 were roughly comparable (Beckett *et al.*, 2007). The pervasive nature of the institutional deprivation meant that we had very limited power to examine differential effects. Nevertheless, the unusually high rate of attentional difficulties did suggest the possibility that scholastic attainment might be especially impeded as a consequence of such attentional difficulties above and beyond any effect of overall cognitive skills. In the event, that is not what our results showed (Beckett *et al.*, 2007). The relative deficit in attainment in reading and arithmetic at 11, as compared with the domestic adoptees group, was markedly diminished once IQ level was taken into account. There was a further, but very slight, reduction when attentional difficulties were taken into account. Taken together, IQ and inattention accounted for close to all, but not quite all, of the deficit in scholastic attainment. It may be concluded that institutional deprivation had a detrimental effect on scholastic attainment, but that this was part and parcel of the overall effect on global intellectual functioning.

Quasi-autism

One of the really surprising initial findings from the study of Romanian adoptees was the markedly high rate of autistic-like patterns involving problems in social reciprocity and communication, together with unusual circumscribed interests (Rutter *et al.*, 1999). At age 4, the features seemed indistinguishable from 'ordinary' autism but, by age 6, there seemed to be important differences in terms both of the decrease in autistic features (as compared with a comparable longitudinal study of individuals with 'ordinary' autism) and the unusual degree of social approach. Our recent follow-up to age 11 (Rutter *et al.*, 2007) has cast further light on the meaning of this pattern. On the one hand, about a quarter of the children lost their autistic features and in another quarter they diminished greatly. Only a minority of the individuals who had shown quasi-autistic patterns when young showed a clearly autistic pattern at 11 (apart from the four children who continued to show significant cognitive impairment). On the other hand, only a few were free of impairment at 11. Most showed either disinhibited attachment or evidence of poor peer relationships and most were receiving some form of educational or mental health service provisions. The reasons why some children developed quasi-autistic patterns (about 12% of the institutional-reared adoptees showed a clear pattern, plus another 8% with minor features) is by no means clear. The patterns were largely confirmed by investigator-based ratings, by some impairments in Theory of Mind functioning, and by service provision, but that does not explain their origin. It does not seem to be a function of non-institutional deprivation because no Romanian adoptee who had not experienced institutional care developed the pattern and because, although the pattern has been observed in other samples of institutionally deprived children (Hoksbergen *et al.*, 2005), it has not been a feature of studies of non-institutionalized abused or neglected children. Possibly, it constitutes a response to profound lack of interpersonal interactions and conversations. The general lack of this feature in ordinary samples of children with an autism spectrum disorder suggests that the findings cannot be generalized to the broader run of autism spectrum disorders. On the other hand, the findings are relevant for the concept that linguistic and perceptual deprivation is involved in the genesis of autism whether due to an intrinsic impairment – that is, an internal deficit that is basic (as in most cases of ordinary autism) or extrinsic restrictions in input (meaning the effects of inadequate experiences), as in these cases.

Disinhibited Attachment

In some respects, the outcome most specifically associated with institutional deprivation was disinhibited attachment – a disorder involving a lack of clear differentiation among familiar and unfamiliar adults, a lack of wariness with strangers, a lack of checking back with parents in anxiety-provoking situations, and a physical and social violation of conventional boundaries in interactions with other people. This was strongly evident in the findings at age 4 and 6 years (O'Connor *et al.*, 1999, 2001; O'Connor, Rutter and the English and Romanian Adoptees Study Team, 2000) and was equally striking at age 11 (Rutter *et al.*, 2007a). The parental reports suggested some lessening of disinhibited attachment between 6 and 11 but the standardized investigator ratings suggested that some of the reduction was artefactual (reflecting the lesser developmental appropriateness of the reports at 11 than at age 6). Two features of the findings warrant special emphasis. First, mild (but *not* severe) indications of disinhibited attachment were quite common in the domestic comparison group at age 6 but, in almost all cases, the features were no longer present at age 11. By contrast, mild, as well as severe, disinhibited attachment in the institution-reared group usually persisted to age 11. Putting the findings together, it may be concluded that caution needs to be exercised about the meaning of mild disinhibited features found in the absence of institutional care and, second, that the assessment needs to be based not just on parental report but also on investigator observations of inappropriate social interaction and ignoring of the usual conventions of social boundaries. It might be argued that the disinhibited features were no more than an adaptation to the very unusual situation of institutional deprivation, but two findings negate that supposition. First, the effects of institutional care were as strong at age 11 as they had been at 4 and 6 years of age. Second, at age 11, disinhibited attachment was associated with a much increased rate of malfunction in other psychological domains. It constitutes a disorder and not just a stylistic variation.

A further query is whether the disinhibited attachment pattern represents a variety of attachment insecurity. Several features indicate that it does not. To begin with, there was only a weak association with attachment insecurity as assessed in the usual way by a version of the 'strange situation' procedure modified for use in the home. Second, what was atypical was *not* the style of reunion with the mother but rather the response to the stranger. Third, the most striking features concerned the intrusive social approach and disregard of social boundaries rather than the response to overtures of comfort. Finally, insecure attachment has usually been found to alter with changes in parenting, whereas disinhibited attachment did not.

Inattention/Overactivity

Perhaps unexpectedly in view of the evidence of the high heritability of Attention Deficit Disorder with Hyperactivity (ADHD) (Taylor and Sonuga-Barke, 2008), at age 6 inattention/overactivity (I/O) was much more frequent among Romanian adoptees than in the comparison group; it was also associated with duration of institutional deprivation (Kreppner *et al.*, 2001). At age 11, however, although the group of Romanian institution reared children as a whole continued to show significantly higher levels of I/O in both home and school settings when compared with the UK adoptees, the children adopted over the age of 6 months from Romania were at particular risk. This group showed significantly elevated levels of I/O, whereas those under the age of 6 months were indistinguishable in this respect from both the UK adoptees and those Romanian children who had not experienced institutional deprivation (Stevens *et al.*, 2008). Moreover, many of the Romanian children with I/O had received clinical services for ADHD (Castle *et al.*, 2006). What was different at age 11, as compared with age 6, is that there was no dose–response association with duration of deprivation beyond the 6-month point. As already noted, this applied similarly to other outcomes. A pilot study comparing I/O in Romanian adoptees with 'ordinary' varieties of ADHD showed that, in males, the behavioural patterns and neuropsychological features were very similar, but the severity tended to be greater in the Romanian adoptees (Sonuga-Barke and Rubia, 2008). By contrast, the features in females did not differ markedly from controls.

Emotional and Conduct Disturbance

At age 6, the Romanian adoptees and the domestic comparison group did not differ significantly in the rates of overall emotional and conduct disturbance as measured by questionnaire (Rutter, Kreppner, O'Connor and the ERA Study Team, 2001). The situation at age 11 was slightly different (Colvert *et al.*, in press). Conduct disturbance at both age 6 and age 11 was slightly more frequent in the Romanian adoptees but the differences fell short of statistical significance, and the group difference did not increase between 6 and 11. By contrast, emotional disturbance was no different between the groups at age 6 but was significantly more frequent in Romanian adoptees at age 11. The key questions were whether the apparent increase over time meant that it had been manifest in a different way at age 6 (with the increase by 11 artefactual), whether there had been a true increase and (if there had) whether this was a function of institutional deprivation or rather some aspect of the post-adoption environment.

The findings were clear-cut in one respect and ambiguous in a second respect. The straightforward finding was that the higher rate of emotional disturbance in the Romanian adoptees at age 11 was largely a consequence of the relatively deprivation-specific patterns already evident at age 6. This association with deprivation-specific patterns was as evident in those whose emotional disturbance remitted after age 6, began after age 6 or continued between the two ages. In other words, the increase in emotional disturbance associated with deprivation-specific problems was independent of age and these deprivation-specific features did not account for the increase between 6 and 11. Nevertheless, there was an increase in emotional disturbance (albeit a small one) in children who had *not* shown a deprivation-specific pattern at age 6. There was no evidence that it constituted a delayed response to institutional deprivation but, equally, there was no definite indication of an origin in post-adoption circumstances.

Services

As already indicated, the overall group of Romanian adoptees needed and received considerable mental health and educational input (Castle *et al.*,

2006). Overall, almost a third of the children from Romania placed after 6 months received mental health provision, compared with 11 to 15% in the groups adopted before the age of 6 months. There were similar findings for special educational provision. Our evidence indicates that this was needed and well justified. The children who received help from community services were largely those for whom our research measures indicated that they needed help. What was striking, however, was that in the great majority of cases the help was provided for unusual problems that were relatively specific to institutional deprivation. Because of that there was a very limited understanding of the types of interventions likely to be beneficial (Rutter, 2007).

Theoretical Implications

The most obvious and important theoretical findings are, first, that following profound institutional deprivation lasting up to 3.5 years of age there can be, and usually is, a huge improvement in functioning following removal to a generally well-functioning family home. Second, although there is often a quite rapid initial improvement, continuing gains continue for up to two years and, sometimes, even much longer than that. Such gains did not appear to be a function of the relatively minor variations in the quality of the adoptive family environment. Third, despite the severity of the subnutrition experienced by most of the Romanian adoptees, the relative severity of that subnutrition had only a minor effect on the psychological outcomes. However, we lacked good data on the relative *quality* of the nutritional intake and it may be that specific types of malnutrition were more influential than the overall degree of undernutrition.

Fourth, although the overall degree of impairment at the time of leaving the institution proved to be of very weak predictive power, the findings suggested that even a very low level of language, as indexed by the presence of the rudimentary skill of being able to imitate speech sounds, constituted a worthwhile protective feature with respect to cognitive (but not social) development.

Fifth, although, in most ordinary circumstances the adverse consequences associated with psychosocial stress, adversity and deprivation are relatively non-specific in diagnostic terms (McMahon *et al.*, 2003), this does not appear to be the case with profound institutional deprivation. Rather it is relatively specifically associated with quasi-autistic patterns and disinhibited attachment, and to a lesser extent with cognitive impairment and inattention/overactivity (the lesser extent being mainly a consequence of their greater incidence in individuals who have not experienced institutional deprivation).

Policy and Practice Implications

Seven policy implications dominate. First, it is obvious that a systematic paediatric and psychological assessment prior to adoption ought to be routine. This is needed in order to alert both professionals and families to the features that need either investigation or treatment (this applies particularly to health problems – see Beckett *et al.*, 2003). Second, both professionals and prospective adoptive parents need to be made aware of both the nature and frequency of psychological (and health) problems that are common in children adopted from severely depriving conditions. Third, there must be an awareness that, at least for some families, the service needs last far longer than the early months post adoption. Adoptive parents need to be able to ask for, and receive, ongoing help over a much longer period of time. Fourth, both parents and professionals need to understand the unusual nature of many of the adverse consequences of profound institutional deprivation. There should be specialists available to give advice on how best to help with these problems. Fifth, it has to be accepted that, at present, our knowledge of what interventions are most effective is rudimentary. Further research is essential. Sixth, many of our adoptive families would not have proved acceptable for domestic adoption at that time (because they were too old or because they already had biological children of their own). The study of home features will be the subject of separate reports, but it is clear that much more flexible, wider criteria are possible for successful adoption. Finally, despite all the hazards and difficulties (which were considerable), the great majority of the families remained committed to their adoptive children and made a success of the adoption. There were only two breakdowns up to age 4 and only one further breakdown by age 11 (Castle *et al.*, 2006) – a rate far lower than is usual with late adoptions.

Policy in Romania

It is obvious from the total number of children in institutions in Romania (or other countries) that intercountry adoption cannot possibly provide any general solution to institutional deprivation. Other investigators are tackling the issues in the host countries more directly (Zeanah *et al.*, 2005) but our findings are important in indicating the potential. Three conclusions stand out. First, assessment of the degree of impairment of the children whilst in the institution provides a very poor indication of the potential for recovery. Attempts to divide institutional children into the irrecoverable and the recoverable are not likely to be accurate other than to a very limited extent. Second, the remarkable improvements following intercountry adoption suggest the considerable potential in Romania (and other host countries) for relative recovery if the right conditions outside institutions can be provided. Third, the long-term findings underline the fact that, if this is to happen, considerable help to families will be needed, and such help will need to be provided over a substantial period of time.

References

Ames, E.W. (1997) *The Development of Romanian Orphanage Children Adopted to Canada*, Final report to Human Resources, Canada. Simon Fraser University, Burnaby, BC.

Beckett, C., Bredenkamp, D., Castle, J. *et al.* (2002) Behavior patterns associated with institutional deprivation: A study of children adopted from Romania. *Journal of Developmental and Behavioral Pediatrics*, **23**, 297–303.

Beckett, C., Castle, J., Groothues, C. *et al.* (2003) Health problems in children adopted from Romania: Association with duration of deprivation and behavioural problems. *Adoption & Fostering*, **27**, 19–29.

Beckett, C., Maughan, B., Rutter, M. *et al.* (2006) Do the effects of early severe deprivation on cognition persist into early adolescence? Findings from the English and Romanian Adoptees study. *Child Development*, **77**, 696–711.

Beckett, C., Maughan, B., Rutter, M. *et al.* (2007) Scholastic attainment following severe early institutional deprivation: A study of children adopted from Romania. *Journal of Abnormal Child Psychology*, published online 21 July 2007.

Castle, J., Groothues, C., Bredenkamp, D. *et al.* (1999) Effects of qualities of early institutional care on cognitive attainment. *American Journal of Orthopsychiatry*, **69**, 424–37.

Castle, J., Rutter, M., Beckett, C. *et al.* (2006) Service use by families with children adopted from Romania. *Journal of Children's Services*, **1**, 5–15.

Children's Health Care Collaborative Study Group (1992) Romanian health and social care system for children and families: Future directions in health care reform. *British Medical Journal*, **304**, 556–9.

Colvert, E., Rutter, M., Beckett, C. *et al.* (2008) Emotional difficulties in early adolescence following severe early deprivation: Findings from the English and Romanian Adoptees Study. *Development and Psychopathology* **20**, 547–67.

Croft, C., Beckett, C., Rutter, M. *et al.* (2006) Early adolescent outcomes of institutionally-deprived and non-deprived adoptees. II: Language as a protective factor and a vulnerable outcome. *Journal of Child Psychology and Psychiatry*, **48**, 31–44.

Gunnar, M.R., van Dulmen, M.H. and The International Adoption Project Team (2007) Behaviour problems in postinstitutionalized internationally adopted children. *Development and Psychopathology*, **19**, 129–48.

Haugaard, J.J. and Hazan, C. (2003) Adoption as a natural experiment. *Development and Psychopathology*, **15**, 909–26.

Hawkins, A., Beckett, C., Castle, J. *et al.* (2007) The experience of adoption. I. A study of intercountry and domestic adoption from the child's point of view. *Adoption & Fostering*, **31**, 5–16.

Hoksbergen, R., ter Laak, J., Rijk, K. *et al.* (2005) Post institutional autistic syndrome in Romanian adoptees. *Journal of Autism and Developmental Disorders*, **35**, 615–23.

Ivaldi, G. (2000) *Surveying Adoption: A Comprehensive Analysis of Local Authority Adoptions 1998–1999 (England)*, British Association of Adoption and Fostering, London.

Kreppner, J., O'Connor, T.G., Rutter M. and the English and Romanian Adoptees Study Team (2001) Can inattention/overactivity be an institutional deprivation syndrome? *Journal of Abnormal Child Psychology*, **29**, 513–28.

Kreppner, J., Rutter, M., Beckett, C. *et al.* (2007) Normality and impairment following profound early institutional deprivation: A longitudinal follow up into early adolescence. *Developmental Psychology*, **43**, 931–46.

Maclean, K. (2003) The impact of institutionalization on child development. *Development and Psychopathology*, **15**, 853–84.

Marcovitch, S., Cesarone, L., Roberts, W. and Swanson, C. (1995) Romanian adoption: Parents' dreams, nightmares and realities. *Child Welfare*, **7**, 993–1017.

McMahon, S.D., Grant, K.E., Compas, B. *et al.* (2003) Stress and psychopathology in children and adolescents: Is there evidence of specificity? *Journal of Child Psychology and Psychiatry*, **44**, 107–33.

Mehta, M.A., Golembo, N.I., Nosarti, C. *et al.* Structural alterations of the corpus callosum and amygdala, but not hippocampus, in adolescence following institutional deprivation in early childhood (submitted).

O'Connor, T.G., Bredenkamp, D., Rutter, M. and the English and Romanian Adoptees Study Team (1999) Attachment disturbances and disorders in children exposed to early severe deprivation. *Infant Mental Health Journal*, **20**, 10–29.

O'Connor, T.G., Rutter, M., Beckett, C. *et al.* (2001) Early deprivation and later attachment-related behaviour: Lessons from the English and Romanian Adoptee Study, in *Parenting: Applications in Clinical Practice* (eds W. Yule and O. Udwin), Occasional Papers No. 18. Association of Child Psychology and Psychiatry, London.

O'Connor, T.G., Rutter, M. and the English and Romanian Adoptees Study Team (2000) Attachment disorder behavior following early severe deprivation: Extension and longitudinal follow-up. *Journal of the American Academy of Child and Adolescent Psychiatry*, **39**, 703–12.

Reich, D. (1990) Children of the nightmare. *Adoption & Fostering*, **14**, 9–15.

Rutter, M. (2006) *Genes and Behavior: Nature-Nurture Interplay Explained*, Blackwell Scientific, Oxford.

Rutter, M. (2007) Proceeding from observed correlation to causal inference: The use of natural experiments. *Perspectives on Psychological Science*, **2**, 377–95.

Rutter, M., Andersen-Wood, L., Beckett, C. *et al.* (1999) Quasi-autistic patterns following severe early global privation. *Journal of Child Psychology and Psychiatry*, **40**, 537–49.

Rutter, M., Colvert, E., Kreppner, J. *et al.* (2007) Early adolescent outcomes for institutionally-deprived and non-deprived adoptees. I. Disinhibited attachment. *Journal of Child Psychology and Psychiatry*, **48**, 17–30.

Rutter, M. and the English and Romanian Adoptees Study Team (1998) Developmental catch up and deficit following adoption after severe global early privation. *Journal of Child Psychology and Psychiatry*, **39**, 465–76.

Rutter, M., Kreppner, J., Croft, C. *et al.* Early adolescent outcomes of institutionally deprived and non deprived adoptees. III. Quasi autism. *Journal of Child Psychology and Psychiatry*, **48**, 1200–7.

Rutter, M., Kreppner, J., O'Connor, T. and the ERA Study Team (2001) Specificity and heterogeneity in children's responses to profound privation. *British Journal of Psychiatry Special Issue*, **179**, 97–103.

Rutter, M., Moffitt, T.E. and Caspi, A. (2006) Gene-environment interplay and psychopathology: Multiple varieties but real effects. *Journal of Child Psychology and Psychiatry*, **47**, 226–61.

Rutter, M., Pickles, A., Murray, R. and Eaves, L. (2001) Testing hypotheses on specific environmental causal effects on behavior. *Psychological Bulletin*, **127**, 291–324.

Sonuga-Barke, E.J.S., Beckett, C., Kreppner, J. *et al.* (2008) Is subnutrition necessary for a poor outcome following severe and pervasive early institutional deprivation? Brain growth, cognition and mental health. *Developmental Medicine & Clinical Neurology*.

Sonuga-Barke, E.J.S. and Rubia, X. (2008) Inattentive/overactive children with histories of profound institutional deprivation compared with standard ADHD cases: A brief report. *Child Care, Health and Development*. **34**, 596–602.

Stevens, S., Sonuga-Barke, E.J.S., Asherson, P. *et al.* (2006) A consideration of the potential role of genetic factors in individual differences in response to early institutional deprivation: The case of inattention/overactivity in the English and Romanian Adoptees study. *Occasional Paper: Association of Child and Adolescent Mental Health*, **25**, 63–76.

Stevens, S., Sonuga-Barke, E.J.S., Kreppner, J. *et al.* (2008) Inattention/overactivity following early severe institutional deprivation: Presentations and associations in early adolescence. *Journal of Abnormal Child Psychology*, **36**, 385–98.

Taylor, E. and Sonuga-Barke, E. Disorders of attention and activity (2008), in *Rutter's Child and Adolescent Psychiatry*, 5th edn (eds D. Bishop, D. Pine, M. Rutter, S. Scott, J. Stevenson, E. Taylor and A. Thapar), Blackwell, Oxford pp. 521–42.

van IJzendoorn, M.H. and Juffer, F. (2006) The Emanuel Miller Memorial Lecture 2006: Adoption as intervention. Meta-analytic evidence for massive catch-up and plasticity in physical, socio-emotional, and cognitive development. *Journal of Child Psychology and Psychiatry*, **47**, 1228–45.

Wickett, J.C., Vernon, P.A. and Lee, D.H. (2000) Relationships between factors of intelligence and brain volume. *Personality and Individual Differences*, **29**, 1095–122.

Zeanah, C.H., Smyke, A.T., Koga, S.F. *et al.* (2005) Attachment in institutionalized and community children in Romania. *Child Development*, **76**, 1015–28.

8

International Adoption Comes of Age: Development of International Adoptees from a Longitudinal and Meta-Analytical Perspective*

Femmie Juffer and Marinus H. van IJzendoorn

Introduction

In 1948, at a session of the United Nations it was decided to make a study of the needs of homeless children. These children were described as "children who were orphaned or separated from their families ... and need care in foster-homes, institutions or other types of group care" (Bowlby, 1965, p. 7). The World Health Organization then offered to conduct a study on the mental health aspects of this problem. Child psychiatrist John Bowlby took up temporary appointment with the World Health Organization in January 1950, and during that year Bowlby visited the United States and several countries in Europe. In a now famous report, Bowlby (1951) concluded that children suffered from the effects of institutional care, even

* We gratefully thank the following persons who contributed to the work described in this chapter: Marian Bakermans-Kranenburg, Nicole Bimmel, Caroline Klein Poelhuis, Maartje Luijk, Linda van den Dries and Angy Wong. The longitudinal international adoption study is supported by Stichting Kind en Toekomst and Wereldkinderen. The Adoption Meta-Analysis Project (ADOPTION MAP) is supported by grants from VSBfonds, Fonds 1818, Fonds Psychische Gezondheid, and Stichting Kinderpostzegels Nederland to F.J. and M.H.vIJ in cooperation with the Adoptie Driehoek Onderzoeks Centrum (ADOC; www.adoptionresearch.nl). Femmie Juffer holds the Chair for Adoption Studies supported by Wereldkinderen, The Hague. Marinus van IJzendoorn is supported by the NWO/SPINOZA Prize of the Netherlands Organization for Scientific Research.

when their physical needs (food, clothes) were met adequately. The children were deprived of parental care and missed out opportunities to develop stable and continuous attachment relationships (Bowlby, 1982). According to Bowlby, parental deprivation leads to compromised child development and sets the stage for various mental health problems in children.

As viable alternatives for institutional care, Bowlby (1982) recommended foster care and adoption, as both provide children with 'substitute' parents. Regarding adoption, Bowlby (1965) stated that scientific studies on adoption were largely lacking: "Yet very little serious study has been given to the problems of adoption, and it is only gradually becoming recognized as a process requiring scientific understanding and professional skill (. . . .) Once again scientific studies of the subject are conspicuous by their scarcity" (p. 123). In his report for the World Health Organization, summarized in the book *Child Care and the Growth of Love*, Bowlby (1965) could only cite one study in New York on 50 adoptees (p. 131). According to Bowlby, only six cases of parents (12%) in this study were not positive about their adoption. Bowlby (1965) continued that these figures did not provide the evidence to make a final judgement and he ends his chapter on adoption with: "From these meagre facts it may be supposed that in skilled hands adoption can give a child nearly as good a chance of a happy home life as that of the child brought up in his own home" (p. 132). In the current chapter, Bowlby's statement will be the basis for our working hypothesis.

More than 50 years after Bowlby's famous report, and after about 50 years of international adoption, we can now test and extend Bowlby's statement as a working hypothesis: Is adoption an adequate option, not only *instead* of institutional care but also *after* institutional care, meaning the adoption of children who may be scarred by the consequences of early neglect and deprivation? Some 50 years after its beginning, international adoption comes of age. It's time to take stock of what international adoption means for children's development. We tested this hypothesis in two ways: First, through a longitudinal study in which we followed and observed a group of internationally adopted children growing up and coming of age. And second, by conducting a series of meta-analyses of adopted children's development and adjustment following their life after adoption.

Catch-up and Delays in Adoptees

Adoption, defined as the legal placement of abandoned, relinquished or orphaned children within an adoptive family, can be characterized as a situation with risk and protective factors. According to the theory of risk and

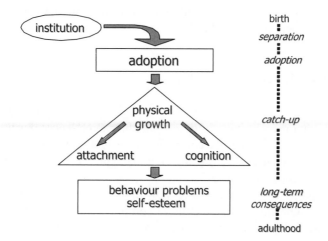

Figure 8.1 A catch-up model of adoption (from van IJzendoorn and Juffer, 2006, p. 1229).

protective factors, an accumulation of risk factors (e.g. early neglect and abuse) leads to less optimal child development, whereas protective factors (e.g. a secure attachment relationship with a supporting parent) may buffer the negative effects of the risks, resulting in resilience in children (Rutter, 1987, 1990; Werner, 1993, 2000). We are interested in the possibilities for catch-up and delays in adoptees, and in the long-term consequences of adoption. For many adoptees, their life after separation from their birth parents starts in institutional care. After the child has been adopted, sometimes to another country (international adoption), there are possibilities for catch-up (see Figure 8.1). Relevant for this chapter is the catch-up in physical growth, in attachment security, and in cognition (see also van IJzendoorn and Juffer, 2006). The long-term consequences of being adopted are also relevant: Do adopted children show behaviour problems, and do they develop adequate levels of self-esteem? Coming back to Bowlby's statement (see Introduction), the central question is: Are adopted children developing nearly as well as their non-adopted peers?

Compared with their non-adopted counterparts, adopted children may meet more adversity and risks in the beginning of their life. They may have had problems around their birth, they certainly experienced the loss of their birth family (Brodzinsky, 1990; Leon, 2002), and in many cases they were involved in group care in an institution. Institutional care is often qualified by a lack of sensitive care and a risk of malnutrition, neglect and abuse (Gunnar, Bruce and Grotevant, 2000; Miller, 2005). These experiences may have negative consequences for children's physical growth, their attachment security and their cognitive development.

The Case of Institutional Care

Before examining the catch-up and possible delays of adoptees *after* adoption, it is important to take into account their experiences during institutional care *before* adoptive placement. Focusing on the effects of institutional care on physical growth, attachment and cognitive development, can a general conclusion be drawn?

A first parameter of child development is physical growth. Based on findings in eight studies (n = 919), we computed that the longer children are in institutional care, the more delayed their height will be, finding a strong negative correlation, $r = -0.62$ (van IJzendoorn, Bakermans-Kranenburg and Juffer, 2007). In the same vein, in an ongoing study in a children's home in India, we measured children's height, weight and head circumference in the institution, and if they were adopted by Dutch families we measured them again after adoptive placement. Findings on 18 children showed that during their stay in the institution, the children were significantly delayed in height for age, weight for age and head circumference, compared with World Health Organization norms. We were able to assess these 18 children again after an average of nine months in their adoptive family and we found a significant catch-up in physical growth (Van Geest and Juffer, 2007). In another study we found substantial delays in physical growth in institution-reared children in the Ukraine compared with family-reared children in the same country (Dobrova-Krol *et al.*, 2008).

In infancy, formation of a secure attachment relationship is a major developmental milestone (Bowlby, 1982). The frightening nature of severe insensitivity and enduring unresponsiveness in institutional settings may trigger insecure disorganized attachment in children (Solomon and George, 1999), a category of insecure attachment with major psychopathological consequences (van IJzendoorn, Schuengel and Bakermans-Kranenburg, 1999). In an empirical study, Vorria *et al.* (2003) indeed found that 66% of institutionalized Greek infants at the age of 13 months demonstrated disorganized attachment, an extremely high over-representation compared with the 15% rate of disorganized attachment found in normative groups (van IJzendoorn, Schuengel and Bakermans-Kranenburg, 1999). These findings were replicated in a study by Zeanah *et al.* (2005), examining institutionalized Romanian children's attachment at the age of 24 months, which showed a remarkably similar rate of disorganized attachment (65%).

An important aspect of children's cognitive development is their intelligence. Recently we conducted a meta-analysis of intelligence (IQ) of children in institutions (van IJzendoorn, Luijk and Juffer, 2008). In this meta-analysis we collected 75 studies (including n = 3888) on IQ of children in institutions (children's homes, orphanages and other group homes). Different measures for IQ were used in these studies such as the Wechsler Scales, the non-verbal Raven Test of Progressive Matrices and other intelligence tests. Children in institutional care were compared with non-institutional children or with norms. For these 75 studies we found a large, significant effect ($d = -1.10$; see next section for an explanation of effect size d). This outcome means that on average children in institutions develop an IQ of about 84, which can be considered a delayed cognitive development (the mean IQ of normative children is 100 with a standard deviation of 15).

We conclude that institutional care appears to have a negative impact on children's physical development, attachment security and on their cognitive development. In the same vein, neurobiological studies have suggested that institutional high-stress environments may affect children's brain development and their attachment behaviour, leading to cognitive and socio-emotional delays (Chugani *et al.*, 2001; Gunnar and Kertes, 2005; Rutter, O'Connor and the English and Romanian Adoptees Study Team, 2004). It is therefore important to know whether adopted children are able to recover from these delays when they are offered the environment of a usually nurturing adoptive family (see also Johnson, 2002; Palacios and Sánchez-Sandoval, 2005; Tizard, 1977). Are they able to catch up regarding physical growth, attachment security and their cognitive development? And how do adopted children adjust in the long run with respect to behaviour problems and self-esteem? In the next part of this chapter we examine these aspects of development, each time starting with evidence from our longitudinal international adoption study and continuing with meta-analytic evidence on the same subject. Before we focus on the developmental domains of adoptees, we will introduce our longitudinal adoption study and some aspects of the meta-analytical methods.

A Longitudinal and Meta-Analytical Approach

In our longitudinal study, 160 internationally adopted children were followed from infancy to age 14 (75 boys and 85 girls). The adoptive families were randomly recruited through Dutch adoption organizations and the adopted children were not selected based on present or expected future problems (Juffer, 1993). The children were adopted from Sri Lanka (n = 86), South Korea (n = 49) and Colombia (n = 25), and placed in the adoptive families before the age of 6 months (M = 11 weeks; SD = 5.5). The adoptive parents were white, and in all families the mother was the primary caregiver. At the time of adoption the mean age of the adoptive fathers was 35 years (SD = 3.5) and the adoptive mothers 33 years (SD = 3.5). The adoptive families were predominantly from middle-class or upper middle-class backgrounds (Stams, Juffer and van IJzendoorn, 2002). The adopted children were neither selected by nor matched to the characteristics of their future adoptive parents. Placement of a particular child in an adoptive family was contingent upon the adoptive parents' place on the waiting list of an adoption organization.

In the first stage of the study, a short-term attachment-based intervention was tested, starting when the child was 6 months of age. The parents were not aware of the intervention when they entered the study. The intervention aimed at enhancing parental sensitivity, with the ultimate goal of promoting secure infant–parent attachment relationships. Parents received a 'personal book' (the name of the child was integrated in the text) with suggestions for sensitive parenting and playful interactions, and they were involved in three sessions of video feedback. The intervener showed the mother a videorecording of herself interacting with her child, and commented on selected fragments of the film. In her comments the intervener focused on sensitivity: providing security by reacting sensitively to the child's (attachment) behaviour and also offering opportunities for the child's exploration (play) behaviour. The intervention with the personal book and video feedback (in 50 of the 160 families) appeared to be effective in promoting maternal sensitive responsiveness and reducing infant disorganized attachment (see for details Juffer, Bakermans-Kranenburg and van IJzendoorn, 2005, 2008b). The intervention was not repeated in subsequent years of the study. We followed the children from the time that they were 6 months with several assessments during early childhood, again at the age of 7, and finally at the age of 14.

By examining a group of children who were internationally adopted at the earliest possible time, without serious pre-adoption adversities, we hoped to be able to estimate the effects of adoption *per se*. In case of the children from Sri Lanka: they had not been in institutional care (these infants stayed with their birth mother until the meeting with the adoptive family), and the children from Korea and Colombia came from relatively favourable children's homes, supported by Western adoption agencies.

We also studied the effects of adoption through a meta-analytical approach. In a meta-analysis, all available empirical studies on a particular subject (e.g. adopted children's attachment security) are systematically reviewed, analysed and synthesized. We included more than 270 empirical studies (n > 230 000) that examined adopted children's adjustment in our meta-analytic database (see also van IJzendoorn and Juffer, 2006). With this Meta-Analysis Project (ADOPTION MAP) we aimed to map out several important aspects of adopted children's development.

For the meta-analyses described in this chapter we report effect sizes in terms of Cohen's d: the standardized difference in means between the adopted group and their non-adopted comparisons. According to Cohen's (1988) criteria, d's up to 0.20 are considered small effects, d's of about 0.50 moderate effects, and d's of about 0.80 and higher can be seen as large effects. A positive d means an advantageous development of the adoptees compared with siblings or peers who remained behind in the institution or family of origin. A negative d indicates a delay of the adoptees compared with their current, environmental peers or normative comparison groups.

Physical Growth

Regarding the domain of physical growth, the adopted children in the longitudinal study showed a substantial catch-up in the first year after their adoption: they gained more in height and weight than their non-adopted peers (Juffer, 1993). We did not measure their height and weight in adolescence but we found that at the age of 14 years, 35 adolescents (of 153; 23%) were dissatisfied with their short stature. The findings in our longitudinal study point to catch-up of physical growth shortly after adoption, and a (small) delay in later childhood and adolescence. However, the children in the longitudinal study were adopted at a very young age. Can our findings be generalized to older-placed adoptees? A meta-analysis can address this issue.

In recent decades, physical growth of adopted children has been studied in 33 empirical studies, including more than 3500 international adoptees. A series of meta-analyses revealed that adopted children showed serious delays in height, weight and head circumference when they arrived in their adoptive families (for details, see van IJzendoorn, Bakermans-Kranenburg and Juffer, 2007). The children's mean chronological age at adoptive placement in the pertinent studies was 30 months in the case of height assessments, and 23 months for weight assessments. The combined effect sizes for the lags in height, weight and head circumference at adoptive placement were large (see Figure 8.2), $d = -2.39$ to $d = -2.60$ (15 to 27 studies; 1331

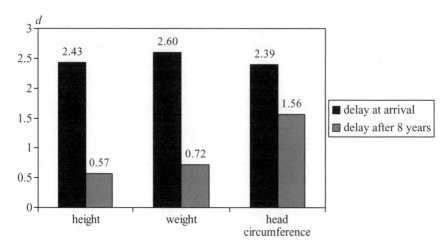

Figure 8.2 Reduction of physical growth delays for internationally adopted children after an average of eight years in the adoptive family.

to 3753 adoptees). There were no differences between children adopted before or after their first birthday.

After an average of eight years in their adoptive families, the internationally adopted children showed a remarkable catch-up in height and weight (Figure 8.2; van IJzendoorn, Bakermans-Kranenburg and Juffer, 2007). The lags in height and weight had decreased to $d = -0.57$ and $d = -0.72$, respectively (23 and 18 studies; 3437 and 3259 adoptees, respectively). For children adopted before their first birthday, the catch-up in height (but not for weight) was complete ($d = -0.03$). Remarkably, some years after adoption the combined effect size for the lag in head circumference compared with the reference population remained large, $d = -1.56$ (6 studies; 527 adoptees). Thus, the catch-up in height and weight was much more impressive than the catch-up in head circumference.

To further study this issue, four studies with longitudinal data were identified and included in a meta-analysis. The set of studies including 448 adopted children, again showed that the catch-up of head circumference across a similar average period of 19 months (mean chronological age at adoptive placement) to 49 months (mean chronological age at follow-up assessment) was significantly smaller than the catch-up of height and weight. We concluded that catch-up of head circumference, indexing possible early brain damage, was slower and remained incomplete, even several years after adoption (van IJzendoorn, Bakermans-Kranenburg and Juffer, 2007; see also Miller, 2005; Rutter, O'Connor and the English and Romanian Adoptees Study Team, 2004).

Regarding long-term effects on physical growth, our series of meta-analyses showed some evidence that, in particular, height of adoptees seemed to lag more behind the reference population from nine years of age onwards. We argued that precocious puberty may be one of the causes for this lower final height than may be expected on the basis of the rapid catch-up before puberty (van IJzendoorn, Bakermans-Kranenburg and Juffer, 2007). Based on our series of meta-analyses, we conclude that adoptees show catch-up, as well as some delays, in physical growth.

Attachment

In our longitudinal sample we assessed infant attachment security at 12 months with the Strange Situation Procedure (Ainsworth *et al.*, 1978). Our longitudinal adoption study started out as an intervention project (see above), examining the effects of a personal book and video feedback on parental sensitivity and children's attachment security (Juffer, Bakermans-Kranenburg and van IJzendoorn, 2005; Juffer *et al.*, 1997). To give a realistic picture – without the intervention effects – we used only the control group in the study (n = 80) for this analysis. We found 74% of the children demonstrated secure attachment (Juffer and Rosenboom, 1997), which is comparable with the normative percentage of 65% (van IJzendoorn and Kroonenberg, 1988). We also identified 22% of the adopted children with disorganized attachment (Figure 8.3; Juffer, Bakermans-Kranenburg and van IJzendoorn, 2005), again not significantly different from the normative percentage of disorganized behaviour 15% (van IJzendoorn, Schuengel and Bakermans-Kranenburg, 1999). We thus found no risk of insecure or disorganized attachment for this group of early-adopted international adoptees. But can these findings be generalized to adoptees placed at a later age, or to domestic adoptees?

In a series of meta-analyses, we included 17 empirical studies that examined attachment security in more than 750 adopted children using the Strange Situation Procedure (or the Attachment Q-sort; Walters and Deane, 1985). Overall, adopted children did not differ from their non-adopted counterparts with respect to attachment security (Van den Dries *et al.*, in press). Children who were adopted before their first birthday showed secure attachments as often as non-adopted children did. However, children adopted after 12 months of age showed significantly less attachment security than did non-adopted children. There was no difference between

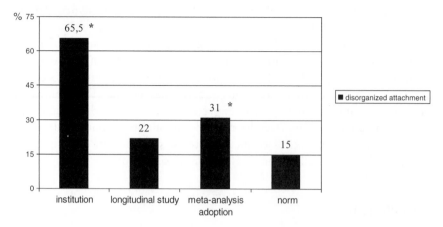

Figure 8.3 Percent of children demonstrating disorganized attachment for institutionalized children, a longitudinal study of international adoption, a meta-analysis of adoption studies and normative groups. *: Significantly different from the norm.

international and domestic adoptees. In another meta-analysis of 11 empirical adoption studies including more than 450 adoptees, we examined the risk of insecure disorganized attachment and found that more adopted children showed disorganized attachment, compared with their non-adopted counterparts (Van den Dries *et al.*, in press). No differences were found for age at placement (before or after 12 months) or between domestic and international adoption. To further examine the issue of disorganized attachment, we computed that 31% of adopted children showed disorganized attachment, significantly more than the 15% found in normative samples (see Figure 8.3). At the same time, it should be emphasized that there seems to be an impressive catch-up too, because children in institutions do show much higher rates of disorganized attachment (Vorria *et al.*, 2003 and Zeanah *et al.*, 2005: 66 and 65%, respectively). Thus, for attachment there is a considerable catch-up compared with the children in institutions, but also delays compared with current peers.

Cognitive Development

In our longitudinal study of early-adopted children we found normative IQs and school achievement in middle childhood (Stams *et al.*, 2000). Also, learning problems were in the normative range. Intelligence was measured

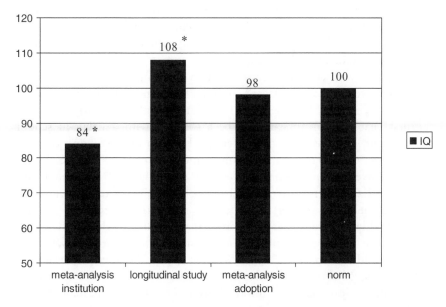

Figure 8.4 Mean IQ for adopted children in three studies: A meta-analysis of institutionalized children, a longitudinal study of international adoption, a meta-analysis of adoption studies, and in normative groups. *: Significantly different from the norm.

at the age of 7 years with the Revised Amsterdam Child Intelligence Test (RACIT; Bleichrodt *et al.*, 1987). The raw scores were transformed to standardized intelligence scores with a mean of 100, and a standard deviation of 15 (for more details, see Stams *et al.*, 2000). The mean IQ of the adopted children in the longitudinal study (M = 108; SD = 14; n = 146; range: 56–145) was significantly higher than the mean IQ in the Dutch norm group, t (145) = 6.68, p < 0.001 (see Figure 8.4). In particular, the IQ of the Korean children (M = 115) was higher than that of the norms (Juffer and van IJzendoorn, 2007b). Similar outcomes for Korean adoptees were found in a study in Belgium (Frydman and Lynn, 1989) and a study in the United States (Kim, 1995).

Did we find comparable outcomes with our meta-analytic approach for adoptees in general? Again we found massive catch-up of the adopted children compared with the children left behind in the institutions, both for IQ (d = 1.17; 6 studies; 253 children) and school achievement (d = 0.55; 3 studies; 523 children) (van IJzendoorn and Juffer, 2005; van IJzendoorn, Juffer and Klein Poelhuis, 2005). At the same time, in a large set of studies we found that adopted children's IQ was not different from their current peers ($d = -0.13$; 42 studies; 6411 children; see Figure 8.4). This was equally true for domestic and international adoptees, and for children adopted before or after their first birthday.

Compared with current peers, we found small but significant delays in school achievement ($d = -0.19$; 52 studies; 78 662 children) and in language abilities ($d = -0.09$; 14 studies; 15 418 children). Only later adoption (after the first year of life) appeared to be associated with a delay in school achievement, but there was no difference between domestic and international adoption. Furthermore, a considerable number of adoptees were found to have learning problems ($d = -0.55$; 8 studies; 3018 adopted children) (van IJzendoorn, Juffer and Klein Poelhuis, 2005). Adoptive families seek more help and support to cope with the learning problems of their child. The higher rate for learning problems may also be due to the lower threshold for adoptive parents to seek assistance for the problems of their adopted child (Miller *et al.*, 2000; Warren, 1992). Adopted children who had experienced serious pre-adoption adversity such as severe neglect in Romanian institutions, were more delayed in school achievement than children without extreme trauma.

Concluding, based on our series of meta-analyses we found massive catch-up in IQ and school achievement of adopted children compared with children in institutions. Compared with current peers we found normative IQs, small delays in school achievement (but only for children adopted after their first birthday) and language abilities, and a large risk of learning problems.

Behaviour Problems

How do adopted children adjust several years after their adoption? Behavioural adjustment may be considered one of the indices of the long-term consequences of being adopted (e.g. Bimmel *et al.*, 2003; Nickman *et al.*, 2005; Tieman, Van der Ende and Verhulst, 2005; Verhulst, Althaus and Versluis-den Bieman, 1990). In the longitudinal adoption study we assessed children's behaviour problems at the age of 7 years. The Child Behavior Check List (CBCL; Achenbach, 1991a) and Teacher's Report Form (TRF; Achenbach, 1991b) were administered to the mother and teacher of the adoptee involved. Both standardized questionnaires assess the child's externalizing behaviour problems, such as aggressive behaviour, internalizing problems, such as depressed behaviour, and total behaviour problems (a compilation of all kinds of difficulties). The CBCL and the TRF both

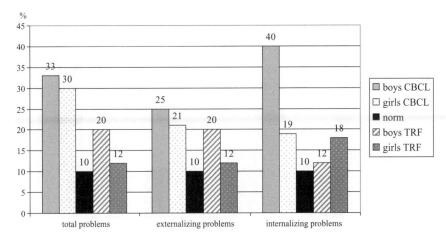

Figure 8.5 Percent of behaviour problems in the clinical range as reported on the Child Behavior Check List (CBCL) and Teacher Report Form (TRF) for the longitudinal study of international adoption and a normative group.

contain 118 problem items, which are scored on similar 3-point scales. Mothers and teachers indicated whether behavioural descriptions were (0) not at all true, (1) somewhat true or (2) very true of their child. The CBCL and TRF provide criteria to determine percentages of children falling in the clinical range. The incidence of behaviour problems in children exceeding the clinical cut-off criterion is likely to equal the incidence of behaviour problems in children who have been referred to clinical settings. We used cut-off points that were based on a sample of 2227 children between age 4 and 18, drawn from the Dutch general population (for more details, see Stams *et al.*, 2000).

Whereas in normative samples about 10% of the children fall in the clinical range, we found that according to parent report the adopted children – boys as well as girls – showed significantly elevated rates of externalizing, internalizing and total behaviour problems. According to teacher report, however, no significant risks were found (Stams *et al.*, 2000; see Figure 8.5).

Is the over-representation of behaviour problems reported by the parents of adopted children a unique outcome or a general pattern also found in other adoption studies? In a comprehensive meta-analysis including 25 281 adoptees and 80 260 non-adopted comparisons, adoptees (both within and between countries) presented more externalizing, internalizing and total behaviour problems, but effect sizes were small (*d*: −0.16 to −0.24; Juffer

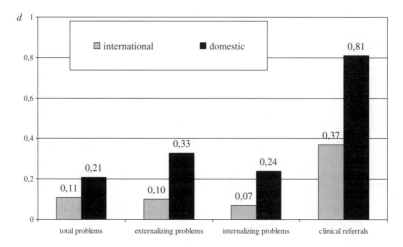

Figure 8.6 A meta-analytic comparison of international and domestic adoptees on behaviour problems and clinical referrals.

and van IJzendoorn, 2005). Adoptees (n = 5092) were over-represented in mental health services, and this effect size was large ($d = -0.72$). Among 15790 cases and 30450 controls, international adoptees showed more behaviour problems than non-adopted controls but effect sizes were small (d: -0.07 to -0.11). Remarkably, international adoptees showed fewer total, externalizing and internalizing behaviour problems than domestic adoptees did (see Figure 8.6). Also, international adoptees were less often referred to mental health services, $d = -0.37$, than domestic adoptees, $d = -0.81$ (Figure 8.6; Juffer and van IJzendoorn, 2005).

How can the significant differences between international and domestic adoptions be explained? First, it is possible that physical differences between parents and international adoptees are so obvious that the fact of the adoption was never a secret, resulting in more communication and trust in the family (Juffer and van IJzendoorn, 2005). Second, families choosing international adoption may have different parenting qualities compared with parents in domestic adoptions. No systematic information about parenting abilities was available in our meta-analytic dataset. However, in most countries parents undergo a 'screening' procedure to assess their potential fitness for parenting and receive (some) preparation. Third, genetic risks may differ between international and domestic adoption. Whereas children in international adoption are often adopted because of lack of resources and poverty (Selman, 2000), relinquishment in local adoption may (also) involve mental health problems in the birth parent, such as substance abuse or psychiatric disorders. Although reasons for relinquishment may overlap, genetic risks predisposing for mental health problems may be less prevalent in international adoptees (Juffer and van IJzendoorn, 2005).

International adoptees with severe pre-adoption adversity, for example children adopted from Romanian or Russian orphanages, showed more total problems and externalizing problems than international adoptees without evidence of extreme deprivation. For children adopted as infants (0–12 months) compared with children adopted after their first birthday, there were no differences for total behaviour problems, externalizing problems or internalizing problems. Examining children adopted before or after 24 months resulted in similar outcomes. We also found that international adoptees presented more total behaviour problems in childhood than in adolescence ($d = 0.23$ versus $d = 0.09$, respectively). Finally, children who had been with their adoptive family for more than 12 years showed fewer total and externalizing behaviour problems than children who had been in their adoptive home for less than 12 years.

To conclude, based on our series of meta-analyses, adoptees show more behaviour problems than their non-adopted peers but the effects are modest, meaning that the large majority is well adjusted. Furthermore, international adoptees present fewer behavioural difficulties than domestic adoptees. In the group of international adoptees we found no differences between children adopted as infants and children adopted at an older age. Remarkably, in international adoptees we found more behaviour problems in childhood years than in adolescence.

Self-Esteem

Another, maybe ultimate, long-term consequence of being adopted is the self-esteem of adoptees. Adopted children are hypothesized to be at risk for low self-esteem. They may suffer from the consequences of neglect, abuse and malnutrition in institutions before adoption (Gunnar, Bruce and Grotevant, 2000; Johnson, 2000; Miller, 2005). They have to cope with their adoptive status implying lack of resemblance to their adoptive parents (e.g. Brodzinsky, 1990). Additionally, transracial and international adoptees may feel less integrated in their family due to cultural differences (Lee *et al.*, 2006). Therefore, adoptees may be at risk of non-optimal self-esteem. In our longitudinal study we found, however, that in middle childhood the internationally adopted children had similar levels of self-esteem as their classmates (Stams *et al.*, 2000). The self-esteem score was derived from the

California Child Q-Set (Block and Block, 1980), completed by the child's teacher.

Can we generalize this finding to other groups of adoptees? Especially transracial and (older-placed) international adoptees may find it harder to develop positive self-esteem, because they have a different appearance and because they may be hindered by negative experiences in their early childhood years. Also, problems may be found in adolescence because adoptees often start thinking about their identity in that life stage. To address this issue we conducted a meta-analysis of adoptees' self-esteem (Juffer and van IJzendoorn, 2007a). We included generally accepted standardized self-esteem measures, such as the Harter Self-Perception Profile for Children (Harter, 1985) and the Rosenberg Self-Esteem Scale (Rosenberg, 1979), or related measures to examine self-esteem.

Surprisingly, we found no difference in self-esteem between adoptees (n = 10 977) and non-adopted comparisons (n = 33 862) across 88 studies (Juffer and van IJzendoorn, 2007a). This was equally true for international, domestic and transracial adoptees. We found no differences in self-esteem between children adopted before or after their first birthday, nor did self-esteem assessments of adoptees in childhood, adolescence or adulthood differ. Moreover, studies that used the view of the adoptees themselves (self-report measures) showed the same outcomes as studies that relied on the perception of teachers or parents (other-report measures).

Across 18 studies including 2198 adoptees no differences in self-esteem were found between transracial and same-race adoptees. In contrast, in a small set of three studies (n = 300) adoptees showed higher levels of self-esteem than non-adopted, institutionalized children (Juffer and van IJzendoorn, 2007a).

Contrary to expectations, our series of meta-analyses shows that adopted children are able to develop normative levels of self-esteem, and this appears to be the case throughout specific groups of adoptees (placed before or after their first birthday, international or domestic adoptees, transracial or same-race adoptees), across the lifespan, and independent of informant (self or other report). Our findings may be explained by adoptees' resilience to overcome early adversity, supported by the large investment of adoptive families.

Conclusions and Suggestions for Adoption Practice

More than 50 years after Bowlby's (1951) comments on adoption in his famous report for the World Health Organization, and after more than 50 years of international adoption and adoption research, we are able to answer the question: Is adoption an adequate option, not only *instead* of but also *after* institutional care? Empirical evidence from our longitudinal international adoption study and our meta-analyses show massive catch-up after adoptive placement in all developmental domains, including physical growth, attachment, cognitive development, behaviour problems and self-esteem. We conclude that adoption indeed is an adequate option *instead* of institutional care. At the same time our meta-analyses, and to a lesser degree our longitudinal adoption study, show that *after* institutional care adoptees are not able to catch up completely with their current peers (see also van IJzendoorn and Juffer, 2006). We therefore also conclude that adoptive families and adoptees need assistance and support to help them cope with the delays and difficulties of the adoptees. The catch-up and delays found in our empirical and meta-analytic evidence convincingly illustrate how adoption provides both risk and protective factors. The influences of institutional care, loss and separations on adopted children's development constitute major risk factors, whereas the influences of the adoptive family may function as protective factors.

As suggested above, our prospective, longitudinal study may show the effects of international adoption *per se*, without accumulative deprivation. The children in this study were adopted at a very young age of 11 weeks on average, and they showed normative development and functioning regarding attachment security and attachment disorganization, cognition, and self-esteem. Their physical growth, however, lagged somewhat behind and in adolescence several adoptees were dissatisfied with their short stature. The adopted children also showed more behaviour problems in middle childhood, internalizing as well as externalizing problems.

Do the findings from our longitudinal study converge with our meta-analytic evidence? As the children in our longitudinal study were adopted (long) before 12 months of age, we focused in the pertinent meta-analyses on the age factor 'placement before versus after 12 months'. The findings on physical growth indeed converge: both times we found considerable catch-up but also partial delay, particularly in adolescence. Attachment shows a mixed picture: based on the longitudinal study and the meta-analysis there is no elevated risk of insecure attachment for children adopted before their first birthday, but according to the meta-analysis there is an increased risk of disorganized attachment independent of age at placement. In the longitudinal study we did not find an elevated rate of attachment disorganization, but this may be explained by the very young age at placement in this study (11 weeks on average). We found a convergent picture for self-esteem: the longitudinal study and meta-analysis do not point to a risk of low self-esteem. For behaviour problems the findings again converge: children adopted before their first birthday show elevated rates of behaviour problems compared with non-adopted counterparts according to the longitudinal study and the meta-analyses. Our meta-analyses also show that the rate of behaviour problems may be higher in childhood than in adolescence (Juffer and van IJzendoorn, 2005). In our longitudinal study this also appeared to be the case: at the age of 14 years, the adoptees showed fewer behaviour problems than at the age of 7 years, although still significantly more than their non-adopted peers (Jaffari-Bimmel *et al.*, 2004).

Our longitudinal study is not illustrative of older-placed adopted children. The meta-analytic approach showed that children placed after their first birthday may be at risk of insecure and disorganized attachment. They do not catch up completely with respect to height growth and head circumference. They may show less optimal school achievement and present relatively many behaviour problems. At the same time, it should be emphasized that children adopted after 12 or 24 months also showed considerable gains compared with the children left behind in institutional care. For example, older-placed adoptees present significantly less attachment disorganization and appear to have higher IQs than children in institutions.

The elevated risks of attachment insecurity and school achievement in children placed after their first birthday, and the elevated risks of attachment disorganization and behaviour problems in adoptees independent of age of placement, suggest that adoptive families should be supported to prevent or reduce attachment insecurity and disorganization and to reduce behaviour problems. In previous studies we found that early attachment relationships in the adoptive family and sensitive parenting predict adopted children's later social adjustment in middle childhood and adolescence (Jaffari-Bimmel *et al.*, 2006; Stams, Juffer and van IJzendoorn, 2002). The video-feedback programme, Video-feedback Intervention to promote Positive Parenting (VIPP), that our team of Leiden University researchers developed to promote sensitive parenting and attachment security and to enhance sensitive discipline to reduce externalizing behaviour problems (VIPP-SD; Juffer, Bakermans-Kranenburg and van IJzendoorn, 2008a; Mesman *et al.*, 2008; Van Zeijl *et al.*, 2006) proved to be successful. Therefore, intervention programmes like VIPP seem to be promising avenues to help adoptive families. As an illustration, based on our experimental study on video-feedback intervention in adoptive families (Juffer, Bakermans-Kranenburg and van IJzendoorn, 2005, 2008b), adoptive parents in our country now can apply for video-feedback support after adoptive placement.

The finding that adoptees show more internalizing and externalizing behaviour problems independent of their age of placement suggests that the process or features of adoption itself may be involved in the aetiology of behaviour problems (apart from potential genetic and pre- and perinatal risks). We indeed found evidence that adopted children's problem behaviour in middle childhood (assessed by mother *and* teacher report) was predicted by the wish of the adoptees to be white and the wish that they were born in the adoptive family (Juffer, 2006; Juffer, Stams and van IJzendoorn, 2004). An explanation for these wishes 'not to look or to be different' may be found in attachment theory (Juffer, 2006). A common theme in both wishes may be that adopted children feel frustrated in their tendency to identify with their parents, which is a normative tendency in middle childhood and a logical consequence of early parent–child attachment relationships (Bowlby, 1982).

In our meta-analyses we found that adoptees are more often referred to mental health services and facilities for learning problems or special education. There are some indications that adoptive parents have a lower threshold to ask help and support for their problems (Miller *et al.*, 2000; Warren, 1992). On the other hand, adoptive parents may be more open for advice, which can be seen as a positive characteristic. For adoption practice the substantial referral rates for mental health problems and learning difficulties mean that counsellors, psychologists, and social workers may expect more requests from adoptive families and adoptees. Adoption clinicians should be prepared to adequately address the needs of adoptive families and adoptees, and our meta-analyses and longitudinal study provide some guidelines about which problems and topics can be expected and which developmental domains might need extra support.

In conclusion, adoption is a vivid illustration of both risks and protective factors. We found empirical evidence of mostly modest delays in adoptees with respect to physical growth, attachment, school achievement and behaviour problems. At the same time we documented massive catch-up and gains in all developmental domains including self-esteem, demonstrating that adoption – as an alternative for institutional care – is a very successful intervention in children's lives (van IJzendoorn and Juffer, 2006).

References

Achenbach, T.M. (1991a) *Manual for the Child Behavior Checklist/4-18 and 1991 Profiles*, University of Vermont, Department of Psychiatry, Burlington, VT.

Achenbach, T.M. (1991b) *Manual for the Teacher's Report Form and 1991 Profiles*, University of Vermont, Department of Psychiatry, Burlington, VT.

Ainsworth, M.D.S., Blehar, M.C., Waters, E. and Wall, S. (1978) *Patterns of Attachment: A Psychological Study of the Strange Situation*, Erlbaum, Hillsdale, NJ.

Bimmel, N., Juffer, F., van IJzendoorn, M.H. and Bakermans-Kranenburg, M.J. (2003) Problem behavior of internationally adopted adolescents: A review and meta-analysis. *Harvard Review of Psychiatry*, **11**, 64–77.

Bleichrodt, N., Drenth, P.J.D., Zaal, J.N. and Resing, W.C.M. (1987) *RAKIT-handleiding: Revisie Amsterdamse Kinder Intelligentie Test* [Revised Amsterdam Child Intelligence Test], Swets & Zeitlinger, Lisse.

Block, J.H. and Block, J. (1980) The role of ego-control and ego-resiliency in the organization of behavior, in *Minnesota Symposium on Child Psychology* (ed. W.A. Collins), Erlbaum, Hillsdale, NJ, pp. 39–101.

Bowlby, J. (1951) *Maternal Care and Mental Health*, World Health Organization, Geneva.

Bowlby, J. (1965) *Child Care and the Growth of Love*, 2nd edn based by permission of the World Health Organization on the report *Maternal Care and Mental Health*, Penguin Books, Harmondsworth, UK.

Bowlby, J. (1982) *Attachment and Loss, Vol. 1: Attachment*, 2nd edn, Basic Books, New York (original work published in 1969).

Brodzinsky, D.M. (1990) A stress and coping model of adoption adjustment, in *The Psychology of Adoption* (eds D.M. Brodzinsky and M.D. Schechter), Oxford University Press, Oxford, pp. 3–24.

Chugani, H.T., Behen, M.E., Muzik, O. *et al.* (2001) Local brain functional activity following early deprivation: A study of postinstitutionalized Romanian orphans. *Neuroimage*, **14**, 1290–301.

Cohen, J. (1988) *Statistical Power Analysis for the Behavioral Sciences*, 2nd edn, Academic Press, New York.

Dobrova-Krol, N., van IJzendoorn, M.H., Bakermans-Kranenburg, M.J. *et al.* (2007) Physical growth delays and stress dysregulation in stunted and non-stunted Ukrainian institution-reared children. *Infant Behavior and Development*, **31**, 539–53.

Frydman, M. and Lynn, R. (1989) The intelligence of Korean children adopted in Belgium. *Personality and Individual Differences*, **10**, 1323–5.

Gunnar, M.R., Bruce, J. and Grotevant, H.D. (2000) International adoption of institutionally reared children: Research and policy. *Development and Psychopathology*, **12**, 677–93.

Gunnar, M.R. and Kertes, D.A. (2005) Prenatal and postnatal risks to neurobiological development in internationally adopted children, in *Psychological Issues in Adoption* (eds D.M. Brodzinsky and J. Palacios), Praeger, London, pp. 47–65.

Harter, S. (1985) *Manual for the Self-Perception Profile for Children*, University of Denver, Denver, CO.

Jaffari-Bimmel, N., Juffer, F., van IJzendoorn, M.H. and Bakermans-Kranenburg, M.J. (2004) *Problem behavior of internationally adopted adolescents: Do behavior problems in middle childhood predict later maladjustment?* Poster presented at the SRA Biennial Meeting, Baltimore, MD.

Jaffari-Bimmel, N., Juffer, F., van IJzendoorn, M.H. *et al.* (2006) Social development from infancy to adolescence: Longitudinal and concurrent factors in an adoption sample. *Developmental Psychology*, **42**, 1143–53.

Johnson, D.E. (2000) Medical and developmental sequelae of early childhood institutionalization in eastern European adoptees. *Minnesota Symposia on Child Psychology*, **31**, 113–62.

Johnson, D.E. (2002) Adoption and the effect on children's development. *Early Human Development*, **68**, 39–54.

Juffer, F. (1993) *Verbonden door adoptie. Een experimenteel onderzoek naar hechting en competentie in gezinnen met een adoptiebaby* [Attached through adoption. An experimental study of attachment and competence in families with adopted babies], Academische Uitgeverij, Amersfoort, the Netherlands.

Juffer, F. (2006) Children's awareness of adoption and their problem behavior in families with 7-year-old internationally adopted children. *Adoption Quarterly*, **9** (2/3), 1–22.

Juffer, F., Bakermans-Kranenburg, M.J. and van IJzendoorn, M.H. (2005) The importance of parenting in the development of disorganized attachment: Evidence from a preventive intervention study in adoptive families. *Journal of Child Psychology and Psychiatry*, **46**, 263–74.

Juffer, F., Bakermans-Kranenburg, M.J. and van IJzendoorn, M.H. (eds) (2008a) *Promoting Positive Parenting: An Attachment-based Intervention*, Lawrence Erlbaum/Taylor and Francis, New York.

Juffer, F., Bakermans-Kranenburg, M.J. and van IJzendoorn, M.H. (2008b) Supporting adoptive families with video-feedback intervention, in *Promoting Positive Parenting: An Attachment-based Intervention* (eds F. Juffer, M.J. Bakermans-Kranenburg and M.H. van IJzendoorn), Lawrence Erlbaum/Taylor and Francis, New York, pp. 139–53.

Juffer, F., Hoksbergen, R.A.C., Riksen-Walraven, J.M.A. and Kohnstamm, G.A. (1997) Early intervention in adoptive families: Supporting maternal sensitive responsiveness, infant-mother attachment and infant competence. *Journal of Child Psychology and Psychiatry*, **38**, 1039–50.

Juffer, F. and Rosenboom, L.G. (1997) Infant-mother attachments in internationally adopted children in the Netherlands. *International Journal of Behavioral Development*, **20**, 93–107.

Juffer, F., Stams, G.J.J.M. and van IJzendoorn, M.H. (2004) Adopted children's problem behavior is significantly related to their ego resiliency, ego control, and sociometric status. *Journal of Child Psychology and Psychiatry*, **45**, 697–706.

Juffer, F. and van IJzendoorn, M.H. (2005) Behavior problems and mental health referrals of international adoptees: A meta-analysis. *JAMA – Journal of the American Medical Association*, **293**, 2501–15.

Juffer, F. and van IJzendoorn, M.H. (2007a) Adoptees do not lack self-esteem: A meta-analysis of studies on self-esteem of transracial, international and domestic adoptees. *Psychological Bulletin*, **133**, 1067–83.

Juffer, F. and van IJzendoorn, M.H. (2007b) A longitudinal study of Korean adoptees in the Netherlands: Infancy to middle childhood. In *International Korean Adoption. A Fifty-Year History of Policy and Practice* (eds K.J.S. Bergquist, M.E. Vonk, D.S. Kim and M.D. Feit), Haworth Press, Binghamton, NY, pp. 263–76.

Kim, W.J. (1995) International adoption: A case review of Korean children. *Child Psychiatry and Human Development*, **25** (3), 141–54.

Lee, R.M., Grotevant, H.D., Hellerstedt, W.L. *et al.* (2006) Cultural socialization in families with internationally adopted children. *Journal of Family Psychology*, **20**, 571–80.

Leon, I.G. (2002) Adoption losses: Naturally occurring or socially constructed? *Child Development*, **73**, 652–63.

Mesman, J., Stolk, M.N., Van Zeijl, J. *et al.* (2008) Extending VIPP to parental discipline: The early prevention of antisocial behavior, in *Promoting Positive Parenting: An Attachment-based Intervention* (eds F. Juffer, M.J. Bakermans-Kranenburg and M.H. van IJzendoorn), Lawrence Erlbaum/Taylor and Francis, New York, pp. 171–91.

Miller, B.C., Fan, X., Grotevant, H.D. *et al.* (2000) Adopted adolescents' overrepresentation in mental health counseling: Adoptees' problems or parents' lower threshold for referral? *Journal of the American Academy of Child and Adolescent Psychiatry*, **39**, 1504–11.

Miller, L.C. (2005) *The Handbook of International Adoption Medicine. A Guide for Physicians, Parents, and Providers*, Oxford University Press, Oxford.

Nickman, S.L., Rosenfeld, A.A., Fine, P. *et al.* (2005) Children in adoptive families: Overview and update. *Journal of the American Academy of Child and Adolescent Psychiatry*, **44**, 987–95.

Palacios, J. and Sánchez-Sandoval, Y. (2005) Beyond adopted/nonadopted comparisons, in *Psychological Issues in Adoption: Research and Practice* (eds D.M. Brodzinsky and J. Palacios), Praeger, Westport, CT, pp. 117–44.

Rosenberg, M. (1979) *Conceiving the Self*, Basic, New York.

Rutter, M. (1987) Psychosocial resilience and protective mechanisms. *American Journal of Orthopsychiatry*, **57**, 316–31.

Rutter, M. (1990) Psychosocial resilience and protective mechanisms, in *Risk and Protective Factors in the Development of Psychopathology* (eds J. Rolf, A.S. Masten, D. Cichetti, K.H. Nuechterlein and S. Weintraub), Cambridge University Press, Cambridge, pp. 181–214.

Rutter, M., O'Connor, T.G. and the English and Romanian Adoptees Study Team (2004) Are there biological programming effects for psychological development? Findings from a study of Romanian adoptees. *Developmental Psychology*, **40**, 81–94.

Selman, P. (2000) The demographic history of intercountry adoption, in *Intercountry Adoption: Developments Trends and Perspectives* (ed. P. Selman), British Agencies for Adoption and Fostering (BAAF), London, pp. 15–39.

Solomon, J. and George, C. (1999) The place of disorganization in attachment theory: Linking classic observations with contemporary findings, in *Attachment Disorganization* (eds J. Solomon and C. George), Guilford, New York, pp. 3–32.

Stams, G.J.J.M., Juffer, F., Rispens J. and Hoksbergen, R.A.C. (2000) The development and adjustment of 7-year old children adopted in infancy. *Journal of Child Psychology and Psychiatry*, **41**, 1025–37.

Stams, G.J.J.M., Juffer, F. and van IJzendoorn, M.H. (2002) Maternal sensitivity, infant attachment, and temperament predict adjustment in middle childhood: The case of adopted children and their biologically unrelated parents. *Developmental Psychology*, **38**, 806–21.

Tieman, W., Van der Ende, J. and Verhulst F.C. (2005) Psychiatric disorders in young adult intercountry adoptees: An epidemiological study. *American Journal of Psychiatry*, **162**, 592–8.

Tizard, B. (1977) *Adoption: A Second Chance*, The Free Press, New York.

van den Dries, L., Juffer, F., Van IJzendoorn, M.H. and Bakermans-Kranenburg, M.J. (in press) Fostering security? A meta-analysis of attachment in adopted and foster children. *Children and Youth Services Review*.

Van Geest, S. and Juffer, F. (2007) Van tehuis naar thuis: groeiachterstand en inhaalgroei na adoptie [From children's home to family: Growth delay and catch-up after adoption]. *Adoptietijdschrift*, **10** (3), 18–9.

van IJzendoorn, M.H., Bakermans-Kranenburg, M.J. and Juffer, F. (2007) Plasticity of growth in height, weight and head circumference: Meta-analytic evidence of massive catch-up after international adoption. *Journal of Developmental and Behavioral Pediatrics*, **28**, 334–43.

van IJzendoorn, M.H. and Juffer, F. (2005) Adoption is a successful natural intervention enhancing adopted children's IQ and school performance. *Current Directions in Psychological Science*, **14**, 326–30.

van IJzendoorn, M.H. and Juffer, F. (2006) Adoption as intervention: Meta-analytic evidence for massive catch-up and plasticity in physical, socio-emotional and cognitive development. The Emanuel Miller Memorial Lecture 2006. *Journal of Child Psychology and Psychiatry*, **47**, 1128–245.

van IJzendoorn, M.H., Juffer, F. and Klein Poelhuis, C.W. (2005) Adoption and cognitive development: A meta-analytic comparison of adopted and non-adopted children's IQ and school performance. *Psychological Bulletin*, **131**, 301–16.

van IJzendoorn, M.H. and Kroonenberg, P.M. (1988) Cross-cultural patterns of attachment: A meta-analysis of the strange situation. *Child Development*, **59**, 147–56.

van IJzendoorn, M.H., Luijk, M.P.C.M. and Juffer, F. (2008) IQ of children growing up in children's homes: A meta-analysis on IQ in orphanages. *Merrill Palmer Quarterly*, **54**, 341–66.

van IJzendoorn, M.H., Schuengel, C. and Bakermans-Kranenburg, M.J. (1999) Disorganized attachment in early childhood: Meta-analysis of precursors, concomitants, and sequelae. *Development and Psychopathology*, **11**, 225–49.

van Zeijl, J., Mesman, J., van IJzendoorn, M.H. *et al.* (2006) Attachment-based intervention for enhancing sensitive discipline in mothers of one- to three-year-old children at risk for externalizing behavior problems: A randomized controlled trial. *Journal of Consulting and Clinical Psychology*, **74**, 994–1005.

Verhulst, F.C., Althaus, M. and Versluis-den Bieman, H.J.M.V. (1990) Problem behavior in international adoptees: I. An epidemiological study. *Journal of the American Academy of Child and Adolescent Psychiatry*, **29**, 94–103.

Vorria, P., Papaligoura, Z., Dunn, J. *et al.* (2003) Early experiences and attachment relationships of Greek infants raised in residential group care. *Journal of Child Psychology and Psychiatry*, **44**, 1–13.

Walters, E. and Deane, K.E. (1985) Defining and assessing individual differences in attachment relationships: Q-methodology and the organization of behavior in infancy and early childhood. *Monographs of the Society for Research in Child Development*, **50**, 41–65.

Warren, S.B. (1992) Lower threshold for referral for psychiatric treatment for adopted adolescents. *Journal for Child Psychology and Psychiatry*, **31**, 512–7.

Werner, E. (1993) Risk, resilience, and recovery: Perspectives from the Kauai Longitudinal Study. *Development and Psychopathology*, **5**, 503–15.

Werner, E. (2000) *Protective factors and individual resilience, in Handbook of Early Childhood Intervention*, 2nd edn, (eds J.P. Shonkoff and S.J. Meisels), Cambridge University Press, Cambridge, pp. 115–32.

Zeanah, C.H., Smyke, A.T., Koga, S.F. *et al.* (2005) Attachment in institutionalized and community children in Romania. *Child Development*, **76**, 1015–28.

9

Attachment Representations and Adoption Outcome: On the Use of Narrative Assessments to Track the Adaptation of Previously Maltreated Children in Their New Families

Miriam Steele, Jill Hodges, Jeanne Kaniuk, Howard Steele, Kay Asquith and Saul Hillman

This chapter describes our findings from a longitudinal study of adoptive parents and their newly placed, previously maltreated children. This study offered a unique opportunity to study the process by which an adult becomes a parent to a child with a previous history of abuse and neglect which led to their permanent separation from birth parents. Similarly unique is the opportunity to observe changes in the adopted children as they form an attachment relationship with new adults who promise to provide, what these children have not yet known – that is, a permanent family constellation or 'home'. We relied primarily on attachment theory as outlined by John Bowlby (1969/1982, 1973, 1980) to formulate our expectations, and measure the contribution of each (adoptive parent and child) to our study of these new relationships. This chapter begins with a discussion of the relevance of an attachment perspective to the study of family relationships generally, and particularly those in the context of adoption. We then describe the Adult Attachment Interview (AAI) (George, Kaplan and Main, 1984–1996; Main, Hesse and Goldwyn, 2008; Main, Kaplan and Cassidy, 1985) and the Story Stem Assessment Profile (SSAP)

(Hodges *et al.*, 2002a), which we relied upon to access aspects of the study participants' representations of attachment relationships. We then present empirical findings from our investigation, the 'Attachment Representations and Adoption Outcome Study' together with a qualitative portrait of two families from the study, sharing narrative excerpts from the mothers' AAIs and their children's responses to the SSAP that was administered early in the placement and then again two years later. This provides a window on the history each (parent and child) brought to this new relationship and a sense of the early trajectory of the mother–child relationship in the new adoptive home.

Bowlby's theory has given rise to a thriving industry of attachment research reaching over 30 years that is still growing (e.g. Ainsworth *et al.*, 1978; Main, Kaplan and Cassidy, 1985; Steele and Steele, 2008a, 2008b; van IJzendoorn and Bakermans-Kranenburg, 2008). Studying adoptive families, where a school-aged child with a history of maltreatment has recently been placed, affords the exceptional possibility to understand how such new relationships are fundamentally different from, but also similar to, more typical parent–child attachment relationships. The AAI serves as our assessment measure of how an adult's attachment state of mind can help in understanding aspects of parenting the next generation at this unique 'late' starting point. The SSAP (Hodges *et al.*, 2002a) is a catalyst that permits close observation of children's verbal and non-verbal responses to emotive prompts, allowing for the assessment of the child's attachment representations. That we can observe inter-generational concordances between biologically unrelated children who are older when they come to be parented by these adults offers compelling new evidence regarding the social transmission of attachment patterns from parent to child.

An attachment framework offers much to workers in the field of adoption, foster care and general social work as it places central emphasis on major issues of common interest such as implications of trauma, loss, separation for the individual as well as a focus on family process and inter-generational transmission. Bowlby emphasized the deeply ingrained species-specific need for the young to look to a parent for protection and care. If this care is of the 'good enough' variety, the tendency will be for the individual to build an organized and secure 'internal working model' leading the child to have 'good' expectations of others and a positive model of the self as worthy of attention and affection. By contrast, when the habitual pattern of care received is neglectful and rejecting, the child may not surprisingly have impoverished expectations of others, and a weak, negative sense of self (Bowlby, 1980).

The Use of the AAI in the Study of Parent–Child Relationships

In the context of adoption, where the change in the all-encompassing environment of a new caregiving experience, the concept of internal working models, is vital to understanding both the way in which the potential prospective adopter might take on the parenting role, and the way in which the late-adopted child may respond. The Adult Attachment Interview (AAI) has demonstrated psychometrically robust features as an index of how childhood experiences are represented in the adult mind (Hesse, 1999; Main, Hesse and Goldwyn, 2008), and thus has enormous merit for use when the evaluation of parenting capacities and qualities are sought. The initial Berkeley study showed how AAI classifications from parents of 6-year-olds mapped (backward) on to the well-known infant patterns of attachment available for their children from prior assessments made of these children's attachment relationships with mother (at 12 months) and with father (at 18 months). Subsequent AAI studies showed how parents' responses map forward from pregnancy assessments to later observations of infant–mother and infant–father attachment (Steele, Steele and Fonagy, 1996), and more broadly, across cultures and diverse language groups, the association between parents' AAIs and infant–parent attachment has been replicated extensively (van IJzendoorn, 1995).

More recently, these same correlates have been observed in the context of foster care (Bick and Dozier, 2008; Dozier *et al.*, 2001), underlining how young infants respond promptly and differentially to changes in caregivers, depending on the caregiver's state of mind about attachment indexed by the AAI. The infants, most of who had suffered early neglect and some of whom had previously suffered from abusive parenting, were significantly likely to adapt quickly and well when placed with foster mothers provided these 'new' mothers had secure-autonomous states of mind, as demonstrated in response to the AAI. The Dozier *et al.* work showed that there was a 72% match between foster mother state of mind and child attachment. Only 21% of autonomous foster mothers had children with disorganized attachment, compared with 62.5% of non-autonomous foster mothers. Interestingly the child's age at placement was not associated with infant attachment, but these infants were all within the age of infancy (3–20 months of age). Based upon these findings, the authors propose that foster children organize and reorganize their attachment around the availability of their foster parents.

The AAI covers a range of issues encompassing the experience of one's childhood history and current state of mind regarding these experiences.

Several of the questions are, as Mary Main describes, aimed at "surprising the unconscious". The interview achieves this, with its unique set of 18 questions that tend to catch respondents in a situation of having to 'think on their feet'. For example, one such question that is asked early on is "What did you do when you were upset as a child?" Although adopters have normally already undergone extensive interviewing in the context of the selection process, the AAI is still likely to be experienced as unusual. The questions can be divided into those that probe the probable experiences of childhood, asking for the individual to provide five adjectives that describe their early relationship with mother and then with father, what happened when they were ill or physically hurt. Questions about separation, experience of loss and abuse are also carefully probed. Throughout the individual is asked to think back to his or her experiences of childhood and at the same time organize these thoughts and memories into a coherent enough narrative so that the interviewer and then subsequently the raters can comprehend what probably happened during their childhood. An important feature of the interview is the probing for both semantically driven descriptors as in the adjective query, followed up with requests to give specific examples or episodic accounts to back up what they say. In this way, the AAI is able to assess the individuals' representation of their childhood experience as they tell it in their own words, which contrasts distinctively from self-report questionnaire-based measures. From the narrative responses to these questions, the rater assigns a score of how loving, rejecting, neglecting the parents were experienced. The responses to the AAI questions are also rated for the individual's current state of mind with regard to attachment as manifested in the degree of idealization, derogation, or anger the individual expresses in relation to both mother and father or alternate caregiver. The central most revealing feature of the interview is the designated rating of qualities of the narrative in terms of coherence. This rating encompasses features of discourse analysis including the ideas of the psycholinguist Grice who postulated four maxims of coherent collaborative conversation: truth, economy, relation and manner. In the AAI context, the match between the overarching semantic descriptors (the adjectives provided to describe childhood relations with each parent) is contrasted with the individual's ability to provide memories or incidents as evidence for these global representations. Truth and relation are satisfied when a clear fit or match is observed between specific sensory experiences and evaluations (adjectives provided).

Two AAI questions in particular tap into the extent to which speakers can remain coherent and also show a depth of understanding about human motivation and relationships: "Why do you think your parents behaved as they did during your childhood?" and "How do you think your childhood experiences have influenced your adult personality?" These two questions are aimed at both probing for the individuals' current attachment state of mind but also for evidence that they are equipped with a capacity for reflective functioning, that is, the ability to put themselves in their parents' shoes and to think about the thoughts, feelings, intentions their parents may have had as they parented them. The concept of reflective functioning first formulated by Fonagy *et al.* (1991) has provided a further source for understanding the possible underlying mechanisms underlying inter-generational transmission of attachment patterns (see Steele and Steele, 2008a).

Interviews are scored both on rating scales capturing the quality of probable past experiences, and current state of mind regarding attachment. Finally, an overall AAI classification as *secure*-autonomous or insecure (*dismissing or preoccupied*) is assigned, and where loss or trauma is concerned a judgement is made as to whether the interview is resolved or unresolved. The majority of the low-risk, middle-class parents observed by Main, Kaplan and Cassidy (1985) were in the *secure* group, having provided coherent narratives about family life, and showing an overall valuing of attachment. These parents were those with the highest probability of having babies who responded to them in a secure manner at 1 year of age in the Ainsworth strange situation (Ainsworth *et al.*, 1978). Other parents insisted they had difficulty in recalling childhood attachment experiences, showing a tendency towards defensive idealization of the past, and leaving the listener/reader with an impression of neglect or rejection in their experience – stored implicitly but not readily available to awareness. These parents' state of mind about attachment, termed insecure-*dismissing*, has been shown to be highly likely of having babies who avoid them, move or turn away, in the reunion episodes of the strange situation (Ainsworth *et al.*, 1978; Main, Kaplan and Cassidy, 1985; Steele, Steele and Fonagy, 1996; van IJzendoorn, 1995). A third classification, which also typifies some incoherent narratives, provided in response to the AAI is that said to have a *preoccupied* state of mind about attachment. These interviews err on the side of speaking too much about negative (often overly involving) aspects of the past that intrude on present functioning such that the speaker often seems highly angry, and their infants in the strange situation also seem angry or petulant, a pattern of infant attachment termed *insecure resistant* or *ambivalent*.

Specific questions regarding the experience of loss and trauma provide additional critical information to the AAI judge as they allow for the coding of mental states concerning loss or trauma, which have been demonstrated to have a significant influence upon mental health and qualities of parenting, with unresolved mental states concerning loss or trauma being especially common in clinical populations (van IJzendoorn and Bakermans-Kranenburg, 2008). These 'unresolved' parents have been shown to be especially prone to having infants who are *disorganized/disoriented* in the Ainsworth strange situation (Main and Solomon, 1990) with one probable mechanism of influence being frightened or frightening behaviour by the caregiver towards the child (Main and Hesse, 1990; Schuengel *et al.*, 1999).

Attachment Story Completions as an Index of the Inner World (and Past Attachment Experiences) of Children and Correlates with Parental Adult Attachment Interviews

Inter-generational patterns of attachment between parents' narratives in response to the Adult Attachment Interview and their infants' responses to the Strange Situation paradigm have been demonstrated as cited above. Attachment assessments with older children have also yielded compelling concordances. This work has shown meaningful and statistically significant overlap between Adult Attachment Interviews of mothers and story completions of their genetically linked – and raised from birth – children (Gloger-Tippelt *et al.*, 2002; Steele *et al.*, 2003). When AAIs from primiparous biologically related mothers were compared with their children's narrative story completions at age 5, it was confirmed that mothers whose AAIs were judged secure-autonomous had children demonstrating similar narrative qualities (Steele *et al.*, 2003). Such children provided story completions that depicted the kind of routine events that might happen in everyday family life, and caregivers who provide help in the face of distress and who are able to set limits firmly and fairly. Where parents' attachment narratives had been previously observed to be strikingly lacking in coherence and correspondingly insecure (dismissing or preoccupied and/or unresolved), we observed elevated levels of reference to attachment figures who were inconsistent, ineffective or overly (physically) punitive in setting limits.

Studies using story stem assessment with high-risk clinical groups of children, including many with a history of maltreatment, reveal an inner world that appears highly dysregulated. This is evident in story completions that include themes depicting parents and children as frightened, chaotic, abusive, absent, helpless and violent (e.g. Murray, 2007; Robinson, 2007; Robinson *et al.*, 2000; Toth *et al.*, 1997). These studies led us to expect high levels of insecurity and disorganization in the story completions we would collect from the recently adopted children in our study, with an amelioration of these troubling themes over time as they settled into the adoptive home, with possible individual differences being linked to the adoptive parents' responses to the AAI immediately prior to the adoptive placement.

The Attachment Representations and Adoption Outcome Study[1]

Our study, conducted with Jeanne Kaniuk (Coram Family) and Jill Hodges (Great Ormond Street Hospital), represents one of the first to look at inter-generational patterns of attachment in non-biologically linked parents and children. The study highlighted the specific characteristics that each member of the parent–child dyad brings to this new and developing attachment relationship. It was longitudinal in nature, so that the changes in the child, both in terms of their behaviour and their thoughts and feelings about attachment relationships could be observed (Hodges *et al.*, 2003, 2005; Steele *et al.*, 2003). The study's design included administering the Adult Attachment Interview to both prospective adoptive parents before a child was placed with them. Then, within three months of placement, the mothers were administered the Parent Development Interview, alongside several questionnaire measures of child behaviour problems and indices of parenting stress. The children were assessed using the Story Stem Assessment Profile (Hodges *et al.*, 2002a).

The study also included a comparison group of 48 children, matched in age with the late-placed maltreated group who shared adoption as a feature of their family life but were placed in the first 12 months of their lives. Inclusion of these early-placed children allowed for comparisons between the groups where the duration and often the intensity of adversity was vastly exaggerated in the late-placed maltreated children and confirmed the importance of designing research that is both longitudinal and moves beyond comparisons of adopted versus non-adopted samples (Palacios and Sanchez-Sandoval, 2005). A further important and unique feature of the study was the inclusion of fathers, so often left out of developmental and social work research but who undoubtedly have a vital role to play in the development of their children.

Sample

The main sample comprised 58 children who were 'late placed', between the ages of 4 and 8 years, mean = 5.5 years, SD = 1.4 years. These 58

[1] We are grateful for the generous support received from the Sainsbury Family trusts (the Tedworth Charitable Trust and the Glass-House Trust).

children were adopted by 41 mothers, 25 of whom adopted one child, 15 of whom adopted sibling pairs and one who adopted a trio of siblings. Five of the adopters were single, and the rest were married. The mean age of the mothers was 40 years (SD = 6); mean age of the fathers was 43 (SD = 7).

The sample of children comprised 43% boys and 85% were Anglo-European. The children had all suffered serious adversity, including neglect, physical abuse and sexual abuse. A global tally for type and severity of abusive experiences yielded an index with a range from 2 to 5, where the mean was 3.2 (SD = 0.7), indicating that all children had experienced at least two or more of the following types of abuse (physical, sexual, severe neglect). The number of carers they had experienced ranged from 2 to 18 different placements, mean = 5.2, SD = 2.8.

The comparison group of children adopted in infancy consisted of 48 children; half of them are boys. Ten were singletons, the rest were part of a sibling group. The mean age at first assessment was 5 years, 9 months and they were followed up for two years, just like the maltreated group of children.

The core of the adult assessments included the administration of the Adult Attachment Interview to both parents before the child (or children) was placed and the administration of the Parent Development Interview to the mothers at placement, one year and two years later. The AAI was administered to 40 of the 41 adoptive mothers and 34 of the 36 adoptive fathers. By the time of the two-year follow-up, two adoptive placements had broken down, and there were AAIs available for 32 couples whose 47 children provided attachment story completions. The 74 interviews were audio-recorded and transcribed verbatim for later study by a trained, experienced and reliable rater (M. Steele). Twenty of these transcripts (from 8 fathers and 12 mothers) were independently rated (by H. Steele) and there was 100% two-way agreement (insecure versus secure) with the primary rater. High three-way (90%) and four-way (100%) agreement was also achieved. In two cases (10%) of this reliability set, where there was agreement that the interviews were Unresolved with respect to loss, conferencing was required to agree the best-fitting Insecure alternate (Dismissing or Preoccupied). A Can't Classify (CC) designation was also considered (see Hesse, 1999) for these rare cases that combined both dismissing and preoccupied themes. In the results below these two interviews are included in the Insecure category.

The core of the assessments administered to the children across three different points in time from early in the adoptive placement, and then one and two years later, was the SSAP (Hodges *et al.*, 2002a). This measure that has been demonstrated to be an effective tool for accessing younger children's internal working models of parental figures, particularly where custodial decisions need to be made, has been developed by Jill Hodges for use with children who have suffered trauma and adversity (Hodges and Steele, 2000). The SSAP is comprised of 13 story beginnings or stems which include five stories developed by Jill Hodges and eight stories which comprise the MacArthur Story Stem Battery (Bretherton, Ridgeway and Cassidy, 1990; Oppenheim, Emde and Warren, 1997). The stories cover a range of developmentally appropriate scenarios that cover many facets of children's lives. A proportion of the stories have clear attachment themes such as one from the SSAP, the 'Little Pig' story, where a little pig leaves the other pigs and goes on a long walk past all the other animals, then exclaims he is lost, can't see the other pigs and doesn't know how to get back. The interviewer then asks the child to "show me and tell me what happens next?". The themes of the MacArthur Story Stem battery depict common routines such as 'spilt juice' where a family is seated around the dinner table, the mother pours juice for everyone, child reaches across the table and spills the juice. The interviewer then asks the child to "show me and tell me what happens next?". Scoring of the transcriptions involves consideration of 30 coding categories, which have been reduced to four reliable composites: Security, Insecure Aggression, Avoidance and Disorganization (Hodges *et al.*, 2005). Coding the children's responses has been manualized and a training package is available for researchers and clinicians.

Results

Adoptive Parent Adult Attachment Interviews and Their Childrens' Story Stem Narratives

We have found interesting associations between the adoptive mothers' Adult Attachment Interview classifications and their newly placed adoptive children within three months of the placement. We compared discrete themes of children who were placed with mothers whose AAIs were independently rated as Insecure (either Dismissing or Preoccupied) as opposed to Secure, and found that that at the earliest assessment phase, the children placed with them had significantly more of each of the following themes in their attachment narratives: catastrophic fantasies, child aggresses, adult aggresses, throwing out or throwing away, bizarre or atypical content, child injured or dead, adult injured or dead, and adult actively rejects child (Steele *et al.*, 2003).

When we turned these variables into a composite, internally consistent score for 'aggression', further links to the maternal AAIs were observed (Steele *et al.*, 2003). Aggression themes as coded in the children's story stem narratives, three months into the adoptive placement, correlated significantly with a number of the 9-point interval scales indexing the speaker's 'state of mind' concerning attachment (Main, Hesse and Goldwyn, 2008; Main, Kaplan and Cassidy, 1985). For example, the children's higher aggression score correlated significantly with the AAI rating of mothers' *insistence on the inability to recall* their childhood, a linguistic form pointing to denial and repression, a signal feature of the Insecure-Dismissing interview pattern. Similarly, children's aggression themes correlated positively with mothers' *derogation* of their own fathers and correlated *negatively* with the hallmarks of an Autonomous-Secure interview pattern, that is, ratings of *coherence of mind and coherence of transcript.*

Looking at which themes were most prevalent in the children's story completions (early in the placement) if they were placed with mothers whose AAIs were classified as Unresolved with regard to Loss/Trauma, we observed a number of significant differences such that they scored highest (in comparison with those children placed with non-Unresolved mother) for the following themes: parent appearing child-like, adult aggression, throwing out or throwing away. This group of children placed with Unresolved mothers also scored significantly lower for the positive themes of realistic mastery and sibling or peer helps (Steele *et al.*, 2003).

These findings suggest that unresolved mourning in a parent may exacerbate the emotional worries of a recently adopted child with a history of maltreatment. Adoptive mothers with prior loss or trauma appear less able to help their newly placed child use an organized strategy to deal with the kinds of conflict depicted in the story stem prompts. The most compelling feature of these results was that we were able to observe differences in the children within a very short period of time since being introduced to their adoptive parents, that is, within three months (Steele *et al.*, 2003). These results confirm Mary Dozier *et al.*'s (2001) findings in a much younger group of children, but with almost equally rapid results.

In terms of what happens across the first two years of the adoptive placement, we have recently reported on these longer-term outcomes for this late-adopted group (Hodges *et al.*, 2005). Firstly, in relation to the non-maltreated comparison group of children who were the same age as the maltreated children when assessed, there were differences in their story stem assessment narratives that fit with differences in their experiences. For example, the previously maltreated group showed more avoidance and more disorganized themes as a strategy to resolve the dilemmas in the stories. At first glance, while not surprising that even after two years of placement in a more settled and hopefully 'good enough' family, the previously maltreated children did not fully 'catch up' to their non-maltreated peers. However, despite continuing to have higher levels of the more negative indicators of avoidance and disorganization in comparison with the non-maltreated group, overall they showed decreases when compared with their assessments at the time when they were first placed (Hodges *et al.*, 2005). Secondly, all the children in the previously maltreated group showed increases in their 'secure' themes. This important finding highlights the success of the adoption intervention in this high-risk sample. It also highlights an important aspect concerning the nature of mental representations. That is, it seems much easier to accommodate and take on positive representations than to 'extinguish' negative representations as indicated by the persistence of avoidance and disorganized themes. This has obvious and important implications for clinical work with both children and adults.

In order to give a more detailed picture of the material that is gleaned from using attachment narrative assessments, two cases are presented below, one in which the mother's Adult Attachment Interview was classified as autonomous-secure and one in which the mother was classified as dismissing. Following the AAI transcript excerpts are their children's story stem narrative examples from early in the placement and then at the two-year follow-up stage.

Case 1: The Jones Family   Mr and Mrs Jones were interviewed with the Adult Attachment Interview prior to having 7-year-old Samantha placed with them. The following excerpt is from Mrs Jones' AAI, where she gives an indication of the availability of her mother, especially when distressed.

INTERVIEWER: **When you were upset as a young child what would you do?**

MRS. JONES: "I went to my mother. I mean my memories of my mother rushing out of bed, when I was calling out because I was having bad dreams and coming to me, when I was distressed. I always knew she'd do something about it. Or when you were ill, you always felt very looked after. I mean if we were poorly, you got to sleep in their double bed, and you got bought special books and there'd be teddies brought to you."

Later in the same interview she is asked, "Why do you think your parents behaved as they did during your childhood?"

MRS. JONES: "Oh, it's the things in their childhood and the people that they were, and the things that had happened to them, in life. I mean we were always aware, I was always aware of the impact that the war had had on my family, my mum as well as my dad. My dad's life, being the one who was sent away from his family at such a young age. His dad had been very close to him but his mum wasn't, and his mum actually interfered in the relationship between my dad and his dad a great deal. No, she was quite a nasty woman, my grandmother, really, when I think about it. A very self centered, self absorbed woman. As we got older we were very much aware of how much that shaped my dad, and his attitude to family life. My mum's family, because it was, was also very close. Although they fell in and fell out with each other, all these people who were spread all over the world, yet they were very close."

These two short selections convey some of the important features of the Adult Attachment Interview that highlight this mother's state of mind with regard to attachment. It is interesting for example that her immediate response to the question, as if she had no need to think about what happened when she was upset as a child was, "I went to my mother". It is one of the hallmarks of attachment security, as Mary Main's (1990) comments as to what might differentiate the securely from the insecurely attached infant in the Strange Situation is that when distressed the securely attached infant has only one consideration in mind, where is mother? By contrast, the insecurely attached infant has also to consider the caregiver's state of mind. Mrs Jones also shows a capacity for reflective functioning in her response to the interview question about why she thinks her parents behaved as they did, making the link to *their* own experiences of childhood. Here she is able to discuss some of the less positive features of her own family, letting us know that she is thinking about the relationships and personalities involved as she contemplates her paternal grandmother's rather pernicious influence upon her father. This ability to speak about attachment relevant issues in a balanced, objective way, illustrating both positive and negative features further marks her narrative as autonomous-secure.

Samantha's Story Stem Conducted Within Three Months of Being Placed with the Thompson's   The following excerpt was taken from the transcribed narrative of the 'Little Pig' story which is introduced as follows:

Groups of animals are arranged in front of the child. The interviewer says:
"Once there was a little pig and it lived here with all the other pigs, big ones and little ones. And the cows lived here, the lions lived here, the crocodile lived here. And the camels lived here. One day, the little pig went for a long walk. He went a long way, past the cows, past the lions/tigers, past the crocodile, past the camels. (interviewer shows little

pig as far away as possible from all the other animals) Then he said, "Oh! Oh! I'm lost! I can't see the other pigs! I don't know how to get back!". Show me and tell me what happens next?

SAMANTHA: He gets lost, even more lost.

INTERVIEWER: **He gets lost even more lost! What does he do then?**

SAMANTHA: He searches around and he gets more lost.

INTERVIEWER: **He keeps searching around and he gets more lost! So what do you think happens to him?**

SAMANTHA: Uhm . . . I don't know.

INTERVIEWER: **Do you think he stays there? Does he ever get home?**

SAMANTHA: He tries all day.

INTERVIEWER: **He tries all day. And what happens?**

SAMANTHA: He finds them.

INTERVIEWER: **I see – but how does he find them because I thought he was lost?**

SAMANTHA: Because he saw some cows and then he just goes . . .

INTERVIEWER: **Oh I see he saw the cows and he found his way back home. So he got back home. Did the other pigs say anything to him when he got back home?**

SAMANTHA: They didn't notice

INTERVIEWER: **They didn't notice. Did they know that he'd gone for a walk?**

SAMANTHA: No.

INTERVIEWER: **They didn't know that he'd gone for a walk. I see. Okay. Is that the end of that story?**

SAMANTHA: Yeah.

This story stem narrative was coded using the Story Stem Assessment Profile (Hodges *et al.*, 2002b). In particular we can note how Samantha shows some hesitation in providing a response to the narrative as she answers with "I don't know" in relation to what happens to the lost pig. Samantha has the pig try and find his way home, which without explanation he somehow does, although interestingly and quite emphatically Samantha conveys that the other pigs (usually understood to represent adults) don't notice that the lost pig is gone. This theme of the narrative was coded as 'adult unaware', an obviously important marker for assessing the quality of attachment representations – that is, that even when lost, the adults are not available to help with the apparent distress. If we look ahead at the way Samantha responds to the exact same story stem, two years later we are able to witness elements of change.

Follow-up Visit Two Years into Placement 'Little Pig' Story

INTERVIEWER: **Can you show and tell me what happens next?**

SAMANTHA: Well he goes all the way round . . .

INTERVIEWER: **but I thought he was lost? What happens?**

SAMANTHA: But . . . cos they always have dinner together All the pigs always have dinner together

INTERVIEWER: **What is this big pig doing?**

SAMANTHA: I don't know . . . And they always had that order. That's the daddy, that's the mummy, that's the little one . . . and that could be the grandfather. And in real life, they always had 5. So he knows that one pig is missing. They had lived with each other for 5 years.

Samantha has the pigs go through the animals.

Interviewer verbalizes this and says "So they all go and look, one looks in the camels, one looks in the tigers, one looks in the lions . . . So all the pigs go to different animals to find out where the little pig is.

SAMANTHA: And then they realize he is not there. Then they find this gap in a hedge. And he goes grunt grunt. The big pig goes grunt grunt And cos its been like 25 minutes, he goes through the hedge wondering where he has gone. This little one is just crying.

INTERVIEWER: **The lost pig is crying**

SAMANTHA: And he goes on and on, trying to find his way but then he real-izes, I am lost, then he has to go all the way back. So big pig has to go all the way back and hasn't found little pig. And because he always made an instruction of staying together, he goes and looks for this one, he goes and looks for this one. So the big pigs are finding each other and then the other little pig. But they still can't find the lost pig. Then they just realized, the hedge.

Then they all see the hedge now. They heard a weeping noise (repeated by interviewer)

In the hedge, cos they know he likes to go in hedges

INTERVIEWER: **Oh, I see.**

SAMANTHA: They just find the little pig . . . a surprise . . . hello . . . they look

INTERVIEWER: **They find little piggy. Is that the end of that story?**

SAMANTHA: Yeh. And then they all go home

The narrative Samantha provides now two years later demonstrates a rather different set of themes. The narrative was coded as displaying themes of siblings/peers being helpful when all the pigs including seemingly same-age pigs are all out looking for the little pig. The narrative also conveys that Samantha's attachment representations include adults who can both acknowledge distress in the child and provide comfort and help. Finally there is a portrayal of family life, which conveys a sense of Samantha being able to conjure up in her mind examples of how families might be together, with instructions to stay together and all going home at the end of the story. The rather dramatic shift between the first assessment conducted soon after Samantha was placed and the one conducted two years later exemplifies some of the strongest findings from our study as mentioned earlier. If we compare the themes that Samantha expressed at the first assessment, we see that there was an 'initial aversion' to producing a response and then more than anything, the little pig is left lost, without the adults being aware of the distress. Two years later, the themes that emerge are indicative of attachment security, namely that the adults are aware of the distress and are able to provide the necessary help and comfort.

Case 2: The Thompson Family   Mr and Mrs Thompson were both interviewed with the Adult Attachment Interview shortly before they had 6.5-year-old Stacy placed with them. The following excerpts are from Mrs Thompson's interview:

INTERVIEWER: **When you were upset as a child what would you do?**
MRS. THOMPSON: Uhm– if I was upset, uhm, I would probably do my best to avoid letting anyone know I was upset in case it was seen as, uhm, as a sign of weakness.
INTERVIEWER: **Could you give me a specific time when you were emotionally upset?**
I think again, uhm, I, I can't remember exactly when it was, but I do remember going, uhm, getting, again as I said to you before maths wasn't my best subject and I got, I had a test at school and I got something like 70% in the test which I thought was marvelous for me, and I showed my mum and she said "Well what happened to the other 30. It's maths. You should have got 100%" uhm, so and it, you know, uhm, and what I'm trying to say is that I've, basically most of my emotional upset at that stage I think would be put down to the fact that I always felt that I was being told that I was stupid all the time and I would just have to deal with that in my own way.
Later in the same interview . . . .
INTERVIEWER: **Why do you think your parents behaved as they did during your childhood?**
MRS. THOMPSON: Why? Because that's the way that everybody else behaved. I wouldn't, I mean I, I probably my childhood but I, it, it was, the way that my parents behaved was no different from the way that other people of my age's, where I lived, parents behaved. Uhm, they, er, it was probably the way that their parents brought them up and they just passed that on uhm, so they, you know, their, their behaviour and just sort imposed that on their children.

The Adult Attachment Interview responses that Mrs Thompson provided were classified as belonging to the Insecure-Dismissing group. The features of the interview that led to this classification include the extreme reliance on a personal strength, especially in times of distress when one would expect to rely on adults to offer comfort or help. The derogating quality of the discourse was evident when describing mother, who showed such disappointment with her math grade and led the subject to feel stupid. Another one of the hallmark features of a Dismissing interview, especially where there are also indications of low reflective functioning is her response to the question, which often produces a reflective response, "why do you think your parents behaved as they did?" Here she is able to come up with relatively little, apart from suggesting that all parents of that era behaved in the same way.

The following transcript narrative was collected from Stacy when she was first assessed, early in her placement with the Thompsons.

Time 1 Assessment: 'Crying Outside' Story   This story is introduced as follows: Here is (child 1 doll) who lived in a house with her mom and dad little sister. One day they were all sitting in their house and this little girl went out and she went right around the back of the houses, we cannot see her anymore but now listen (interviewer makes crying sounds) What's happening?

STACY: Uhm . . . who's that one again?
INTERVIEWER: **This is Emma, big sister Emma. So what do you think happens?**
STACY: Uhm . . .
INTERVIEWER: **It's your story . . .**
STACY: Monster comes . . .
INTERVIEWER: **What did she do?**
STACY: Monster comes
INTERVIEWER: **Monster comes! What does the monster do?**
STACY: Eh, eats her
INTERVIEWER: **So the monster comes – and what did he do? He eats her?**
STACY: Yeah!
INTERVIEWER: **And what happens to her?**
STACY: Umm – that's it.
INTERVIEWER: **What does this monster look like?**
STACY: Umm . . . he's small and purple.
INTERVIEWER: **He's small and purple. So he eats up Emma . . .**
STACY: Yes . . .
INTERVIEWER: **And what happens to Emma after that, do you think?**

STACY: Uhm . . . uh . . . they looked for her.

INTERVIEWER: **They look for her**

STACY: Yes . . . and then Mummy cooks the dinner, and then she tells Emma to come and get her dinner, and then the monster comes in there, and eats her dinner.

INTERVIEWER: **The monster comes, they can't find Emma?**

STACY: No

INTERVIEWER: **Oh I see – so the monster comes and has her dinner. So, what happens to Emma?**

STACY: Umm . . . I don't know.

INTERVIEWER: **Any more to the story?**

STACY: No

This narrative was coded for themes, which conveyed a defensive quality so that Stacy initially tries to avoid giving a narrative (initial aversion code) and then later tries to finish it all up before even really getting started (premature foreclosure code). The child protagonist in the story is depicted as injured/dead through being eaten, which is also coded as extreme aggression magic/omnipotence and catastrophic fantasy. Alongside these codes which fall into the 'insecure' and 'disorganized' clusters, the presentation of Emma being 'looked for' and 'Mummy cooks the dinner' also show evidence of the adult providing help which is a code in the 'secure' cluster.

Let's look now at this same child's response to the same story, two years later:

INTERVIEWER: **Could you show and tell me what happens now?**

STACY: Louise gets up and follows Annette (repeated by interviewer) And then she finds her. And then they hear her crying.

INTERVIEWER: **Who hears the crying?**

STACY: Mummy and Daddy hear her crying. Then daddy follows to see what they are up to (repeated by interviewer) Then mummy hears another cry, even louder (repeated by interviewer) Then she goes out (repeated by interviewer) In front of them, is a big space bat angel dragon (repeated by interviewer) It's a black dragon and its got really big wings like an angel and the wings were black as in the shape of a bat and it came down from space (repeated by interviewer)

STACY: And it was roaring 'cos it wanted food so Louise and Annette went in.

INTERVIEWER: **And what do they do?**

STACY: And sat on the sofa . . . lay down (repeated by interviewer)

Then mum and dad came and they got up and they all helped to lift the sofa (repeated by interviewer)

And they had to feed the space angel dragon.

INTERVIEWER: **They feed the sofa to the dragon. I see.**

STACY: And he says he is still hungry so he eats dad (repeated by interviewer) with the sofa

And then he eats Louise on the sofa (repeated by interviewer)

INTERVIEWER: **What about Mum and Annette?**

STACY: Mum and Annette found a new house and they did not know they were there. They left their old settee.

INTERVIEWER: **I thought the settee got eaten**

STACY: Yeh . . . they went to get the remains of their old settee in the garden and they went to a new house and they found the sofa and 2 people lying on it faced down and they then realised, at first they didn't know who it was, then when they questioned these two people, they realised it was Dad and Louise (repeated by interviewer)

The sofa was exactly like the old one so they went back to their old house and there were just bones on the remains of the old sofa

INTERVIEWER: **So is that the end of the story?**

STACY: Yeh.

Here we see evidence in Stacy of one of the main findings from the longitudinal study where children, who were placed with a parent who was classified as insecure or unresolved with regard to experiences of loss and/or trauma, were more likely to have children who while showing an increase in positive secure themes in their story stems, continued to show a preponderance of the negative themes belonging to the insecure, disorganized and avoidant clusters. In Stacy's case while we see that there were themes of acknowledgement of distress and siblings/peers being helpful, there were also the following themes coded: adults appearing injured/dead; child appearing injured dead; adult being unaware of distress; extreme aggression; catastrophic fantasy; bizarre/atypical; magic omnipotence; back to life and moving house themes. As was discussed earlier, secure themes can flourish in these children despite their early experiences of adversity once placed in permanent adoptive homes. However, the confluence of the parent's insecure state of mind with regard to attachment with their child's existing attachment representation makes it less likely that the negative themes to be ameliorated.

Messages for Good Practice in Adoption and Social Work from an Attachment Perspective

Much can be learned from the use of person-near narrative assessments whether they be collected from adults or children. The use of narrative-based measures, as described in this chapter, merits strong consideration for inclusion among the tools used in the assessment and decision-making process for children in foster and adoptive care. While it is clearly not practical to think that all social workers, clinical psychologists, child psychotherapists, child psychiatrists and so on, should be trained in these assessment procedures, much can be gained from educating the practitioner in the narrative methods of the AAI and SSAP together with the approaches to scoring followed by researchers. Certainly, having access to a core of practitioners who are trained in these specialist assessment techniques could enhance any multidisciplinary team. In the current climate to utilize evidence-based interventions and assessments, to have the entire teams' attention trained to identify certain empirically derived features of narratives is not only possible but also desirable. When skills in the administration and coding of these assessments are not available within a clinical team, there may well be occasions when decision making is especially challenging, and outside consultation with a specialist in attachment, narrative tasks may be wisely sought to obtain an additional perspective on the problem, on the model of secondary consultations that are not infrequently sought.

An example of how an AAI-based consultation may assist social workers or clinicians working with prospective adopters or foster parents concerns the topics of loss and trauma insofar as the AAI pays close attention to language and mental states regarding these experiences. And, one of the chief clinical features of the AAI rating system (Main, Goldwyn and Hesse, 2003) is the attention given to identifying *unresolved* mental states concerning past loss or trauma, for example, physical, emotional and/or sexual abuse. Further, as the current study confirms, such lack of resolution of mourning is linked to profound difficulties in the parenting role, so it seems prudent to ascertain whether such difficulties accompany an adoptive parent, and if so, to offer relevant therapeutic support (e.g. Stovall-McClough and Cloitre, 2003). In an AAI, blatant examples of unresolved speech may occur, but a speaker is equally if not more likely to reveal unresolved mental states in subtle ways that are only discernable upon viewing and reviewing the written text. It is for this reason that one is not advised to jump to the conclusion of considering a client 'unresolved' without the benefit of information that follows from administration and reliable coding of the Adult Attachment Interview. At the same time, knowledge of the indices may go a long way to attune social workers to features that may complement their social work skills and enhance their overall assessment work.

The story stem narrative assessments are of complementary value to those working within a foster care or adoption context. The vast majority of assessments of children in care do not often involve gathering data from the child themselves but rather are gathered from those familiar with the child, for example, Child Behavior Checklist or questionnaires filled in by the child's social worker. The story stem procedure by contrast offers a unique opportunity for children to express in their own words and play aspects of their inner world, especially those most pertinent to aspects of their current state of mind with regard to attachment relationships. The range of indices that are covered by the coding of story stems in terms of representations of adults being able to provide care or acknowledge distress, or indications of a propensity to violent and aggressive fantasies or bizarre atypical themes, are obviously of interest to those working clinically with or making decisions about future care plans for children where permanence is not yet of feature of their lives.

Conclusion

The 'Attachment Representations and Adoption Outcome' study provides a rich set of longitudinal data following the developmental trajectory of more than 100 families. The findings to date indicate the value of an attachment perspective in providing a framework to understand some of the central issues that underpin these unique parent–child relationships. Central to the attachment perspective are the range of assessment techniques relying on observation of behaviour as well as interview narratives, which provide reliable and valid tools. We have found evidence for the 'adoption as intervention' phenomenon whereby all the children express more security in their story stem narratives across the two years of the study. We have also found that by knowing the attachment state of mind of the parent, one can predict qualities of the relationship from the child's perspective early in the placement, and two years later. Specifically, knowledge of the parents' attachment classification as insecure or unresolved (versus secure) was associated with their children's story stem narratives being scored significantly higher for such themes as aggression and disorganization.

The work described in this chapter underlines the potential to enhance social work practice through the dissemination of knowledge gleaned from the use of empirically driven assessments of attachment representations. While translating attachment research findings into daily social work practice is not necessarily an easy one, the benefits surely outweigh the costs.

References

Ainsworth, M., Blehar, M., Waters, E. and Wall, S. (1978) *Patterns of Attachment: A Psychological Study of the Strange Situation*, Erlbaum, Hillsdale, NJ.

Bick, J. and Dozier, M. (2008) Helping foster parents change: The role of parental state of mind, in *Clinical Applications of the Adult Attachment Interview* (eds H. Steele and M. Steele), Guilford Press, New York.

Bowlby, J. (1969/1982) *Attachment and Loss (Vol. 1): Attachment*, Basic Books, New York.

Bowlby, J. (1973) *Attachment and Loss (Vol. 2): Separation, Anxiety and Anger*, Basic Books, New York.

Bowlby, J. (1980) *Attachment and Loss (Vol. 3): Loss: Sadness and Depression*, Hogarth Press and Institute of Psycho-Analysis, London.

Bretherton, I., Ridgeway, D. and Cassidy, J. (1990) Assessing internal working models of the attachment relationship: An attachment story completion task for 3-year-olds, in *Attachment in the Preschool Years* (eds M.T. Greenberg, D. Cicchetti and E.M. Cummings), University of Chicago Press, London, pp. 273–308.

Dozier, M., Chase-Stovall, K., Albus, K. and Bates, B. (2001) Attachment for infants in foster care: The role of caregiver state of mind. *Child Development*, **72**, 1467–77.

Fonagy, P., Steele, M., Steele, H. *et al.* (1991) The capacity for understanding mental states: The reflective self in parent and child and its significance for security of attachment. *Infant Mental Health Journal*, **12**, 201–18.

George, C., Kaplan N. and Main, M. (1996) *The Adult Attachment Interview*, 3rd edn, Unpublished manuscript. University of California, Berkeley (1984, 1st edn; 1985, 2nd edn).

Gloger-Tippelt, G., Gomille, B., Kooenig, L. and Vetter, J. (2002) Attachment representations in 6-year olds: Related longitudinally to the quality of attachment in infancy and mother's attachment representations. *Attachment & Human Development*, **4**, 318–99.

Hesse, E. (1999) The adult attachment interview: Historical and current perspectives, in *Handbook of Attachment: Theory, Research and Clinical Applications* (eds J. Cassidy and P.R. Shaver), Guilford Press, New York, pp. 395–433.

Hodges, J. and Steele, M. (2000) Effects of abuse on attachment representations: Narrative assessments of abused children. *Journal of Child Psychotherapy*, **26**, 433–55.

Hodges, J., Steele, M., Hillman, S. and Henderson, K. (2002a) *Coding Manual for LP Story Stem Narrative Responses, GOS/AFC/CORAM Study*, The Anna Freud Centre, London (unpublished manuscript).

Hodges, J., Steele, M., Hillman S. and Henderson, K. (2002b) Mental representations and defences in severely maltreated children: A story stem battery and rating system for clinical assessment and research applications, in *Narrative*

Processes and the Transition from Infancy to Early Childhood (eds R. Emde, D. Wolf, C. Zahn-Waxler and D. Oppenheim), University of Chicago Press, Chicago.

Hodges, J., Steele, M., Hillman, S. *et al.* (2003) Changes in attachment representations over the first year of adoptive placement; narratives of maltreated children. *Journal of Clinical Child Psychology and Psychiatry*, 8, 351–67.

Hodges, J., Steele, M., Hillman, S. *et al.* (2005) Change and continuity in mental representations of attachment in adoption, in *Psychological Issues in Adoption: Research and Practice* (eds D. Brodzinsky and J. Palacios), Praeger, Westport, CT.

Main, M. (1990) Cross-cultural studies of attachment organization: Recent studies, changing methodologies, and the concept of conditional strategies. *Human Development*, **33**, 48–61.

Main, M., Goldwyn, R. and Hesse, E. (2003) *Adult Attachment Classification System Version 7.2*, University of California, Berkeley (unpublished manuscript).

Main, M. and Hesse, E. (1990) Parents' unresolved traumatic experiences are related to infant disorganised attachment status: Is frightened and/or frightening parental behavior the linking mechanism? in *Attachment in the Preschool Years: Theory, Research, and Intervention* (eds M.T. Greenberg, D. Cicchetti and E.M. Cummings), University of Chicago Press, Chicago, IL, pp. 161-82.

Main, M., Hesse, E. and Goldwyn, R. (2008) Studying differences in language usage in recounting attachment history: An introduction to the adult attachment interview, in *Clinical Applications of the Adult Attachment Interview* (eds H. Steele and M. Steele), Guilford Press, New York, pp. 31–67.

Main, M., Kaplan, N. and Cassidy, J. (1985) Security in infancy, childhood, and adulthood: A move to the level of representation, in *Growing Points in Attachment Theory and Research* (eds I. Bretherton and E. Waters), Monographs of the Society for Research in Child Development, 50 (1-2, no. 209) pp. 66–104.

Main, M. and Solomon, J. (1990) Procedures for identifying infants as disorganized/disoriented during the Ainsworth strange situation, in *Attachment in the Preschool Years: Theory, Research, and Intervention* (eds M. Greenberg, D. Cicchetti and E.M. Cummings), University of Chicago Press, Chicago, IL.

Murray, L. (2007) Future directions for doll play narrative research: A commentary. *Attachment & Human Development*, 9, 287–393.

Oppenheim, D., Emde, R.N. and Warren, S. (1997) Children's narrative representations of mothers: Their development and associations with child and mother adaptation. *Child Development*, **68**, 127–38.

Palacios, J. and Sanchez-Sandoval, Y. (2005) Beyond adopted/non-adopted comparisons, in *Psychological Issues in Adoption: Research and Practice* (eds D. Brodzinsky and J. Palacios), Praeger, Westport, CT.

Robinson, J.L. (2007) Story stem narratives with young children: Moving to clinical research and practice. *Attachment & Human Development*, 9, 179–85.

Robinson, J., Herot, C., Haynes, P. and Mantz-Simmons, L. (2000) Children's story stem responses: A measure of program impact on developmental risks associated with dysfunctional parenting. *Child Abuse and Neglect*, 24, 99–110.

Schuengel, C., van IJzendoorn, M., Bakermans-Kranenburg, M. and Bloom, M. (1999) Frightening, frightened and/or dissociated behaviour, unresolved loss, and infant disorganization. *Journal of Consulting and Clinical Psychology*, 67, 54–63.

Steele, M., Hodges, J., Kaniuk, J. *et al.* (2003) Attachment representations in newly adopted maltreated children and their adoptive parents: Implications for placement and support. *Journal of Child Psychotherapy*, 29, 187–205.

Steele, H. and Steele, M. (2008a) On the origins of reflective functioning, in *Mentalization: Theoretical Considerations Research Findings, and Clinical Implications* (ed. F. Busch), The Analytic Press, New York.

Steele, H. and Steele, M. (2008b) Ten clinical uses of the Adult Attachment Interview, in *Clinical Applications of the Adult Attachment Interview* (eds H. Steele and M. Steele), Guilford Press, New York, pp. 3–30.

Steele, H., Steele, M. and Fonagy, P. (1996) Associations among attachment classifications of mothers, fathers, and their infants: Evidence for a relationship-specific perspective. *Child Development*, 67, 541–55.

Steele, M., Steele, H., Woolgar, M. *et al.* (2003) Children's emotion narratives reflect their parents' dreams, in *Narrative Processes and the Transition from Infancy to Early Childhood* (eds R. Emde, D. Wolf, C. Zahn-Waxler and D. Oppenheim), University of Chicago Press, Chicago.

Stovall-McClough, K.C. and Cloitre, M. (2003) Reorganization of traumatic childhood memories following exposure therapy [Special issue: Roots of mental illness in children]. *Annals of the New York Academy of Science*, 1008, 297–9.

Toth, S.L., Cicchetti, D., MacFie, J. and Emde, R.N. (1997) Representations of self and others in the narratives of neglected, physically abused, and sexually abused preschoolers. *Developmental Psychopathology*, 9, 781–96.

van IJzendoorn, M.H. (1995) Adult attachments representations, parental responsiveness, and infant attachment: A meta-analysis on the predictive validity of the Adult Attachment Interview. *Psychological Bulletin*, 117, 387–403.

van IJzendoorn, M.H. and Bakermans-Kranenburg, M.J. (2008) The distribution of adult attachment representations in clinical groups: A meta-analytic search for patterns of attachment in 105 AAI studies, in *Clinical Applications of the Adult Attachment Interview* (eds H. Steele and M. Steele), Guilford Press, New York, pp. 69–96.

10

Adopted Adolescents: Who and What Are They Curious About?

Gretchen Miller Wrobel and Kristin Dillon

Curiosity is a natural part of every child's experience. The inquisitive mind seeks out new information and opportunities to deepen understanding of the world. Adopted children have a unique experience that captures their curiosity, being born into one family and raised in another. In the adoption literature, curiosity has often been tied to searching for one's birth parents, but curiosity is actually a much broader topic that underpins several important adoption issues. Development of an adoptive identity, seeking out information about one's birth family, and communication in the family about adoption are all processes fuelled by children's curiosity about their birth history. Contact in adoption has been identified as one way to satisfy children's curiosity about their birth histories by providing information about, or relationships with, birth family members. Yet, the nature of children to be curious will always move them from one answered question to the next unanswered one. Curiosity is a component of human nature that can be modified or deepened rather than eliminated by connectedness or increased information.

Theoretical Conceptions of Curiosity

Curiosity is a part of our human existence that provides motivation to engage the world through an individual's desire to answer complex questions of daily life and engage in new, complex physical and social experiences (Reio *et al.*, 2006). Thus, curiosity is important for understanding an individual's approach to the world. The benefits of curiosity are many. Kashdan, Rose and Fincham (2004) found curiosity to be associated with "positive evaluations of the self, world and future; beliefs that goals are attainable and obstacles can be circumvented; general tendencies to enjoy effortful cognitive endeavors and be open to new experiences and ideas" (p. 301). Curiosity can also predict positive relationship outcomes (Kashdan and Roberts, 2004).

Psychologists conceptualize curiosity as motivational energy that fuels exploratory activity (Kashdan, Rose and Fincham, 2004; Loewenstein, 1994). Berlyne's (1954) classic work emphasizes the motivational capability of curiosity to promote exploration through the identification of two types of curiosity: perceptual curiosity and epistemic curiosity. Perceptual curiosity is defined as "the curiosity which leads to increased perception of stimuli" (p. 180) and is evoked by sensory stimulation and reduced by continued exposure to the stimuli. Epistemic curiosity is a "drive to know" (p. 187) that motivates one to gain a depth of knowledge. Additionally, Berlyne (1960, p. 80) posited two types of exploratory behavior: diversive behavior motivated by boredom, which seeks out new experience and challenge, and specific exploratory behavior, which is motivated by curiosity with the direct goal of acquiring new and particular information.

Litman and Spielberger's (2003) work to specifically assess epistemic curiosity found empirical support for the dimensions identified by Berlyne. Loewenstein (1994) offers another conceptualization of specific epistemic curiosity, which is less focused on the status of curiosity as a drive to be reduced. Loewenstein's integrative approach theorizes an "information gap" account of curiosity as "an intrinsically motivated desire for specific information" (p. 87). An information gap is defined by the difference between "what one knows and what one wants to know" (Loewenstein, 1994, p. 87) and is related to an individual's subjective information reference point. When the reference point of what information is desirable becomes higher than actual knowledge, a state of dissatisfaction arises. The resulting dissatisfaction or deprivation is identified by Loewenstein as curiosity. Loewenstein suggests that the information reference point helps us understand why similar knowledge may "evoke or not evoke curiosity depending on the level of one's reference point" (p. 87) in relation to actual knowledge. Thus, curiosity is a response to an individual's focus on a specific gap in information and motivates the individual to obtain the missing information, so the gap can be filled and dissatisfaction eliminated. Yet, Loewenstein identifies two situations when curiosity may not be the response to an information gap. First, the information gap must be salient. An individual must care about the missing information enough that it induces a feeling of dissatisfaction. Second, individuals will not focus on an information gap when there is only a small likelihood that curiosity will be satisfied. The evaluation that sought-after information may be unobtainable makes the curiosity that arises from dissatisfaction too difficult to engage.

Loewenstein (1994) highlights two fundamental implications of the information gap perspective. First, curiosity is positively related to information that can fill the gap. One will be more curious about specific pieces of information missing in the information gap. Second, curiosity is positively related to actual knowledge. As information is gained, an individual will focus more on what is unknown than known so that the information gap can be closed. The qualitative shift of focus from known to unknown information is the beginning of curiosity. Loewenstein acknowledges that the relationship between information and curiosity is not simple, because, as knowledge is gained, an individual's reference point can shift and influence the perceived information gap. For example, one may seek out and obtain a sufficient, but not exhaustive, amount of information to fill the gap and reduce dissatisfaction.

Specific curiosity with its desire for particular information to fill an information gap flows from epistemic curiosity and is the emphasis of discussion in this chapter. This chapter will address the role that specific curiosity, in this case information about one's adoption, plays in the development of adopted adolescents.

Adoption and Curiosity

The formation of an adoptive family establishes an adoption kinship network (AKN) that includes the child, the child's extended family by birth and the child's extended family by adoption (Grotevant and McRoy, 1998; Grotevant *et al.*, 2007). While parental rights and responsibilities reside with the adoptive parents, there are still ties to the birth family, even if birth and adoptive family members are not known to each other. From the perspective of the adoptive family, the role of the birth family in the adoptive kinship network can vary from that of genetic parent only to a vital member of extended family. Whatever role the birth family possesses in the adoption kinship network, the birth family is still an entity that needs to be integrated into the adopted person's representation of family. This integration requires specific knowledge and positions the birth family as a focus of the child's curiosity.

Adoption Information Gap and Curiosity

Adoption curiosity results from the information gap associated with an individual's knowledge about his or her adoption and is, therefore, a normative experience for adopted individuals. Yet, there is wide variation among adopted persons in the content of curiosity, the intensity of curiosity, and action taken to seek out additional information. Loewenstein's (1994) concept of a specific information reference point can help explain the variation of adoption curiosity expressed among adopted persons. When the information known about one's adoption matches the desired information, there is no adoption information gap and, thus, little curiosity. Changes to an adoption information reference point, making it higher than known information, thus, creating a state of adoption curiosity, can result from many factors. Developmentally, as the child grows older and begins the process of identity formation, integrating an adoptive identity may require more information than is available. An adopted person can encounter another adopted person (perhaps a sibling) who has more adoption information then he or she possesses. This comparative difference may increase a desire for more information. As adopted adolescents approach the age at which their birth mother gave birth to them, they may reflect upon what that experience may have been like and want to know specifically what their birth mother was feeling, and how she made her decision to place her child for adoption. Adoptive parents may reveal information unknown to their child about his or her adoption, and the child may want to know even more. Each adopted individual has a unique adoption information reference point, and a unique set of known adoption information, that can result in an adoption information gap.

One significant influence on the amount of adoption information possessed by the adopted person is the amount of contact in his or her adoption. Current adoption practice includes many different types of contact between birth and adoptive families. International infant adoptions typically have no exchange of information beyond placement records. Older children adopted from foster care because of difficult birth family histories may have continued contact, sometimes supervised, with birth parents or birth relatives. Infant placements in the United States most often include arrangements for exchange of information with the child's birth family or face-to-face contact among adoptive kinship network members. For example, there may be contact with one's birth mother and little known about the birth father. In other adoption kinship networks, the birth grandmother may maintain contact. Varying contact arrangements allow for wide ranging amount and type of known adoption-related information. Yet, it is important to remember that all adopted individuals, regardless of the amount of known adoption information, can be curious about their adoptions. It is not the amount, or even type, of unknown information that fuels curiosity, but the unique adoption information gap perceived by the individual.

Information seeking undertaken to fill the information gap also varies among adopted persons. The content of the desired information can influence the action taken. Someone who wants to know his birth parent's name may seek out original birth records. Another who wants to meet her birth parents will conduct a search with reunion as the goal. An adopted person who has meetings with his birth mother and wonders about his birth father's role in the adoption decision can ask his birth mother if he feels comfortable posing the question.

Some may not seek out additional information to fill the adoptive information gap. If the desired information seems unobtainable, it can be frustrating to focus on what is unknown (Loewenstein, 1994). This can be one of several reasons some adopted persons feel they are 'not ready' to seek out additional information. There are unique barriers to information associated with adoption. In the United States, adoption records are not uniformly available. In some cases, they are permanently closed; in others, the age of majority must be obtained in order to access them. The records themselves also vary in content and detail, reflecting adoption practice at the time of placement. Also, adopted persons may not want to seek out additional information, especially if it includes contacting a birth mother, if they feel that action may hurt the feelings of their adoptive parents, or that the birth mother may not desire contact. The removal of barriers to information may allow the adopted person to focus on the information gap leading to action. For example, information seeking can increase closer to the age of majority when records may become accessible (Wrobel, Grotevant and McRoy, 2004). It is important to remember that some adopted persons may not perceive an information gap and, as such, do not seek out additional information.

Information Seeking and Adoption

Despite curiosity as a normative experience, and its acknowledged impact upon development, scant attention has been paid to the concept of curiosity in adoption literature. Most often, the desire for adopted individuals (usually adults) to seek out and meet their birth mother is used as a single indicator of curiosity (Howe and Feast, 2001; Müller, Gibbs and Ariely, 2002; Sobol and Cardiff, 1983). Yet, the expression of curiosity differs across developmental stages (Brodzinsky and Pinderhughes, 2002). In the pre-school period, telling of the adoption story leads to curiosity and questions about birth, reproduction, and the child's origins. Curiosity about origins continues to grow during the school years, with a more intense reflection upon the birth parents' identities and their motivations for placement. At adolescence, curiosity can express itself as preoccupation with adoption with possible subsequent desire to search for birth parents. Kohler, Grotevant and McRoy (2002) conceptualized preoccupation with adoption, defined as intense reflective thinking about one's adoption, and implementation of a birth parent search as broad markers of curiosity. With regard to preoccupation, over 80% of their sample reported thinking about their adoption at least once a month, with 27% reporting weekly frequency. Girls were more preoccupied with their adoptions than boys, regardless of how much contact they may have had with birth family members. As adults, women tend to think more about their birth mothers than birth fathers (Müller, Gibbs and Ariely, 2002) and more women search with the goal of reunion than men (Müller and Perry, 2001). Lastly, adulthood brings legal status to access adoption records in many circumstances. The ability to access records legally removes a barrier to information and may provide impetus for adults to take action to satisfy their curiosity.

Given the various expressions of curiosity in childhood, adolescence and adulthood, curiosity must be conceptualized as more than a birth parent search. It is important that all aspects of curiosity receive attention. Curiosity in the adoptive context includes thinking about one's adoption; the content of that reflection or wondering that can determine an adoption information gap; and actions taken to gain desired, yet missing, information. The ability to reflect about what one wants to know, to determine the process for obtaining that information, and, finally, to integrate the information can influence adoptive identity and one's representation of family. Work regarding preoccupation with adoption (Kohler, Grotevant and McRoy, 2002) has taken a first step towards understanding the intensity of reflection reported by adopted adolescents. The field's emphasis on understanding the search and reunion process has brought about great gains in our understanding of a particular segment of the adoptive population: those without direct contact with their birth parents who desire that type of interaction (Howe and Feast, 2001; Müller, Gibbs and Ariely, 2002; Sobol and Cardiff, 1983).

Yet, the many forms of adoption, including openness in adoption, international adoption and older child adoption, require a broadening of the traditional view of searching. It is no longer the case that searching for an unknown birth parent has to be the lone behaviour observed to fill an information gap. Adoption with varying levels of contact provides differing types and amounts of available information to adopted persons, creating qualitatively different knowledge gaps. The adopted person with no information about her birth family may wonder what her birth mother looks like and what interests she has. Someone adopted internationally may like to know what role cultural influences played in his birth mother's placement decision. A child adopted at an older age from the foster care system may wonder how her birth family is currently doing. Each individual is seeking different information. Thus, searching as a means to satisfy curiosity should be re-conceptualized into the more inclusive construct of information seeking.

Information seeking is defined as the gathering of information previously unknown to the adopted person about his or her adoption and birth family. This definition accounts for the diversity of information sought by adopted individuals experiencing varying adoption forms. Little attention has been paid to the content of knowledge gaps that provide motivation to seek out unknown adoption information. The specific information desired, and the amount of information sought, can influence what action is taken to find that information. For example, the desire for information does not always lead to a search for a birth parent. Desired information may be found in previously unseen adoption or birth records. Younger children can often have their questions answered by information available to their adoptive parents. What one is curious about matters and motivates the adopted person to seek out that information, but it is important to remember there are multiple sources with the potential for filling in the information gap.

Adoptive Family Communication as It Promotes Child Questioning and Information Seeking

The adoptive kinship network is an important context in which children and adolescents experience curiosity about their adoptions. The type of contact within the kinship network, be it confidential with no information exchange between birth and adoptive families, agency facilitation of non-identifying information exchange, or direct contact between birth and adoptive families, influences the type of information available (and thus unavailable), and the means by which information can be gathered. For example, individuals with direct contact have the opportunity to ask their birth mother what they want to know, and others can have the adoption agency mediate their request, while those with no contact may seek out the birth mother or other birth relative in order to request the information. Understanding the dynamics of adoptive family contact with the birth family on the development of the adopted person is an emphasis of the Minnesota/Texas Adoption Research Project (MTARP). (For a full description of this project see Grotevant and McRoy, 1998; Grotevant, Perry and McRoy, 2005; and Chapter 13).

One focus of this longitudinal study has been adopted children's curiosity expressed about their birth relatives. During the first wave of MTARP, adopted children across all openness arrangements reported being curious about their birth parents. Even those children with direct contact with their birth parents reported curiosity about them. Contact with a birth parent does not eliminate a child's natural curiosity (Wrobel *et al.*, 1996). Parents' responses to the adopted child's curiosity are an important influence on their subsequent information-seeking behaviour. One way parents can respond is through their active communication about adoption with the child. An example of how children can engage parents in active communication about adoption through their questioning is found with children from Wave 1 of MTARP who had mediated contact (Wrobel *et al.*, 1998). All children in this group expressed curiosity about their birth parents, with ratings ranging from 'curious' to 'very curious'. Breadth of curiosity was determined by counting the number of adoption-related issues about which adoptive parents were questioned. Children who had more information about their birth parents were more curious and asked significantly more questions than those children with less birth parent information. Interestingly, all adoptive mothers reported actively responding to their child about adoption-related issues regardless of how many questions they were asked. A different pattern was observed for adoptive fathers. Fathers reported more active communication about adoption-related issues when their children reported being more curious and had more birth family information.

Adoption communication is an ongoing process that should consider the unique specific curiosity of each individual child. The Family Adoption Communication (FAC) model (Wrobel *et al.*, 2003) provides a useful framework for conceptualizing this ongoing communication process. FAC has three phases of communication that are child focused: Phase I – telling the adoption story, Phase II – responding to adopted child questioning, and Phase III – adopted child independent information gathering. It is the adopted child's reflection about adoption and behaviour directed towards gaining unknown information that is the impetus for movement through the model. Early phases of the model can be re-entered as the adopted person desires. Someone who has begun an independent search for birth parents may also ask his or her parents again for information. Information the child has access to will shape his or her specific curiosity, which, in turn, will shape the content and intensity of the child's questioning. This questioning directly influences family communication about adoption. In Phase II, when children ask their adoptive parents about their adoption, a decision must be made by adoptive parents about how they will respond and support their child's specific curiosity. Four options are available: (i) share all available information; (ii) share all available information while seeking more; (iii) share some information and withhold other information; and (iv) withhold all available information. Each of these responses is influenced by the amount of information the parents possess, the child's developmental level and intensity of curiosity, and what information the parents are willing to share or desire to withhold.

Positive communication about adoption, in general and in response to a child's specific curiosity, can support active information seeking. At adolescence (Wave 2), the information-seeking intentions of those who had no direct contact with their birth parents were examined to determine who chooses to seek out new information and who does not (Wrobel, Grotevant and McRoy, 2004). Adoptive family functioning and adolescent psychological adjustment in relation to information seeking were also explored. Adopted adolescents who had no desire to seek out new information, or who desired new information, or who had already taken action to obtain new information, were included in the study. In general, families were described by parents and adolescents as functioning well. Those most likely to search were older adolescents who were the least satisfied with the amount of contact and were the most preoccupied with their adoption. Information seeking was not fuelled by poor psychological adjustment or negative family relationships, but occurred in the context of positive family functioning.

Direction of Current Research

The current chapter moves our emphasis on adoptive curiosity to include the content of the information gap. Previous MTARP studies have focused on the adopted adolescent's reflection or preoccupation with adoption and the intent or action taken to seek out new information. Loewenstein (1994) suggests desiring unknown information creates a dissatisfaction that fuels curiosity and motivates one into action. It is then essential that the content of specific adoptive curiosity be described. Such a description will allow adoption professionals and adoptive families to become aware of what specific adoptive curiosity motivates an individual's information seeking.

In the analyses presented in this chapter, we will describe: all aspects of adoptive curiosity; the content of that specific curiosity; the intensity of curiosity regarding birth mothers and birth fathers; and how curiosity is related to information seeking. A unique aspect of the present analyses is a differentiation of adoptive curiosity to include desire for information about both birth mothers and birth fathers. A focus on each specific birth parent recognizes the unique place each birth parent has in the adoption kinship network.

Our specific research questions are:

1. How curious are adopted adolescents with different openness arrangements about their birth mothers and birth fathers?
2. What are adopted adolescents curious about in relation to their birth parents?
3. How does birth parent curiosity influence information seeking?

Method

Participants and Procedure

Participants in this study were 153 adopted adolescents (74 male, 79 female, mean age = 15.7 years) who were interviewed during the first two waves of the Minnesota/Texas Adoption Research Project (Grotevant and McRoy, 1998). Interviews were conducted during a home visit at which time other measures and interviews were administered to the adoptive parents.

Measures

Adopted Child Interview (Wave 1) and Adopted Adolescent Interview (Wave 2)   The interviews were designed to elicit open discussion of the participant's experiences, feelings, knowledge, and attitudes about his or her adoption, adoptive family situation and birth parents. The interviews covered general adoption issues as well as questions specific to the level of openness in the participant's adoption. The adolescent interview also addressed issues of adoptive identity and openness topics, including the breadth and diversity of persons within the adoptive kinship network with whom the adolescent has or has not had contact, changes in openness arrangements, withholding of information or contact by parents, and frequency of contact.

Coding

Coding schemes were developed to assess several issues of interest (described below), and ratings for variables were based on the entire transcript of the interview. Coders made judgements that required moderate to high levels of inference. Two coders coded each interview independently; disagreements were resolved through discussion.

Variables

Adoptive Family Degree of Openness   Openness arrangements were coded into four groups using adolescent and parent reports of contact:

1. No contact – No contact with birth relatives has occurred, and no information has been shared beyond six months post-placement (n = 42).
2. Stopped contact – Information sharing and contact between birth and adoptive families had stopped by the time of study participation at Wave 2 (n = 33).
3. Contact without meetings – Adopted adolescent and/or family has had mediated or direct contact with birth mother, but adolescent has not had face-to-face contact; contact has not stopped (n = 26).
4. Contact with meetings – Adopted adolescent has had face-to-face contact with birth mother at least once; contact has not stopped (n = 52).

Adopted Child Curiosity about Birth Mother and Birth Father
Wave 1   The child's overall level of curiosity about birth parents was coded from the adopted child interview. The children's responses were judged to fall into one of four broad categories. Curiosity about birth parents was rated (inter-rater reliability = 0.82) on a scale where 1 represented 'not curious because avoidant or fearful of birth parents' (n = 3), 2 'not curious' (n = 11), 3 'curious' (n = 79), and 4 'very curious' (n = 34). A group of children was also coded as 'other' (n = 24). Although this scale did not finely discriminate between children's levels of curiosity, it accurately represented the range of curiosity expressed. For the current study, the children who were coded as avoidant, or fearful, or other were omitted from the analyses. The remaining scores were then recoded so that 0 represented 'not curious', 1 represented 'curious', and 2 represented 'very curious'.

Wave 2   Children's curiosity about each birth parent was again derived from the adopted child's interview. For this wave of data collection, curiosity about birth mothers and curiosity about birth fathers were coded separately. Curiosity was coded on a 4-point scale; 0 represented no evidence of curiosity (birth mother, n = 14; birth father, n = 19), 1 represented low curiosity (birth mother, n = 12; birth father, n = 18), 2 represented moderate curiosity (birth mother, n = 52; birth father, n = 63), and 3 represented strong curiosity (birth mother, n = 44; birth father, n = 43). There were three participants missing curiosity data about their birth mothers. Seven participants were missing curiosity data about their birth fathers. A distinct category of 'not curious because already know everything' (birth mother, n = 27; birth father, n = 3) was also coded. For this study, those in this category were examined separately and excluded from the larger models.

Information Seeking   Information seeking is defined as the gathering of information previously unknown to the adopted person about his or her birth mother or birth family. A text analysis of the adolescent interview was conducted to determine the breadth of the continuum and points of demarcation of adolescents' information-seeking intentions or behaviour. The initial information seeking focus was on the 93 adolescents in our sample who did not have direct, ongoing contact with their birth mother. Future text analyses will be broadened to include those adolescents with direct, ongoing contact. The 93 adolescents were assigned to one of four information-seeking groups. Adolescents in group 1 (will not seek information/weak interest) made strong statements that they would not seek information in the future or stated that they most likely would not seek information but left open a small possibility that they might (n = 22). Group 2 (weak interest) was comprised of the adolescents who indicated a slight interest in eventually seeking information in the future (n = 10). The adolescents in group 3 (moderate interest) said they might seek information about or search for birth relatives in the future and included those adolescents who left open the possibility of information seeking but expressed ambivalence about it (n = 23). Adolescents in group 4 (strong interest) said they would definitely seek information or search for birth parents in the future (n = 26). Group 5 (actively seeking information) adolescents had already embarked on an active search for information or contact with birth relatives (n = 12).

Curiosity over Time   To determine the movement of curiosity about birth parents across two waves of data, a curiosity difference score was calculated by subtracting the three-level Wave 1 curiosity scale from the four-level Wave 2 curiosity scale. In Wave 1, the curiosity score was based on the birth parents together, while the Wave 2 curiosity score was separated into curiosity about birth mother and curiosity about birth father. For the curiosity change over time, the curiosity about birth mother score from Wave 2 was used because, within the interviews, participants tend to discuss birth mothers more, and we believed that the Wave 1 scores were primarily geared towards curiosity about the birth mother. The resulting difference scores ranged from −2 to +3, with negative scores indicating a greater curiosity at Wave 1 than at Wave 2. A positive score indicates a greater curiosity at Wave 2 than at Wave 1. A score of zero represents either no curiosity at either time point or a slightly lower level of curiosity at Wave 2. Only one adolescent received a −2, eight received a −1, 13 received a 0, 42 received a 1, 20 received a 2, and one received a 3. The remaining adolescents were excluded because, in Wave 2, they knew everything about their birth parents (n = 28), in Wave 1 they were coded as avoidant or fearful, uncodeable or other (n = 34), or they did not participate in Wave 1 despite participating in Wave 2 (n = 6).

Content Categories of Birth Parent Curiosity Two questions from the adopted adolescent interview were used to determine adolescent curiosity regarding their birth parents: "What more would you like to know about your birth parents or their families?" and "If you could ask your birth parents three questions, what would they be?" From the verbatim transcripts, a team of researchers developed a list of 36 content categories. The categories were not mutually exclusive, and some responses were coded under multiple categories. For instance, the response "Does my birth father have other kids?" was coded as both "specific questions for the birth father" and "other children he/she is parenting". For each category, a participant was given 1 point if they explicitly stated that they had questions in that topic area in either of the questions listed above. All of the adopted adolescents endorsed at least one area of curiosity.

Results

How Curious Are Adopted Adolescents about Their Birth Parents?

Overall, the adopted adolescents in this study displayed a great deal of curiosity about their birth parents. Over 78% (n = 96) of the adolescents who were given a curiosity score (122 for birth mothers and 143 for birth fathers) indicated that they had a moderate or strong curiosity about their birth mothers, and 74% (n = 106) indicated a moderate or strong curiosity about their birth fathers. Only 12% (n = 14) showed no evidence of any curiosity about their birth mothers, and only 13% (n = 19) showed no curiosity about their birth fathers.

To test differences in curiosity about the birth mother versus curiosity about the birth father, a repeated-measures ANOVA was used. In this case, the same measure about two different, but highly dependent, variables (curiosity about birth mother and curiosity about birth father) was treated as the repeated measure. The role of gender was of particular interest in this model because of the greater rate of preoccupation with adoption and searching with a reunion goal among females. As such, gender was treated as the independent variable, while age and openness were covariates. When examining the between-subject effects of gender, age and openness on curiosity levels, none of these variables significantly predicted curiosity on its own.

Overall, when examining the within-subject effects, there was not a significant difference in how curious the adolescents were about their birth mothers versus their birth fathers. Curiosity level was moderate to moderately high for both birth parents (birth mother $M = 2.03$; birth father $M = 1.91$). However, there was a significant relationship between curiosity about birth mothers versus curiosity about birth fathers across age (F $(1, 113) = 4.637$, $p = 0.033$). Older adolescents were more curious about birth mothers. There is a highly significant interaction between curiosity about birth mothers versus curiosity about birth fathers across gender (F $(1, 113) = 7.295$, $p = 0.008$). When considering the means for each group (male curiosity about birth mother, male curiosity about birth father, female curiosity about birth mother and female curiosity about birth father), it is clear that males have similar levels of curiosity about both their birth mothers ($M = 1.778$, $SD = 0.945$) and birth fathers ($M = 1.796$, $SD = 0.959$), whereas females have more curiosity about their birth mothers ($M = 2.222$, $SD = 0.958$) than their birth fathers ($M = 1.921$, $SD = 1.052$) (see Figure 10.1).

Adolescents who were not curious about their birth mother fell into one of two categories: not curious because they stated they 'knew everything' ($n = 27$), indicating their knowledge gap had been satisfied, and 'not curious', indicating that there was no identified knowledge gap to satisfy. Of those who 'knew everything' about their birth mother, 89% ($n = 24$) indicated curiosity about their birth father. Only 2 of the 27 (7.4%) adopted adolescents who reported knowing everything about the birth mother also said they knew everything about their birth father, and 1 (3.7%) showed no curiosity about the birth father, despite not knowing everything.

In comparison, the 'not curious' ($n = 14$) group who demonstrated no curiosity about their birth mothers and no information gap showed little curiosity about their birth fathers. All but one of these participants expressed no curiosity about their birth fathers. The remaining adolescent demonstrated moderate birth father curiosity.

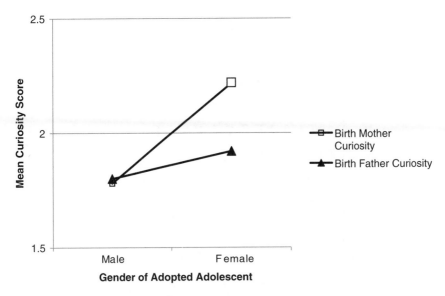

Figure 10.1 Birth parent curiosity by gender.

What Are Adopted Adolescents Curious about in Relation to Their Birth Parents?

The five most commonly identified items of specific adoption information about which the adolescents were curious were: (i) reasons for placing the child (n = 62); (ii) other children he/she is parenting (n = 58); (iii) appearance/physical characteristics (n = 52); (iv) how they are doing (n = 51); and (v) personalities/behaviours (n = 43).

Table 10.1 indicates significant differences in the top five items of specific adoption information across gender, age and openness arrangements. Only one significant gender difference appeared. Between male and female respondents, the category of 'appearance/physical characteristics' showed significance (χ^2 (1, n = 153) = 5.184, p = 0.023). More females expressed curiosity about appearance (43.42%), than males (25.00%). Between age groupings, none of the top five categories showed significant differences. There were three categories that showed significant differences between openness groups. For the categories of 'reasons for placing child' and 'appearance/physical characteristics', significantly fewer adolescents who had the highest level of adoptive openness exhibited curiosity than those in the other openness groups (χ^2 (3, n = 153) = 16.47, p = 0.001 and χ^2 (3, n = 153) = 8.184, p = 0.033, respectively). With regard to curiosity about

Table 10.1 Adopted adolescents' curiosities across gender, age and openness groups.

Top ranked items of curiosity		Gender			Age				Openness level				
		Male	Female	x^2 (df = 1)	11–13	14–16	17–21	x^2 (df = 2)	1	2	3	4	x^2 (df = 3)
1 Reasons for placing child	n	31	31	0.018	14	29	19	1.495	24	16	12	10	16.47[b]
	%	41	40		34	41	48		59	49	46	19	
2 Other children he/she is parenting	n	26	32	0.765	16	25	17	0.594	17	19	7	15	8.764[a]
	%	35	42		39	35	43		42	58	27	29	
3 Appearance/physical characteristics	n	19	33	5.184[a]	13	26	13	0.349	17	13	12	10	8.184[a]
	%	25	43		32	37	33		42	39	46	19	
4 How they are doing	n	23	28	0.553	13	25	13	0.170	15	12	9	15	0.846
	%	31	36		32	35	33		37	36	35	29	
5 Personalities/ behaviours	n	22	21	0.080	15	19	9	2.134	9	10	8	16	1.114
	%	29	27		37	27	23		22	30	31	31	

[a] p < 0.05.
[b] p < 0.001.

other children the birth parents were parenting, the two groups with the greatest openness demonstrated less curiosity than the two groups with the lowest levels of openness (χ^2 (1, n = 153) = 8.764, p = 0.033).

How Does Birth Parent Curiosity Influence Information Seeking?

There was a great deal of variation across levels of search intentions. Over one-third of the participants with an information seeking score (34.5%, n = 33) had no or weak interest in information seeking, while a quarter (24.7%, n = 23) had a moderate interest, 28% (n = 26) had a strong interest, and 13% (n = 12) had already started seeking out additional information. In order to understand how curiosity across time can influence information seeking, a curiosity change score was created for the 85 adopted adolescents with Wave 1 and Wave 2 interviews to determine how their level of curiosity about their birth parents had changed from the first wave of data collection to the second. This change score was heavily skewed towards participants showing greater curiosity in Wave 2 than in Wave 1 (74.1%, n = 63), although 15.3% (n = 13) showed no change in curiosity, and 10.6% (n = 9) were more curious in Wave 1 than in Wave 2. By using these two variables that necessitated omitting a large number of participants for reasons such as having had contact with birth parents, not participating in Wave 1, or not showing curiosity because they already know everything about their birth parents, only 72 of the 153 interviewed participants were included in this model. To determine if those excluded varied significantly from those included, we tested ages and genders between the included and excluded groups. There was no significant difference in genders between the two groups (χ^2 (1, n = 72) = 0.606, p = 0.514). However, there was a practically insignificant (essentially a one year mid-adolescence age difference) but statistically significant difference in ages between the groups (t (150) = -3.641, p < 0.01), with those included being older (M = 16.16, SD = 1.89) than those not included (M = 14.98, SD = 2.12).

An exploratory regression analysis was used to test the influence of age, gender, openness and curiosity change on information-seeking intention at adolescence (see Tables 10.2 and 10.3 for summary statistics). The analysis revealed that the model significantly predicted adolescent search intentions (F (4,67) = 13.957, p < 0.001, adj R^2 = 0.422). Both openness (β = 0.468, p < 0.001) and curiosity change (β = 0.521, p < 0.000) significantly predicted adolescent information-seeking intention and accounted for 14.2 and 25.8%, respectively, of the variance in information seeking. Both increased openness and curiosity were associated with greater information seeking.

Table 10.2 Regression analysis summary for variables predicting information seeking.

	B (SE)	β	Sig.	R² change
Age	0.050 (0.072)	0.065	0.490	0.054
Gender	0.018 (0.272)	0.006	0.948	
Openness	0.727 (0.147)	0.468	0.000	0.142[a]
Curiosity change	0.818 (0.145)	0.521	0.000	0.257[b]

[a] $p < 0.001$.
[b] $p < 0.0001$.

Table 10.3 Intercorrelations, means and standard deviations for regression variables.

Variable	M	SD	1	2	3	4
Age	15.67	2.07	—	−0.116	0.011	0.192
Openness level	2.49	1.19		—	−0.132	0.399[a]
Curiosity change	0.88	0.96			—	0.468[a]
Information seeking	2.96	1.37				—

[a] $p < 0.001$.

Age and gender did not independently, significantly predict information-seeking intention.

Conclusion

Curiosity is an important part of adoptive life and can provide energy to engage in information seeking. In our sample, the vast majority of adolescents expressed moderate to high amounts of curiosity about one or both birth parents, and over half had moderate to strong intentions to seek out unknown information. Given the prevalence of birth parent curiosity, it would be wrong to assume that all adopted persons are curious about their birth parents. Not all adopted persons exhibit the same amount of curiosity about their adoptions, and some display none at all. Thirteen adolescents in our study expressed no curiosity about either birth parent. Yet, all adopted individuals engage in some level of psychological work related to curiosity (Wrobel, Grotevant and McRoy, 2004), if only to consider whether they would like to know more adoption-related information than they possess. For those who would like to know more, each curious individual seeks different specific adoption information. How, then, given all the possible individual specific manifestations, should curiosity be studied in order to examine its impact on development?

Adoption Curiosity Pathway Model (ACP)

Although each person's experience with adoption curiosity is unique, there is similarity across adopted persons in the process used to define adoptive curiosity and make a decision to seek out specific adoption information. The Adoption Curiosity Pathway Model (ACP) is a process model that addresses the expression of adoption curiosity. The ACP draws on the work of Loewenstein (1994), applying his conceptualization of curiosity, including an information gap, to the unique context of adoption and desire for adoption-specific information. There are three steps on the pathway: identifying an information gap, determining intensity of curiosity and seeking out desired adoption information.

Identifying an Adoption Information Gap

Loewenstein (1994) describes curiosity as the motivation to fill a perceived information gap, and the ACP begins with an adopted person's reflection regarding the amount of known adoption information. It is our belief that each adopted individual engages in such reflection with two possible outcomes: the adopted person would either like more specific adoption information or would not. Preoccupation with adoption (Kohler, Grotevant and McRoy, 2002) is one indicator of the level of reflection about adoption-related issues. When known specific adoption information matches the desired information, there is no perceived information gap and no curiosity. The wide variation in adoption type provides differing ways for information needs to be met. For example, a person in an adoption with face-to-face birth parent contact may feel that the relationship has provided all one needs to know. Another person may be satisfied with the content of placement records. At the same time, another adopted person with similar information may express curiosity. Despite what is known, there is desire for more information. It is important to remember that the amount of known information does not determine the information gap. Rather, the driving factor is the perception of unknown information relative to expectations of desired information. At that point, the adopted person considers the specific content of their curiosity, thus, defining his or her perceived adoption information gap.

Specific Items of Curiosity Identified by the Adolescents   Our study is the first to systematically identify the content of specific adoption information contained in the adoption information gap. The identification of common themes among the group of adolescents is important for understanding decisions made further along the ACP to seek out that information. The most common item of curiosity identified by the adolescents was 'why was I placed for adoption'. This question is subjective, and, in many cases, can only be answered by the birth parent; the inability to access this complete information from another source may account for the large number of responses identifying this piece of specific information. Interestingly, during the interview, each of the adolescents was able to recite their adoption narrative, given to them as they were growing up, which offered an explanation of why they were adopted. The adolescents' strong interest in this question indicates that they did not feel that their adoption story was adequate to satisfy their current curiosity. Developmentally, information that may have been adequate at an earlier age may not be at older ages. The reference point of what is desired information shifts, and an information gap forms where there may not have been one before.

For the top five specific items of curiosity reported by the entire adolescent group, males and females differed in prevalence of endorsement on only one item, 'appearance/physical characteristics', with females identifying this item as the subject of their curiosity more frequently than males. Females may be more attuned to body image as well as more inclined to wonder about what they may look like as they enter adulthood. Furthermore, as females move from childhood into adulthood, they may be more sensitive to growing differences in how they look compared with their adoptive parents. The different openness groups offered the greatest statistical variation on the same top five curiosity items. Adolescents without birth parent meetings overwhelmingly identified as content of their curiosity the item 'reasons for placing child' responses in comparison with those with contact with meetings. Those individuals in the contact with meetings group are likely to be able to ask a birth parent the reason for being placed, which would satisfy this particular curiosity. This explanation could also account for the significantly fewer adolescents in the contact with meetings group who were curious about the appearance of their birth parents. Those with contact including meetings would have seen their birth parent, thus satisfying their curiosity about appearance. Some questions, such as other children the birth parents are parenting, would not require a face-to-face meeting to be answered and would explain why both contact groups (those with and without meetings) did not identify curiosity about biological siblings as often as those without contact.

Content and Intensity of Curiosity   Absence of curiosity about one aspect of adoption does preclude there being an information gap about another aspect of adoption. Our findings related to those adolescents who 'knew everything' about their birth mothers, yet were curious about their birth fathers, highlight the diversity of content that can be the object of curiosity. Especially interesting was the difference between the 'knew everything' group and 'no curiosity' group. Many in the 'knew everything' group, who at present had their curiosity satisfied about their birth mothers, were very interested in knowing more about their birth fathers. Success in filling the information gap about one's birth mother could prompt one to engage in the same process for one's birth father. Birth mother information is often more available than information about the birth father, accounting for the continued information gap about birth fathers after satisfying the birth mother information gap. In the 'no curiosity' group, all but one of the adolescents who did not identify an information gap about their birth mothers were also not curious about their birth fathers. For this group, there was no information seeking. They had not moved onto the Adoption Curiosity Pathway.

Salience of the desired information for the adopted person is also an important consideration for how curious an adopted person may be about his or her adoption information gap. Developmentally, different issues present themselves as central to the adopted child's growth (Brodzinsky and Pinderhughes, 2002) and can reset the reference point (Loewenstein, 1994) used to identify an information gap. The information in the adoption narrative may be all a young child desires to know, but as he or she grows into adolescence, the desire for a more detailed or differentiated narrative may arise. If desired information is important to the adopted person, there will be greater desire to obtain that information.

Intensity of Curiosity

Once an adoption information gap is identified, the next step on the ACP is to evaluate the intensity of curiosity (desire to obtain the unknown information). The intensity of desire to fill the information gap can be influenced by several factors, including age, gender and openness arrangement. The present study examined these influences on general curiosity about the birth mother and birth father.

Differences in Curiosity about Birth Mother and Birth Father   Differences in curiosity about the birth mother and birth father were not observed across age, gender and openness arrangements. All groups equally expressed moderate to moderately strong curiosity about both birth mother and birth father. Yet, when looking within subjects, differences did emerge. Age became an important influence; older adolescents were more curious about birth mothers than about birth fathers, whereas younger adolescents had similar curiosity about both. As the adopted adolescent grows older, the desire to fill the information gap concerning the birth mother intensifies. One or both of the following reasons can contribute to the increased desire for birth mother information by the older adolescents: known information about the birth mother increases, and information about the birth mothers appears to be more available. Sometimes, adoptive parents will withhold information from their child until 'the time is right to share', usually identified as when their child is older. Revelation of previously unknown information to the adolescent could trigger the desire for more answers. Having some information can motivate the seeking out of more information as the adolescent focuses on what is left to fill their identified specific adoption information gap. Most often, adoptive parents have the greatest amount of information about birth mothers to share, thus increasing the focus on the birth mother over the birth father. Secondly, information about the birth father may seem unobtainable, and the desire for that information could produce more frustration than the adolescent wants to engage, especially if unknown information about the birth mother seems more obtainable.

Gender also influenced a difference in curiosity about the birth mother and birth father. Males expressed similar curiosity about both birth parents, whereas females expressed greater curiosity about birth mothers, mirroring the experience of adult adopted women (Müller, Gibbs and Ariely, 2002; Müller and Perry, 2001). Both males and females at this age are developing their identity as a man or woman. One marker of adulthood for women is the ability to bear children. Many of the adolescents in this study were of similar age to their birth mothers when they gave birth. For adolescent girls, their own capacity for pregnancy may lead to reflection about what it might have been like for their birth mother to give birth to them. Their own birth story is held by the birth mother, and the adolescent girl may desire that information to fill her gap in knowledge. Reproductive issues may not be as salient for males at this age, and, as such, males may not yet have encountered a specific adoption information gap that, despite being curious about both birth parents, produces a greater desire for information about one birth parent over the other.

Adoption Information Seeking

Once curiosity for specific adoption information is identified, steps can be taken to obtain the desired information. At this point on the ACP, barriers or facilitators can influence movement to information seeking.

Adoption Barriers and Facilitators to Information Seeking Adoption brings unique experiences and contexts that can influence the acquisition of unknown specific adoption information. In accordance with Loewenstein (1994), the perceived ease in which information may be obtained also influences the intensity of desire for specific adoption information and subsequent action taken to obtain that information. Encountering barriers to information can either enhance or diminish intensity of curiosity depending upon the individual's response to the barrier. Frustration because one cannot access desired adoption information is inherent when encountering a barrier. That frustration may energize one adopted person to find ways to overcome the barrier, whereas, to another, the barrier seems insurmountable, and that person may pull back from seeking out desired information, thus avoiding frustration. Barriers and facilitators to information seeking can be found in the contexts of legal requirements, adoption agency practice and policy, cultural expectations, and the adoption kinship network.

Legal access to adoption records and original birth records varies from state to state in the United States, and from country to country in other parts of the world. Records vary in the detail that is available and the age at which they might become accessible. Limited to no access to records is a barrier to information seeking. In places where these barriers do not exist, acquiring knowledge from birth records can provide specific adoption information that may, in turn, facilitate the acquisition of further adoption knowledge. For example, finding out the name of one's birth mother from an original birth certificate can increase the chances of finding her for a face-to-face meeting.

Agency practice and policy also influence the information-seeking process. Barriers to information seeking can include agency policy against direct birth family contact. Even if agency policy has become more supportive of contact over the years, a restrictive policy at time of placement could have discouraged members of the adoption kinship network from leaving information that could facilitate contact. Agency fees charged for information-seeking assistance are a barrier for some adopted persons to engage in information seeking, especially those who have a goal of reunion. When fees are a barrier, information seeking must often wait until adequate monetary resources are available. This can be very frustrating to those adopted persons with high curiosity and few discretionary funds. Agency policy supportive of information sharing and positive adoption agency relationships are facilitators of information seeking. When the adoption agency has been supportive in the past, there is an expectation that this type of relationship will continue. If the agency is determined to be important for information seeking, either as a source of information or as a facilitator of the process, a supportive agency can be seen as a helpful resource to the adopted person.

Cultural influences can be both domestic and international. Societal attitudes towards adoption and its practice that are accepting of the complexity of the adoption kinship network, and the communication possibilities that exist, are supportive of information sharing. When adoption is seen as a solution to a moral indiscretion (see Chapter 11), or as a way to meet the need of birth parents to place a child and an adoptive family to parent a child (with express purpose of moving on with their individual lives after placement), those attitudes can be a barrier to information seeking. In international adoptions, language barriers, different cultural attitudes towards adoption, differing adoption practice, and record keeping can make information seeking difficult. Domestic adoption in countries other than the United States will present ACP barriers and facilitators that look very different from those cases in North America and Europe.

Barriers and facilitators to information seeking also reside within the adoption kinship network (AKN). The openness arrangement implemented influences the exchange of information. The amount of information exchanged can range from basic medical information given at placement, to non-identifying, agency-mediated exchange, to face-to-face meetings among members of the AKN. Attitudes of individual members can also influence information seeking. All members of the AKN can hold attitudes that could be considered barriers and facilitators of information seeking. Birth parents may leave messages with agencies indicating whether or not they would welcome future contact, or they may leave no information at all, making their wishes unknown. As identified by the Family Adoption Communication model (Wrobel *et al.*, 2003), adoptive parents have the choice, when asked for more information by their child, to either withhold all or part of what they have, share all they have, or seek out unknown information themselves. The course of action taken can convey an attitude of support, reluctance, indifference or dislike for information sharing. The issue of withholding information brings complexity to information seeking as only certain adoption-specific information may be seen as acceptable to seek out.

The adopted persons may find positive attitudes held by their adoptive parents influencing their own attitude towards information seeking. Not wanting to hurt the feelings of adoptive parents who are less than enthusiastic about information seeking may cause the adopted persons to avoid seeking out the information they desire. Another concern that may inhibit information seeking is fear that the birth parent will not want to be found or share the desired information. The latter may especially apply when there is birth mother contact, and curiosity is focused on the birth father, with whom the birth mother had a difficult relationship. At times, the adopted persons may feel they are 'not ready' to find out the desired information without being able to specify why, other than the time is not right. Often, a point in the future is identified as the time for information seeking.

Moving Ahead with Information Seeking Contexts of legal requirements, adoption agency practice and policy, cultural expectations, and the adoption kinship network, in conjunction with content and intensity of curiosity, influence information seeking. Obviously, when barriers to information seeking exist, the process becomes more difficult and can lead to a postponement of obtaining desired, specific adoption information. Interestingly, our results showed that 28% of our adolescent group who did not have contact with birth parents indicated that they had a strong intention to seek out information in the future. Reaching the age of majority that could open adoption records directly to them could be one factor for the identification of future information seeking. We also found that intensity of curiosity increased across time, with 74% of our sample, for whom we could calculate a curiosity change score indicating greater intensity of curiosity at adolescence. Our exploratory regression analyses support the idea that both context and intensity of curiosity influence information seeking. Both greater curiosity at adolescence and greater openness predicted more information seeking. Information seeking is a culmination of the motivations and experiences encountered along the ACP.

Future Research and the ACP

Future research of the ACP should be focused at each step of the pathway. Preoccupation with adoption is an important factor to explore further as an expression of reflection about adoption knowledge. Content of the adoptive information gap should be related to preoccupation with adoption. Are specific types of adoption information related differentially to preoccupation with adoption? Describing the strength of impact of various barriers and facilitators on information seeking should also be explored. The ACP provides a framework to answer these and other questions about the role adoption curiosity plays in the life of the adopted individual.

Implications for Practice

Practitioners will find the ACP useful for describing the curiosity of adopted individuals. The ability to conceptualize curiosity as both motivation and content of information seeking will help adoption professionals to assist adopted persons in that endeavour by helping them to identify what they would like to know, ways in which to anticipate and remove barriers, and use facilitators to enhance information seeking. Yet, the ACP explains why some adopted persons do not desire more information. All adopted persons reflect upon their adoption knowledge, and a lack of adoption-related curiosity should be viewed as satisfaction with their current knowledge, not a denial of curiosity.

Curiosity is dynamic and changes over time. As such, our results provide motivation for adoption professionals to keep information available by placing updates in files and facilitating contact as desired by members of the adoption kinship network. Following are some suggestions to assist practitioners in supporting the curiosity of adopted persons:

1. Particular attention should be paid to the content of curiosity. For our sample, reasons why the child was placed topped the list of curiosity content. It appears that the childhood adoption narrative no longer satisfies the adopted adolescent. At this stage of development, adolescents have more questions about their placement stories, and the answers may be difficult to convey. Adoption practitioners should be ready to support birth parents in telling a more sophisticated placement story at adolescence. This can be done through the writing of a 'later in adolescence' letter to be shared during the teenage years, or, for those adopted adolescents with birth parent meetings, the birth mother can follow the lead of the adopted child by answering specific questions.

2. Many adopted adolescents who express curiosity are curious about both birth parents. It is important to consider ways of making information about birth fathers more accessible. Adoption practitioners can help birth mothers sort through a difficult relationship with the adopted child's birth father to determine appropriate information to be placed in the file or to share directly with the adopted child. If possible, birth

fathers can also be supported to share information they feel is important with the child.

3. For adoption arrangements with contact, it is important for there to be flexibility in the amount and type of information shared. Adoption practitioners can help members of both adoptive and birth families be aware of changing information needs as the adopted child grows, supporting them in their approaches to meet those needs.

4. It is important for practitioners, as well as birth and adoptive family members, to remember that once an information gap is identified, and curiosity about the missing content is satisfied, curiosity may move to new content. The dynamic nature of curiosity should not be forgotten. One should be ready for the possibility that, as one question is answered, another may be asked.

The ACP provides guidance to researchers and practitioners alike for understanding the implications of curiosity for the adopted person. The model encompasses curiosity as both content and motivator, and recognizes the diversity of individual experience. Curiosity is an important factor in the experience of adopted persons and as such requires thoughtful reflection about its impact. Hopefully, this model will move our understanding of adoption curiosity forward and facilitate continued dialogue between adoption researchers and adoption practitioners.

References

Berlyne, D.E. (1954) A theory of human curiosity. *British Journal of Psychology*, 45, 180–90.

Berlyne, D.E. (1960) *Conflict, Arousal, and Curiosity*, McGraw-Hill, New York.

Brodzinsky, D.M. and Pinderhughes, E. (2002) Parenting and child development in adoptive families, in *Handbook of Parenting* (ed. M. Bornstein), Erlbaum, Hillsdale, NJ, pp. 279–311.

Grotevant, H.D. and McRoy, R. (1998) *Openness in Adoption: Connecting Families of Birth and Adoption*, Sage, Newbury Park, CA.

Grotevant, H.D., Perry, Y. and McRoy, R. (2005) Openness in adoption: Outcomes for adolescents within their adoptive kinship networks, in *Psychological Issues in Adoption: Research and Practice* (eds D. Brodzinsky and J. Palacios), Praeger, Westport, CT, pp. 167–86.

Grotevant, H.D., Wrobel, G.M., VonKorff, L. *et al.* (2007) Many faces of openness in adoption: Perspectives of adopted adolescents and their parents. *Adoption Quarterly*, 10 (3/4), 79–101.

Howe, D. and Feast, J. (2001) The long-term outcomes of reunions between adult adopted people and their birthmother. *British Journal of Social Work*, **31**, 351–68.

Kashdan, T.B. and Roberts, J.E. (2004) Train and state curiosity in the genesis of intimacy: Differentiation from related constructs. *Journal of Social and Clinical Psychology*, **23**, 792–816.

Kashdan, T.B., Rose, P. and Fincham, F.D. (2004) Curiosity and exploration: Facilitating positive subjective experiences and personal growth opportunities. *Journal of Personality Assessment*, **82**, 291–305.

Kohler, J.K., Grotevant, H.D. and McRoy, R. (2002) Adopted adolescents' preoccupation with adoption: The impact on adoptive family relationships. *Journal of Marriage and Family*, **64**, 93–104.

Litman, J.A. and Spielberger, C.D. (2003) Measuring episteic curiosity and its diversive and specific components. *Journal of Personality Assessment*, **80** (1), 75–86.

Loewenstein, G. (1994) The psychology of curiosity: A review and reinterpretation. *Psychological Bulletin*, **116** (1), 75–98.

Müller, U., Gibbs, P. and Ariely, S. (2002) Predictors of psychological functioning and adoption experience in adults searching for their birthparents. *Adoption Quarterly*, **5** (3), 25–53.

Müller, U. and Perry, B. (2001) Adopted persons' search for and contact with their birthparents I: Who searches and why? *Adoption Quarterly*, **4**, 5–37.

Reio, T.J., Petrosko, J.M., Wiswelll, A.K. and Thongsukmag, J. (2006) The measurement and conceptualization of curiosity. *The Journal of Genetic Psychology*, **167**, 117–35.

Sobol, M.D. and Cardiff, J. (1983) A socio-psychological investigation of adult adoptees' search for birth parents. *Family Relations*, **32**, 477–83.

Wrobel, G.M., Ayers-Lopez, S., Grotevant, H.D. *et al.* (1996) Openness in adoption and the level of child participation. *Child Development*, **67**, 2358–74.

Wrobel, G.M., Grotevant, H.D. and McRoy, R. (2004) Adolescent search for birthparents: Who moves forward? *Journal of Adolescent Research*, **19** (1), 132–51.

Wrobel, G.M., Kohler, J.K., Grotevant, H.D. and McRoy, R. (1998) Factors related to patterns of information exchange between adoptive parents and children in mediated adoptions. *Journal of Applied Developmental Psychology*, **19**, 641–57.

Wrobel, G.M., Kohler, J.K., Grotevant, H.D. and McRoy, R. (2003) The Family Adoption Communication (FAC) Model: Identifying pathways of adoption-related communication. *Adoption Quarterly*, **7** (2), 53–84.

11

Emerging Voices – Reflections on Adoption from the Birth Mother's Perspective

Ruth Kelly

Intercountry and domestic adoption is currently seen as a child welfare solution that provides permanent family care for children who cannot be cared for by their birth families. The positive impact that adoption can make on children's life chances has been well documented. The consequences of adoption for birth families of adopted children have been less often been studied. However, if adoption is conceived of as creating an extended kinship network, then the experience and welfare of birth family members ought to be an important consideration. This is true no matter whether an adoption is open or closed, because in all types of adoption, the birth family remains psychologically relevant to the child and indeed to the adopted adult.

Within the last decade, a small but growing body of knowledge has emerged about mothers who parted with a child for adoption. This research, which has been undertaken with mothers who relinquished in a number of different circumstances, has begun to give us some insight into how these mothers have fared in the aftermath of relinquishment. One group of mothers who have been studied are those who relinquished their child during times and in places where the stigma attached to out-of-wedlock pregnancy was intense (Dorow, 1999; Fessler, 2006; Howe, Sawbridge and Hinings, 1992; Inglis, 1984; Kelly, 2005) and for whom therefore, even if they had wished to be a parent, there was no option or choice available. Whereas many of these studies have been small in nature, the information gathered through qualitative interviews (or postal questionnaires) has been rich in the detail recorded about the mothers' subjective experience of relinquishment. One significant theme that emerges from this body of research is that whereas these relinquishments were, when viewed within a strict legal framework, voluntary relinquishments, the lack of choice that mothers believed they had in relation to the act of parting with their child, belies *their* belief in the voluntary nature of this relinquishment (Fessler, 2006; Howe, Sawbridge and Hinings, 1992; Kelly, 2005; Wilson, Lordan and Mullender, 2004). In addition, the system of closed adoption, which was the only choice available to these mothers, left them with no information about the circumstances of their child, causing them to worry and be fearful about the continuing welfare of their child. These mothers describe lives, in the aftermath of the adoption, in which they were required to engage in the ongoing management of feelings of loss, guilt and shame, and that this had to be done without the aid of any support or assistance. Whereas the intensity of these emotions diminished for some mothers over the course of time, there continue to be various life events, including that of reunion, when many conflicting and painful emotions again rise to the surface. As a result it has often been very difficult to come to any resolution about or adjustment to the adoption decision (Condon, 1986; Kelly, 2005; Mullender and Kearn, 1997; Robinson, 2000; Triseliotis, Feast and Kyle, 2005; Winkler and Van Keppel, 1984).

A further group of mothers who have been studied are those who have relinquished in a climate within which there has been a greater degree of choice. A sample of these mothers has taken part in a large, longitudinal study that is currently being undertaken by Grotevant, McRoy and colleagues. In their analysis of Wave 2 of this study, Henney *et al.* (2004) present the findings from interviews with 127 birth mothers who had placed their children for adoption within the previous 20 years. These women had relinquished their children voluntarily, and had done so with contact arrangements along a continuum of openness. These contact arrangements ranged from confidential adoptions where only non-identifying information was shared, to fully disclosed adoptions, which involved direct communication and full disclosure of identifying information. For the majority of these birth mothers (76%), the principal motivation for relinquishment was that they did not believe they were ready to be parents. They also believed that adoption placement with a two-parent family would give their child more opportunities (77%) and a more stable financial situation (63%). In addition, mothers also cited their marital status (55%), age and lack of emotional maturity (54%), problems with the birth father (44%) or their own family (34%) as factors in their decision to place.

Within this study, one measure of adjustment to the adoption decision was birth mothers' satisfaction or dissatisfaction with the openness arrangement, which obviously included information exchange about how the child was faring. Fifty-two percent of mothers involved in confidential adoptions where there was little openness were dissatisfied or very dissatisfied with their arrangement, whereas for mothers who were involved in more open arrangements the satisfaction rating was 79%. The primary problem for mothers in confidential adoptions appeared to be that they had generalized worries about their adolescent child. Because they had no information they were fearful for their child's welfare. In contrast, birth mothers who had information and who knew what had happened to their child, appeared to have less worries post adoption, and so had some measure of ease with their decision. When measuring these mothers' continuing experiences of grief in relation to relinquishment, Henney *et al.* (2007) found that in the 12–20 years following the placement of the child, most birth mothers continued to experience some feelings of grief and loss, with 13.4% of mothers still experiencing a high degree of grief and loss, and 59% experiencing some or a moderate degree. In contrast, 27.6% reported no current feelings of grief pertaining to the adoption, demonstrating that a resolution of painful feelings is possible.

A third group of mothers who had yet another experience of relinquishment are those who have been involved in non-consenting or enforced adoptions, that is, mothers whose children were adopted within the care system (Lindley, 1997; Neil, 2007). For children in this type of adoption, contact with birth relatives in some form or another is now the usual plan in England and Wales (Neil, 2002). Reporting on the second wave of the 'Contact after Adoption Study', Neil (2007) presents the accounts of 72 birth relatives, including 32 birth mothers. Seventy-five percent of the sample was 'non-consenting' adoptions, that is, the decision about adoption had been made by social services and not by the parents. The remaining group was 'requested' adoptions. Neil suggests that the qualitative analysis of her data showed a wide variety of ways in which birth mothers and birth relatives came to terms with or accepted the child's adoption, and also notes that the 'type' of adoption did not predict acceptance. Within the study, acceptance (or not) of adoption took three main forms: 'positive acceptance', 'resignation' and 'anger or resistance'. Positive acceptance was associated with type of contact arrangements, which involved three types of contact: face-to-face contact, mediated letter contact with meeting and mediated letter contact with no meeting. Relatives who had face-to-face contact were most likely to positively accept adoption, and those who had mediated letter contact without a meeting were least likely. The grandparents, rather than parents (32 birth mothers, 13 birth fathers) were more likely to be involved in face-to-face contact, possibly explaining why grandparents were more likely to positively accept the adoption than birth parents. For many of the birth mothers, however, resignation or continued anger appeared to be more the norm, possibly, Neil suggests, due to the feelings of having been 'forced' into adoption by social services or by their circumstances at the time. Subjective feelings about a lack of choice and control led to painful emotions of self-condemnation and guilt or anger.

The evidence from the studies reviewed above suggests that for birth mothers, the impact of adoption does bring a particular and difficult grief reaction. Whereas this grief reaction appears to vary over time, it includes feelings of profound loss, sadness, guilt, shame, anger, depression, anxiety and worry. A common theme to emerge is that the emotional reaction to adoption and adjustment to the adoption decision is often complicated by the circumstances necessitating the adoption. Birth mothers who believed they had little choice or control in relation to the adoption decision often, in addition to the feelings of loss, experience ongoing feelings of anger, guilt and depression. Mothers whose pregnancy and motherhood were stigmatized due to the societal norms of the time, again in conjunction with profound feelings of loss, often have to contend with additional feelings of shame and guilt for their act of relinquishment. Mothers whose children were adopted from care are also affected by stigma, as their parenting has been publicly judged as inadequate.

A further common theme to emerge within these studies has been that various forms of openness and post-adoption contact do appear to assist mothers in their adjustment to adoption. For mothers who experienced no openness or who had no information about their child, the grief that they continued to experience was further complicated with the additional worry and anxiety about what had become of their child. However, for mothers who experienced various forms of mediated arrangements through adoption agencies (ranging from letter box contact with limited disclosure, to face-to-face meetings with full disclosure), some further adjustment to the adoption decision appeared to take place. However when considering openness, it is important to note that decisions about openness need to be flexible and case sensitive as contact (and openness) is a dynamic and transactional experience (Neil, 2007). In addition, it is important to consider that not only is one type of openness not right for everyone, but that, in relation to grief and loss, the 'right amount' of openness may change depending on the person's life stage or situation (Henney *et al.*, 2007).

Having identified some of the themes that have emerged from the literature in relation to the impact of relinquishment and adjustment to the adoption decision, it is interesting to examine how, or if, the emotional costs of adoption may come to impact on reunions. Using the author's (Kelly, 2005) small qualitative study of mothers who have been through a reunion as a case study, it is possible to gain an insight into some of the challenges involved for birth mothers within reunions and post-reunion relationships.

The Research

This qualitative study was undertaken with a group of 18 Irish birth mothers, who relinquished their children during the years 1956 to 1979. These three decades were a period in Irish history when to consider becoming a lone parent was a cultural anathema and a challenge to the prevailing ethos. However, in the 1990s, changing attitudes within adoption, particularly in relation to information about birth and relinquishment history, meant that increasing numbers of adopted people and birth mothers presented to adoption agencies requesting a contact service. Because of the social opprobrium that had existed towards women who had given birth outside marriage, and the secrecy that existed in relation to placing a child for adoption, little was known about this group of women, or what had become of them subsequent to their having relinquished. Adoption agencies had not, in the years since relinquishment, offered a service to these women, and so there was little knowledge available to social work practitioners about the issues involved for birth mothers when approaching a reunion. As a practising adoption social worker encountering a similar lack of knowledge, the author (Kelly, 2005), decided to undertake a small qualitative study with a group of these mothers.

The sample of mothers who took part in the study were recruited through five separate registered adoption agencies, in both urban and rural areas, throughout the island of Ireland. Experience, which had been gained through practice, meant that the author had an understanding of the complex issues involved in relinquishment and reunion with this group of women, and this included an appreciation of the skills and sensitivity required for interview. Familiarity with the processes involved also meant that decisions about sampling and subsequent access to the sample were made with knowledge of agency practices and procedures. When approached, each of the agencies issued invitations to mothers who had had a reunion facilitated through their agency and mothers self-selected to take part. Through a semi-structured interview schedule, the views of mothers on their subjective experience of adoption and reunion were sought. Interviews, of up to three hours duration, took place in the homes of the birth mothers.

In order to gain a long-term perspective, mothers were asked to give an account of their experience of pregnancy, relinquishment, their lives post relinquishment, their reunions, the relationships that they had formed with their child in the aftermath of reunion and their own reflections on how adoption had impacted on their lives. At the time of pregnancy, the age range of mothers was between 16 and 31, with five mothers being under 18, 12 mothers being between 18 and 24, and one mother who was aged 31. At the time of reunion, periods of 18 to 40 years had elapsed since relinquishment. Birth mothers initiated contact with the wish to effect a reunion in six instances, and the adopted child (now adult) in 12 instances. Reunion meetings had taken place within periods of between one and nine years prior to interview. No particular patterns emerged in relation to age of mothers and time since relinquishment or reunion.

Analysis of the data followed the core principles of qualitative and feminist analysis. This was achieved through identifying the salient, grounded categories of meaning held by the participants in the setting and the experience they had been through. Emerging themes and patterns were noted and then categorized. The analysis was therefore contextual, experiential, socially relevant, and inclusive of emotions and events as experienced by the mothers (McCarl Neilson, 1990). A full account of the study is given in Kelly (2005).

The Irish Context

The introduction of adoption to Ireland in 1952 was heralded as a child welfare policy that would promote the best interests of children. Similar adoption laws had been enacted in many other jurisdictions over the previous 30 years and Ireland was in fact catching up with the rest of the world. As had been the proven experience of adoption in other countries, the possibility of adoption for children who had previously been cared for in fostering placements brought permanency for the children and security for the parents. Closed adoption, the model of adoption that results in the total severance of any ongoing connection between the birth mother and the child she relinquished, was both the philosophy and the practice that underpinned the law that was enacted in Ireland and the policies that were implemented as a result.

At the time of the introduction of the legislation, despite extravagant displays of religious fervour, Ireland was in fact a grim, inward-looking and deeply repressive society (Cooney, 1999). Irish society's attitudes to sexual activity were shaped by Catholic social teachings, which deemed sexual intercourse outside marriage to be sinful and immoral. The Catholic Church provided both the religious and moral discourse through its control of schools and its pervasive influence in many state institutions and government. Catholic moral theology was particularly strict in relation to women and sexuality. In the game of love and lust, it was the task of single women to remain chaste and virginal, and certainly not to become pregnant. The ultimate shame, for both the young single woman *and* for her family, was to become pregnant outside marriage. These teachings were enforced within state institutions and within families through a series of strategies based on creating shame, embarrassment and guilt. The perception was that to have given birth to an 'illegitimate child' a social problem had been created, and that this was a social problem that affected both the moral climate of the State and the social status of the family (Kelly, 2005; Wilson, Lordan and Mullender, 2004). In the event that a single woman did become pregnant therefore, both for herself and for her family, it was imperative that the potential problem of a non-marital child be concealed.

For the majority of women and their families, the system of closed adoption offered a solution to non-marital pregnancy. In fact, during the 20-year period from 1954 to 1974, the percentage of non-marital children placed for adoption was never less than 50%; indeed in 1967 it was as high as 97% (Adoption Board, 2005). The vast majority of these children were adopted within the Irish State, though a small percentage was sent to Irish Catholic families in the United States.[1] As it was not the practice of adoption agencies within the existing system of adoption to inform mothers as to whether their child had been adopted within the state or had been sent abroad, mothers rarely knew what in fact had become of their child.

Key Themes from the Interviews

Pregnancy – A Crisis

As a result of the social climate that existed in Ireland pregnancy for a single woman manifested as an immediate crisis. When remembering the time they discovered they were pregnant, all of the mothers (n = 18) recalled vivid

---

[1] Ireland was at one time a sending country for international adoption. Between 1951 and 1973, a total of 1993 'adoption passports' were issued by the Irish government for children who were adopted abroad. The majority of these children were adopted by people of Irish heritage in the United States (Milotte, 1997).

memories of their own upset and fear. They did not know where to turn, and they knew that there was little prospect of support:

> I was terrified, on my own, could tell no one.

> I was very upset, I didn't know what to do, hadn't a clue what I was going to do.

The vast majority (n = 16) of women were living at home or visited their family almost every weekend and so were well integrated. As a result, they immediately understood that their pregnancy was also a crisis for their families:

> My father was awful upset, very upset, my mother was in a state of shock.

> My mother found out and she hit me and thumped me and called me all the names under the sun.

For half of the women (n = 9) the reaction of their boyfriends to the news of pregnancy was unsupportive:

> The father didn't want to know, I told him and my mother told an aunt of his, and he absconded, he went, he disappeared.

A number of mothers (n = 5) recalled that they were in fact denied the opportunity to tell their boyfriend or for that matter any of their friends. The fear of the stigma that would attach to families meant that the young pregnant women were immediately sent away to relatives, sent abroad, or brought to Mother and Baby Homes where contact with the outside world was discouraged or forbidden:

> The guy didn't know I was pregnant, he hadn't a got a clue, he didn't know. All he knew was that I had vanished off the face of the earth and I was apparently supposed to be over in London.

> I was put there because of neighbours, because of what neighbours thought, you know you were evil, you were wrong, you know Litany of Saints was put on to you as well.

The Adoption Decision

As the figures quoted above demonstrate, once adoption had been introduced to Ireland, it immediately became the solution to out-of-wedlock pregnancy for a large proportion of women who found themselves in that position. For all of the women in this study, a similar path was taken, though none of the mothers believed that it had been a solution of choice for themselves or their child. Rather, the memory of all of the mothers was that they had been coerced into signing the relinquishment papers, this coercion having been experienced through the manner in which both families and state agencies pressured them to choose adoption:

> I won't say I signed, rather I was forced to sign, because as far as I am concerned my son was taken from me, he wasn't given, because I had no choice in the matter, my father saw to all of that.

> I remember saying to the social worker, 'I don't know about this adoption', and she saying to me, 'well do you have any more money today than you had yesterday?'. I said, 'I don't' and she said, 'well what can you do for a child?'. . . . so you see no matter where I turned . . .

Motherhood Silenced

In the aftermath of relinquishment, strategies to ensure that the discredited action of pregnancy outside marriage remained a secret became part of the plan that had to be implemented. This required that all those who had known of the pregnancy, including family, adoption agencies, and other state agencies became complicit in ensuring that the birth would remain a secret and never become public.

For parents and families who were fearful of the stigma that would attach to them within the neighbourhood, it was believed that the imposition of a 'silence' about what had occurred would be the most effective way of ensuring that the social disgrace, would not occur. As a result, measures that ensured that the facts and reality of what had happened be restricted to family were activated. Mothers described how parents took charge and made decisions that were experienced as unsympathetic and even cruel:

> My father came down and collected me and drove me home. He said, 'Straighten yourself up now, think about the neighbours. We will never talk about this again'.

> My father said: 'I do not want to hear about you or your bastard ever again . . . it will not be discussed and you will not be asked about it'.

In addition to the collusion about secrecy that was put in place by families, the mothers themselves had to come up with their own strategies that would protect their secret. In his analysis of the presentation of self in everyday life, Goffman (1959) describes how people are constantly employed in various kinds of 'preventative practices' to avoid embarrassment. He suggests that if these preventative practices are not sufficient, 'corrective practices' are employed to compensate for discrediting occurrences that have not been successfully avoided. These preventative and corrective practices comprise of the techniques employed to safeguard the impression fostered by individuals during their presence before others, especially within families, communities and neighbourhoods. Mothers in this study gave descriptions of preventative and corrective actions that they undertook within their day-to-day lives:

> I didn't do anything with my girlfriends. I wouldn't dare even change my nurse's uniform because of the stretch marks. I was hiding myself the whole time.

And mothers further recounted how they maintained the image of themselves as a person who was not a mother, this often having been done through the erection of what Hochschild (1990) describes as a 'protective sixth sense', the psychological equivalent of a status shield. Erecting such a protective shield gave them some fortification or defence from the past and stigmatizing event. However, the ongoing emotional costs were high:

> You had a mask on the whole time, you were the happiest person in this world, and your heart was breaking, but what could you do?

The Impact of Relinquishment

Once the pregnancy and birth had effectively been silenced, the mothers were left with their own intense and personal grief. When asked to reflect on how living with this grief had affected their day-to-day lives, they all had a lot to say. One mother was quite graphic and asked: "How long is your tape?". All of the mothers described 'overwhelming pain and sadness', which became their lot throughout the post-adoption years. They had no information about their child and so wondered, for example, if their child was nearby or had been sent abroad. They recalled that they thought about their child constantly, despite, on occasion, having to deny their existence:

> I was thinking every day about where was he gone, who had him, was he in Ireland or where was he? . . . they never told you anything.

> And mentally you are thinking, I have another girl. You are saying (aloud) you have two children, but you have three, but really you only have two.

Mothers also recalled experiencing feelings of anger, shame and self-reproach. They felt this both for themselves and for what they believed they might have inflicted on their child:

> I always felt I had done a terrible thing, that it was a major sin. The darkness was always there.

> Not only did I bring this terrible shame to me, but I brought this terrible burden to him as well.

Throughout the years post relinquishment, the protective strategies of denial and repression that they employed meant that their sense of powerlessness remained high:

> She belonged to someone else, I had no rights.

> I felt inferior because I had signed him away and because I had had him out of wedlock, and I lacked a lot of confidence because of that.

As a result of feeling disempowered, a number of mothers (n = 8) recounted how they did not even contemplate trying to make contact in the years post relinquishment. For these women to try to think of themselves as the mother of their absent child was too painful:

> Throughout the pregnancy I always thought this child is for someone else, I know that is terrible, but that is the way it was . . .

A small number of mothers (n = 4) did make some efforts to regain control. They wrote to adoption agencies with the purpose of enquiring about their child or to register details of their own changed circumstances. Most often these mothers received no response or acknowledgement from the agencies.

Mother and Child Reunited

Until relatively recently, for mothers who had relinquished children to the adoption system, it was most often presumed that birth mothers would forget about their child and continue with their lives as if the child did not exist. For many mothers, including the mothers in this study, this was not the case, and their wish to know what had happened to their child remained with them. When, for whatever reason, the possibility of contact and reunion became a reality therefore, they immediately came forward as being available for contact or reunion.

An adoption reunion is a journey into uncharted waters. It is a rite of passage for which there are few rules and no traditions. Generally, it is not just a single event, but rather a process which is highly charged due to the range of conflicting emotions which are brought to the table. For mothers who had not seen or heard of their child for long periods of time, there will obviously be great joy and happiness. In addition, however, there will also be the more difficult emotions of fear, sadness, guilt and apprehension in relation to deeds of the past and how to explain the act of relinquishment. The mothers in this study described having a range of emotional reactions throughout the reunion process. For example, being contacted in the first instance by an agency brought joy, emotional relief and a sense of reality about an extremely important life event that had been denied, or at least suppressed for many years:

> It was very exciting, to me it was very exciting. I was totally and utterly on a high. I was bursting with excitement.

> It brought it home to me when I got the photos that he really does exist.

However, as they reflected on the possibility of a reunion meeting, their emotional reactions were also those of fear and apprehension:

> How could I possibly start now to meet someone I had given away? I could not ask him to forgive me. I just didn't know where to start.

These mothers had managed to suppress their emotions throughout the years. Ongoing feelings of grief, pain and anger had become normalized for them. They now began to realize they had buried their sadness and anger:

> A lot of pain, a lot of anger, a lot of hurt came through. . . . you know after 21 years you had found him. The anger, the hurt, everything just kept flowing through.

The actual reunion meetings were also highly charged and full of conflicting emotion, which for some mothers were hard to control. Their emotional states were raw and unpredictable:

> It was a joyful occasion, again mixed emotions.

> It was just that I cried my eyes out, it's just I don't know what came over me. . . . there was great sadness involved.

And the end of these meetings had the effect of re-igniting their feelings of fear:

> I just had that awful feeling that maybe that's it, she has met me now and that's it.

Life After Reunion

Subsequent to the reunion meeting almost all of the mothers went on to have a relationship with their child. In just one instance no relationship developed as the child terminated contact immediately after the meeting, so despite the mother wishing to have a relationship there was no opportunity to do so. The qualitative analysis of the mother's interviews showed that for all mothers there were 'ups and downs' in their relationships with their child. Overall relationships were proving to be either satisfactory, which was the case for a majority (n = 10), or unsatisfactory which was the case for the remaining seven mothers.

The building of a satisfactory relationship between two people who are so intimately related but who are, through the effects of closed adoption, strangers to each other, must invariably be a complex task. Giddens (1991) suggests that for any relationship to work it requires a number of 'anchoring features', a principal one of which must be that of trust. He notes that what matters in the building of trust in a relationship is that one can rely on what the other says and does. In addition, he suggests that in relationships that are satisfactory, it is likely that one is able to rely on regularly eliciting certain sorts of desired responses from the other. Giddens also identifies friendship as being an important feature of a relationship, defining a friend as someone who has a relationship unprompted by anything other than the rewards that the relationship provides. Within the post-reunion relationships of the mothers in the study, it was possible to identify a number of anchoring features that appeared to determine what was making relationships satisfactory or not.

Relationships Satisfactory Mothers whose relationships were satisfactory described a number of anchoring features that appeared to be giving stability to the relationship. The first of these features was when mothers believed there **'was a patterned and predictable structure attached to how the relationship functioned between mother and child'**:

> I cannot go any more than two weeks without giving her a buzz and I know that she can't either. If I don't ring her she will ring me, so I kind of know

she needs to talk to me every now and then and I need to talk to her ... I know the contact is there and I am not afraid of it.

A second factor that contributed positively to the relationship working well appeared to be an ability on the part of the mothers to have realistic expectations of what *kind* of relationship might develop with her child. For these mothers what appeared to be helpful was **'when the relationship between the mothers and their child closely resembled a friendship'**:

We are the best of friends, we have better than mother and son relationship in the sense that I can tell him anything, he could tell me anything.

A third positive influence was when there was **'an acceptance by mothers that they could not and never would be the kind of mother they might have wished to be to their child'**. An important part of this feature was birth mothers having an acceptance of the adoptive status of their child, and recognizing that they had attachments to another family. A number of mothers in this study had in fact met the adoptive parents and the meetings had gone well:

It is going well. Absolutely. I mean I certainly would not take over and try and step in and act as his mother.

There are so many stories that I had heard about adopted children and I was wondering if she had gone to the wrong hands. But I am so delighted today. I have a lot to be thankful for to those people, her adopted parents, and at the end of the day, they are her parents.

The fourth and final feature that mothers felt was influencing relationships positively was when **'a good relationship had developed between the child who had been adopted and other children born to the mother post relinquishment'**:

The first weekend she came down here we went for a spin and the three of them were playing football together. I was sitting on this little mound and I had tears running down my eyes and I was thinking, 'God the three of them are really together' ...

Relationships Unsatisfactory   On the other hand, a minority (n = 7) of the mothers were experiencing their relationships as 'unsatisfactory'. The relationships that were unsatisfactory displayed a number of features that appeared to be impeding good progress.

Firstly when mothers **'felt disempowered'** within the relationship and the balance was askew, they did not feel sufficiently confident in themselves to either take the initiative or make demands about contact. In addition, their own self-esteem was low in relation to how they perceived who was responsible if things were not going according to plan:

> So when he made no contact, I didn't feel I should make a move. It was up to him to make the decisions.

> But what you are actually feeling is 'What did you do? What did you say? You've said something, he has found some fault in you', and that is reeling around in your head for months and months.

A second feature that brought dissatisfaction was when there were **'haphazard and erratic contact patterns upon which it was difficult to rely'**. In conjunction with this, for some mothers **'the frequency and nature of contact was also disappointing'**:

> It happened there at Christmas, he said 'I'll be down for Christmas, I'll be down for New year', I really had my heart set on that but he didn't come down and there was no explanation why.

The third feature of unsatisfactory relationships occurred when there were **'unrealistic expectations'** about what the post-reunion relationship would, or could, deliver:

> I think I had these expectations that everything was going to be hunky dory, I was thinking he might move down here eventually.

Reflections on Reunion and Post-Reunion Relationships

Following on from sharing their perceptions of the ongoing relationships with their child, mothers in the study were asked to reflect on their own emotional well-being as their lives progressed post reunion. All mothers were happy that they had met their child again, and in their initial responses mothers reported that this final breaking of the silence around their identity as a mother made them feel more confident, self-assured and they believed their own self-image had improved:

> I wanted to tell the whole world, because it wasn't a secret any longer. It was a secret, a heartbreaking secret for so long.

> I am more secure than I was, more happy in myself than what I was. I know I am not the bad egg I was told I was.

However, despite whether they identified their relationships as having been satisfactory or unsatisfactory, they also reported that the denial of their child and the consequent grief and sadness with which they had to cope throughout their lives had always had an impact and continued to do so. Whereas they believed that feelings of guilt (for example) had eased, the reality was that it had not disappeared:

> You carry this awful guilt around with you, you carry it like you are carrying a suitcase full of lead, and it never goes, it just gets easier, but it never goes.

It was also painful for mothers when they reflected on their past adoption decision in the light of the current choices for lone parents, where stigma is much reduced and state and family support is available:

> How sad it was to have missed her all those years. I just wish things could have been different and if it had been a few years down the line it would have been different.

In addition post-reunion relationships brought new and difficult emotions for mothers. Having always had to practise emotional restraint and engage in the management of their emotions, the need to continue this practice did not diminish. And this was despite whether the relationship with their child was proving satisfactory or not:

> We are more or less friends really, rather than mother and daughter. Sometimes that hurts, that hurts, you know it hurts me.

> Because no matter how much you say, 'Ok this doesn't matter or that doesn't matter to you', it does matter to you, it matters that you are his mother and that you are not his birth mother as they want to call you.

The need for further emotional restraint was also evident in relation to how open and honest they could be about the joys of having a relationship with their child who was now an adult. Their grief remained their own and their loss continued to be profound. In the end, whereas reunion brought some closure and emotional relief, ultimately what had been lost could never be retrieved:

> You are never prepared for the fact that it was a child you handed up and what you got back was an adult.

It is like when I met her it was this tall blond slim young woman and I had left a six-day-old baby and there is more of me needed to hold the baby than the relationship with this young woman.

What emerges from the descriptions and experience of these mothers is that no matter how good the experience of reunion and the relationship post reunion, the existence of such relationships can only offer partial relief to a mother who relinquished her child through adoption. Reunion cannot change the past and give mothers back their baby, and as a result some measure of the pain, disempowerment and sadness which had been created by relinquishment remained.

Discussion

This research records the subjective experience of a small group of 18 Irish birth mothers, all of whom had had a reunion with their adopted child as an adult. The accounts of these women highlight the importance of understanding the context in which adoption takes place. These mothers relinquished their children in circumstances they experienced as coercive and shameful; the birth and subsequent loss of their child became a secret. As well as being denied the opportunity to actually mother their child, these women also had to deny their status as mothers. The emotional costs of this denial were high and the resultant difficulties apparent. Albeit that for many mothers the feelings of loss, guilt, shame and self-condemnation did ease, it is evident that some measure of these emotions continued to be an ongoing part of their lives, and it was only through continuous emotional management that they remained hidden. Having to maintain such denial was, for many women disempowering and debilitative, and it often prevented mothers from being true even to themselves. For many of the women these difficult emotions impacted on their decisions about whether or not to seek out their child, and also upon their experience and management of reunion.

It is heartening that the majority of mothers in this study went on to have satisfactory relationships with their children. Looking at these relationships from the birth mothers' point of view, satisfaction seemed to have come about largely because of their having managed to come to terms with some of the principal realities of adoption, that is, that their child had become part of another family and that they were never going to have the mothering role that they might have wished. As a result of such acceptance, there also came an acceptance that the type of relationship that was on offer would be one of friendship. The effects of such acceptance meant that birth mothers became more confident in themselves, their self-esteem was enhanced, and they had a more positive sense of self-worth.

Because the experiences of these Irish mothers were those of a small and particular group who relinquished children in specific circumstances, the findings in this study cannot claim to be representative of all birth mothers. There are many questions that the study does not and cannot answer. In order to gain a more complete picture, there is a need for a large-scale study of mothers who, historically, have relinquished in similar circumstances. In addition to those women who relinquished in the past, there are an estimated 40 000 women per year who are relinquishing children to the system of international adoption (Selman, 2006). From the inadequate and often unsubstantiated knowledge we have of these mothers, it is possible to speculate that it is unlikely that all of them are making an informed choice about relinquishment, or that they live within systems or structures that offer them the encouragement to do so,[2] and so research is also needed to confirm or deny these speculations. And finally, there is a need to compare these findings with those of the experience of relinquishment and post-reunion relationships for mothers whose children were adopted in other contexts (such as through the care system or where relinquishment involved a greater degree of choice), and where different degrees of openness are attached to the adoption. In conclusion, it is noteworthy that although this study is limited in its sample and scope, many of the key themes that have emerged echo and endorse those of other studies, suggesting that small-scale practitioner led research can be useful and valid.

Implications for Policy and Practice

The Fair Treatment of Birth Mothers   As has been demonstrated in this and other studies, not all relinquishing mothers will have freely and fairly planned adoption for their child, and the ongoing detrimental effects of this experience have been illustrated. We are not yet living in a world where the position of women is such that they may always have a choice about relinquishment. Within many cultures and societies, women continue to be denied equal rights or status, and stigma in relation to pregnancy outside marriage also persists in many communities. In such an imperfect world, despite the best efforts of governments to honour the spirit of international

---

[2]   Recent reports in the media concerning birth mothers in Korea, for example, indicate that they have begun to protest about government policies that favour intercountry adoption (e.g. Trenka, 2007).

agreements such as the UN Convention on the Rights of the Child (which calls for a child's right to know and to be cared for by his or her birth parents), it is likely that adoption and intercountry adoption will continue to exist. As long as adoption exists, birth mothers (and birth relatives) will exist and their fair treatment within the system needs to be safeguarded. Such safeguards must come through both domestic and international legislation, which will have extra complexities within the forum of international adoption. The foundations for such legislation are already laid through such international agreements as the Hague Convention on Intercountry Adoption, Article 4 of which requires that consent to adoption must be: given only after the child's birth; given freely, legally and without inducements; and that mothers must be counselled as to the effects of adoption and the giving of their consent. Whereas the enactment of such legislation may not guarantee that systems will be perfect, and indeed such legislation would require constant monitoring to ensure that it was serving the needs of an ever-changing environment, it could go a long way in acknowledging the importance and perspective of each party within adoption.

With these rights must also come policies and services that offer support to mothers who choose to relinquish. It is fair to say that within the developed world, services to birth mothers and in some instances to birth relatives, have improved. These improvements have mainly been in the areas such as counselling for mothers who are contemplating adoption, support services for those involved in post-adoption contact arrangements, and in the provision of information and tracing services for those wishing to try to reconnect with their child. In some countries these improvements have come about with the aid of legislation, but in most they have been driven by adoption agencies engaging in a more enlightened practice as a direct result of the lessons learned from the past.

Despite these improvements, there are still a number of areas remaining where current adoption practice falls short in fulfilling its duty of care to birth mothers, particularly for mothers who having relinquished in what were experienced as coercive circumstances. Whereas the needs of mothers whose children were adopted through the care system have begun to be addressed in England and Wales for example through the Adoption and Children Act 2002, recent research shows that the implementation and provision of the required services to birth parents has been mixed and substantial challenges still exist in maximizing support service take-up by birth relatives (Sellick, 2007).

Supporting Adoption Reunions Through the reflections of the birth mothers in the study, we begin to gain an insight into the manner in which the ongoing influences of relinquishment can affect post-reunion relationships. This study concurs with other research illustrating both the complexities and joys of reunions for birth mothers (e.g. Triseliotis, Feast and Kyle, 2005). The mothers in this small sample came to the reunion process with a range of emotions and feelings which for many years, had to be kept backstage or repressed. Indeed for most of their adult lives they had been practising emotional restraint, but reunion meetings reopened the emotional floodgates. As reunions progressed, birth mothers were often faced with new dilemmas and further conflicting emotions. A yearning for 'what might have been', for example, was a common emotion expressed by the mothers who had relinquished in an era when there was little choice, especially when compared with the situation today where lone parenthood is supported by the state, and where adoption is seen as less preferable to abortion (Mahon, Conlon and Dillon, 1998).

Some anchoring features of both successful and unsuccessful reunions have been identified within the research, and a central theme to emerge is that mothers who accepted the realities of adoption were those most likely to have successful relationships with their child. But such successful relationships require skills and fortitude to manage the ongoing emotional confusion. And it is important to remember too that achieving a satisfactory relationship after reunion may be hard to achieve for many birth mothers. These are mothers who cannot, for their own reasons, ever come to terms with how their child will be within a post-adoption relationship, and so often their feelings of powerlessness and perhaps ongoing anger and self-reproach remain with ongoing consequences in terms of lack of confidence and self-esteem. For these mothers, the influences of relinquishment will continue to resonate and perhaps be unresolved.

Such findings suggest that comprehensive support services need to be available to help birth mothers through the process of reunion. It is important that such services must, for example, have the ability to: support women who have, as the research is telling us, repressed or hidden feelings of loss for many years; provide preparation and information for mothers in anticipation of reunion; offer assistance in achieving balanced and satisfactory post-reunion relationships; and, in the event that reunion relationships do not work out for birth mothers (or their adopted children) provide ongoing counselling or support for these mothers.

Openness in Adoption   For the mothers who took part in the current study, the social and historical context that necessitated the placement of their babies for adoption also ruled out the possibility of them having any subsequent information or contact with their adopted child (at least until the child was an adult). These adoptions were 'closed' on more than one level: not only was there no possibility of post-adoption contact, but neither could mothers be open in society about their feelings and experiences. This, and the lack of information, reinforced feelings of loss and stigma for the mothers. The possibility that the effects of relinquishment do not always have to be overwhelmingly sad and painful is suggested in other research, and, as discussed in the Introduction, the part that openness can play in helping birth mothers adjust to the loss of their child is beginning to be identified. This echoes with this current study of reunions, as meeting and getting to know the adoptive parents was a factor in increased satisfaction within post-adoption relationships. At the very least it appears that knowing what happened to your child and who is caring for them enhances adjustment to the adoption decision. And even when it is not possible for birth mothers to have identifying information about, or the chance to meet adoptive parents, at the very least non-identifying information about the adoptive family should be available.

It is important that openness arrangements include the means for birth mothers and the adopted child to make contact once the child is an adult. Many countries have now legislated in favour of state-sponsored Contact Registers. Through such registers a birth mother may record a wish to make contact with the adopted person. However the numbers of birth mothers whose children are currently being adopted in intercountry arrangements, will, in most cases, be relinquishing to what are in fact closed adoption systems. As a result, these mothers will become the newly silenced and disempowered part of the adoption kinship network. When the circumstances and position of these birth mothers are considered, it seems that few lessons have been learned and that many of the mistakes of the past are being repeated. If, or when, these mothers (and children) wish to reconnect, there are currently no national or international systems or registers in place to enable this to happen, either as a right or even as a service. Surely it is time that there be an onus on receiving countries to establish state-sponsored registers where birth mothers and birth family members can be facilitated to lodge details of their existence and circumstances? This would provide an adopted child with the possibility of having such information. Such registers could, in addition, have up-to-date information about an adopted child so that a mother might at least be able to enquire if her child was alive and faring well.

Openness of course may also include contact with the adoptive parents and/or the child (either direct or indirect) that is ongoing from the time the child is placed. In facilitating such contact there may be difficult times that will require support, skills and negotiation as maintaining comfortable contact arrangements over time is not always straightforward, as Chapters 12 and 13 demonstrate. Thus, support for post-adoption contact should be an essential ingredient of post-adoption support services. This may be especially pertinent when children have been adopted through the care system, as these parents may have additional needs (e.g. mental health problems, literacy problems, substance misuse problems) and negative feelings about the adoption, both of which can impact on the quality of post-adoption contact (Lindley, 1997; Mason and Selman, 1997; Neil, 2007).

Conclusion

There have been many changes in Ireland in the past three decades and the particular social climate that compelled the 18 women in the outlined study to place their children for adoption no longer exists. However, the findings from this research are currently relevant both because many of the mothers who placed their children in this historical period (not just in Ireland but around the world) are still living. Furthermore, adoptions are still being made today (in both domestic and intercountry arrangements) where mothers and other birth relatives may have little or no choice over the placement of their child. Creating and maintaining an ethical climate within adoption involves ensuring that all those in any way affected by adoption are recognized, accounted for and visible within the system. It means that adoption practice must be shaped by adherence to values such as fairness, equity and accountability, and that these values must always be at the forefront when providing a service to those most affected. When both past and many current adoption policies and practices, particularly those as applied to birth mothers, are examined and measured against these values, there are glaring and obvious shortfalls. The reality of today's world is that there are now sufficient knowledge, information, skill and resources available to rectify this situation, and in fairness to birth mothers it is time that this is done.

References

Adoption Board (2005) *Annual Report*, Government Publications, Dublin.
Condon, J.T. (1986) Psychological disability in women who relinquished a baby for adoption. *Medical Journal of Australia*, **144**, 117–9.
Cooney, J. (1999) *John Charles McQuaid: Ruler of Catholic Ireland*, O'Brien Press, Dublin.

Dorow, S. (ed.) (1999) *I Wish for You a Beautiful Life: Letters from the Korean Birth Mothers of Ae Ran Won to Their Children*, Yeong & Yeong, Minnesota.

Fessler, A. (2006) *The Girls Who Went Away*, Penguin, New York.

Giddens, A. (1991) *Modernity and Self-Identity*, Polity Press, New York.

Goffman, I. (1959) *The Presentation of Self in Everyday Life*, Anchor Books, New York.

Henney, S.M., Ayers-Lopez, S., McRoy, R.G. and Grotevant, H.D. (2004) A longitudinal perspective on changes in adoption openness: The birth mother story, in *Contact in Adoption and Permanent Foster Care* (eds E. Neil and D. Howe), British Agencies for Adoption and Fostering, London, pp. 26–45.

Henney, S.M., Ayers-Lopez, S., McRoy, R.G. and Grotevant, H.D. (2007) Evolution and resolution: Birth mothers' experience of grief and loss at different levels of adoption openness. *Journal of Social and Personal Relationships*, **24**, 875–89.

Hochschild, A. (1990) Ideology and emotion management: A perspective and path for future research, in *Research Agendas in the Sociology of Emotion* (ed. P. Kemper), SUNY Press, New York.

Howe, D., Sawbridge, P. and Hinings, D. (1992) *Half a Million Women: Mothers Who Lose Their Children by Adoption*, The Post Adoption Centre, London.

Inglis, K. (1984) *Living Mistakes: Mothers Who Consent to Adoption*, George, Allen and Unwin, Sydney.

Kelly, R.J.A. (2005) *Motherhood Silenced – The Experiences of Natural Mothers on Adoption Reunion*, Liffey Press, Dublin.

Lindley, B. (1997) Partnership or panic? A survey of adoption agency practice on working with birth families in the adoption process. *Adoption & Fostering*, **21** (4), 23–33.

Mahon, E., Conlon, C. and Dillion, L. (1998) *Women and Crisis Pregnancy*, Government Publications, Dublin.

Mason, K. and Selman, P. (1997) Birth parents' experiences of contested adoption. *Adoption & Fostering*, **21** (1), 21–8.

McCarl Neilson, J. (ed.) (1990) *Feminist Research Methods*, Westview Press, Colorado.

Milotte, M. (1997) *Banished Babies: The Secret History of Ireland's Baby Export Business*, New Island Books, Dublin.

Mullender, A. and Kearn, S. (1997) *"I'm Here Waiting": Birth Relatives' Views on Part II of the Adoption Contact Register for England and Wales*, British Agencies for Adoption and Fostering, London.

Neil, E. (2002) Contact after adoption: The role of agencies in making and supporting plans. *Adoption & Fostering*, **26**, 25–38.

Neil, E. (2007) Coming to terms with the loss of a child: The feelings of birth parents and grandparents about adoption and post adoption contact. *Adoption Quarterly*, **10** (1), 1–23.

Robinson, E. (2000) *Adoption and Loss: The Hidden Grief*, Clova Publications, New South Wales.

Sellick, C. (2007) An examination of adoption support services for birth relatives and for post-adoption contact in England and Wales. *Adoption & Fostering*, **31** (4), 17–26.

Selman, P. (2006) Trends in intercountry adoption: Analysis of data from 20 receiving countries, 1998-2004. *Journal of Population Research*, **23** (2), 183–204.

Trenka, J. (2007) Korean Adoptees from Abroad and Birth Mothers Protest Overseas Adoption, *The Hankyoreh*, 5 August 2007, http://jjtrenka.wordpress.com/category/resistance/ (accessed December 2007).

Triseliotis, J., Feast, J. and Kyle, F. (2005) *The Adoption Triangle Revisited*, British Agencies for Adoption and Fostering, London.

Wilson, M., Lordan, N. and Mullender, A. (2004) Family, community, church and state: Natural parents talking about adoption in Ireland. *British Journal of Social Work*, **35** (5), 621–49.

Winkler, R. and Van Keppel, M. (1984) *Relinquishing Mothers in Adoption: Their Long-Term Adjustment. Monograph No. 3*, Institute of Family Studies, Melbourne.

12

The Corresponding Experiences of Adoptive Parents and Birth Relatives in Open Adoptions*

Elsbeth Neil

Introduction

Post-adoption contact arrangements between adopted children and their birth family members are a central feature of many, if not most, contemporary domestic adoptions in countries such as the United Kingdom and the United States, both when children are placed for adoption by their birth parent/s and when children are adopted via the public care system (Child Welfare Information Gateway, 2003; Henney *et al.*, 2003; Neil, 2002; Parker, 1999). Such contact arrangements may involve face-to-face meetings or contact by phone, letters, e-mail, and these types of contact can be either directly managed by families or mediated by an adoption agency. Regardless of contact type, these arrangements propel adoptive parents and birth relatives into relationships with one another. Each person brings his or her own characteristics and experiences to this relationship and these factors can affect how well contact works. At the same time, the experience of contact can change how adoptive parents and birth relatives feel: it is a dynamic and transactional phenomenon (Neil and Howe, 2004). Understanding the dynamics of the relationships between adults is central in understanding how contact might be experienced by the child, as children are unlikely to be comfortable when the adults involved are tense or unhappy and when relationships are strained. Not all planned post-adoption contact arrangements endure over time, and of those that do, not all are

* Support for this research is acknowledged with thanks, from the Nuffield Foundation, London.

experienced positively. It is important to try and understand why some contact arrangements work and why others do not, and this chapter explores these issues from the perspective of adoptive parents and birth parents and grandparents.

A number of studies have looked at the qualities of adoptive parents and birth relatives that are associated with contact arrangements that work well. With adoptive parents an open attitude towards maintaining contact, based on an inclusive and empathic view of the birth family and an understanding of adoption-related issues for their child, seems important. Brodzinsky (2005, 2006) has argued that structural openness (actual contact arrangements) is less important for the healthy development of adopted children than the communicative openness of adoptive parents, which he defines in terms of their ability to create "an open, honest, non defensive, and emotionally attuned family dialogue" (2005, p. 151). Adoptive parents can be communicatively open regardless of what contact may be happening, but the two types of openness often overlap, with parents who are communicatively open choosing and maintaining more structurally open arrangements (Brodzinsky, 2006; Neil, 2007a). For birth relatives, it seems important that continued concern for the child is conveyed alongside an acceptance of the child's place in the adoptive family, and of the adopters as the child's new psychological parents (Neil, 2007b; Neil and Howe, 2004).

Only a few studies of post-adoption contact have included both adoptive parents and birth relatives, and even when this is the case, analysis of corresponding interviews does not necessarily take place. There are some notable exceptions to this however, not least of which is the discussion of emotional distance regulation in adoptive kinship networks by Grotevant (Chapter 13). An earlier paper by Grotevant *et al.* (1999) explored collaboration between adoptive parents and birth mothers in domestic infant adoptions in the United States. Characteristics of networks rated as high on this construct were effective management of the logistics of openness, management of people's own fears and anxieties, appropriate involvement of and communication with the child, mutual empathy between adoptive parents and birth mothers, management of boundaries, and willingness to compromise. In highly collaborative arrangements, adoptive parents and birth mothers mutually worked out the 'comfort zone' within which they related to each other. Further work at the adolescent follow-up stage of this longitudinal project used an intensive case study design to analyse eight adoptive kinship networks (Dunbar *et al.*, 2006). This analysis focused on the reasons behind changes in agency-mediated contact arrangements. In four cases contact had changed to become fully disclosed (i.e. adoptive parents and birth relatives exchanged identifying information and contacted each other directly) and in the other four cases it had stopped. Where contact had stopped, adoptive parents and birth mothers tended to disagree about who had stopped the contact, each blaming the other. Where adoptive parents had controlled changes in contact, they tended to be satisfied with these changes. Where birth mothers or adolescents had initiated change, adoptive parents' satisfaction was lower. Birth mothers were often anxious not to violate these boundaries set by adoptive parents, even when they wanted a greater level of openness. The role of the mediating agency was also highlighted, as a lack of efficiency in organizing exchanges between the parties could create or exacerbate misunderstandings about the other person's needs and wishes.

Some similar findings to this American research have emerged from Logan and Smith's study of direct contact in UK adoptions (Logan and Smith, 2005), mostly involving children placed from public care. They analysed a subsample of 11 triangulated cases (adoptive parents, birth relatives and adopted children), including a wide range of children in terms of their age at placement (from 0 to 11 years) and age at interview (from 4 to 18 years). In these 11 'triangles', good relationships were characterized by mutual acceptance, but whereas adoptive parents expressed 'sympathy' towards birth relatives, birth relatives showed 'gratitude' towards adopters, suggesting or reflecting a power imbalance between the two. This theme of power and control also emerged when looking at people's satisfaction with the level of contact, with birth relatives tending to want more contact than adoptive parents were happy with. Relationships between adoptive parents and birth relatives were complex and although mutual liking and respect was an important theme, some relationships 'worked' in the absence of these, as people managed their more difficult feelings about the other person. The transactional nature of contact was illustrated. Adoptive parents felt positive when birth relatives gave them 'permission to parent', and birth relatives responded positively to adoptive parents allowing them an ongoing role in the child's life. On the other hand, when birth mothers found it hard to accept the adoptive parents' role, adoptive mothers found this very difficult. In two kinship networks there was little direct communication between adult parties, and relationships lacked most of the characteristics of working arrangements. In these two cases children expressed an awareness of and unhappiness about the tension between their two families. This study illustrates some of the potential complexities of post-adoption contact for older children, who may have loyalties to both their families but very complicated feelings and memories about time spent in their birth family.

The research reported in this chapter adds to this small body of previous work with an analysis of 30 matched cases where both adoptive parents and birth relatives involved in post-adoption contact arrangements were interviewed. These cases were taken from an English study of post-adoption contact. The study followed up children (under age 4 at placement) for whom either face-to-face or agency-mediated letter contact with birth relatives was planned. This research sought to answer questions about how these two types of contact were experienced by birth relatives, children and adoptive parents approximately seven years into the child's placement, and to explore whether post-adoption contact was impacting the development and adjustment of children, adoptive parents and birth relatives (Neil, 2006). The analysis reported in this chapter is exploratory in nature. It seeks to understand how the individual qualities that adoptive parents and birth relatives bring to contact can affect the dynamics of contact, exploring whether different combinations of birth relatives and adoptive parents might give rise to differences in how contact progresses.

Methodology

Sample

This paper is based on interview data from the 'Contact after Adoption' study. This project began in 1996 following up a group of children adopted or placed for adoption in 1996–1997 and has collected data from adoptive parents, birth relatives and adopted children. This paper is based on the follow-up of some of these families on average seven years after the child was placed for adoption.

In 30 cases in the study both the adoptive mother and the corresponding birth relative were interviewed, and these 'matched' cases are the focus of this paper. All the children in the study were placed for adoption under the age of 4 years. In the 30 cases, the mean age of the children at placement was 19.9 months (SD = 15.9) and their age at the follow-up was 8.4 years (SD = 1.9). In 16 cases the planned contact was face-to-face between the adoptive parents and child and the birth relative. In the other 14 cases the contact plan was for letter contact, mediated by the adoption agency, between adoptive parents and birth relatives. Within both of these broad types of contact precise arrangements could vary quite widely, but generally speaking almost all contact was relatively low frequency (between one and four times a year). Adoptive mothers in all 30 cases were interviewed. Five of these mothers were lone parents, either because they were single, widowed or separated or divorced. Of the 30 birth relatives, 21 were birth parents (15 mothers, 6 fathers) and 9 were grandparents (2 grandfathers, 7 grandmothers). In 21 of the 30 cases the child had been adopted from public care, and in nine cases he or she had been placed at the parents' request.

The analysis reported in this paper builds on the coding of adoptive parent and birth relative interviews, using this coding to sort matched cases into groups. The analysis was carried out in four stages, outlined below.

Stage 1: Birth Relative Interviews Were Explored and Coded in Relation to 'Acceptance of Adoption'

In-depth, semi-structured face-to-face interviews were carried out with birth relatives. People were asked to talk about why their child (or grandchild) had been adopted, how they felt about the child, the adoptive parents and the adoption itself, over time and up to the present date. Respondents were also asked to talk through all the arrangements for contact – how these had arisen and how they had worked out in practice. These interview data were then explored qualitatively using a process of thematic analysis (Boyatzis, 1998), the focus of which was the birth relative's current feelings about the adoption, including their acceptance of the child's place in the adoptive family (for full details see Neil, 2007b). This analysis resulted in the identification of three patterns: *positive acceptance, resignation,* and *anger and resistance.*

Stage 2: Adoptive Parent Interviews Were Used to Code Their 'Adoption Communicative Openness' (ACO)

Adoptive parent interviews were semi-structured and face-to-face. Parents were asked to explore in detail their feelings about post-adoption contact and their experiences of such contact – including their feelings about birth relatives, and patterns of communication about adoption within the adoptive family. The whole of the interview was used to rate ACO. The method of qualitative analysis followed the process of theory-driven thematic coding outlined by Boyatzis (1998) (for full details see Neil, 2007a). Starting with Brodzinsky's (2005) definition of adoption communicative openness, a rating scale was developed (Neil, Grotevant and Young, 2006). Brodzinsky's construct was broken down into five constituent dimensions: communication with the child about adoption; comfort with and promotion of the child's dual connection to birth and adoptive family; empathy for the

Table 12.1 Cross-tabulation of adoptive mother communicative openness groups with birth relative 'acceptance' groups.

	Birth relative positively accepting	Birth relative NOT positively accepting
Adoptive mother HIGH on ACO	n = 9	n = 3
Adoptive mother MODERATE on ACO	n = 5	n = 3
Adoptive mother LOW on ACO		n = 10

adopted child; communication with the birth family; and empathy for the birth relative. Adoptive mothers were rated from 1 to 5 on each of these scales (1 being low and 5 being high). From this a total score for ACO for each adoptive mother was calculated, the possible range being 5–25.

Stage 3: Identifying Groups of Cases

It was decided to divide adoptive mothers into three groups (high, moderate and low) on the basis of their ACO scores: the choice of three groups (as opposed to two) was taken in order to reduce variability within each group. Twelve mothers scored as 'high' (21–25), 8 as 'moderate' (15–20) and 10 as 'low' (14 and below). Birth relatives were split into two groups, those who positively accepted the adoption (n = 14) versus those who did not, that is, the 'resigned' and 'angry' groups (n = 16). The decision was made to combine the resigned and angry groups because both of these categories indicate a lack of resolution of the difficult issues associated with adoption, whereas in the positive acceptance group there were several indicators of resolution. Cross-tabulating the three adoptive mother groups with the two birth relative groups produced five groups of matched cases (see Table 12.1). The sixth potential group (adoptive parents low on communicative openness, birth relatives accepting of adoption) was empty.

Stage 4: Further Analysis of the Five Groups

Having identified groups of matched cases, further qualitative analysis was then undertaken. The approach used was based on the process of data-driven thematic analysis as described by Boyatzis (1998), and the stages of this analysis are outlined more fully below.

Results

Birth Relative Acceptance of Adoption

All birth relatives except one (a parent with learning disabilities) showed an understanding and acceptance of the legal realities of adoption: they understood the child's placement was permanent and their own legal rights terminated. However, whether parents and grandparents had reached a point of emotionally accepting the child's adoption was another matter, and three main patterns emerged from the interview data. In the 'positive acceptance' group (n = 14), birth relatives accepted that the child was now also part of another family. They expressed positive feelings about the adoptive parents and pleasure about the new life their child was enjoying. They were realistic about their current and future role in their child's life. On balance they felt that however hard the adoption had been, things had worked out for the best. The 'resignation' group (n = 10) consisted of birth relatives who felt very unhappy about the adoption but they resigned themselves to the loss. They saw themselves as worthless and unable to help or protect their child. Their current feelings about the adoption were marked by sadness, guilt and anxiety about their child. In the 'angry and resistant' group (n = 6), people expressed the view that although the adoptive parents were the legal parents, they were the *real* parents. They felt the adoption had happened unfairly and anger and blame were directed towards others, for example, family and friends, adoptive parents, social workers and judges. Grandparents were significantly more likely to be in the positive acceptance group than birth parents. The full results of this analysis are reported in Neil (2007b).

Adoption Communicative Openness

In these 30 cases, adoptive mothers' adoption communicative openness scores ranged from 9 to 25 (the possible range was 5–25). The mean score was 18.2 and the standard deviation 5.5. A full report of adoption communicative openness scores across the whole sample is given in Neil (2007a).

Thematic Analysis of Matched Cases

By using the five groups of matched cases (see Table 12.1), the next process was an exploratory qualitative analysis of these matched cases. The form

Table 12.2 Key themes from each group of matched cases.

	Birth relative positively accepting	Birth relative NOT positively accepting
Adoptive mother HIGH on ACO	**'Mutual supporters'** • Collaboration and flexibility over arrangements • Toleration and management of difficulties • Both adult parties manage own feelings • Mutual trust, respect and liking • Active involvement of children • Contact seen as beneficial for all • Positive evolution of contact plans	**'Adopter managed contact'** • Unresolved feelings of birth relatives 'spill over' into contact • Adoptive parents tolerate birth relatives' difficulties and persist with contact • Good communication not always achieved • Doubts about benefits of contact • Arrangements ongoing but static
Adoptive mother MODERATE on ACO	**'Birth relative managed contact'** • Birth relatives skilled at managing relationships with adoptive parents and wider birth family • Adoptive parents' anxieties are manageable because birth relatives are supportive • Arrangements static or evolving positively – contact settles at level of adoptive parents' comfort • Cautious satisfaction with contact on both sides	**'Unrealized potential'** • Contact very painful for birth relatives • Adoptive parents initially willing but become discouraged • Contact stops or is very minimal
Adoptive mother LOW on ACO		**'Downward spirals'** • Both sides ambivalent about value of contact • Mutual confusion about arrangements • Lack of opportunities for adult relationships to develop • Mutual lack of tolerance • Fears and threats • Children excluded from contact • Arrangements stopped or minimal

this took was an adapted version of Boyatzis's (1998) model of data-driven thematic analysis, the key stages of this being:

- Stage 1: Deciding on design issues and selection of subsamples (in this case, the five groups outlined above).
- Stage 2: Reduction of raw data by detailed note taking and writing case summaries.
- Stage 3: Reviewing reduced data in each subsample to generate a list of common themes (summarized in Table 12.2).
- Stage 4: Comparing and contrasting themes from the five groups to develop overarching themes.

In the current study, the analysis was undertaken as a supplementary analysis sometime after the end date of the project. Hence the author was the sole researcher, and there was no opportunity for a second person to be involved in the qualitative analysis. However, the detailed reporting of themes below which uses raw data to illustrate, allows the readers of this chapter to take a view as to the appropriateness of the themes.

'Mutual Supporters' – Adoptive Mother Is High on Communicative Openness, Birth Relative Is Accepting of Adoption   Of the nine cases in this group, six of the birth relatives involved in contact were parents and three were grandparents. Seven of the children had been adopted from public care and the other two at their parent's request. All cases in this group were involved in face-to-face contact arrangements. This group was characterized by positive spirals of interaction between mutually supportive birth relatives and adoptive parents, and children who were fully involved in arrangements. This group seemed to contain two types of cases: those where birth relatives had showed positive acceptance of the adoption from the start (e.g. grandparents who approved of the adoption plan) and those where initially unhappy birth relatives (usually birth parents) had been 'won over' by open contact arrangements with tolerant and welcoming adoptive parents.

Collaboration and Flexibility over Contact Arrangements.   Both adoptive parents and birth relatives worked together to negotiate the details of contact meetings and to agree on how issues to do with the child should be managed, for example, how a birth relative might answer any questions the child has about his or her past. There was not an expectation that birth relatives should automatically fall in with whatever adoptive parents suggested (or vice versa). Each party took the needs and wishes of the other adults and the child into consideration.

There was flexibility from both adoptive parents and birth relatives about who was involved in contact arrangements, indicating an acceptance that the child was connected to another 'family' not just other parents. For example, the two families might share special events, children could be introduced to wider members of their birth family, or birth relatives took an interest in other children in the adoptive family.

Toleration and Active Management of Difficulties.   If any problems were encountered, both sides showed an ability to tolerate difficulties and to either overlook or accommodate the problem, or take active steps to resolve the issue. For example, even though one adoptive mother asked the birth mother not refer to herself as mummy during meetings with the child, she overlooked occasions when the birth mother forgot this: *"She does slip up sometimes and she says 'come and see mummy'. . . but I never correct her, I just leave it – there is no point, there is no point in making meetings tense or sad. He [the child] knows what is what anyway."*

Both Adult Parties Can Manage Difficult Feelings.   In situations where meetings evoked uncomfortable or painful emotions, adoptive parents and birth relatives were able to tolerate and manage these. For example, one adoptive mother said, *"I suppose it just feels like loads of responsibility really primarily to [the child]. . . but I am very pleased we have it, it is quite stressful but I am very pleased we have it. . ."* In other cases birth relatives tolerated feelings of loss or envy engendered by seeing the close relationship their child or grandchild enjoyed with the adoptive parents, and took care not to let their feelings negatively impact on the child or adoptive parents. As one birth mother said: *"For the first bit of time it was hard, and it still is in a way, still hard . . . it hurts."* Despite these difficult feelings, she remained committed to carrying on the contact with her son: *"I'll be there for him, he knows that. I'll always be there."*

Mutual Trust, Liking and Respect for Boundaries.   Both adoptive parents and birth relatives raised the issue of trust. Reflecting the reality that all these contact arrangements were voluntary (as opposed to court mandated), meaning that adoptive parents had the power to adjust or stop contact if they wished, the issue of trust was somewhat different when viewed from the perspective of the birth versus adoptive family. Hence mostly adoptive parents talked about how they *trusted* the birth relative to respect boundaries, and birth relatives talked about the importance of *being trustworthy* and *feeling trusted* by the adoptive parents. The following example shows the interaction between the adoptive mother's trust and the birth relative's desire to be trusted:

> [Birthmother]'s always worried she is saying the wrong thing and she'll look at me and say "Should I have said that, I'm sorry. . . Am I allowed?" . . . and I say "Well you know today we are sharing him, today he is more yours, you take him on the roundabout". . . I will let him go off with her for a little while. (adoptive mother)

Positive interactions building trust could be initiated by a gesture from birth relatives or, as in the following example, adoptive parents:

> As soon as they got [the child] adopted, [the adoptive mum] wrote . . .She put her name, addresses, everything and phone number. She said "You can phone at any time you want and see [grandchild] whenever you want. . ." They invited me into their family and I have been there ever since. (grandmother)

Although birth relatives and adoptive parents made decisions about contact jointly, birth relatives were realistic about the power imbalance, acknowledging and accepting that adoptive parents ultimately have more say than they do. As one birth relative put it: *"At the end of the day it's up to [the adoptive mother]; she holds the top card."*

Adoptive parents and birth relatives liked, valued and cared about each other. In some cases people said their relationship was like a friendship, or like 'family' or 'extended family'. Other people, especially when contact was less frequent, had not developed a close relationship but they did talk about qualities and characteristics they valued in the other person. It was common that people showed concern for the welfare of the other person, beyond issues to do with the adoption or the contact. As one adoptive parent said, *"it is not just a, a cold contract any more."*

Active Involvement of Children in Contact. Adoptive parents facilitated their children's development of a direct relationship with their birth family members in two ways. Firstly, they encouraged them to write or phone birth family between meetings. Secondly, they allowed children to spend time alone with their birth relatives during contact meetings. In some families this was a matter of the child going off to their bedroom with their birth parent or grandparent for a while, or walking down to the nearby shop together. In other families the children were allowed to visit their birth family alone, even staying overnight or for a few days. Underpinning these arrangements was the trust that had developed between adoptive parents and birth family members, the valuing of the child's membership of the 'other' family, and the confidence of adoptive parents in their own relationship with the child:

> I am pleased that she is able to have that bond because it makes her a whole person really... it doesn't make me feel any the less loved at all because I know the fact that she loves other people doesn't mean she loves me any less. (adoptive mother)

Contact Seen as Having Benefits for Everyone.   People spoke of contact as an experience that was beneficial for everyone and this strengthened their motivation to keep arrangements going. Adoptive parents talked not just of how the contact might help the child or birth family, but they identified benefits for themselves such as feeling contact strengthened their relationship with the child, being able to have access to information about the child's background, and feeling reassured that the birth family approved of them. Similarly, birth relatives thought about contact not just in terms of their own need or desire to see the child, but also about the benefits they hoped would follow for the child and adoptive parents. For example, one birth mother talked about her belief that contact can help adopted children to understand the reasons why they were adopted and avoid feelings of rejection: *"... to put the child's mind at ease that they've still got a mum out there and that the mum still loves them. And they've got to understand why they were taken off them in the first place..."*

Positive Evolution of Contact Plans – Upward Spirals.   In this group face-to-face contact had been the starting plan in all cases, and moves towards greater openness (in terms of frequency or duration of meetings, disclosure of identifying information and involvement of more people) had occurred over the seven years or so since the placement to a certain extent in all cases.

'Adopter Managed Contact' – Adoptive Mother Is High on Communicative Openness, Birth Relative Is Not Accepting of Adoption   There were three cases in this group all involving mediated letter contact that was two-way between birth parents and adoptive parents. Two of the children had been adopted from care and the third was placed at the parent's request. These were cases where adoptive parents were positive about contact from the start, and they made efforts to make arrangements work (including involving the child) despite the fact that birth parents had not reached a point of

positively accepting the adoption. To some extent adoptive parents 'carried' the contact onwards (contact was ongoing in all three cases), but were unable to make it spiral upwards.

Unresolved Feelings of Birth Relatives Spill over into Contact.   The three birth mothers in this group all had their children adopted in very difficult circumstances and all three were left with intense feelings of anger, grief or guilt. Although all three mothers said they were glad to have some contact rather than none, contact with adoptive parents did not diminish these emotions, and painful feelings were having an impact on how the birth mothers saw contact. For example, one birth mother felt resentful of the adoptive parents for taking over her role as mother, and she believed their relationship with the child could never equal her own. In two of three cases, birth mothers showed little interest in improving their relationship with adoptive parents. They addressed their letters to the child, not the adoptive parents. They were eager to get anything back that was directly from the child, or even just to get a photo of him or her, valuing this more highly than a letter from adoptive parents.

Adoptive Parents Tolerate Birth Relative's Difficulties.   In all three of these cases, adoptive parents had been initially quite positive about the prospect of post-adoption contact. Faced with evidence of unresolved feelings in birth parents, adoptive parents were empathic and tolerant. For example, one adoptive mother explained that the birth mother's letters were 'too adult' for the child (then aged 6) because she poured out her feelings of loss and regret. Yet she tolerated this and understood why letter writing was hard for the birth mother saying: *"I think it's easier for us to write to her than for her to write to us."*

Effective Communication Not Always Achieved.   In all three of these cases, although adoptive parents and birth parents were continuing to write to each other, 'communication' was not always effective. Key concerns were about letters not arriving on time or containing the type of information desired, not knowing whether or how the letter had been received, and (for birth relatives) not knowing if the child was included in the contact. Adoptive parents tried to see such situations from the birth parent's point of view, and often took steps to try and improve things. Neither their commitment to maintaining contact nor their empathy for birth parents was significantly diminished. For birth parents however, any problems with contact seemed to confirm their worries or difficult feelings.

Uncertainty about the Benefits of Contact.   There was not a sense of shared understanding that everyone had something to give and gain from contact. For example, one birth mother enjoyed hearing how her child was getting on, but did not think that her child would get anything out of hearing from her. She also worried that contact was a burden for the adoptive parents, and feared they would rather have a closed adoption.

'Birth Relative Managed Contact' – Adoptive Parents Are Moderate on Communicative Openness, Birth Relatives Are Accepting of Adoption   Of the five cases in this group, four involved face-to-face contact with grand-parents, and one was letter contact with a birth mother. In all five cases contact was ongoing and involved the child. Two of the children had been placed at their parent's request and three were adopted from care. Contact arrangements were working out quite well; arrangements continued over time and children were involved and said to enjoy and benefit from meetings or letters. Birth relatives were playing a key role in making contact work, reassuring adoptive parents about their anxieties. Adoptive parents were generally cautious about opening up arrangements further, tending to keep the level of openness well within their own comfort range.

Adoptive Parent's Anxieties Are Manageable Because Birth Relatives Are Supportive.   All five birth relatives were able to demonstrate their approval and support for adoptive parents from the start of the placement. The adoptive parents had all approached contact with a mixture of hopes and caution. The subsequent success of contact was then dependent upon their hopes being realized and their fears disconfirmed. The behaviour and attitudes of birth relatives reassured adoptive parents in a number of ways, for example, by approving of their parenting and emphasizing their status as parents, by confirming that they were happy the child had been adopted, and by allowing them to stay in control of boundaries.

> [Grandmother] is always . . . full of how lovely [the children] look and, their clothes or whatever. I always remember the first, the very first [meeting] . . . because we were scared stiff obviously, and she actually came up to us and said "It is for the best and I know it's for the best". (adoptive mother)

Birth Relatives Are Skilled at Managing Relationships with Adoptive Parents and the Wider Birth Family.   In all cases there were examples of birth relatives recognizing and tolerating or trying to actively manage adoptive parents' anxieties. As one grandmother put it, *"I mean we had to really tread carefully and, you know, fortunately, we're older and we had a lot more wisdom and tact, we didn't put demands on [adoptive mother] . . . I had to go at her pace . . . and she has cooperated all the way along the line."* Birth relatives in this group seemed skilled at managing relationships, and many played a central role in both facilitating and controlling the involvement in contact of other members of the birth family. Once reassured by birth relatives, some adoptive parents in this group were happy to open contact up, but in other cases contact arrangements had remained static over the years.

Cautious Satisfaction with Contact.   All parties involved identified aspects of contact they were happy with, or things they felt were beneficial about the openness. But adoptive parents tended to express both positives and negatives about contact, or their satisfaction was measured rather than enthusiastic. Where there was the greatest variety in opinions was in terms of how the adoptive parents felt that contact impacted on them personally. Some adoptive parents identified an increase in their comfort with contact over time, for example, *"Although it upped the angst initially we can see how it has made a difference and it does get easier over time."* Other adoptive parents were maintaining contact and they identified benefits for the child, but they continued to feel uncomfortable with some aspects of contact personally, as one parent said, *"Twice a year, it's a reminder that she's adopted and not ours."* Some birth relatives did desire a greater level of contact, but all were prepared to work within the adoptive parent's comfort zone.

'Unrealized Potential' – Adoptive Parents Are Moderate on Communicative Openness, Birth Relatives Are Not Positively Accepting of the Adoption   There were three quite diverse cases in this group. In two cases the contact plan was for face-to-face contact with birth parents. In one of these, all contact had ceased with the birth mother (though it continued with other relatives). In another, face-to-face contact was ongoing but was very infrequent. In the third case the contact involved an exchange of written contact between adoptive parents and birth grandparents; the two parties had never met each other. This contact was ongoing but the exchange of information was quite minimal. Two of the children in this group had been adopted from care and the third at the parent's request. In this group the angry or sad feelings of birth relatives were acting as barriers to contact working well. Adoptive parents did not know why birth parents acted in the way they did, having little knowledge of how they really felt. All three adoptive parents had attempted to involve children in contact, but the extent to which this was possible was constrained by the limited involvement of birth relatives in contact.

Birth Relative's Participation in Contact Hampered by Their Painful Feelings.   Birth relatives found that contact aroused very difficult feelings, and these feelings prevented them from maintaining contact (in one case) or becoming more than only minimally involved (two cases). In all three cases birth relatives had wanted to parent the child themselves (including the grandparent), but had been prevented for various reasons from doing so. Two birth relatives talked of how painful they found contact, either because it brought back feelings of loss, or they resented the adoptive parents usurping their role. Two of the birth relatives also identified very strong feelings of anger in relation to the rules or boundaries of contact. For example, one birth mother disliked the adoptive parents being present during meetings: *"I couldn't face going because they were there all the time . . . And I didn't like it, I didn't like it at all because it was hurtful, it was hurtful for me."*

Adoptive Parent's Initial Willingness Diminishes.   Two of the adoptive parents had started off feeling very positive about and committed to contact, but after the partial or complete withdrawal of birth relatives from arrangements they had effectively stopped trying. As one adoptive mum said: *"I used to ring quite a lot and then time's gone by I've thought – Is this really what they want? . . . I should really stand back and wait for her."* In the third case, the adoptive parents had not particularly wanted contact to begin with. They did not find contact problematic and they were happy to continue exchanging cards with the grandparents, but they did not seek any deeper communication.

'Downward Spirals' – Adoptive Parents Are Low on Communicative Openness, Birth Relatives Do Not Accept the Adoption   In this group of 10 cases, seven of the children were adopted from care and three at their parent's request. The planned contact was face-to-face in four cases and letterbox in six cases – in all cases the contact had spiralled downwards over time. Looking at the four cases where the planned contact was face-to-face, in all of these the contact meetings had stopped. In two of these some contact via letters was being maintained and in the other two cases there was no longer any contact at all. Where contact was planned to be by letter, in all six cases the contact was either only happening at a very minimal level, or it had stopped. There were no examples where letter contact involved a regular two-way exchange of information including the adopted child.

Ambivalence on Both Sides about the Value of Contact.   Both adoptive parents and birth relatives expressed ambivalence about the value of post-adoption contact. Several adoptive parents said that they had never been enthusiastic; they had agreed to plans either because they thought the contact proposed was very minimal or because they thought they needed to agree in order to have a child placed with them. As one adoptive mother said, *"We would have been happier with no contact [but] . . . it's their ball game, and you have to play."* Other adoptive parents had been initially quite positive about the prospect of contact, but over time they had become increasingly ambivalent or negative, usually because the contact had not worked out they way they expected it to. Whilst most adoptive parents acknowledged that contact might have some benefits for birth relatives, they were less sure of the value for themselves and the child.

Some birth parents and grandparents seemed unconvinced of the value of the contact to others, for example, one mother did not send cards to her son because she felt *"It probably would be confusing when he gets to an older age and starts looking through his cards and thinks – . . . Which one's my mum?"* Other birth relatives seemed unable to tolerate their own pain, for example, one birth mother said about receiving letters, *"I don't want to know how she is getting on with the family . . . I mean it hurts . . . I don't see any purpose in it."*

Confusion about the Contact Arrangements and Wishes of the Other Party.   It was striking how often adoptive parents and birth relatives had different perceptions about what contact was 'supposed' to be happening or why it had stopped. For example, in one case the adoptive mother was keen to receive a letter from the birth mother but the birth mother believed she was 'not allowed' to write back. In another case where contact had started off as face-to-face, both the adoptive parents and the birth parents wanted meetings to continue but each was waiting for the other person to initiate this, a stalemate that had gone on for years.

Lack of Opportunities for Adult Relationships to Develop.   Only two of the six sets of adults involved in letter contact had actually met each other. In several cases there was no actual exchange of letters between birth relatives and adoptive parents: instead people would receive a letter from the agency containing the latest information. In some cases agencies did not pass on information they received – they merely kept it on file in the eventuality that someone would ask to see it. When meetings between adoptive parents and birth relatives did take place, these were not used to discuss the contact plans, nor were any subsequent meetings between parties ever arranged to solve problems when things weren't working well. In this group birth relatives and adoptive parents seemed to lack a real sense of each other – what the other person was like or what they wanted from contact – or any feeling that there was a 'relationship' between them.

Mutual Lack of Tolerance.   In this group people's feelings about each other and about contact had worsened over the years. When problems arose there was often little evidence of tolerance or understanding. Adoptive parents and birth relatives tended to make negative interpretations about the other person's behaviour leading to further withdrawal from contact. Several letter contact cases were in a condition of 'stalemate' with each party refusing to send anything until they received something from the other person. Birth relatives often portrayed adoptive parents as ungenerous or withholding, for example, one birth mother said *"I get angry, I get really angry. Because the least they could do is send me photos. That's the least they could do, seeing as they've got my kid."* Some adoptive parents believed birth parents were uncooperative, disinterested or undeserving: *"To me they're not passionate enough"*, *"She wasn't willing to do anything off her own back; she wanted everything like brought to her on a plate."*

Fears and Threats.   In five cases adoptive parents were reluctant to have contact because they were afraid of birth parents. In two cases contact was highly restricted because birth parents had a history of violent and unpredictable behaviour. But in other cases where no such risk was apparent, anxieties seemed related to feelings of threat about the child's connection to the birth family; *"The involvement of the birth parents just keeps bringing to the fore that he's adopted, that he's not really ours . . . there's something about Birthday cards and Christmas cards from birth parents that is just beyond what we're prepared to deal with."* Most birth relatives emphasized they would not want to do anything to upset the child or adoptive parents, or threaten that placement, but there were two exceptions to this. For example, one birth father said that he would attempt to physically reclaim the child if he had the chance: *"Oh, yeah, I'd take her. Oh yeah, she's my daughter isn't she, I feel like I got a right."*

Children Excluded from Contact.   In seven cases adopted children had no involvement at all in the contact arrangements. Two children were involved in letter contact; these were cases where face-to-face contact had ceased. Adoptive parents' reasons for not involving children were related to their ambivalence about the value of contact; they didn't involve children because they didn't see any particular benefit in doing so at that point in time. Six adoptive parents had not told their children they were having any contact with birth relatives.

Understanding the 'Quality' of Post-Adoption Contact – Overarching Themes The thematic analysis across the five groups of adoptive parent/ birth relative combinations identified six overarching themes, many of which underscore similar themes in other research. These six themes are as follows:

- **Emotional competence.** Post-adoption contact can, and often does, present emotional challenges to adoptive parents and birth relatives. The capacity of adoptive parents and birth parents to recognize and respect the point of view of the other adult party and of the adopted child, and to manage their own feelings (termed 'emotional competence') has emerged as being central in understanding how post-adoption contact works (see also Grotevant *et al.*, 1999). Contact worked best where both adult parties were emotionally competent (as in the 'mutual supporters' group). However, in some situations the emotional competence of one party will compensate for limitations in the emotional competence of the other (e.g. as in the 'adopter managed' and 'birth relative managed' contact groups). Where both parties experience problems in managing difficult feelings, significant problems in contact are evident (as in the 'unfulfilled potential' and 'downward spirals' groups).
- **Relationship skills.** Post-adoption contact requires adoptive parents and birth relatives to relate to each other in order to achieve the desired outcomes for the child. As well as deciding on 'ordinary' issues like where and when to meet, or what and how to write to each other, adoptive parents and birth relatives have to deal with more complex issues, for example, managing emotional distance regulation (see Chapter 13). The skills of the adult parties in managing these relationship issues are key, including the capacity to negotiate, be flexible, compromise and manage boundaries (see also Grotevant *et al.*, 1999). As with emotional competence, the best outcomes are achieved when both parties have these skills, and the worst outcomes, where skills are lacking on both sides. But contact can work if the strengths of one party can compensate for difficulties in the other.
- **Recognition and acceptance of power issues.** Relationships between adoptive parents and birth relatives are not based on an equality of power, but on recognition by birth relatives that adoptive parents have more power and willingness by adoptive parents to share some of this power (see also Dunbar *et al.*, 2006; Logan and Smith, 2005). There is no one right way for these issues to work that applies to all cases, as in different contact networks very different boundaries could be set. What seemed more important was that the level of comfort that adoptive

parents had with regard to contact was acceptable to birth relatives. When this was the case, adoptive parents might then be willing to compromise and share more of their power (e.g. by allowing more frequent contact). But when birth relatives wanted more than adoptive parents were willing to give, contact was uncomfortable for both.

- **Beliefs that contact can benefit all parties.** It was clear that where contact worked best, adoptive parents and birth relatives felt that everyone had something to gain. Doubts about the value of contact for the self, the other adult or the child were associated with less successful arrangements. In some cases these doubts seemed to follow from unsuccessful contact experiences, but in other cases they appeared formative of poor experiences. This suggests that contact is not just about how people feel and how they behave (emotional competence and relationship skills) but is also about how they think about contact; what is it for, who is it for?

- **The involvement of children in contact.** Across all groups it emerged that the quality of relationships between adults related to the involvement of children in contact. Where adult-to-adult relationships were working well, children were active participants in contact and their involvement was supported by their adoptive parents and birth family members. Where the adult relationships were not working well, children were often excluded from contact. Adoptive parents saw children's involvement in contact as either irrelevant to the child or potentially harmful to him or her. Birth relatives on the other hand were disappointed not to have a closer link to the child, valuing this above any relationship with adoptive parents. This suggests that neither thinking about contact either as an arrangement between the birth relative and the child, nor as something concerning only the adoptive parents and birth relative is helpful. Instead contact needs to be thought about (and managed) as an experience in which the adults work together on behalf of the child.

- **Contact arrangements can shape contact quality.** Of the two main types of contact, face-to-face meetings and mediated letter contact, successful and unsuccessful examples of each were identified. However, the most collaborative arrangements ('mutual supporters') were all face-to-face. This could be because positive attributes of birth relatives and adoptive parents make it possible to plan this type of contact. Alternatively, this type of contact might promote communicative openness and acceptance of adoption. There seems evidence that both of these processes could occur (Neil, 2007a, 2007b), although it is also clear from the current analysis that having a face-to-face contact plan does not guarantee success (e.g. 4 of the 10 cases in the 'downward spirals' groups had begun as face-to-face arrangements), especially when there is no opportunity for adoptive parents and birth relatives to directly discuss the contact arrangements outside of the contact meeting itself. Where contact was by letter (especially in cases where adoptive parents and birth relatives had never met each other) effective communication and therefore collaboration was often difficult to achieve (Neil, 2004b). The mediating role of the agency could sometimes make things worse rather than better: inefficiency, negative attitudes or unnecessarily restrictive arrangements could be undermining (Dunbar *et al.*, 2006; Neil, 2004b).

Discussion

This chapter brings together the coding of adoptive parent interview data (focusing on the adoption communicative openness of adoptive mothers) (Neil, 2007a), with the exploration of birth relative's acceptance of adoption (Neil, 2007b). Five different groups representing five different combinations of birth relatives and adoptive mothers on these dimensions were identified and analysed further. The coding of adoptive parent and birth relative data was based on the person's position at the time of interview, several years after the adoption and the groups represent positions people had reached at the time of follow-up. This analysis therefore presents a snapshot of contact but the reality is more like a moving film, as contact is both dynamic and transactional. The transactions (or lack of transactions) over time between adoptive parents and birth relatives had been mutually influential. Neither relationships nor contact plans had always been stable, and positive spirals, negative spirals and static arrangements were all observed.

What this research adds to the existing literature is an understanding of how contact arrangements operate with different *combinations* of adoptive parents and birth relatives. The data suggest that when adoptive parents are highly communicatively open and birth relatives show positive acceptance of the adoption (as in the 'mutual supporters' group), then the stage is set for comfortable and continuing contact with children at the heart of the process. Even when birth relatives find it very hard to positively accept the adoption, to some extent adoptive parents can carry arrangements along, maximizing any possible benefits and preventing downward spirals, as was the case with the 'adopter managed' contact cases. When adoptive parents are moderately communicatively open, a positive attitude of the birth relative is vital. When birth relatives show positive acceptance of the adoption, contact can be maintained and in some cases will become more successful over time, as was seen in the 'birth relative managed' contact group. When birth relatives are resigned or angry and resistant, this tends to reinforce adoptive parents' anxieties and bring about deterioration in contact progress and satisfaction; cases fitting this pattern were described as 'unfulfilled potential' because the positive qualities of adoptive parents often did not result in successful contact arrangements. Contact was least likely to be successful when adoptive parents were low on communicative openness and birth relatives did not positively accept the adoption and 'downwards spirals' involving low satisfaction with and commitment to contact seemed an inevitable outcome.

There were no examples in this study of combinations where adoptive parents were low on communicative openness yet birth relatives showed positive acceptance of the adoption, maybe because this particular combination is not stable. When anxious and defensive adoptive parents who do not feel positive about contact are 'paired' with birth relatives who positively accept the adoption, one of two things might occur: either birth relative's attitudes will have a positive effect on adoptive parents, helping them to feel at least moderately communicatively open, or adoptive parent's attitudes will have a negative effect on birth parents, undermining their positive feelings about the adoption.

The other important factor to consider in understanding contact is of course what the child brings to the arrangements. If children seem comfortable and happy with contact, adults might feel more relaxed and confident, but if children are anxious or disturbed adults might begin to question the value of meetings or letters. It needs to be remembered that the children in this study were young at placement and only in middle childhood at follow-up, and the dynamics of contact may differ for other groups of children. These young placed children seemed to largely take contact with birth relatives for granted – it had been a feature of their life from a young age and they accepted it as normal, and in most cases positive (Neil, 2006). The relatively benign responses of children to contact were generally reassuring for adoptive parents and birth relatives (Neil, 2004a, 2004b; Young and Neil, 2004). For children who are placed at older ages and who have had more involved relationships with birth relatives, or for those who have been traumatically abused, post-adoption contact can be a much more intense experience (e.g. Howe and Steele, 2004; Macaskill, 2002; Thoburn, 2004). The experience of contact for children may also alter as they, as well as their interest in adoption, grow (Grotevant, McRoy and Ayers-Lopez, 2004; Chapter 10).

The analysis of contact arrangements in this chapter bears striking similarity to many of the themes about 'emotional distance regulation' in

Grotevant's work (Chapter 13), in spite of the differences in the samples (infant, relinquished children, versus young children mostly adopted from care). Both analyses highlight the skills and expectations that adoptive parents and birth relatives bring to contact; the development of relationships over time and the upward and downward spirals that can occur depending on whether experiences are positive or negative; the settling of contact at a comfort level acceptable to both; and the role of the agency in socializing people and the issues that can arise with agency-meditated contact. In future research the key themes that have arisen from the current exploratory analysis could now be build on in terms of specific code development that could be used across different samples.

Implications for Practice

When planning post-adoption contact, and the support for such contact, there is a need to think about the *emotional competence, relationships skills* and *beliefs about contact* and *understanding of power issues* of adoptive parents and birth relatives as individuals, and to help people build on positives and address problems in these areas. But the research also suggests a need to think systemically about how the 'combination' of people is likely to work. Where there are positives on both sides, contact arrangements may be successful and self-sustaining. But when this is not the case good outcomes may be unlikely unless appropriate support is available. Support for contact should both help people deal with their individual issues, but also focus on the functioning of the contact network, especially the communication, trust, collaboration and understanding of power issues between adoptive parents and birth relatives.

When considering the type of contact and how contact (especially agency-mediated contact) is managed, there is need to consider how the communication between the adult parties can be facilitated. When contact is to be by letter, extra challenges in achieving communication may exist, and both adoptive parents and birth relatives may value support in writing and receiving letters. If direct contact between the child and birth relative is not deemed appropriate, occasional meetings between adoptive parents and birth relatives that allow adults to develop a relationship with each other may help letter contact plans to succeed. Face-to-face contact will not be appropriate in all cases, but in this study this type of contact often seemed easier than letter arrangements, as meetings facilitated the adults' empathy for each other and left less room for misunderstandings and wrong interpretations. In some cases, even though adults may have the chance to meet each other during contact meetings, further opportunities to meet without the child being present might be needed to facilitate and plan the arrangements.

Although contact ought to be primarily to meet the needs of the child, this analysis suggests unless adults have an understanding of and commitment to the value of contact for all parties, plans are unlikely to endure over time. The adoption agency has an important role to play in helping to socialize adults to their role within the adoption kinship network (Chapter 13). Hence in preparing people for contact, it seems appropriate to focus not just on how contact might help children, but to help people to explore how the experience might benefit themselves and the adults in the child's 'other' family.

References

Boyatzis, R.E. (1998) *Transforming Qualitative Information: Thematic Analysis and Code Development*, Sage, Thousand Oaks, CA.

Brodzinsky, D.M. (2005) Reconceptualizing openness in adoption: Implications for theory, research and practice, in *Psychological Issues in Adoption: Research and Practice* (eds D. Brodzinsky and J. Palacios), Greenwood, New York, pp. 145–66.

Brodzinsky, D.M. (2006) Family structural openness and communication openness as predictors in the adjustment of adopted children. *Adoption Quarterly*, **9**, 1–18.

Child Welfare Information Gateway (2003) *Openness in Adoption: A Bulletin for Professionals*, http://www.childwelfare.gov/pubs/f_openadoptbulletin.cfm (accessed January 2008).

Dunbar, N., Van Dulmen, M.H.M., Ayres-Lopez, S. *et al.* (2006) Processes linked to changes in adoptive kinship networks. *Family Process*, **45**, 449–64.

Grotevant, H.G., McRoy, R.G. and Ayers-Lopez, S. (2004) Contact after adoption: Outcomes for infant placements in the USA, in *Contact in Adoption and Permanent Foster Care: Research, Theory and Practice* (eds E. Neil and D. Howe), British Association for Adoption and Fostering, London, pp. 46–64.

Grotevant, H.D., Ross, N.M., Marcel, M.A. and McRoy, R.G. (1999) Adaptive behaviour in adopted children: Predictors from early risk, collaboration in relationships within the adoptive kinship network, and openness arrangements. *Journal of Adolescent Research*, **14** (2), 231–47.

Henney, S.M., McRoy, R.G., Ayers-Lopez, S. and Grotevant, H.D. (2003) The impact of openness on adoption agency practices: A longitudinal perspective. *Adoption Quarterly*, **6**, 31–51.

Howe, D. and Steele, M. (2004) Contact in cases in which children have been traumatically abused or neglected by birth parents, in *Contact in Adoption and*

Permanent Foster Care: Research, Theory and Practice (eds E. Neil and D. Howe), British Association for Adoption and Fostering, London, pp. 46–64.

Logan, J. and Smith, C. (2005) Face-to-face contact: Views from the triangles. *British Journal of Social Work*, **35**, 3–35.

Macaskill, C. (2002) *Safe Contact? Children in Permanent Placement and Contact with their Birth Relatives*, Russell House Publishing, Lyme Regis.

Neil, E. (2002) Contact after Adoption: The role of agencies in making and supporting plans. *Adoption & Fostering*, **26**, 25–38.

Neil, E. (2004a) The 'Contact after Adoption' study: Face-to-face contact, in *Contact in Adoption and Permanent Foster Care: Research, Theory and Practice* (eds E. Neil and D. Howe), British Association for Adoption and Fostering, London, pp. 65–84.

Neil, E. (2004b) The 'Contact after Adoption' study: Indirect contact and adoptive parents' communication about adoption, in *Contact in Adoption and Permanent Foster Care: Research, Theory and Practice* (eds E. Neil and D. Howe), British Association for Adoption and Fostering, London, pp. 46–64.

Neil, E. (2006) *Contact with Adult Birth Relatives after Adoption: A Longitudinal Study of Children Aged under 4 at Placement. Final Project Report to Nuffield Foundation*, University of East Anglia, Centre for Research on the Child and Family, Norwich.

Neil, E. (2007a) Post adoption contact and openness in adoptive parents' minds: Consequences for children's development. *British Journal of Social Work* (advance access, doi: 10.1093/bjsw/bcm087).

Neil, E. (2007b) Coming to terms with the loss of a child: The feelings of birth parents and grandparents about adoption and post-adoption contact. *Adoption Quarterly*, **10** (1), 1–23.

Neil, E., Grotevant, H. and Young, J. (2006) *Adoptive Parent Communication Openness: Coding Manual* (copy available from author).

Neil, E. and Howe, D. (2004) Conclusions: A transactional model for thinking about contact, in *Contact in Adoption and Permanent Foster Care: Research, Theory and Practice* (eds E. Neil and D. Howe), British Association for Adoption and Fostering, London, pp. 224–54.

Parker, R. (1999) *Adoption Now: Messages from Research*, The Stationery Office, London.

Thoburn, J. (2004) Post-placement contact between birth parents and older children: The evidence from a longitudinal study of minority ethnic children, in *Contact in Adoption and Permanent Foster Care: Research, Theory and Practice* (eds E. Neil and D. Howe), British Association for Adoption and Fostering, London, pp. 224–54.

Young, J. and Neil, E. (2004) The 'Contact after Adoption' study: The perspective of birth relatives after non-voluntary adoption, in *Contact in Adoption and Permanent Foster Care: Research, Theory and Practice* (eds E. Neil and D. Howe), British Association for Adoption and Fostering, London, pp. 46–64.

13

Emotional Distance Regulation over the Life Course in Adoptive Kinship Networks*

Harold D. Grotevant

We used to write daily and call each other weekly, I mean in the beginning. When the children were real little, it was tremendous intensity. And I think as our birth mother became more secure in herself and went on to finish college, her need to have to see them once a week or once a month became less and less. And you know, she feels more comfortable with us, we feel more comfortable with her, and we just know that we always have access . . . You just take it one day at a time. If you want it to work, you'll work at it. We feel it's healthy and want it to work because of our children. (adoptive mother)

This quote describes how a child's adoptive parents and birth mother have worked to achieve a mutually agreeable degree of closeness in their relationships, and how those relationships have evolved over time as the adults became more secure in their own roles and more comfortable with each other. We refer to the process of negotiating, fine-tuning and navigating the dimension of closeness–distance in these relationships as *emotional distance regulation*.

Regulation of emotional distance among members has been recognized as one of the most basic processes engaged in by family systems (Broderick,

* Support for the Minnesota/Texas Adoption Research Project is acknowledged, with gratitude, from the National Institute of Child Health and Human Development; National Science Foundation; William T. Grant Foundation; Office of Population Affairs, United States Department of Health and Human Services; and the Hogg Foundation for Mental Health.

1993; Grotevant and Cooper, 1986, 1998; Hess and Handel, 1959; Kantor and Lehr, 1975; Reiss, 1981). In the case of adoption, this process extends to the regulation of emotional distance over time among members of a child's adoptive and birth families, the adoptive kinship network. Although the task is relevant for all adoptive kinship networks, the participants and the dynamics among them will vary as a function of whether there is direct contact, indirect contact, or no contact between adoptive and birth family members.

In a confidential adoption, even if little or no information is available and contact is impossible, adoptive parents are well aware that their child was born to others, and the adopted child is aware that they have birth parents and perhaps extended family. In other words, the birth family may be psychologically present even if they are physically absent (Fravel, 1995; Fravel, McRoy and Grotevant, 2000). In the case of agency-mediated or indirect contact, shared information and contact may be quite limited. However, participants know that there are others who contributed to the life of the child. In fully disclosed open adoptions, the opportunity is present for extensive contact among extended family members in both the adoptive and the birth family. Despite this opportunity, families with open adoptions vary widely in the frequency and type of contact and in the number of people who are involved in contact with each other (Grotevant, Perry and McRoy, 2005).

Understanding the dynamics of families requires that we understand the individuals who make them up. However, the family system is not reducible to the sum of its members, because when all the individuals come together, emergent family dynamics are created. Nevertheless, qualities that individuals bring to the family make significant contributions to the resulting dynamics. In our work, we have tried not to privilege individuals, dyadic relationships, or families, acknowledging that understanding each of these levels and their interconnections is critically important.

Individuals bring four important elements to the families they create and inhabit: their developmental history, expectations about relationships, expectations about adoption, and relationship skills. *Developmental history* refers to people's experiences in their families of origin and other close relationships. Attachment theory (Bowlby, 1969, 1988; Sroufe, 1979, 1996) specifies how such experiences contribute to the construction of an internal working model of relationships (relationship representations) that guide behaviour in future relationships. *Expectations about relationships* grow out of people's internal working models of relationships, influenced by family of origin experiences as well as contemporary relationship experiences (Sroufe *et al.*, 2005). *Expectations about adoption* are shaped by many things, including personal experience with adoption, media portrayals, friends' stories of adoption, and personal circumstances leading one to consider adoption, such as infertility. *Relationship skills* include perspective-taking ability, empathy, communication skills, and style of relating to others. Taken together across individuals, each of these four elements has significant implications for how an adoptive kinship network will function.

The quote that began this chapter is a clear example of how the participants in one adoptive kinship network arrived at a degree of closeness they were all comfortable with. The adoptive mother reported that there was a 'tremendous intensity' soon after the placement, but then the birth mother's need for contact 'became less and less'. As they have become more comfortable with each other, they gravitated towards a level of intensity of contact that worked for all of them.

Farley (1979) noted that individuals bring to their families a range of tolerance for separation and connection. This comfort zone is influenced by the individual's relationship history, expectations and skills. For each person in the adoptive kinship network, we can ask: How close is 'too close'? How separate is 'too separate'? What is the comfort zone of closeness–distance in which each person operates? What happens when the individuality of each participant comes together to create an adoptive kinship network?

As the members of an adoptive kinship network become acquainted, individual differences in tolerance for separation and connection surface and must be dealt with over time. Of course, this process is not unique to adoptive families. It happens every time we enter or create a new group, whether it be in the work setting, school, neighbourhood or extended family.

Broderick's (1993) writing about couples provides useful ideas for thinking about the formation of adoptive kinship networks. He noted that when couples begin a new relationship, there are three possible scenarios. The partners may have well-matched comfort zones, in which case the relationship can get off to an easy start. Second, if they are not well matched, one person may yield to the other. Or third, the parties may need to negotiate in order to find a level of closeness that works for both of them. 'Negotiate' is not necessarily a conscious, overt process. It is a process that takes place through all the nuanced micro-steps in daily interactions. Broderick (1993) described this process as the "normal, rhythmic alternation of connection and separation in real time" (p. 92); like the contraction and expansion involved in a heartbeat (Hoffman, 1981).

In addition to the dynamics associated with creating new relationships, adoption itself challenges adults' comfort zones because the relationships are incredibly intimate (e.g. with the birth mother of the child you are raising), yet the relationship partner is also a stranger. In an ideal world, members of adoptive kinship networks would be able to evolve a mutually agreeable fit, where participants' comfort zones are compatible or can be stretched to be compatible. In reality, the process works like it does in all families. We develop close relationships with some people and more distant ones with others, and the relationships continue to evolve over time.

The process we have seen over time looks like a relationship dance in which the partners establish a comfort zone of interaction that works for them. The accumulation of interactions leads to increased interdependence among participants, which means that the thoughts, emotions, and behaviours of one participant affect and are affected by the thoughts, emotions and behaviours of another (Kelley *et al.*, 1983).

When interactions are positive and rewarding, participants are willing to risk a bit more the next time. They are willing to let the other come a little closer into their social circle. When interactions seem difficult or challenging, they may erect barriers or defences that constrain the development of further intimacy. This series of interactions builds up over time into a relationship pattern (Kelley *et al.*, 1983; Levinger, 1983).

This is the same process we use as we enter into any new, potentially intimate, relationship. Expectations and interactions lead us to make judgements about how much we like the other person, how trustworthy we believe them to be, how much of a risk we are willing to take to get to know them better, and how much we want them to know us.

Yet the relationship dance in adoption has some distinctive features as well. Adoption establishes a relationship among adults, not only for their own sakes, but also because they believe that having the relationship is good for the child who is at the centre of this adoptive kinship network. Thus, their concerns about trust, caring and commitment to the relationship are about the child as well as about themselves.

This chapter examines the dynamics within adoption kinship networks using the lens of family systems theory. The Minnesota/Texas Adoption Research Project (Grotevant and McRoy, co-principal investigators) will be used as a source of insights.[1] A life-course view of emotional distance regulation will be outlined, focusing primarily on the adult members of the

---

[1]   Names and other identifying information have been changed in order to protect participants' confidentiality.

adoptive kinship network. Special attention will be given to similarities and differences in emotional distance regulation as a function of contact between adoptive and birth family members.

Openness in Adoption: The Minnesota/Texas Adoption Research Project

In the United States, there continues to be a small, yet significant number of adoptive placements of infants by birth parents who voluntarily relinquish their parental rights, typically so that the child will have better opportunities and a more stable family than the birth parents feel they can provide. The Minnesota/Texas Adoption Research Project (MTARP) began in the mid-1980s, when most infant placements were arranged by private adoption agencies – typically non-profit organizations, some of which had religious ties (e.g. Lutheran Social Services, Catholic Charities). MTARP was initiated because some of these agencies began to offer arrangements that allowed the birth mother to choose the family who would adopt her child and then have contact with them as the child grew up.[2] This new paradigm stemmed from the belief that children deserve to know their histories and their birth parents, and that members of the adoptive kinship network are fully capable of forging relationships that would provide nurturing contexts for their children.

The study was launched in order to contribute to understanding of relationships and developmental outcomes for children in adoptive kinship networks that vary in degree of contact between the child's birth and adoptive family members. Each of the families in the project adopted an infant in the late 1970s or early 1980s. Participants were first interviewed between 1987 and 1992 (Wave 1), again between 1996 and 2000 (Wave 2), and most recently between 2005 and 2008 (Wave 3).

Participants were recruited for the study through 35 adoption agencies located across the United States. Families were sought in which there was at least one adopted child between the ages of 4 and 12 years, who was placed for adoption before the child's first birthday. Transracial, international and special needs adoptions were not included because of

---

[2] The initial impetus for post-adoption contact in the United States came from private agencies (McRoy, Grotevant and White, 1988). Public agencies placing children who had been removed from their birth parents' homes because of abuse, neglect, chemical dependency or mental illness have approached the idea of contact much more slowly. Similarly, the idea of openness in international adoptions is only recently being explored.

the additional variance they would introduce into the study design. At Wave 1, the sample included 720 individuals: 190 adoptive mothers, 190 adoptive fathers, 171 adopted children and 169 birth mothers. The racial background of the participating families reflected that of the clients typically served by private adoption agencies at that time: the vast majority were white, Protestant and middle- to upper-middle class. The median age at which the children had been placed for adoption was 2 weeks; the mean age of the children at the time of the Wave 1 interview was 7.8 years. Almost all couples adopted because of infertility. Birth mothers typically placed babies for adoption so that they would grow up in a two-parent family that would offer their child good financial and educational opportunities, and because they felt adoption was preferable to abortion.

Adoptive families were interviewed in their homes across the United States; birth mothers were interviewed in their homes, at the agency or by telephone. Participants completed lengthy individual interviews and a number of standardized questionnaires (see below). Further details about the sample and measures are reported in Grotevant and McRoy (1998). At Wave 2, participants included at least one member of 177 of the original 190 adoptive families (173 mothers, 162 fathers, 156 adolescents) and 127 birth mothers (Grotevant, Perry and McRoy, 2005). The adopted adolescents ranged in age from 12 to 20 years (mean age = 15.7 years). Adoptive families were once again seen in their homes. Participants completed detailed individual interviews, standardized questionnaires, and a family interaction task. Birth mothers completed interviews by telephone and questionnaires by mail. Wave 3 (in progress) involves the young adult adoptees (age range 20–28), the person identified as their closest relationship partner, and their adoptive parents. Young adults and their partners were interviewed via online chat technology and completed standardized questionnaires through a Web interface. Parents were interviewed by telephone and completed questionnaires by mail.

The insights reported in this chapter emerged from the extensive interviews conducted with the adoptive parents and birth mothers, especially those adoptive kinship networks experiencing contact between adoptive and birth family members.

Emotional Distance Regulation across the Life Course

Emotional distance regulation is a dynamic process by its very nature. It can be experienced in moment-to-moment interactions in families. It is also affected by contexts originating in distinctive challenges for adoptive kinship networks across the life course. This section provides examples of distance regulation that begin prior to adoptive placement and continue through adolescence.

Prior to Placement

Emotional distance regulation begins prior to placement, when the individuals who will eventually become an adoptive kinship network are forming mental representations and expectations of what their new family arrangement will be. Most individuals or couples seeking to adopt do so because they want the experience of parenting, and they want to offer something to a child, perhaps a child they were not able to conceive biologically. What images of adoption guide their anticipatory thinking about what their own adoptive family might be like? What kind of family do they intend to create? Daly (1988, 1992) has noted that infertile couples who had planned to have biological children undergo a process of resocialization into adoptive parenthood, during which their thinking about the meaning of parenting necessarily changes. Parents who opt for more open adoptions may also need to undergo another resocialization process, from visualizing themselves as 'traditional' adoptive parents to parents involved as part of a larger kinship network.

Birth parents also have ideas and expectations about what an adoption might mean for them and for their child. Will the placement provide them with reassurance about their child's well-being over the years? What are their expectations about the role they might play in the child's life, now and in the future?

The seeds of the emotional distance regulation process that will play itself out over time are present in these early mental representations of adoption. In the views of the adult participants, what are the proper roles of adoptive parents and birth parents with respect to each other and to the child? These initial views will guide how the key people interpret and evaluate information about adoption that they find on the Internet, discuss with friends and family, and learn from adoption agencies or intermediaries.

Expectations about adoption are also shaped by the interactions that participants have with friends, family members and adoption professionals. If they work with an adoption agency that exclusively brokers open adoptions, they may become socialized into this way of thinking, or they may seek a different type of agency or intermediary whose views are more in line with their own. Selection of the adoption intermediary is one of the early steps in emotional distance regulation, since the way the adoption is structured at the outset will set the tone for how it is to proceed.

Consider the following contrasting views given by adoptive mothers in our study:

> In an open adoption, "you not only have the medical information, but you have the history, which I think is very important for children – to know what great grandpa did and what parts of them are like people in their biological family. And to have them involved in their celebration for birthdays and holidays and major events . . . So I think this gives them history, it gives them a connection and I think as long as there is respect of who are the parents and not co-parents, I think we can manage." (adoptive mother)

> An advantage of confidential adoption is that birth mothers "could be able to move on with their lives and not have something hanging over their heads. You know, adoption to the adoptive parent is not baby-sitting. It's your responsibility to raise, take care of these children, and if there's another mother there, where does it stop, where does the confusion end? I don't know, I don't know." (adoptive mother)

Thus, in many ways, the process of emotional distance regulation has begun, even before the adoptive parents meet the child or birth parents.

Placement and the Earliest Months

The placement itself requires that decisions be made about physical and emotional distance. In uncontested adoptions, it is now common for members of the child's birth family and adoptive family to meet at or around placement, sometimes even before the child's birth. What expectations do these family members have about the future? The child's birth family members may be wondering: Who are these strangers I'm giving my child to? Can I trust them? Will they stay in touch with me, or will they forget me as soon as they have my child? Will they help my child remember me? The new adoptive parents may be wondering: Who is this person who is giving her child to us? Does she expect to be able to see her child? If we have contact with her, will she take advantage of the situation? Will she interfere with our parenting? Will she try to take the child back if her life circumstances change? Will she make demands on my life? What about her parents or the birth father? All of these questions are guided by concerns about the unknown future.

Our data suggest that strangers come together to co-construct a future by first testing the waters of this new relationship with their little toes. Few dive in head first, because they don't know what lurks beneath the surface. New relationships follow predictable patterns that can be described using concepts from Kelley *et al.*'s (1983) close relationships model. Relationship development progresses through five phases: (i) acquaintance, (ii) build-up, (iii) consolidation, (iv) deterioration and (v) ending (Levinger, 1983). In adoptions where no information is shared, relationships do not even proceed to the acquaintance phase. If information is shared, adoptive kinship network members have the option to maintain an acquaintance-like relationship or intensify the relationship. During the build-up phase, participants explore relationships by gathering information, increasing the frequency of interaction, and varying the types and settings of exchanges. If the relationship moves to the consolidation phase, the stability of the relationship often increases and partners become more interdependent. Deterioration occurs if some of the partners become less involved in the relationship, and ending may follow when contact is terminated (Dunbar *et al.*, 2006).

As a child's birth and adoptive parents interact over time, they develop a level of mutual comfort with the degree of closeness and interdependence in their relationship (Grotevant *et al.*, 1994). Fine-tuning of a relational comfort zone requires time, communication, negotiation skill, and attitudes of openness and flexibility to move the relationship from the acquaintance phase to the consolidation phase and then to prevent deterioration (Dunbar *et al.*, 2006).

In addition to the gradual build-up of moment-to-moment interactions, emotional distance may be regulated by verbal or written agreements about the type and frequency of contact. Written contact agreements specify details about how frequent visits may be, where they may occur, who may be present and so on. The legal enforceability of written contact agreements continues to be challenged in the courts (Appell, 2000a, 2000b). Verbal contact agreements are easier to modify over time, but may also lead to missteps if the parties do not communicate well with each other (remember the 'relationship skill' component that participants bring to the table.) Others may improvise as the relationship proceeds. This requires strong communication skills and flexibility. Very few MTARP families had written contact agreements. Rather, over time, they engaged in the relationship dance (mentioned earlier) in which they established a comfort zone of interaction.

Emotional distance regulation can be assisted by rituals. When we were starting our research on openness about 20 years ago, Ruth McRoy and I were invited to witness an adoption placement ceremony. Social workers played a key role in orchestrating the placement, attaching symbolic meanings to its actions, and shaping the expectations that participants took away from the ceremony.

Prior to the ceremony, the prospective adoptive couple and their parents came to the agency and followed their caseworker down the hall to one office. A little later, the birth mother, infant, and her parents came to the agency and went down another hall to meet with their (different) caseworker. At the appointed time, all parties gathered in the conference room, which doubled as an impromptu chapel (since this agency had a religious affiliation). A chaplain presided over the placement, during which the birth mother handed the child to the adoptive parents, and commitments about the child's well-being were publicly stated. Prayers were said to seal the arrangement, pictures were taken, and poignant congratulations were offered. Afterwards, before going their separate ways, the adoptive family members and birth family members met again with their respective caseworkers to process what had happened and what might lie ahead.

This tightly scripted ritual and the surrounding interactions with social workers set the stage for the expectations that all parties might have about the future. In the Vygotskian sense, the professionals provided scaffolding for the fledgling adoptive kinship network, with the assumption that their assistance would be gradually withdrawn and the kinship network members would need to negotiate their own future.

Although most all adoptions have some assistance with the legal details, many adoptions have much less support in the way of relationship scaffolding. Since there are few time-tested scripts for contact after adoption, the parties are left to their own devices to figure out their unique dance. How will they develop this dance? Will they be able to learn from their inevitable missteps, or will one party's unintentional transgression lead to an emotional cut-off by the other? With the placement, the stage is set for how future steps in the dance might look.

Whether the birth parents' rights were terminated voluntarily or involuntarily can have a significant impact on the relationships in the kinship network. If the placement was involuntary (parental rights were terminated by the courts), contact may be forbidden. But that does not mean that the birth family does not exist. And if the child was older at placement, he/she may have vivid memories (both good and bad) about that part of the family. The agency's philosophy about both structural and communicative openness also has a strong impact on participants in the kinship network, who may not have had their own presuppositions about adoption before coming to the agency.

Adoptive parents and birth parents do not participate in the kinship network on an even playing field. The adoptive parents have full legal rights and responsibilities for the child, whereas the birth parents' rights have been terminated through court proceedings, either voluntarily or involuntarily. In open adoptions lacking written contact agreements, the opportunities extended to the birth family members are at the pleasure of the adoptive parents. However, birth family members also have power in the situation because they can decline contact or refuse to participate.

Finally, there are often age, race, and social class asymmetries between adoptive and birth family members, further complicating the task of finding common ground about this kinship network. For example, if the birth mother and adoptive mother are not truly peers, how do they enter into a peer-like relationship? Is there an expectation that the adoptive parents will take on a mentoring role to their child's birth mother? Our data indicate sometimes yes, sometimes no.

The Early Years

Our interviews with adoptive parents and birth mothers revealed that the adults in the adoptive kinship network have different needs for contact and relationships during the early years. For the moment, take the perspective of a child's birth mother. In our interviews, birth mothers told us that they do not put the child out of their minds and 'get on with their lives', as some suggest they should. Many told us that they think about the child every day; that the child is psychologically present to them, even if physically absent (Fravel, McRoy and Grotevant, 2000).

Birth mothers' initial concerns are completely understandable. The birth mothers in our sample elected voluntary placements so that their child would have a better life and would be loved and secure. Many talked about wanting the child to grow up with two parents who could give them better life opportunities. They wondered: How is my child doing? Is my child safe? Can the adoptive parents – strangers – truly love my child? Her need for reassurance, information and perhaps contact is most intense in the early years of the placement. Feeling reassured allows her to invest her emotional energy in other relationships – perhaps a new romantic relationship or other children.

Adoptive parents' perspectives, concerns and needs were different. Most of them had experienced fertility problems and were very excited to finally have the child they had wanted for a number of years. Once the child arrived, their primary interest was in establishing their new family, especially if this was their first adoption. The years of working towards this goal gave the early years of the adoption special intensity.

Some developed a plan for birth family contact from the beginning, often with the assistance of the agency. However, their primary focus tended to remain on the child. Once several years passed and the adoptive parents felt more secure as parents, they found it easier to think about extending their family circle to include the child's birth family.

Ironically, as the adoptive parents felt more comfortable reaching out, the child's birth mother might be pulling back a bit, especially if she is romantically involved or has children she is parenting. Adoptive and birth parents' developmental pathways may not be in synchrony (van Dulmen, Grotevant and McRoy, 1998).

As the adults' diverging paths are getting sorted out, the child may be taking on a more active role in the family drama. His or her developing understanding of the concept of adoption (Brodzinsky, Singer and Braff, 1984) and emerging sense of identity as an adoptive person (Grotevant, 1997) may evoke questions about birth family or desires for contact. The Family Adoption Communication (FAC) Model (Wrobel *et al.*, 2003) outlines the progression from the child's initial adoption story (provided by adoptive parents) to their active questioning of their parents and relatives, to their independent information gathering and possible searching.

The Childhood Years: Life Happens

Once initial adoptive kinship network relationships are established, they will continue to evolve in response to forces internal to the relationship and to the external ecology of the network. Among the most influential external factors are the entrance and exit of people from the kinship network (through birth, adoption, divorce, death), changes in geographical distance, and changes in agency involvement in the relationship. Responses to all these events require the regulation of emotional distance.

Like all families, adoptive families experience a range of membership changes, the details of which are unique for each family. New children join the family through birth or adoption, adults join the family through marriage or commitment, parents divorce and sometimes remarry, family members die, and so on. The child's birth family may experience a similar range of relationship changes.

Our research revealed that marriage of the birth mother has significant potential to change the relationship equilibrium that may have been established in the kinship network. At Wave 1, 57% of the birth mothers were married. By Wave 2, 66% were married and 81.9% were either married or involved in a romantic relationship (McRoy *et al.*, 2001).

The birth mother's marriage (rarely to the child's birth father) may affect the kinship network in varied ways. In some of the cases in our study, the birth mother shared information about the adoption with her new husband, and he was accepting of this and became an active member of the kinship network himself. In other cases, the man wanted to marry the birth mother but had little interest in the adopted child and family, choosing not to participate in their lives. In very rare cases, he forced the birth mother to choose between him and the child, or she kept the adoption secret from him. The latter two situations typically increased the emotional distance between the birth mother and her child and adoptive family, sometimes at great emotional cost.

Emotional distance can also be affected when the birth mother has children in a new relationship. By Wave 2, 76.4% of the birth mothers were actively parenting children (McRoy *et al.*, 2001). Although the vast majority of birth mothers were sharing information about the adoption with their romantic partners, some were not comfortable doing so with their children, but most of them planned to share the information when the children were older. When such information is not shared, the extent of her participation in the adoptive kinship network may suffer as a result.

Divorce of the adoptive parents also has the potential to shift relationships within the kinship network. Thirteen of the original 190 adoptive families experienced divorce or separation between Waves 1 and 2. Some of the divorced adoptive mothers felt very guilty because they knew the birth mothers had made an adoption plan so that the child would be in a two-parent family, and now they were not able to live up to this expectation. In rare cases, contact with the birth mother stopped or changed because the adoptive mother did not want to reveal the divorce.

Emotional distance can also be affected by factors external to the relationship, for example, when a third party is mediating the relationship. As this adoptive mother noted, the plan for mediated contact was interrupted when there was a change in staffing at the adoption agency.

> Our social worker quit the agency. So, she called beforehand and gave us a little information and since that time we've had no contact whatsoever. She gave the little information that she had with the birth mother, and that was the last we've heard. We didn't know the new worker, so I suppose our case was just put in a file and forgotten.

The Adolescent Years

Adolescence brings an ongoing recalibration of closeness–distance within all families (Grotevant, 1998). As adolescents seek more independence in their social lives, school lives and decision making, parents assess how ready they believe their adolescents are to take on such responsibilities. Interviews at Wave 2 revealed that adoptive mothers continued to broker contact between adopted children and birth family, but they anticipated a gradual shift in which the adolescent will take the lead on birth family contact. Interviews with the adolescents, however, suggested that some were not aware that their parents expected them to be taking on more responsibility in this domain (Dunbar *et al.*, 2006).

As adolescents and birth mothers increased the independence of their own relationship (away from mediation by the adoptive parents), they found that it required new relationship work to arrange contact and negotiate how they would interact. Birth mothers who previously had close relationships with the adoptive parents sometimes missed this contact as their relationship with the adopted youth took shape. However, this change also presented the birth mother with the exciting opportunity to build the deeper relationship with the adopted youth that she had long desired (McRoy *et al.*, 2001).

Birth mothers who did not have contact were aware of the upcoming eighteenth birthday of their children and were anticipating that the adolescent might try to contact them. Most birth mothers said they would welcome contact from their children, but did not want to initiate it themselves and risk intruding on the adolescent.

Thus, adolescence is another time when significant recalibrations of emotional distance may occur. The individual characteristics mentioned earlier in this chapter come into play. Expectations about relationships influence people's behaviour along the closeness–distance continuum. If it is anticipated that a particular relationship will be rewarding, behaviour that will bring about more closeness may occur. Conversely, relationships anticipated with fear or concern will elicit distancing. Expectations about adoption also come in to play. What is 'supposed to' happen among members of the adoptive kinship network? Open adoptions are still new enough that there is no relationship template. Although some people may want more guidance from experts, the lack of a template allows the participants to enter into the relationship dance and determine themselves how close they will be. Of course, communication skills are called upon as relationship changes are considered or enacted.

Despite all of these dynamics, it is important to remember that adoptive families are just like most other families raising kids. They deal with school, friends, siblings, jobs, sports, activities and the business of daily life. And during adolescence, as one adoptive mother put it, "teenage things take over".

The Dynamics of Emotional Distance Regulation

Strategies and Interaction Patterns

Interviews with adoptive parents in MTARP revealed a number of strategies used within adoptive kinship networks to regulate emotional distance. In general, adoptive mothers were the 'kin keepers' in our sample, and took on greater responsibility than their husbands for managing contact. Very few birth fathers were involved in their children's lives by mid-adolescence. Thus, these interactions took place primarily between adoptive mothers and birth mothers.

The following strategies were noted: (i) adoptive mothers and birth mothers present a united front to the child; (ii) adoptive mothers and birth mothers recognize each others' unique contributions to the child; (iii) adoptive mothers and birth mothers provide support to each other; (iv) adults establish clear boundaries; (v) adults tolerate the complexity and ambiguity inherent in their relationship; and (vi) adults allow the relationship to grow gradually. This list illustrates the kind of strategies that the adult members of adoptive kinship networks use to regulate emotional distance among themselves, but it is not intended to be exhaustive.

Adoptive and Birth Mothers Present a United Front to the Child Discussions between adoptive and birth parents can identify issues of potential triangulation, especially where the child might try to pit adoptive and birth parents against one another. When the adults agree about how they will approach an issue, they prevent potential difficulties while simultaneously strengthening their own relationship.

> Maddie (Jason's birth mother) is real fearful about Jason's being rejected by his birth father if he ever finds him. And so we kind of chat on the phone about what the psychologist says and what I'm willing to work with and what she's willing to give, so that we don't present this odd picture to him. I would say me and Maddie have gotten pretty close. I mean, we don't talk to each other unless it's about Jason or our families. But she seems comfortable calling if she has questions. (adoptive mother)

Adoptive and Birth Mothers Recognize Each Other's Unique Contributions to the Child Relationships can be strengthened by emphasizing cooperation rather than competition and by realizing that all the adults in the adoptive kinship network can potentially make positive contributions to the child's life.

> We're both two individuals ⟨adoptive mother and birth mother⟩, and we can enrich her life in different ways, so I guess I really don't feel in competition with her ⟨the birth mother⟩ any more. I know that we both have a special place in her heart. (adoptive mother)

> I know that my son as an individual has questions. Same as a lot of my other kids, he's got sensitivities. And she's (birth mother) got the answer. I don't. And she's the key to some of those. And so that's been very satisfying to me to know that he has that access when he wants it. (adoptive mother)

Adoptive and Birth Mothers Provide Support to Each Other Family members can be brought closer together in times of crisis or difficulty. From a family systems perspective, positive, supportive relationships among the adults are likely to be beneficial for the child.

> I'd like to try to be as supportive to her in her experiences as a new mom, as perhaps her mom was to me. Offering support, to help, baby sit. I'd like to be able to do that. (adoptive mother)

Adults Establish Clear Boundaries Sometimes it is not clear where the boundaries in a relationship are, until one party feels that the boundaries have been violated. At that point, clarification of boundaries through open and honest communication will benefit relationships among the adults and with the child.

> I think as long as there is respect of who are the parents and not co-parents, I think we can manage. (adoptive mother)

> The following dialogue drawn from an interview with an adoptive mother illustrates establishment of boundaries:

> Birth mother (BMo) to adoptive mother (AM) following an extended visit: "I can't get enough of ⟨teen⟩ and I'll tell you that right off."
> AM to BMo: "Well, I know you can't."
> BMo to AM: "Well, you let me know when I overstep my bounds."
> AM to BMo: "You will know."
> Teen to BMo: "Oh, come see me sometime."

BMo to Teen: "I'd love that!"
AM to BMo: "I'm not ready for that yet."

In another situation, the BMo called the adoptive family's home, and their daughter answered the phone. BMo asked to speak to her son directly (she had never done this before), and the daughter gave her brother the phone without his knowing who was calling. He didn't know how to respond to her and was somewhat upset. "So we did ask her from then on, to please ask for us, only so that we could tell her whether he was in a mood to talk to her. . . . To offer him the choice rather than picking up the phone and not knowing that it was her on the other end." (adoptive mother)

And even though I'm old enough to be her mother, at one point, she wanted to adopt me as her mom, she even asked at one point if she could move in with us and I said no. . . . No, that's not an option. I was like, I adopted one, I'm not adopting two. (adoptive mother)

Adults Tolerate the Complexity and Ambiguity Inherent in the Relationship   Families choosing open adoptions are still relationship pioneers, even though open adoptions have been available for about 20 years. There are no templates for participants to follow, and a certain amount of trial-and-error is involved. Acknowledgement of ambiguities coupled with good communication and a sense of humour will be beneficial to all network members.

When asked if she thinks it's confusing for her daughter or family to have contact with birth relatives, one adoptive mother said, "I came from a divorced family, and so I have a step-sister; and then my father remarried, and I have another step-sister and two step-brothers, and it doesn't really confuse you, it just adds." (adoptive mother)

There's a funny character to the relationship in the sense that there's a bond that's stronger than almost any, but we don't know each other that well. And we care for each other immensely, but we don't have a relationship. (adoptive mother)

Adults Allow the Relationship to Grow Gradually   Most of the MTARP families with extensive contact did not start out that way. The relationship grew gradually over time as the adoptive parents and birth mother got to know one another. Intimacy and trust expanded as both parties had positive experiences in the relationship.

I went from not knowing them (the adoptive parents) to knowing them, to kind of being a part of their life through their child, to being a part of their life just by being me. (birth mother)

The adoptive parents call and ask me to send cards to Sara. They seem to want more contact, and they keep calling and saying that she is asking a lot of questions. They want me to be more involved than I am. But I just don't have the time to just really devote a lot to her now 'cause I've got so much of my own going on'. (birth mother)

When we first started out with Morgan's birth mother, I asked, "How much contact do you want?" I was real nervous, because I'd heard all these stories that they try to get them back and all this, and you knew you had to wait six months before it was really final. (adoptive mother)

I didn't know if I wanted to go on, maybe just send a picture once in a while, a letter once a year or something. But after we have that initial meeting and can see what they're like and see how the first couple years it goes, I said it was OK. I didn't mind giving information after we got to know her. We let her have our phone number first and then later on, we just wrote letters using the adoption agency's address and then later, we gave her our home address. I was nervous at first (laugh) but not really after we knew her pretty well. (adoptive mother)

Towards a Process Model of Emotional Distance Regulation

This brief exploration of emotional distance regulation in adoptive kinship networks has highlighted the processes whereby individuals within networks modulate their relationships along the closeness–distance dimension over the life course. We hope that the following 10 observations emerging from data from the Minnesota/Texas Adoption Research Project will form a foundation for future theoretical and empirical work in this area.

1. The adoptive kinship network brings together individuals who come to adoption with different developmental histories, expectations of relationships (specific and general), expectations of adoption, and relationship skills.
2. The creation of an adoptive kinship network occurs within adoption-specific contexts that involve traditions, rituals, agencies, policies, laws and public attitudes towards adoption.
3. Contact among members of the adoptive kinship network occurs by various means, among varying people, at differing rates, and with varying degrees of interest.
4. Face-to-face meetings have powerful influence on distance regulation.

5. Each adoptive kinship network is a unique combination of persons and contexts; therefore, one size cannot fit all with respect to contact arrangements. As an adoptive father in MTARP stated, "The same glove does not fit every hand."
6. Positive, rewarding interactions tend to increase contact and the desire for it.
7. Negative, problematic interactions tend to decrease contact and the desire for it.
8. The extent of contact tends to be the level acceptable to all members of the kinship network – that is, the lowest common denominator.
9. The adoptive mother–birth mother relationship is especially important in setting the stage for interactions across the entire adoptive kinship network.
10. In families with more than one adopted child, parents tailor decisions about contact to specific knowledge of, and comfort with, each child's birth family members.

Implications for Practice

A family systems perspective on emotional distance regulation within families illuminates some of the challenges facing adoptive kinship networks and suggests ways in which problems might be anticipated or remedied. Practice implications outlined here are aimed at professionals providing pre-adoption counselling or post-adoption services to members of adoptive kinship networks. These recommendations flow directly from knowledge of what kinship network participants bring as individuals to their families and how interactions among them are shaped across the life course.

1. Help clients think beyond their nuclear family and consider themselves members of a broader adoption kinship network. Even when there is little or no contact between adoptive and birth family (i.e. physical absence), members may be psychologically present to each other, even if the person is fantasized rather than known.
2. Plans for contact and changes in contact should reflect an appreciation of the individual differences among the participants. Individuals will vary in their developmental history, relationship expectations, expectations about adoption, and relationship skills; and these differences will influence their attitudes towards contact and success with it.

3. Adoptive kinship network members can be taught skills that will help them negotiate a comfort zone of interaction that works for all parties. Since the level of contact often sinks to the lowest level commonly accepted by all, the network level of contact could be enhanced by providing skills or new perspectives to those in the network least interested in contact. Teachable skills are suggested by the strategies that adoptive and birth mothers used to regulate distance in their kinship networks (see above); for example, presenting a united front to the child, recognizing each others' unique contributions to the child, providing mutual support, establishing clear boundaries and tolerating the complexity inherent in their relationships.

4. Agency staff and other adoption intermediaries should recognize the special responsibilities and challenges associated with mediating contact in adoptions where identifying information has not been shared. Since the adoptive and birth family members are not known to each other, provisions must be made for mediated contact to continue if the primary staff person becomes ill, goes on vacation or leaves the agency. An agreement to mediate communication between adoptive and birth family members should be viewed as a many-year commitment.

5. Craft individualized contact plans for adoptive kinship networks with built-in flexibility, anticipating that families and their members will change over the life course. Detailed, inflexible plans may work in the short run but not meet anyone's needs in the longer term.

6. In conceptualizing adoptive kinship networks as one type of 'complex family', adoption professionals should stay abreast of advances in working with blended families post-divorce, families built through assisted reproductive technology, long-term foster families, and families of choice. New concepts and accrued practice wisdom concerning one type of complex family might suggest strategies that could be applied to others.

References

Appell, A.R. (2000a) Enforceable post-adoption contact statutes, Part I: Adoption with contact. *Adoption Quarterly*, **4** (1), 81–90.

Appell, A.R. (2000b) Enforceable post adoption contact statutes, Part II: Court-imposed post adoption contact. *Adoption Quarterly*, **4** (2), 101–11.

Bowlby, J. (1969) *Attachment and Loss: Vol. 1: Attachment*, Basic Books, New York.

Bowlby, J. (1988) *A Secure Base*, Basic Books, New York.

Broderick, C.B. (1993) *Understanding Family Process: Basics of Family Systems Theory*, Sage, Newbury Park, CA.

Brodzinsky, D., Singer, L.M. and Braff, A. (1984) Children's understanding of adoption. *Child Development*, 55, 869–78.

Daly, K. (1988) Reshaped parenthood identity: The transition to adoptive parenthood. *Journal of Contemporary Ethnography*, 17, 40–66.

Daly, K. (1992) Toward a formal theory of interactive resocialization: The case of adoptive parenthood. *Qualitative Sociology*, 15, 395–417.

Dunbar, N., van Dulmen, M.H.M., Ayers-Lopez, S. *et al.* (2006) Processes linked to contact changes in adoptive kinship networks. *Family Process*, 45, 449–64.

Farley, J.E. (1979) Family separation-individuation tolerance – A developmental conceptualization of the nuclear family. *Journal of Marital and Family Therapy*, 5, 61–7.

Fravel, D.L. (1995) Boundary ambiguity perceptions of adoptive parents experiencing various levels of openness in adoption. Unpublished Doctoral Dissertation, University of Minnesota, St. Paul.

Fravel, D.L., McRoy, R.G. and Grotevant, H.D. (2000) Birthmother perceptions of the psychologically present adopted child: Adoption openness and boundary ambiguity. *Family Relations*, 49, 425–33.

Grotevant, H.D. (1997) Coming to terms with adoption: The construction of identity from adolescence into adulthood. *Adoption Quarterly*, 1 (1), 3–27.

Grotevant, H.D. (1998) Adolescent development in family contexts, in *Handbook of Child Psychology: Vol. 3. Social, Emotional, and Personality Development*, 5th edn (eds W. Damon [series edition] and N. Eisenberg [volume edition]), John Wiley & Sons, Ltd, New York, pp. 1097–149.

Grotevant, H.D. and Cooper, C.R. (1986) Individuation in family relationships: A perspective on individual differences in the development of identity and role taking in adolescence. *Human Development*, 29, 82–100.

Grotevant, H.D. and Cooper, C.R. (1998) Individuality and connectedness in adolescent development: Review and prospects for research on identity, relationships, and context, in *Personality Development in Adolescence: A Cross National and Life Span Perspective* (eds E. Skoe and A. von der Lippe), Routledge, London, pp. 3–37.

Grotevant, H.D. and McRoy, R.G. (1998) *Openness in Adoption: Connecting Families of Birth and Adoption*, Sage, Newbury Park, CA.

Grotevant, H.D., McRoy, R.G., Elde, C.L. and Fravel, D.L. (1994) Adoptive family system dynamics: Variations by level of openness in the adoption. *Family Process*, 33, 125–46.

Grotevant, H.D., Perry, Y. and McRoy, R.G. (2005) Openness in adoption: Outcomes for adolescents within their adoptive kinship networks, in *Psychological Issues in Adoption: Research and Practice* (eds D. Brodzinsky and J. Palacios), Praeger, Westport, CT, pp. 167–86.

Hess, R.S. and Handel, G. (1959) *Family Worlds: A Psychosocial Approach to Family Life*, University of Chicago Press, Chicago.

Hoffman, L. (1981) *Foundations of Family Therapy*, Basic Books, New York.

Kantor, D. and Lehr, W. (1975) *Inside the Family: Toward a Theory of Family Process*, Jossey-Bass, San Francisco.

Kelley, H.H., Berscheid, E., Christensen, A. *et al.* (1983) *Close Relationships*, W.H. Freeman, San Francisco.

Levinger, G. (1983) Development and change, in *Close Relationships* (eds H.H. Kelley, E. Berscheid, A. Christensen, *et al.*), W.H. Freeman, San Francisco, pp. 315–59.

McRoy, R.G., Ayers-Lopez, S., Henney, S. *et al.* (2001) *Adoption openness: Longitudinal birthmother outcomes*. Final report prepared for the Office of Population Affairs, United States Department of Health and Human Services, University of Texas at Austin School of Social Work, Austin, TX.

McRoy, R.G., Grotevant, H.D. and White, K.L. (1988) *Openness in Adoption: New Practices, New Issues*, Praeger, New York.

Reiss, D. (1981) *The Family's Construction of Reality*, Harvard University Press, Cambridge, MA.

Sroufe, L.A. (1979) The coherence of individual development. *American Psychologist*, **34**, 834–41.

Sroufe, L.A. (1996) *Emotional Development: The Organization of Emotional Life in the Early Years*, Cambridge University Press, New York.

Sroufe, L.A., Egeland, B., Carlson, E.A. and Collins, W.A. (2005) *The Development of the Person: The Minnesota Study of Risk and Adaptation from Birth to Adulthood*, Guilford, New York.

Van Dulmen, M.H.M., Grotevant, H.D. and McRoy, R.G. (1998) The adoptive kinship network, in *Openness in Adoption: Connecting Families of Birth and Adoption* (eds H.D. Grotevant and R.G. McRoy), Sage, Newbury Park, CA.

Wrobel, G.M., Kohler, J., Grotevant, H.D. and McRoy, R. (2003) The Family Adoption Communication (FAC) Model: Identifying pathways of adoption-related communication. *Adoption Quarterly*, **7** (2), 53–84.

14

Connecting Research to Practice

Gretchen Miller Wrobel and Elsbeth Neil

Introduction

Adoption researchers and practitioners hold a common goal: to support the experience and lives of adopted persons and their families. Researchers seek out knowledge that can benefit members of the adoption kinship network while practitioners utilize that knowledge in professional practice. Across the years, both adoption research and practice have responded to the changing needs of birth and adoptive families. As adoption and its many forms continue to evolve, research and practice must continue to change as well.

Common to all forms of adoption is the experience of the adopted child being born into one family and raised in another. Yet, the myriad of adoption types express this fundamental experience in different ways. Children may live with their birth families for a number of years before being adopted into another, be much loved or experience abuse or environments of extreme deprivation, move from one county to another, be adopted by relatives or foster carers, or have varying amounts of contact with their birth families. It is the unique context in which the adoptive kinship network resides and the experiences of its members that inform both research and practice. The research contributions to this volume reflect the diversity of adoptive context and experience, providing unique insight for understanding adoptive families as a complex family form. In this chapter we do not attempt to give specific and detailed practice suggestions (though many chapter authors have done so) but more to point to key themes that reflect the work presented in this volume. The four key themes we shall discuss below are as follows:

- The need to be both optimistic and realistic about what adoption can achieve for children.
- The need to maintain an ethical climate in adoption practice.
- The need for expertise in adoption practice.
- The need for practitioners to facilitate and inform research.

Although we are drawing on the contributions of chapter authors, the views expressed here are our own.

Messages for Practice

The Success of Adoption as a Child Welfare Intervention: Being Optimistic and Realistic

Adoption practice emerges as a worthwhile strategy to meet the needs of children who have no realistic prospect of being raised successfully in their birth family. The message here for practice is really one of encouragement to continue the excellent work of finding a wide range of families for the wide range of children who would otherwise grow up in unsuitable environments. This optimistic message of encouragement to promote adoption must be balanced with realistic and research-informed understanding of factors associated with success, and a commitment to the provision of ongoing services to adopted children and their birth and adoptive families.

The improvements in developmental outcomes for adopted children justify adoption's place in the range of permanency options for children in need. Even children adopted from the poorest of backgrounds often experience very positive adjustment. At the same time, the research reported by the teams led by Rutter (Chapter 7), Juffer (Chapter 8), Steele (Chapter 9) and McRoy (Chapter 5) all illustrate that some children will continue to have ongoing difficulties in their development that cannot be entirely ameliorated by their adoption. These same authors have also illustrated that, in many of these cases, children and parents can experience loving family relationships in spite of these challenges. This suggests that in promoting adoption as a child welfare intervention, practitioners need to balance optimism about adoption, with realism about what adoption can and cannot achieve. The research in this book reinforces messages that have emerged from many studies over the past 40 years or so, that the children likely to need ongoing specialist help are those who have experienced deprivation in an institutional setting, those with high levels of genetic risk, and those who have experienced abuse, neglect or multiple placements. Adoption may provide a child with a family for life, but this does not mean it can be seen as a way to end the responsibilities of either society or adoption agencies towards children with special needs: promoting adoption must be accompanied by promoting post-adoption support services.

Both McRoy *et al.* and Steele *et al.* point out that adoption is most likely to succeed when the needs and wishes of children and adoptive parents are carefully matched. Hence in arguing for the promotion of adoption, we would also argue that care and discrimination needs to be taken at the placement stage. Both the above-mentioned chapters discuss the psychological characteristics of parents who can succeed in parenting children with special needs. For example, Steele *et al.* talk about the need for adoptive parents to have resolved their own issues of trauma and loss. McRoy *et al.* identify characteristics such as commitment, flexibility, determination and a sense of humour. Neil (Chapter 12) identifies open and supportive communication with birth parents as important.

While we advocate paying careful attention to qualities such as these in adults we are considering placing children with, there is also evidence that a wide range of adults can make suitable adoptive parents. We ought not to be unnecessarily restrictive about other characteristics such as age and marital status, as this may exclude those who can parent well. For example, many of the parents in the Rutter *et al.* study who had adopted children from Romanian orphanages had been rejected by British adoption agencies, often on the grounds of age. Yet the adoption breakdown rate in this sample was virtually non-existent. McRoy *et al.*'s report that over one-third of the parents who successfully adopted the older children with special needs in the Collaboration to AdoptUsKids programme, were not 'traditional' married couples. Given these findings it is interesting that Selman (Chapter 3) reports that China is now refusing adoption by single parents. Similarly, Palacios (Chapter 4) has discussed the somewhat random policies different countries have about the maximum age of adoptive parents. Both these observations suggest that what happens in policy and practice is still not yet always informed by research.

Maintaining an Ethical Climate in Adoption

In continuing to encourage adoption, it is vital that practitioners and policy makers maintain 'an ethical climate' (Kelly, Chapter 11). We suggest this means firstly that the social forces – political, institutional and attitudinal

– which help shape adoption experiences, need to be considered by adoption professionals; and secondly that the costs as well as benefits of adoption must be understood and addressed.

Poverty   In Chapters 1 to 4, Howe, Carp, Selman and Palacios have all illustrated that the broader social context in which adoption occurs is vital in determining when, why and where adoption happens. Living in poverty is one social context that makes it difficult and sometimes impossible to raise children. The possibility of a life not dominated by poverty for one's child can provide motivation for relinquishment in both wealthy and economically developing countries. Themes of poverty permeate explanations given to children for their adoption. Adopted children want to know why they were placed for adoption (Wrobel and Dillon, Chapter 10) and when explanation for relinquishment and placement include that one's birth mother "could not take care of you" or "wanted to give you a better life", an underlying assumption is that she did not have the financial resources to provide a home and raise her child. Howe points out that societal representations of adoption found in literature also incorporate escape from poverty and the chance for a better life.

For children adopted from the public care system, such as those discussed by Steele *et al.*, McRoy *et al.* and Neil, poverty is also a feature of their backgrounds. Though poverty is not the sole reason for adoption from care, the birth parents of the majority of these children will have struggled to parent while dealing with a combination of psychosocial disadvantages. Issues such as mental ill health, poor educational outcomes, substance misuse problems and involvement with the criminal justice system can both result from living in materially deprived conditions, and also contribute to social and financial decline.

Given the vast inequalities in resources both between and within countries, the values of both justice and compassion must be central. Promoting adoption as a child welfare response to a range of disadvantages must be undertaken in addition to, not instead of, initiatives that reduce the need for adoption and enable children to be safe and secure in their birth families. When birth mothers consider placing their children for adoption, adoption practitioners must be vigilant in providing information and support that will lead to a fully informed decision. The dark side of birth mother relinquishment is perpetrated by unscrupulous 'baby brokers' who provide payment to birth mothers for placing their children and pay scant attention to informed consent. Providing payment can lead to coerced relinquishment. Lack of adequate explanation can leave the birth mother with the idea that her child may return in the future, not understanding the permanent nature of the arrangement. When children are adopted from care, proper and stringent legal requirements need to be enforced to ensure that this serious and life-changing measure is made fairly and with full consideration of the potential impact for all involved.

Stigma   Social stigma associated with adoption must also be recognized. There have been a number of examples of how stigma relates to adoption in this book. Carp points out that the social stigma attached to adoption was instrumental in closing adoption records in the United States, England, Wales and New Zealand. Protecting a child's illegitimate status from being known and the idea that birth mothers might possibly harass adoptive families both motivated changes in policy to seal records. Carp's historical analysis documents how these broad forces in society shaped the individual experience of adoption triad members as records gradually became closed to adopted people themselves. It is easy to make links with Wrobel and Dillon's chapter, in which they demonstrate the need of adopted people to know about their own history.

The experience of birth mothers is also shaped by social stigma. Kelly has written about the experience of Irish birth mothers in the 1960s who were coerced into placing their child for adoption to avoid the stigma of raising an illegitimate child and bringing shame onto their family. This type of stigma may still be driving adoption in some countries today, as both Kelly and Selman have argued. But even in countries where births outside marriage are accepted, stigma is still a relevant concept from the point of view of birth families. Firstly, as both Kelly and Palacios point out, in societies where keeping one's baby is the norm a mother who chooses to place her child for adoption may be stigmatized as selfish and unwilling to make the sacrifice needed to raise a child. Secondly, as Kelly and Neil discuss, birth parents whose children are adopted from public care are also likely to be affected by shame and social stigma. Their child's adoption rests on a judgement by the state that they have failed as parents; the abuse and neglect of children are transgressions about which few members of society feel sympathetic.

There are also suggestions that stigma about adoption can affect the adoptive family and adopted person, and that adoption itself can be seen as an inferior form of family. Palacios describes the many ways in which this might come about, from the medicalization of infertility making adoption 'third best' (after having biological children naturally, or through fertility treatments) through to a focus on the negative aspects of adoption in both research and the media. There is a danger that if adoptive families feel stigmatized or inferior, they may seek to avoid thinking about or drawing attention to their differences. One possible consequence of this may be the impact it could have on adoptive parents' preference for the type of child they would like to adopt. Children who come with reminders that they are adopted (e.g. because they are older or have special needs, because they need contact with their birth family members, or because they are of a different ethnic group – in short many of the children who most need to be adopted) may not be favoured.

The impact that adoption practitioners can make on social and political forces that shape stigma and poverty is questionable. However, our plea remains that these forces must be at the very least made visible and their impact on children, their adoptive families and their birth families recognized, talked about and, where possible, ameliorated.

Recognizing the Lifelong Impact of Adoption   The lifelong impact of adoption on all parties must always be held in mind, and the ability to empathize with all parties in adoption is vital. This volume has allowed us to learn about adoption from the perspective of adopted children, adoptive parents and birth relatives. What we learn from this is about not just the joys of adoption but also some of the costs.

Although the research in this book is largely optimistic about the gains for children that adoption can bring, it needs to be remembered that the fact of adoption itself can have a price for the adopted person. Wrobel and Dillon's chapter illustrates some of the extra challenges adopted children have to deal with in adolescence, especially in finding answers to the question 'why was I adopted?' Carp outlines the legal barriers that have prevented adopted people from having access to information about *their own* life history. Juffer and van IJzendoorn report how some intercountry adoption children were unhappy that they were not white, and sad that they were not born to their adoptive parents. Selman refers to the difficult feelings children adopted from Korea and China might have about the fact that they could not remain in the country of their birth, let alone in their birth families. Although in many cases these 'costs' may not outweigh the costs of *not* being adopted, practitioners must always recognize the potential drawbacks as well as the anticipated benefits of the placement. This recognition is the first step in taking appropriate steps to reduce later problems. This might entail, for example (as Wrobel and Dillon suggest) maintaining excellent records as a resource to the child, facilitating birth family contact as desired, or as Kelly suggests setting up information exchange systems or contact registers.

The chapters by Kelly and Neil illustrate that for birth parents, grandparents and other relatives, adoption often comes with considerable costs in the form of long-term feelings of anxiety, loss, shame, anger and guilt. Yet Kelly suggests this need not be the case and those birth mothers who have a fair choice about adoption, support to deal with their difficult feelings and access to ongoing information about their child can fare much better. Neil's chapter also illustrates the positive impact that post-adoption contact can have on birth family members.

With adoptive parents, an ethical position is one that recognizes their strengths and contributions, but also acknowledges and supports their needs. The chapters by Steele *et al.*, Rutter *et al.* and McRoy *et al.* especially illustrate the huge challenges and developmental problems that some adopted children can have, and the emotional challenges that adoptive parents can experience. Adoptive families should not be left to deal with these alone, or be made to feel they have to fight or beg for support. Post-adoption services need to be available and accessible.

The Place for Expertise in Adoption Practice

There is a great need for effective pre-placement preparation and assessment and subsequent ongoing support for adopted children, adoptive parents and birth family members. To address these needs we suggest that adoption practice needs to be multidisciplinary, expert and case sensitive.

Palacios includes a discussion about the role of the adoption practitioner in the ecology of the adoptive family. He also highlights the lack of an evidence base about 'what works' in adoption practice. Although there are admittedly few research studies that have particularly studied adoption practice as the central focus, the research included in this volume offers useful suggestions about the nature and type of expertise required by practitioners. It is clear that expertise in adoption practice is required from a range of professional groups including social work, psychiatry, paediatrics, psychology, teaching, social pedagogy, counselling and legal advocacy.

Professionals working within adoption are likely to need very specific skills and expertise together with an excellent understanding of adoption itself. For example, Steele *et al.* describe how positive parental attachment representations allow for flexibility of parenting which in turn promotes positive attachment between adoptive parent and adopted child. They suggest that adoption workers could benefit from an understanding of some of the narrative methods of the adult attachment interview and story-stem techniques when assessing and matching parents and children. Reiss *et al.* (Chapter 6) outline the need for practitioners to have an understanding of genetic risks, and to detect potential problems at an early stage when intervention may be most effective. Juffer and van IJzendoorn outline how video training with feedback can be a useful method for enhancing attachment security between children and adoptive parents. Rutter *et al.* suggest that health professionals need to have an understanding of the unusual patterns of development that can follow early institutional deprivation.

Neil and Grotevant (Chapters 12 and 13) both illustrate the need for adoption practitioners to understand the dynamics of the adoption kinship network and to have skills in facilitating the functioning of these networks. The existence of the adoption kinship network as an inherent aspect of adoption brings complexity to the adoptive family. The management of relationships between the adopted person, the adoptive family and the birth family varies by the amount of contact between the adoption kinship network members. Grotevant discusses how emotional distance regulation is an important part of the process that members of the adoption kinship network use to find the balance of relationships that meets the needs of all. Neil also identifies some of the key skills, attitudes, and emotional qualities held by birth relatives and adoptive parents that underpin sustained, satisfying and child-focused contact arrangements. She discusses how adoptive parents who were highly communicatively open facilitated their children in being actively involved in post-adoption contact, and managed children's feelings when contact was not straightforward.

Practitioners must also understand the dynamics of communication about adoption. Within the complexity of the adoptive family and across types of adoption arrangement, communication about adoption can promote positive development. How communication takes place, the content and effect of that communication, and action taken on behalf of and by the adopted person all influence adoption outcomes. For example, adoptive parents tell the adoption story to their child, and adopted children must learn what adoption means and form an adoptive identity. These tasks can prompt and are prompted by curiosity about adoption and subsequent action to find out the information (Wrobel and Dillon).

As their numbers continue to rise, the unique context of children adopted from foster care, which includes established birth family relationships, must be understood. Most children in foster care become available for adoption as a result of involuntary termination of parental rights because of abuse or neglect and are placed at older ages. These children have difficult histories that must be integrated into their new adoptive families. To facilitate that integration, as appropriate, contact can be maintained with birth families. Neil has described the impact of birth relatives' attitude towards the adoptive placement and adoption communicative openness by the adoptive mother as providing an important context for development of the adopted child in families where contact with birth parents occurs. McRoy *et al.* describe the positive outcomes for both adopted children and adoptive parents as adoptive parents recognize, work with, and integrate the difficult backgrounds of their children.

As the above discussion identifies, practitioner expertise needs to be flexible and case sensitive; adoption is not a uniform experience but one that is unique to each individual and family. All the research reports in this volume illustrate the diversity of peoples' situations, needs and feelings, both between people and within the same individual across time. What works for one family may not be right for the next, even though their situation may appear similar. Also, what any one person needs or wants may require review and adaptation over time.

Working in adoption requires both a sound ethical base and complex skills. Practitioners need to understand, care about and balance multiple perspectives. Hence it is vital that practitioners are understood and cared about in turn by their employers. The need for expertise in adoption practice requires a commitment by governments and adoption agencies to provide ongoing supervision, support and training to practitioners. As research makes new understandings available and identifies new and effective interventions, practitioners need to be allowed the time, and equipped with the skills to learn about and respond to these innovations.

The Contribution that Practitioners Can Make to Research

The contribution that practitioners can and do make to research needs to be valued and promoted.

So many of the studies reported in this book would not have been possible without the cooperation of colleagues in practice settings. Adoption agencies were central in helping research teams recruit their samples in most of the studies. The need to help with recruitment, to provide data (e.g. completing questionnaires, keeping case records or giving access to case files), and in some cases to provide support to individuals to take part in research no doubt places an additional burden on already-stretched professionals. But without this help researchers are severely restricted in what they can achieve, and hence the continued commitment of adoption agencies and workers to research must be supported. Practitioners also have a vital role to play in identifying gaps in knowledge and hence identifying the important research questions. By sharing their practice wisdom, practitioners can suggest solutions for needs identified by research teams.

Effective communication, collaboration, and mutual respect between researchers and practitioners are essential in enhancing the work of each. Many chapter contributors to this volume have a background in practice, and some have retained a practitioner role alongside their research interests. This no doubt informs and enhances the quality of adoption research, and opportunities and funding for adoption practitioners to become involved in research need to be encouraged.

Conclusion

As evidenced by the contributions to this volume from psychologists, psychiatrists, social workers, family scientists, demographers, historians, social pedagogues and behavioural geneticists, adoption holds an interest across many disciplines. Each line of research has pointed out specific content that needs further exploration. Yet, future contribution to our knowledge about adoption will be facilitated when research agendas can be formed with a truly interdisciplinary focus that considers practice implications. After all, a goal of adoption research is to benefit members of the adoption kinship network, as well as enhance the expertise of practitioners and policy makers that support them. A multidisciplinary approach requires commitment to creativity and good communication but has great reward. Bringing multiple perspectives together, including those of practitioners, will help shape qualitatively new ways of thinking, moving our knowledge to new levels.

As adoption researchers and practitioners continue to respond to the dynamic nature of adoption, this volume is an attempt to enhance the connection between research and practice. Adoption in its many forms requires us to think broadly about what adoption can teach us about families and their place in society. Adoption research is poised to move beyond the description of adoption experience to understanding the processes behind the outcomes, resulting in theory development. The resulting knowledge can inform practice and policy that must meet the complex and changing needs of members of the adoption kinship network. There is much to do and research and practice together can make a positive difference for adopted individuals and their families.

Index